TEXT AND INTERPRETATION

Studies in the New Testament presented to Matthew Black

PHOTOGRAPH BY PETER ADAMSON
UNIVERSITY OF ST ANDREWS PHOTOGRAPHIC UNIT

Frontispiece

TEXT AND INTERPRETATION

Studies in the New Testament presented to Matthew Black

EDITED BY
ERNEST BEST
Professor of Divinity and Biblical Criticism, University of Glasgow
AND
R. McL. WILSON
Professor of New Testament, University of St Andrews

CAMBRIDGE UNIVERSITY PRESS
CAMBRIDGE
LONDON · NEW YORK · MELBOURNE

Published by the Syndics of the Cambridge University Press
The Pitt Building, Trumpington Street, Cambridge CB2 1RP
Bentley House, 200 Euston Road, London NW1 2DB
32 East 57th Street, New York, NY 10022, USA
296 Beaconsfield Parade, Middle Park, Melbourne 3206, Australia

First published 1979

Printed in Great Britain at the
University Press, Cambridge

Library of Congress Cataloguing in Publication Data
Main entry under title:
Text and interpretation.
1. Bible. N. T. – Criticism, interpretation,
etc. – Addresses, essays, lectures. 2. Black,
Matthew – Addresses, essays, lectures. I. Black,
Matthew. II. Best, Ernest. III. Wilson,
Robert McLachlan.
BS2395.T4 225.6 78–2962
ISBN 0 521 220211

CONTENTS

Contents

PREFACE

Along with our contributors and his many colleagues and friends, we congratulate Matthew Black on attaining his seventieth birthday and offer to him this volume in token of our gratitude and esteem. In his long career as a scholar, culminating in more than twenty years as Principal of St Mary's College in the University of St Andrews, he has served church and university, contributing a wide knowledge and a wise judgment to both. Many scholars have learned from him the beginnings of their trade. Others have been generously encouraged and guided when they presented their papers to him as Editor of *New Testament Studies*. Under his direction this journal has reached a pre-eminent position and he has thereby made a major contribution to the advancement of New Testament scholarship. He has made another such contribution as one of the editors of the United Bible Societies' text of the New Testament; many of the articles in this volume are a tribute to his interest in this area. It would easily have been possible to choose other areas where he has left his mark on scholarship. A doughty opponent in discussion, a genial friend, a generous encourager of the scholarship of others, a devout Christian, he has now retired from his editorial chair and is about to retire as Principal. We trust that this will leave him free to continue to make his own personal contribution to the study of the New Testament and its related disciplines.

July 1978

ERNEST BEST
R. McL. WILSON

BIBLIOGRAPHY OF MATTHEW BLACK

A bibliography down to 1968 is included in *Neotestamentica et Semitica* (edited by E. Earle Ellis and Max Wilcox, Edinburgh, 1969). The following list, prepared by Miss M. C. Blackwood, brings the record up to date at the end of 1977.

1958:

add to printed list

'The Milqart Stele', 'The Zakir Stele', *Documents from Old Testament Times*, edited by D. Winton Thomas, Nelson, London, pp. 239–50.

1967:

add to printed list

'A Palestinian Syriac Chrestomathy', in *An Aramaic Handbook*, edited by Franz Rosenthal (*Porta Linguarum Orientalium* series), Wiesbaden, pp. 9–28.

Obituary, Paul Ernst Kahle, *Proceedings of the British Academy*, volume LI, pp. 485–95.

1968

In Memoriam Paul Kahle, edited by Matthew Black and George Fohrer, Berlin, 1968. (*Beiheft* 103 to *ZATW*)

'The Development of Aramaic Studies since the Work of Kahle', *In Memoriam Paul Kahle*, pp. 17–28.

'A New Look at the Bible', *Theological Review*, New Zealand, pp. 5–7.

1969

The Scrolls and Christianity: Historical and Theological Significance, editor, London.

'The Dead Sea Scrolls and Christian Origins', *The Scrolls and Christianity*, pp. 97–106.

'The "Son of Man" Passion Sayings in the Gospel Tradition', *Zeitschrift für die Neutestamentliche Wissenschaft*, volume 60, pp. 1–8.

1970

Apocalypsis Henochi Graeca, Études des pseudépigraphes grecs d'Ancien Testament, Leiden.

Chapter on the Biblical Languages, *Cambridge History of the Bible. From the Beginnings to Jerome*, edited by C. F. Evans and P. R. Ackroyd, volume 1, Cambridge, pp. 1–11.

'The Chi-Rho Sign – Christogram and/or Staurogram', *Apostolic History and the Gospel: Biblical and Historical Essays presented to F. F. Bruce*, edited by W. Ward Gasque and Ralph P. Martin, Exeter, pp. 319–28.

'Uncomfortable Words, III. The Violent Word (Mt. 10.34)', *Expository Times*, January, volume LXXXI, no. 4, pp. 115–18.

'Ephatha (Mk 7.34) and Didrachma (Mt. 17.24)', *Mélanges Bibliques: Hommage au Béda Rigaux*, edited by Albert Descamps and André de Halleux, Gembloux, pp. 57–62.

'The Christological Use of the Old Testament in the New Testament', *New Testament Studies*, volume 18, Cambridge, pp. 1–14.

1971

'The Syriac New Testament in Early Patristic Tradition', Colloque de Strasbourg, *La Bible et les Pères*, edited by André Benoit and Pierre Prigent, Presses Universitaires de France, pp. 263–78.

1972

'A Survey of Christological Thought, 1872–1972: The Contributions of New Testament Scholarship', Croall Centenary Lecture, Edinburgh, p. 21.

'The Syriac Versional Tradition', in *Die alten Übersetzungen des Neuen Testaments, Die Kirchenväterzitate und Lektionare*, published in the series *Arbeiten zur neutestamentlichen Textforschung*, Berlin, pp. 120–59.

1973

Epistle to the Romans: Commentary, New Century Bible Series, London, p. 191.

The History of the Jewish People in the Age of Jesus Christ, 175 B.C.–A.D. 135, volume 1, new English version revised and edited in collaboration with Professor Geza Vermes and Dr Fergus Millar of the University of Oxford, Edinburgh, 614 pp.

'A Reconsideration of the Maranatha Formula (1 Cor. 16.22)', *Christ and Spirit in the New Testament: Studies in Honour of Charles Francis Digby Moule*, edited by Barnabas Lindars and Stephen S. Smalley, Cambridge, pp. 189–96.

1974

On Language, Culture and Religion: In Honor of Eugene A. Nida, joint editor with William A. Smalley, The Hague.

'Some Notes on the Longer and Shorter Text of Acts', *On Language, Culture and Religion: In Honor of Eugene A. Nida*, pp. 119–31.

'Judas of Galilee and Josephus's Fourth Philosophy', *Josephus-Studien: Festschrift für Otto Michel*, edited by Otto Betz, Klaus Haacker and Martin Hengel, Göttingen, pp. 45–54.

1975

Chapter on 'The Biblical Languages', *The Cambridge History of the Bible*, volume 1, edited by P. R. Ackroyd and C. F. Evans (revised for first paperback edition), pp. 1–11.

'Die Apotheose Israels: eine neue Interpretation des danielischen Menschensohns', *Jesus und der Menschensohn: für Anton Vögtle*, edited by R. Pesch and R. Schnackenburg, Freiburg, pp. 92–9.

1976

Collaborated with J. T. Milik in *The Books of Enoch: Aramaic Fragments of Qumrân Cave 4*, Oxford.

'The New Creation in I Enoch', *Creation, Christ and Culture: Studies in Honour of T. F. Torrance*, edited by Richard W. A. McKinney, Edinburgh, pp. 13–21.

'Some Greek Words with "Hebrew" Meanings in the Epistles and the Apocalypse', *Biblical Studies: Essays in Honour of William Barclay*, edited by Johnston R. McKay, Jr. and James F. Miller, London, pp. 135–46.

'The Throne-Theophany Prophetic Commission and the "Son of Man": a Study in Tradition History', *Jews, Greeks and Christians* (*Festschrift* for W. D. Davies), edited by Robert Hamerton Kelly and Robin Scroggs, Leiden, pp. 57–73.

'The Parables of Enoch (I Enoch 37–71) and the "Son of Man"', *Expository Times*, October, volume LXXVIII, no. 1, pp. 5–8.

1977

'The U.B.S. Greek New Testament Evaluated: A Reply', *Technical Papers for the Bible Translator*, January, volume 28, no. 1, pp. 116–20.

ABBREVIATIONS

AB	Anchor Bible
AP	*Archiv für Papyrusforschung und verwandte Gebiete*
ASAE	*Annales du service des antiquités de L'Égypte*
ASNTU	Acta seminarii neotestamentici Upsaliensis
ATANT	Abhandlungen zur Theologie des Alten und Neuen Testaments
BBB	Bonner Biblische Beiträge
BDF	Blass–Debrunner–Funk
BETL	Bibliotheca Ephemeridum Theologicarum Lovaniensium
BEvTh	Beiträge zur evangelischen Theologie
BJRL	*Bulletin of the John Rylands Library, Manchester*
BMAP	*The Brooklyn Museum Aramaic Papyri*, E. G. Kraeling
BSAC	*Bulletin de la société d'archéologie copte*
BWANT	*Beiträge zur Wissenschaft vom Alten und Neuen Testament*
BZ	*Biblische Zeitschrift*
BZNW	*Beihefte zur Zeitschrift für die neutestamentliche Wissenschaft und die Kunde der älteren Kirche*
CBQ	*The Catholic Biblical Quarterly*
CIS	*Corpus Inscriptionum Semiticarum*
CSEL	*Corpus Scriptorum ecclesiasticorum Latinorum*
DALC	Dictionnaire d'archéologie chrétienne et de liturgie
DBS	*Dictionnaire de la Bible*, Supplément
Diss.	Dissertation

Ephem. Theol. Lov.	*Ephemerides Theologicae Lovanienses*
ET	*The Expository Times*
ET	English translation
GCS	*Die griechischen christlichen Schriftsteller der ersten drei Jahrhunderte*
HThK	*Herders theologischer Kommentar zum Neuen Testament*
HTR	*The Harvard Theological Review*
HTS	*Harvard Theological Studies*
IDB	*The Interpreter's Dictionary of the Bible* (5 volumes)
JBL	*Journal of Biblical Literature*
JerB	The Jerusalem Bible
JJS	*Journal of Jewish Studies*
JQR	*Jewish Quarterly Review*
JTS	*Journal of Theological Studies*
KNT	Kommentar zum Neuen Testament
MNTC	The Moffatt New Testament Commentary
MT	Masoretic Text
MThZ	*Münchener theologische Zeitschrift*
NEB	New English Bible
NT	*Novum Testamentum*
NTA	*Neutestamentliche Abhandlungen*
NTD	Das Neue Testament Deutsch
NTS	*New Testament Studies*
PG	*Patrologiae cursus completus, series graeca*, edited by J. P. Migne
PL	*Patrologiae cursus completus, series latina*, edited by J. P. Migne
RB	*Revue Biblique*
REJ	*Revue des études juives*
RES	*Revue des études sémitiques*

RHR	*Revue de l'histoire des Religions*
Riv. Bib.	*Rivista Biblica*
RSR	*Recherches de science religieuse*
RSV	Revised Standard Version of the Bible
RTP	Revue de théologie et de philosophie
SB	*Kommentar zum Neuen Testament aus Talmud und Midrasch*, edited by H. L. Strack & P. Billerbeck (5 volumes)
SBA Hist.-philos. Kl.	Sitzungsberichte der bayerischen Akademie der Wissenschaften
SBL	Society of Biblical Literature
SBS	Stuttgarter Bibelstudien
SBTh	*Studies in Biblical Theology*
StTh	*Studia Theologica*
StUNT	*Studien zur Umwelt des Neuen Testaments*
Suppl. *NT*	Supplements to *Novum Testamentum*
TDNT	*Theological Dictionary of the New Testament*, translated and edited by G. W. Bromiley
TEV	Today's English Version
Tg.	Targum
Theol. Stud.	*Theological Studies*
TS	*Texts and Studies*
TU	*Texte und Untersuchungen zur Geschichte der altchristlichen Literatur*
TWNT	*Theologisches Wörterbuch zum Neuen Testament*, edited by G. Kittel and G. Friedrich
TZ	*Theologische Zeitschrift*
USQR	*Union Seminary Quarterly Review*
Vg	Vulgate
VSal	Verbum Salutis
ZATW	*Zeitschrift für die alttestamentliche Wissenschaft*
ZNTW	*Zeitschrift für die neutestamentliche Wissenschaft*
ZTK	*Zeitschrift für Theologie und Kirche*

The twentieth-century interlude in New Testament textual criticism

K. ALAND

Aus prominentem Anlaß (zum Gedenken an den 1972 verstorbenen W. H. P. Hatch) und an prominentem Ort (bei der Jahrestagung der Society of Biblical Literature 1973) hat Eldon Jay Epp unter dem Titel: 'The Twentieth Century Interlude in New Testament Textual Criticism' eine Wertung der gegenwärtigen Situation und Leistung der neutestamentlichen Textkritik vorgetragen. Diese Memorial Lecture ist zunächst im *Journal of Biblical Literature* erschienen (93, 1974, 386–414) und dann als separater Druck vertrieben worden, ihr Titel bezeichnet programmatisch die dort vorgetragene Auffassung.

Diese Auffassung kann nicht ohne Kommentar bleiben. Ich habe lange damit gezögert, obwohl ich in dem Aufsatz zahlreiche Male zitiert und direkt oder indirekt angesprochen werde (Epp kommt S.399 selbst auf den Gedanken, es sei 'not entirely fair to Aland', was er schreibe) und das Münsteraner Institut für neutestamentliche Textforschung trotz formaler Anerkennung in seiner Fähigkeit, die anstehenden Probleme zu lösen – man kann es eigentlich nicht anders sagen: disqualifiziert wird.[1] Die Festschrift für Matthew Black, Gefährte durch Jahrzehnte

[1] Zwar heißt es zunächst (alle folgenden Zitate auf S.414 in einem Abschnitt!): 'Given the ironic twists of national economies, one now has to say – to change the wording slightly – that since textual criticism requires a great deal of manpower and money it has almost entirely been transferred to Germany.' und: 'It is disheartening to say that I doubt whether the working and publishing NT textual critics in all of North America are equal in number to the postdoctoral researchers in the Münster Institut.' Aber was besagt das, wenn der Aufsatz damit schließt: 'In short, NT textual criticism is an area seriously affected by decreasing attention, diminishing graduate opportunities, and dwindling personnel. It is ironic that this state of affairs – a situation contrasting sharply with any during the long life of W. H. P. Hatch – obtains just at the time when methodological advances warrant a renewed optimism for the discipline and offer fresh challenges which, if met, would carry NT textual criticism beyond its 20th century interlude to a new and distinctive period of achievement.' Münster besitzt danach offensichtlich nur 'manpower and money', daß die 'new and distinctive period of achievement' von dort kommen könnte, liegt offensichtlich außerhalb der Vorstellungsmöglichkeit Epps.

auf dem Wege zum neuen 'Standard-Text' und Mitglied des Wissenschaftlichen Beirats des Münsteraner Instituts seit seiner Gründung vor rund 20 Jahren und als solches mitverantwortlich für alles, was dort geschieht, scheint der gegebene Ort, das bisher Versäumte nachzuholen.

Epp stellt eingangs der 'self-confident, optimistic, and resolute' Textkritik des ausgehenden 19. und beginnenden 20. Jahrhunderts die 'diffuse, indeterminate, and eclectic' Textkritik unserer gegenwärtigen Zeit und der jüngsten Vergangenheit gegenüber (S.386f). Es handele sich beim gegenwärtigen Stand eben um ein 'interlude' (diese Bezeichnung präzisiert Epp dahin, er verstehe darunter 'in its classical meaning': 'a performance between the acts of a play or the parts of a composition', genauer gesagt: 'a subsidiary or a secondary and minor performance following a portion of the main event'). Gewiß sei das 20. Jahrhundert keine Epoche der Inaktivität gewesen, die Zahl der Papyri sei z. B. um 600 Prozent über den Stand der Jahrhundertwende gestiegen, der Lektionar-Text sei festgestellt worden, für die Versionen sei 'wide-ranging work' vollbracht und die ermüdende Arbeit der Erstellung neuer kritischer Ausgaben sei wieder ins Leben gerufen worden. Aber das alles sei nicht mehr gewesen als 'an interlude between the grand achievement of Westcott–Hort and whatever significant second act is to follow' (alle Zitate S.387).

Bereits hier fängt man an, sich zu wundern. Kein Wort davon, daß die Zahl der bekannten neutestamentlichen Handschriften in unserer Generation um über 1000, d. h. über 25 Prozent angestiegen ist, kein Wort davon, daß – zum ersten Mal in der Geschichte der neutestamentlichen Textkritik – die Handschriften inhaltlich durchdrungen und die reinen Koine-Handschriften unter ihnen – rund 80 Prozent – festgestellt und ausgeschieden worden sind, und was dergleichen mehr ist. Aber das ist alles nicht in den USA erfolgt (sondern in Deutschland, genauer gesagt in und durch Münster). Sollte Epp sich bei seinem Bericht auf die Fortschritte der Arbeit in den USA beschränken? Was er aufzählt, gehört in der Tat alles zu den Leistungen der nordamerikanischen Textkritik. Das wäre dann aber ein Provinzialismus, der alles übertrifft, was bisher im damit leider reichlich ausgestatteten Deutschland möglich war. Ich weigere mich, daran zu glauben, obwohl es Indizien gibt, die diese Vermutung verstärken, denn in manchen Arbeiten jüngerer Textkritiker aus den USA findet sich eine auffallende Vernachlässigung der nicht im englischen (genauer gesagt: nordamerikanischen) Sprachbereich erschienenen Literatur. Aber gleichviel: die Steigerung der bekannten Papyri seit der Jahrhundertwende um

600 Prozent, von der Epp spricht, ist jedenfalls sowohl quantitativ falsch wie vor allem qualitativ völlig unzureichend erfaßt. Nur ein Papyrus ($\mathfrak{P}^{11}$) ist im 19. Jahrhundert für eine Ausgabe des Neuen Testaments ausgewertet worden, und zwar überaus fragmentarisch, so beträgt die zahlenmäßige Steigerung bis zur Gegenwart nicht 600 Prozent, sondern fast 9,000 Prozent – und die qualitative ein Vielfaches. Aber schweigen wir davon.

Unter den Beweisen, die Epp für das 'interlude' der Gegenwart anführt, steht an erster Stelle 'Lack of Progress in Popular Critical Editions'. Hier hört nun die Verwunderung auf und beginnt das Erstaunen. Denn Epp zählt 10 Ausgaben auf. Das spricht nicht gerade für seine These – aber, so erklärt er (und zwar mit einem Zitat aus einem Aufsatz von Clark, einer der ihn bestimmenden Autoritäten): 'The conclusion is clear: these three most widely used Greek New Testaments of the mid-twentieth century (Nestle–Aland, Merk, and Bover) "show little change from Westcott–Hort and only rarely present a significant variant"' (S.389). Auch das Greek New Testament fällt für Epp unter dieses Verdikt: 'It will be observed at once that its editors began their work on the basis of Westcott–Hort and that the text of the United Bible Societies' edition is close to the text of Codex Vaticanus (B) – Westcott–Hort's primary manuscript – and close, therefore, to Westcott–Hort's text' (S.390).

Es ist bemerkenswert – und charakteristisch – daß Epp unter den zehn von ihm angeführten Ausgaben nicht die Greek–English Diglot von G. D. Kilpatrick anführt, die nun einen wirklich anderen Weg geht (das gleiche dürfte für die in Vorbereitung befindliche Synopse von H. Greeven gelten) – sie hätten in die von ihm beklagte zu große Nähe des Textes zu Westcott–Hort nicht gepaßt. Weiter muß festgestellt werden, und das gilt nicht nur für Epp, sondern auch für manche andere, daß das Reden vom 'Westcott–Hort-Text', den alle modernen Handausgaben böten, falls sie nicht den Textus receptus wiederbelebten, nicht nur 'somewhat oversimplified' sondern schlicht falsch ist. Wenn der Nestle-Text bis zur 25. Auflage Westcott–Hort näher steht als Tischendorf, so liegt das daran, daß die Ausgabe von Bernhard Weiss, die für Eberhard Nestle den Stichentscheid zwischen Tischendorf und Westcott–Hort lieferte, den Codex Vaticanus unter den alexandrinischen Zeugen am höchsten bewertete, man müßte also, wenigstens in bezug auf den Nestle, vom Westcott–Hort–Weiss-Text sprechen. Und was den neuen 'Standard-Text' angeht, den das Greek New Testament von seiner dritten Ausgabe und der Nestle von seiner 26. Ausgabe an gemeinsam bieten, so hat die

Ausgabe von Westcott–Hort zwar als 'Grundlage' gedient, aber nur so wie bei jeder Neuedition eines griechischen Textes eine der vorhandenen Ausgaben als Basis für die Neubearbeitung verwandt wird, gleich wie das Resultat der Neubearbeitung im Verhältnis zur Vorlage aussieht.

In diesem Abschnitt des Aufsatzes von Epp werden die modernen Handausgaben wegen ihrer Nähe zu Westcott–Hort getadelt, im nächsten wird dann die Textauffassung und -theorie beider als bisher größte und bleibende Lösung gepriesen (vgl. u. S. 5f), wie man das beides zusammenbringen kann, ist mir ein Rätsel. Gewiß ist der neue Standardtext 'close to B', wenigstens mit Epps 'somewhat oversimplified' Maßstäben gemessen, aber ebensosehr gehört es zu seinen Charakteristika, daß er den Text fast immer da geändert hat (und zwar im Gegensatz zu Westcott–Hort und dem 19. Jahrhundert), wo dieser nur auf einer ℵ B-Bezeugung beruhte. Der Codex Vaticanus ist vom Herausgeberkomitee genau so kritisch betrachtet worden wie jede andere Handschrift auch, nur da ist ihm (und den ihn begleitenden Zeugen!) gefolgt worden, wo die Fülle der angewandten äußeren wie inneren Kriterien seinen Text als richtig erwies (was, wie bekannt, in den Evangelien häufiger der Fall ist als beim restlichen Neuen Testament).

Im übrigen: der 'Standard-Text' der beiden neuen Ausgaben ist gewiß nicht unfehlbar. Daß seine Grundlinie aber richtig ist, erfährt nachdrückliche gerade jetzt eine Bestätigung. Im Münsteraner Institut ist nämlich vor einigen Monaten mit einer Neukollation aller Papyrus- und Pergamentfragmente aus der Zeit bis zum 3./4. Jahrhundert begonnen worden, weil wir für sie im Normalfall nur die in der Regel mit Mängeln behaftete Erstedition besitzen (die durch ihre Wiederholung in späteren Ausgaben bzw. Untersuchungen nicht besser geworden ist). Nur an ganz wenigen Stellen weichen zahlreiche dieser frühen Zeugen, soweit sie bisher untersucht sind, vom 'Standard-Text' ab, und da jedesmal zu Unrecht. $\mathfrak{P}^{75}$ steht nicht allein, sondern wird von der Fülle der Zeugen aus der Zeit unterstützt, bevor der Einfluß der großen Textgruppen beginnt. Nur die ganz wenigen Zeugen für den D-Text fallen aus der Norm heraus, die vielfach verbreiteten Konstruktionen von Textgruppen im 3. Jahrhundert (und sei es in der Form von Prae-Texten) finden keine Bestätigung – ganz auf der in meinen 'Studien zur Überlieferung des Neuen Testaments und seines Textes' mehrfach bezeichneten Linie. $\mathfrak{P}^{45}$, $\mathfrak{P}^{46}$, $\mathfrak{P}^{66}$ charakterisieren den 'Frühtext' des 2. Jahrhunderts, was danach folgt, ist offensichtlich viel einheitlicher als bisher angenommen.

Aber, kehren wir zu dem von Epp beklagten Mangel an Taschenausgaben des Neuen Testaments zurück: welchen Sinn hat diese Klage? Soll man Taschenausgaben nur deshalb produzieren, um einen verschiedenen Text zu haben – während anerkanntermaßen das Neue Testament ursprünglich nur *einen* Text besessen haben kann? Die Ausgaben von Vogels, Merk, Bover, um nur diese zu nennen, sind seit ihrer letzten Auflage (1955, 1964, 1968) nicht mehr fortgesetzt worden, die Diglot-Edition von Kilpatrick begann 1958 heftweise zu erscheinen, ist aber 1964 abgebrochen worden. Alle wurden von verschiedenen Verlagen publiziert, wenn diese bisher keine Neuausgabe (und sei es einen unveränderten Nachdruck) vorgelegt haben, so doch wohl deshalb, weil sie keinen Bedarf – oder mindestens keinen buchhändlerisch lohnenswerten Bedarf – dafür wahrnahmen. Nicht einmal das Verdikt verfängt, die Bibelgesellschaften hätten den Markt erdrückt. Denn die Ausgabe von Kilpatrick wurde von der British and Foreign Bible Society verantwortet, bei ihrem Beginn gab es den 'Standard-Text' noch nicht, trotzdem brach die BFBS das Unternehmen ab – wir sind heute eben, entgegen den Ausführungen von Epp, nach der allgemeinen Überzeugung mit dem 'Standard-Text' dem ursprünglichen Text des Neuen Testaments offensichtlich ein entscheidendes Stück nähergerückt. Bereits dieses Faktum reicht aus, um die These von Epp, das 20. Jahrhundert stelle nur ein 'interlude' der neutestamentlichen Textkritik dar, von vornherein in Frage zu stellen.

Epps zweites Argument ('a second strong indication', S.391) für seine These ist der 'Lack of Progress toward a Theory and History of the Earliest NT Text'. Hier rücken nun Westcott/Hort – wegen der Nähe zu ihrem Text waren sämtliche Ausgaben des 20. Jahrhunderts bisher kritisiert worden – in den höchsten Rang: ihr 'classical statement' wird gerühmt, 'and particularly their (actually Hort's) clear and firm view of the early history of the NT text'. Sie kehren mit ihren Theorien wieder, so als ob nicht 100 Jahre seit dem Erscheinen ihrer Ausgabe vergangen wären. Vom 'neutral text' und vom 'western text' ist bei Epp immer wieder die Rede, und zwar *ohne* Anführungszeichen (wenn auch Anm. 13 zu S.391 leichte Vorbehalte für die zweite Bezeichnung anmeldet), während allgemein keinerlei Zweifel daran besteht, daß es keinen 'neutralen' Text gibt, sondern selbst B im Evangelienteil seine Vorlage einer *Revision* (bei Epp gehen die Begriffe Rezension und Revision ständig durcheinander) unter stilistischem Vorzeichen unterzieht und auch die energischsten Verteidiger des zweiten Typs das Wort 'westlich' in Anführungszeichen gebrauchen. Denn der Codex Bezae Cantabrigiensis ist, nach dem Urteil der führenden Vertreter der lateinischen Paläographie, keineswegs im

Westen geschrieben und seine Vorläufer im 3. Jahrhundert, beispielsweise $\mathfrak{P}^{38}$ und $\mathfrak{P}^{48}$, stammen eindeutig aus Ägypten. Nun möchte ich aus dem Gebrauch des Terminus 'neutraler Text' durch Epp nicht mehr ableiten als seine völlige Verwurzelung in den Vorstellungen Westcott–Horts, aber das ist charakteristisch genug. Für Epp gibt es nur zwei frühe Texte, den von B – $\mathfrak{P}^{75}$ und den von D repräsentierten. Mit aller Unbefangenheit geht Epp davon aus, 'that the earliest text known to us is Western in its character', so wie Westcott–Hort das taten. 'This is where we stand, and this is precisely where Westcott–Hort stood', kann Epp erklären und selbst die Papyri können ihn darin nicht irre machen: 'In this respect the extraordinary papyrus discoveries of the past three quarters of a century do not alter our basic dilemma as to whether Neutral or Western better represents the original NT text – at least they provide no new objective criteria to bear on the solution' (S.399). Schon bei dieser Formulierung weiß man nicht, was man sagen soll; nimmt man eine andere aus demselben Abschnitt hinzu, in dem beim Bericht über Westcott–Hort ausgeführt wird, man finde 'two early texts competing in the 2nd century church, one corrupted by paraphrastic expansions [d. h. D] and the other virtually untouched in its course of transmission from the original [d. h. B]' (S.392), wird man endgültig sprachlos.

Nun kann hier auf das überaus komplizierte Problem des sog. 'westlichen Textes' nicht in Ausführlichkeit eingegangen werden. Zunächst einmal wären klare Definitionen notwendig, um der bisherigen Sprachverwirrung ein Ende zu machen: zum D-Text, wie er besser zu nennen wäre (wie es mehrfach schon früher, aber bisher ohne endgültigen Erfolg, durchzusetzen versucht wurde), kann nur gerechnet werden, was dem Rezensionscharakter des Bezae Cantabrigiensis entspricht oder ihm wenigstens verwandt ist: in seinen großen Textauslassungen und -zufügungen, in seinen radikalen sonstigen Eingriffen in den Text, die bis zum Umschreiben ganzer Verse gehen und was dergleichen mehr ist. In dem Augenblick erst, wo das geschieht, kommt Übersicht in die Probleme und kann eine Lösung versucht werden – die dann allerdings wesentlich anders aussehen wird als das nach Epp scheint. Tatsächlich hat sich ja – wovon bei Epp überhaupt nicht die Rede ist – die Gesamtsituation im Vergleich zu Westcott–Hort entscheidend verändert: für sie waren die Vetus Syra und die Vetus Latina die entscheidenden Stützen für die Frühdatierung des D-Textes. Aber diese Stützung durch die altlateinische Überlieferung fällt weg, denn der lateinische Text von D ist nach allgemeiner Ansicht vom griechischen abhängig und nicht umgekehrt, wie man früher meinte. 'Jedenfalls fällt der lateinische Text von d (5) aus dem Rahmen der sonstigen lateinischen Bibel heraus', erklärt Bonifatius Fischer, der beste Kenner der Materie ('Die alten Übersetzungen des Neuen Testaments, die Kirchenväterzitate und Lektionare', *Arbeiten zur neutestamentlichen Textforschung* 5, Berlin, 1972, S.42). Und auch die Vetus Syra ist völlig anders zu werten als im vorigen Jahrhundert. 'There seems to be general agreement that the earliest possible date for the copying of S and C was the beginning of the fifth century: they were presumably copied for use from an archetype which cannot have been so very much older, possibly dating from the middle of the fourth century', stellt Matthew Black selbst fest (ebda. S.132f). Im zweiten Jahrhundert und einige Zeit danach hat es außer dem Diatessaron keinen anderen syrischen Text des Neuen Testaments gegeben, dieser Schluß ist nach allen Kenntnissen, die wir besitzen, unausweichlich (grundlegend dafür Barbara Ehlers (=B. Aland), 'Kann das Thomasevangelium aus Edessa stammen? Ein Beitrag zur Frühgeschichte des Christentums in Edessa', *Novum Testamentum* 12, 1970, 284–314). Bereits damit hat sich die Grundposition entscheidend verändert. Wie erklärt Epp: 'This is where we stand, and this is precisely where Westcott–Hort stood'?

Mehr als diese kurzen Bemerkungen sind hier nicht möglich. Auch zum Cäsarea-Text, auf den Epp ausführlich eingeht, können hier nur wenige Sätze gesagt werden. Ich bin weit davon entfernt zu behaupten, wie Epp es von mir sagt, 'that no Caesarean text-type existed' (S.394). Ich habe vielmehr immer erklärt, daß ein solcher Texttyp angesichts der Funktion des Scriptoriums von Cäsarea zur Zeit des Euseb von Cäsarea aus methodischen Gründen nahe liege. Aber solange der 'Cäsarea-Text' nicht in den Schriften des Origenes und Euseb, mindestens aber denen des zweiten, nachgewiesen werde, und solange seine behauptete Existenz nicht eine breitere Basis als bisher erhalte, sei mir seine Existenz äußerst zweifelhaft. Wenn Epp, und zwar durch kursiven Druck, hervorhebt, daß Hurtado seine Untersuchungen '*throughout* Mark and not merely in sample chapters' angestellt habe, so finde ich eine solche Basis (um zunächst dabei zu bleiben) immer noch viel zu schmal – aus dem Scriptorium von Cäsarea sind keine Handschriften von Einzelevangelien ausgegangen, sondern mindestens vom Tetraevangelium, ja aus methodischen Gründen (vgl. den Bericht bei Euseb über die große Handschriftenlieferung zur Ausstattung der Kirchen von Konstantinopel) sogar überwiegend Vollhandschriften des Neuen Testaments (und das Markusevangelium umfaßt nur rund ein Zwölftel davon). Immerhin kann ich Epps Meinung, durch Hurtados Arbeit erhielten die 'negative conclusions concerning the Caesarean text . . . both a broader and firmer basis than previously possible' (S.394), nur registrierend und seine Zusammenfassung zustimmend zur Kenntnis nehmen: 'In short, the so-called "pre-Caesarean" witnesses are neither pre-Caesarean nor Caesarean at all' (S.395).

Wenn Epp nun weiter, um den Bericht über die 'deficiencies' abzuschließen, den 'Lack of Progress in Major Critical Editions/ Apparatuses' (S.401ff) und den 'Lack of Progress in the Evaluation of Readings' (S.403ff) als Beweis für seine These vom 'interlude' anführt, so muß das erste Argument eigentlich erstaunen. Denn Epp muß in diesem Zusammenhang von der in Münster begonnenen Arbeit an der Novi Testamenti graeci editio critica maior wie von dem amerikanisch-englischen International Greek NT Project sprechen. Daß das amerikanisch/englische Unternehmen sich auf den Abdruck des Textus receptus und eine Wiedergabe der Varianten im Apparat beschränkt, ist eine andere Sache. Das sei ein 'more cautious and methodical approach', meint Epp, er sei aus der resignierenden Erkenntnis entstanden: 'we simply do not have a theory of the text' (S.403). Nun können hier die Einzelheiten nicht diskutiert werden, immerhin sei aber bemerkt,[1] daß auch in den USA lange Zeit hindurch eine kritische Ausgabe angestrebt wurde, und zwar 'from its very beginning'. Colwell, der Promotor und Motor des Unternehmens meinte sogar, daß diese kritische Ausgabe zwei Jahre nach dem Abschluß der Variantensammlung vorliegen würde. Wenn Epp es außerdem 'not only curious but striking' nennt, daß ich das amerikanisch/englische Unternehmen als Anachronismus bezeichnet hätte und v. Dobschütz 40 Jahre früher genau den gleichen Ausdruck in bezug auf Streeters Plan, den Textus receptus als Kollationsbasis für eine neue Ausgabe zu verwenden, gebraucht habe, so kommt das nicht daher, daß ich vor meiner Stellungnahme den Aufsatz von Dobschütz in der *ZNTW* von 1926 gelesen hätte, sondern aus der Sache (in der ich unverändert der seinerzeit vorgetragenen Meinung bin). Wenn man will, kann man das anders als möglicherweise Epp, vielleicht sogar – nicht ohne Befriedigung – als Indiz dafür ansehen, daß die deutsche Textkritik von heute in der Tradition der Generation vor ihr steht, die viele große Namen aufzuweisen hat.

Aber gleichviel, die bloße Tatsache schon, daß die beiden Unter-

[1] In bezug auf das Münsteraner Unternehmen einer kritischen Ausgabe spricht Epp nämlich von der 'boldness with which it is pursued, and the courage which lies behind it' (S.403), wobei sicher nicht nur die erste Charakteristik kritisch gemeint ist.

nehmen in unserer Generation in Gang gesetzt werden konnten, scheint mir ein eindeutiger Hinweis darauf, daß Epps Grundauffassung falsch ist. Er übersieht ja auch völlig den Bereich der Versionen, ganz davon zu schweigen, daß bei ihm nicht einmal die amerikanische Szene voll sichtbar wird. Denn z. B. die Vorbereitungen V. Dearings für eine Ausgabe der Evangelienhandschriften der ersten zehn Jahrhunderte mit Hilfe des Computers werden nirgendwo erwähnt. Nun muß man hier die Resultate abwarten, fest steht jedenfalls, daß die Arbeiten in vollem Gange sind und daß Dearing bei der Untersuchung einiger bisher vernachlässigter kleinerer Majuskeln bemerkenswerte Resultate erzielt hat. Aber zurück zu den Versionen: Auf dem lateinischen Sektor beispielsweise hat unsere Generation den entscheidenden Fortschritt erzielt. Bei der Itala-Ausgabe der vier Evangelien unter dem Namen Jülichers (den man der vorigen Generation zurechnen muß) stammt mit Ausnahme der Leitzeile (die man nicht als gültige Rekonstruktion, sondern nur als interessanten Beitrag dazu ansehen kann) alles von Angehörigen dieser Generation. Das gewaltige Projekt der Beuroner Ausgabe der Vetus Latina ist ebenfalls in dieser Generation in Angriff genommen worden, die Katholischen Briefe und ein Teil der Paulusbriefe liegen bereits vor. Auch der Hieronymus-Text der Vulgata ist – in der Stuttgarter Ausgabe – von dieser Generation neu festgestellt worden. Und schließlich ist auch von dieser Generation die Ausgabe von Wordsworth–White abgeschlossen worden (Fasz. 2 des 3. Bandes mit den Katholischen Briefen erschien 1949, Fasz. 3 mit der Apokalypse 1954). So könnte man fortfahren: in Leiden ist eine kritische Neuausgabe der Peschitta im Erscheinen (wenn auch – hoffentlich nur zunächst – auf das Alte Testament beschränkt), in Münster sind Vorarbeiten für eine neue Ausgabe der Harclensis begonnen, in bezug auf das Diatessaron sind die für die Rekonstruktion entscheidenden Ausgaben erschienen, diese selbst ist weit fortgeschritten.

Wenn wir uns dem zuwenden, was Epp in seinem zweiten hier zu besprechenden Abschnitt über die '"eclectic" method' sagt, so ist zu bemerken, daß er das erste Wort mit Recht in Anführungszeichen setzt, man könnte diese Methode – wenigstens in der von Epp beschriebenen Form – vielleicht besser 'subjective method' nennen, so objektiv zu sein sie vorgibt. Denn wenn sie mit 'particularly intrinsic probability' arbeitet, 'with heavy emphasis on harmony with the author's style or suitability to the context' (S.404), geht sie weithin von dem aus, was *sie* dafür hält. G. D. Fee hat – mit Recht – einen 'rigorous eclecticism' von einem 'reasoned eclecticism' unterschieden – aber sollten wir nicht vielleicht den Ausdruck 'Eklektizismus' im Zusammenhang mit der eigentlichen textkritischen Arbeit überhaupt aufgeben und die Bezeichnung anderen überlassen? Denn wie ist z. B. bei der Erarbeitung des neuen 'Standard-Textes' verfahren worden (und wie verfährt ordnungsgemäße textkritische Arbeit überhaupt)? Am Anfang steht die Sammlung der Varianten und ihrer Bezeugung in den griechischen Handschriften, den Versionen wie bei den in beiden Bezirken in Betracht kommenden Kirchenvätern. Dann folgt – ganz wie in der klassischen Philologie – die Anwendung der genealogischen Methode, nur mit dem Unterschied, daß das aufgestellte Stemma nicht für die ganze Schrift, sondern nur für die zur Debatte stehende Stelle (und ihre Textumgebung!) gilt. Das geschieht zu Recht, denn der 'lebende' Text des Neuen Testaments, welcher der ständigen Beeinflussung durch die verschiedensten Kräfte unterliegt, folgt anderen Gesetzen als der von Gelehrten und Schulmeistern tradierte 'tote' Standard-Text eines klassischen Schriftstellers. So kann eine Handschrift beinahe von Stelle zu Stelle eine verschiedene Wertigkeit aufweisen. Der erfahrene Praktiker, der zahllose Kollationen selbst durchgeführt hat und in ständigem Umgang mit den Varianten und Variationsmöglichkeiten der neutestamentlichen Überlieferung steht und von daher ein Urteil über den Wert der Aussagen der einzelnen Handschriften besitzt,[1] wird beim Anblick der Varianten zu einer Stelle und ihrer Bezeugung sich zwar im allgemeinen sehr bald darüber klar sein, wo der ursprüngliche Text zu suchen ist. Trotzdem wird er in jedem Fall sorgfältig der Genealogie dieser Varianten nachgehen – die, aus der alle anderen sukzessive zu erklären sind, muß den ursprünglichen Text ergeben –, wobei er alle inneren Kriterien (Wortgebrauch, Stil und theologische Dimension der betr. neutestamentlichen Schrift usw. usw.) gleichzeitig voll in Betracht zieht. So hat das Herausgeberkomitee des neuen 'Standard-Texts', wie er in der 3. Ausgabe des *Greek New Testament* und der 26. des *Novum Testamentum graece* von Nestle–Aland in Erscheinung tritt, jedenfalls gearbeitet. Nur der Laie kann meinen, daß das im Gegensatz zur Arbeit der klassischen Philologie stehe. Zwar ist diese im allgemeinen in der Lage, ein Stemma zu erstellen, d. h. eine Übersicht über die Textgeschichte, welche die Zahl der für die Textherstellung in Betracht kommenden Handschriften radikal

[1] Im Gegensatz zu den 'Amateuren', die im allgemeinen von der Theorie leben – eigentlich sollte jedoch niemandem eine verantwortliche Äußerung zum Text des Neuen Testaments erlaubt sein, der nicht selbst mindestens einen großen Papyrus, je eine wichtige Majuskel und Minuskel, sowie wenigstens Teile der Überlieferung in den Versionen und Kirchenvätern vollständig kollationiert hat.

auf die geringe Zahl der Vorlagen beschränkt, seien es reale, seien es hypothetische, von denen die anderen Handschriften abhängen. Aber wer glaubt, daß die hier festgestellten 'Musterhandschriften' mechanisch ausgewertet würden, befindet sich in einem grundlegenden Irrtum, vielmehr werden hier die gleichen Methoden angewandt wie in der modernen neutestamentlichen Textkritik, deren Arbeitsweise man vielleicht (das ist nur ein Vorschlag) als lokal-genealogische Methode bezeichnen sollte. Wenn Epp, wie es scheint (vgl. S.401), der Meinung ist, die Erforschung der frühen Textgeschichte würde Handschriften ergeben, welche die Funktion der 'Musterhandschriften' der klassischen Philologie erfüllen, so träumt er einen unerfüllbaren Traum. Die Zeit der Leitsterne (B für Westcott–Hort, א für Tischendorf), die dem Textkritiker den direkten Weg zu seinem Ziel des 'New Testament in the original Greek' wiesen, wie der Naivität, die dahinter steht, ist unwiederbringlich vorbei.

Wenn Epp zum Abschluß seiner Darlegungen dann zu der Frage übergeht: 'What are the prospects of moving from it [d. h. der von ihm beschriebenen Situation] into a new phase?' (S.406), so ist seine Antwort darauf allerdings einigermaßen dekouvrierend. 'The chances are considerably better than they were a generation ago', erklärt Epp (S.407), um dann fortzufahren: 'Naturally, the papyrus discoveries have contributed to this hopeful situation, but I refer more directly to developments in method which will aid in the reconstruction of the early history of the text' (S.407). Angesichts dieses Satzes befällt einen wieder das große Staunen, denn wenn diese 'early history of the text' irgendwo sichtbar wird, dann doch wohl direkt und umittelbar nur bei den rund 40 Papyri und Majuskeln aus der Zeit bis zum 3./4. Jahrhundert. Hier kann sie am Original studiert werden, alle anderen Arbeiten müssen rekonstruierende Theorie bleiben. Und welche Methoden meint Epp, von denen er die Erkenntnis der frühen Textgeschichte erhofft? Er nennt zwei: Die 'Quantitative Method' Colwells und die in Claremont (auf Initiative Colwells, dessen entscheidende Rolle dabei nicht zu sehr hinter dem Namen derer zurücktreten sollte, die diese Methode dann tatsächlich im einzelnen entwickelt haben) ausgebildete 'Profile Method'. Epp gibt zu: 'The Profile Method is applicable particularly to the location of Byzantine sub-groups' (S.410), woher kann dann von der 'Profile Method' Hilfe bei der 'reconstruction of the *early* history of the text' kommen? Und die quantitative Methode – ich weiß von eigenen Versuchen auf dem Gebiet her genau, wovon ich rede – ist in der theoretischen Darstellung zwar eindrucksvoll. Aber in dem Augenblick, wo sie nicht nur (wie bisher) auf sorgfältig eingegrenzte Gebiete bzw. wenige Handschriften, sondern auf die ganze Breite der für die frühe Textgeschichte aussagefähigen Zeugen angewandt werden soll, wird sie wegen des damit verbundenen Arbeitsaufwandes unanwendbar. Von den über 5,000 griechischen Handschriften des Neuen Testaments müssen nämlich mindestens 600 auf die beschriebene Weise untersucht werden ('each manuscript in the study must be measured against every other one', S.408); das ist selbst bei Einsatz des Computers (von dem Epp selbst sagt: 'it hardly has been touched by North American scholars', S.413) nicht zu bewältigen, weil ungeheure Arbeit (und dementsprechende Kosten) erfordernd. Außerdem dürften die Resultate zum Schluß nicht mehr übersichtlich, im besten Fall diffus sein (was Epp S.394f über die Resultate Hurtados berichtet, 'based . . . on the latest quantitative methods', gibt einen lebhaften Eindruck davon, obwohl hier nur wenige Handschriften herangezogen wurden).

Vor allen Dingen aber muß man erst einmal wissen, welche Handschriften als Material für diese Untersuchung der frühen Textgeschichte in Betracht kommen. Daß das für die Papyri und Majuskeln als geschlossene Gruppe gilt, das ist von vornherein klar, aber die entscheidende Frage ist doch, welche von den rund 2,800 Minuskeln und welche von den rund 2,200 Lektionaren dazu gehören. Sie muß man doch erst einmal kennen, bevor man versucht, die quantitative Methode in größerem Stil anzuwenden. Eine Antwort darauf gibt es nur in Münster, denn hier ist die Masse der Minuskeln auf ihren Textwert untersucht worden, und zwar mit Hilfe des Teststellensystems, das bei Epp nicht einmal erwähnt ist, obwohl es ihm (aus den Darlegungen in meinen 'Studien zur Überlieferung des Neuen Testaments und seines Textes' von 1967 und den mehrfachen Berichten über die seitdem erzielten Fortschritte in den Jahresberichten der Stiftung zur Förderung der neutestamentlichen Textforschung) wohl bekannt sein dürfte. Das gleiche gilt für das Münsteraner Projekt: 'Das Neue Testament auf Papyrus'. Hier werden – im System von Jülichers Itala – alle Texte auf Papyrus wiedergegeben, im kritischen Apparat werden die Resultate einer Vollkollation aller Majuskeln geboten. Auch dieses Hilfsmittel zur Untersuchung der Frühgeschichte des neutestamentlichen Textes bleibt bei Epp völlig unerwähnt, und zwar ebenfalls unverständlicherweise. 1955–6 ist in München das dreibändige Werk von Josef Schmid erschienen, welches die gesamte griechische Überlieferung der Apokalypse bis hin zur letzten Minuskel untersuchte, klassifizierte und textgeschichtlich einordnete, 1968 in Lund das Werk von R. Kieffer, 'Au delà des recensions ?', welches auf der Basis von Joh. vi.52–71 'l'évolution de la tradition textuelle' untersuchte. Daneben wären noch manche anderen Arbeiten zu nennen, aber all das begegnet in Epps Bericht nicht. Entweder will er nur über den Stand der neutestamentlichen Textforschung in den USA berichten, dann hätte er das im Titel und/oder im Text zum Ausdruck bringen müssen. Aber dieser ist ebenso allgemeingültig formuliert wie die zahlreichen Feststellungen und Urteile im Text. Bleibt also nur ein Provinzialismus, der nichts eigentlich zur Kenntnis nimmt, was sich außerhalb seines eigenen Kreises abspielt, und seinen engen Bezirk (vgl. die S.1 Anm. 1 zitierten Urteile Epps über die amerikanische Szene) für die Welt hält? Ich hoffe nicht. Für Epps Darstellung gilt seine Charakteristik der modernen NT-Textkritik, wie sie sich ihm darstellt: 'diffuse, indeterminate, and eclectic' (S.387). Die Ursache dafür ist gewiß nicht allein bei ihm zu suchen, sondern auch – ja vor allem – bei seinen Lehrern. Aber ich kann nicht glauben, daß das Bild, das sich auf diese Weise ergibt, repräsentativ für die NT-Textkritik und die Textkritiker der USA ist. Daß die zentrale Position erst Chicagos und dann Claremonts der Vergangenheit angehört, ist außerordentlich bedauerlich. Aber kann nicht jederzeit anderswo – sei es in Harvard, Yale, Princeton oder an anderem Ort – ein neues Zentrum der Textkritik entstehen (Hilfe dabei, falls erwünscht, steht jederzeit zur Verfügung), damit das 'interlude' der Textkritik in den USA (falls es sich um ein solches handelt) ein Ende nimmt? Dem geschätzten Kollegen Epp[1] möchte man wünschen, daß die pessimistische, ja beinahe 'defätistische' Grundhaltung, aus der heraus er Stellung genommen hat, inzwischen einer 'self-confident, optimistic, and resolute' Position gewichen ist und der Erkenntnis, daß die neutestamentliche Textkritik der Gegenwart, vollständig gesehen, keineswegs ein 'interlude' darstellt, sondern daß ihr die Möglichkeiten und Mittel zur Verfügung stehen, weit über frühere Generationen hinaus dem ursprünglichen Text des Neuen Testaments nahezukommen, und daß sie auf diesem Wege bereits erhebliche Schritte voran getan hat. Wenn das weiter geschehen soll, muß sie sich allerdings dieser Möglichkeiten und Mittel auch bedienen und die Konsequenzen daraus in bezug auf die Vergangenheit ziehen, d. h. sich von denjenigen ihrer Voraussetzungen lösen, die nun einmal im Entscheidenden überholt sind. An Epp – und an die Adresse mancher Kollegen in den USA und anderswo gerichtet, welche die Loslösung noch nicht oder noch nicht vollständig vollzogen haben – kann ich nur

[1] Was hier notwendigerweise an Polemik gegen ihn vorgetragen werden mußte, entspricht nicht der persönlichen Beziehung des Verf. zu ihm und seiner Gesamteinschätzung Epps als Gelehrter, aber: magis amica veritas.

die Schlußworte meines Vortrags zum 100jährigen Jubiläum der Society of Biblical Literature 1964 wiederholen:[1] None of us would entrust himself to a ship of the year 1881 in order to cross the Atlantic, even if the ship were renovated or he was promised danger money. Why then do we still do so in NT textual criticism?

[1] Epp zitiert sie vollständig und gibt zu, die Frage sei damals 'appropriate' gewesen und heute 'both a valid and an embarrassing question' (S.390), so sei dieses Selbstzitat gestattet.

Is there a theological tendency in Codex Bezae?

C. K. BARRETT

The student of Acts, even though he may lack many of the qualifications and skills of such a professional textual critic as Matthew Black, nevertheless finds himself obliged by the text he is studying, beset as it is by so many notorious textual problems, at least to follow the arguments of his better equipped colleagues, and from time to time even to reach some provisional conclusions regarding the opinions they have set forth. He cannot escape the fact that Acts lies before him in two forms, the Old Uncial and the Western, and again and again he must make a decision, though it may often be a hesitant and tentative decision, about their respective merits and the relation of the one to the other. 'Two forms' is, of course, an over-simplification; the establishment of an 'Old Uncial Text' and especially of a 'Western Text' on the basis of the diverse material we possess is itself a task of very great complexity. This essay therefore, in order to be manageable, is confined to one MS of the Western Text, though it must at once be added that D itself, important as it is, does not offer us a 'pure' Western Text; we shall however gain a good deal in objectivity as well as brevity by confining our attention to a group of readings (or rather, to a small number out of a group of readings) actually existing in ink on vellum in the University Library at Cambridge.

A little more than fifty years ago J. H. Ropes wrote, 'Of any special point of view, theological or other, on the part of the "Western" reviser it is difficult to find any trace.'[1] It is true that he goes on to speak of 'a Gentile's feeling that any statement is inadequate which implies that Christianity in the Apostolic age was limited to Jewry',[2] and of a similar 'desire on the part of the editor to indicate that the "sebomenoi" won by the apostles were converted from the status of heathen to the true

[1] J. H. Ropes, *The Beginnings of Christianity*, Part I, *The Acts of the Apostles*, volume III, *The Text of Acts* (London, 1926), ccxxxiii.

[2] *Ibid.*, citing xiv.5; xxiv.5; also ii.17; ii.47.

God through Christ, not merely from Jewish faith to Christianity',[1] but he makes it clear that the tendency, if it exists, is not a notable one, and also discounts the suggestion that much of the distinctive Western material was Montanist in origin.

It may be said at once that the view taken in this essay is that Ropes was substantially right, and one more quotation may be allowed which says or implies as much as can usefully and confidently be said about the Western Text. 'If a reviser had had the Old Uncial text of Acts at his disposal, and had wished to rewrite it so as to make it fuller, smoother, and more emphatic, and as interesting and pictorial as he could, and if he had had no materials whatever except the text before him and the inferences he could draw from it, together with the usual religious commonplaces, it must be admitted that moderate ingenuity and much taking of pains would have enabled him to produce the "Western" text'.[2] Other writers however have not been content with Ropes' position, and two outstanding contributions to the question must now be considered.

P. H. Menoud, who deals with the Western Text as a whole rather than with D, begins by discussing the so-called Apostolic Decree of xv.29 (cf. xv.20; xxi.25).[3] He argues that its original form, designed simply to facilitate table-fellowship between Jewish and Gentile Christians, must have dealt only with food regulations; in fact only one thing was necessary, 'that Gentile Christians should observe the Jewish rule of eating only *kosher* meat' (p. 23). So the earliest form of the Decree, not actually preserved in any of our authorities, charged those to whom it was addressed 'to abstain from what has been sacrificed to idols and from blood'. This basic requirement was expanded by various additions. The addition of *καὶ πνικτοῦ*, hardly more than a verbal alteration, was intended to include in the prohibition all flesh improperly slaughtered. But, beyond this, the tradition found it good to extend the authority of the apostles over further areas of Christian life; hence, in due course, the prohibition of *πορνεία*, and then the addition of the Golden Rule, and finally the reference to the power that makes the moral life possible, the Holy Spirit. Thus the Decree gains a significance wider than its original Jewish context. Menoud sums up the observations he has made: 'The writer of this Western reading reveals here his chief intention: to emphasize the newness of the Christian faith as regards Judaism, and to do so both negatively and positively. Negatively

[1] *Ibid.*, citing xx.21, xvi.15.

[2] *Ibid.*, ccxxv.

[3] P. H. Menoud, *Studiorum Novi Testamenti Societas, Bulletin* II (1951).

in denouncing and condemning the unbelief of the Jews: there is an undeniable anti-Jewish tendency peculiar to many Western readings. Positively, by insisting on the greatness and unity of the church, and on the authority of the apostles, and also simply by mentioning with predilection the grandeurs which separate Christianity from Judaism, that is to say, the Holy Spirit and Jesus as Christ and Lord' (pp. 27f). Menoud proceeds to illustrate the points he has made under four heads. (1) Jews and Christians: here he brings out (from the Western text) the responsibility of the Jews for the death of Jesus (iii.17) and for attacks on the church (iv.9; xiii.45; xiv.2–7; xviii.12, 13), and their powerlessness in making such attacks (v.39; vi.11; iv.14; v.38). (2) The apostles and the church: the variations in the quotation from Joel (ii.17ff) show a universalizing tendency. Paul acts under the guidance of the Spirit (xix.2; xx.3). 'The emphasis in the D reading of Acts xv.2 is not against Paul but in favour of the authority and unity of the church' (p. 29). (3) The Holy Spirit: this is a varied paragraph. Menoud cites xix.2; xx.3 again, to show the overruling of Paul's plans by the Spirit (also viii.39). He rejects the suggestion that this interest points to a Montanist origin for the Western text, and quotes Ropes' argument that this suggestion is inconsistent with a Western anti-feminist tendency. He himself, however, thinks that the anti-feminist tendency is not a major trend in the Western recension. (4) The Lord Jesus Christ: there is little material to note here except the multiplication of titles; in general D tends to prefer 'The Lord Jesus Christ' to 'Jesus' or 'the Lord', or any other simpler designation.

Some of these points will be taken up below. Here, in passing, one (but it is of fundamental importance) will be mentioned. Menoud begins from the Council and the Decree of Acts xv, observing (see above) that only one thing was necessary if Gentile Christians were to be acceptable to Jewish Christians: they must restrict themselves to *kosher* food. In itself, this may be true, though in fact it was not their food alone that made Gentiles unacceptable to Jews. But was this question, of social and religious intercourse, the only issue under consideration at the Council? Was it *the* issue with which the Council was concerned? As a question in its own right this would lead us far from the theme of the present essay, and is therefore not to be discussed. But it is quite clear that the author of Acts (in whatever text we read him) did not think that it was the sole or even the main point at issue. The Council took place because Jewish Christians went from Jerusalem to Antioch and insisted that unless men were circumcised and instructed to keep the law of Moses they could not be saved (xv.1, 5). The question therefore –

for Luke – was of salvation, the question whether Gentiles as such might be converted and included in the church, whether their hearts were cleansed by faith alone, or only by the observance in whole or in part of the law. I am not contending that the Western text of the Decree is the original Lucan text, or that the original Lucan text, whatever that may have been, was historically accurate; but if the Western editor, or successive Western redactors, added references to fornication and the Golden Rule as summing up the divine requirement, he was taking up and developing something that was implicit (even if in a muddled way) in the original Lucan narrative. He was not introducing a new theme, but expanding, amplifying, clarifying, underlining, what was already there. This observation, made about the passage from which Menoud begins his argument, provides the theme of this paper.

A much more extensive treatment of the characteristics of D has been written by E. J. Epp,[1] who comes however to conclusions very similar to those of Menoud. To trace his argument in full would require a book of equal length, and it will be impossible to do justice to it here except by way of example. There is, he claims, a fundamental theological tendency in D in Acts; the MS shows 'a decidedly heightened anti-Judaic attitude and sentiment' (p. 165).[2] This tendency is disclosed in three ways. (1) D portrays the Jews as more hostile to Jesus and more responsible for his death than does the Old Uncial text. Correspondingly it lays a positive emphasis on Jesus as Lord and Messiah. (2) D minimizes the response of the Jews to the Gospel and the importance of Jewish institutions to the new faith. Correspondingly there is a greater Gentile interest, a stronger emphasis on universalism, and a stress on features (such as the Holy Spirit) that distinguish the new faith from the old. (3) D represents the Jews as more hostile to the apostles; correspondingly, the apostles are made to stand out as leaders of the church, and Roman officials are treated as relatively free from blame.

Dr Epp stresses the fact that his evidence is not confined to the few evidently anti-Jewish passages cited by his predecessors.[3] In addition to these he finds a tendency that expresses itself in small variations,

[1] E. J. Epp, *The Theological Tendency of Codex Bezae Cantabrigiensis in Acts*. SNTS Monograph Series 3 (Cambridge, 1966). See my review in *London Quarterly Review* 192 (1967), pp. 345f; also my *New Testament Essays* (London, 1972), pp. 103f. There is an excellent bibliography of the subject in Epp, *The Theological Tendency*, pp. 172–85.

[2] It may be questioned whether an attitude and a sentiment add up to a theological tendency. It may be that Hort (cited by Epp, *The Theological Tendency*, p. 1) was, after all, not very far wrong!

[3] On pp. 166f of *The Theological Tendency*, Epp mentions P. Corssen, D. Plooij, M. J. Lagrange, A. F. J. Klijn, and P. H. Menoud.

which, though previously undetected, show a prevailing cast of thought. Taken separately they might not, perhaps, be thought to supply definite evidence; taken together they form an unmistakable picture. It is only fair to recognize that this means that it is in the nature of things impossible to do justice to Dr Epp in an article: the strength of his case rests not upon the cogency of individual examples but upon their multiplicity. We may however by way of illustration run rapidly through his opening discussion of 'The Jews and Jesus' (pp. 41–64). He begins with the addition in iii.17 of πονηρόν: what the Jews did, though done in ignorance, was wicked. Further, D has ἐπιστάμεθα (B: οἶδα), 'we, the apostles, representing the Christian movement, know', and adds ὑμεῖς μέν, 'you Jews, over against God' (ὁ δὲ θεός, iii.18). A similar point arises in xiii.27, where D, by omitting B's ἀγνοήσαντες, takes away the plea of ignorance that might have excused the Jews. From this we move to xvii.30 where after ἀγνοίας D adds ταύτης: it was this ignorance, the ignorance of the heathen Athenians (and by implication not that of the Jews, who should have known better) that God overlooked. Dr Epp now turns to the context of passages he has already examined. At iii.14, where B has ἠρνήσασθε, D has ἐβαρύνατε. Many explanations (mostly based on the hypothesis of variant translations of a Semitic source) have been offered; Dr Epp takes ἐβαρύνατε to mean that 'the Jews not merely said "no" (ἀρνεῖσθαι) to Jesus' release, as in B, but as if with a vengeance they took positive action against him, they "weighed down", "oppressed", or "tormented" (βαρύνειν) him' (p. 53). The addition of Χριστόν in iii.13 minimizes the excuse of ignorance. Turning to chapter xiii, Dr Epp believes the complicated variants of verses 28f to indicate that 'the D-text shows the Jews in a more active role in the death of Jesus than does B' (p. 58).

Here for the present we leave Dr Epp's learned and ingenious work. Is any over-all tendency to be observed in D? Did the editor, or editors, of the Western Text, of whose work the MS D may be taken as a reasonable though certainly imperfect representative, have some theological or ecclesiastical axe to grind? We may begin from the observation that the author of Acts undoubtedly manifests a number of tendencies, including those that we have just seen attributed to the Western Text. These tendencies appear in Acts (and, *mutatis mutandis*, in the Third Gospel) whatever text we use.

Inevitably Luke manifests an anti-Judaic tendency. It was a simple historical fact that the Jews had rejected Jesus and were in large measure responsible for his death.[1] They brought before Pilate an

[1] That is, to Luke. I do not raise the actual historical question.

accusation which, substantiated, could lead to nothing but execution (Luke xxiii.2); they demanded the release not of Jesus but of Barabbas (xxiii.18), and insisted that Jesus should be crucified (xxiii.21). Pilate's sentence is given in the form: He handed Jesus over to their will (xxiii.25). Acts says no more than this. At ii.23 B and D are united in saying, *τοῦτον . . . προσπήξαντες ἀνείλατε*. At vii.52 they agree in representing Stephen's charge against his judges: he speaks of the Righteous One, of whom you have now become betrayers and murderers. Further, Luke could hardly avoid the simple definition that 'the Jews' were those who did not accept the apostolic message. Those who did accept it became Christians, 'brothers', 'disciples', 'those who belonged to the Way'. In the nature of things, the Jews were 'them' over against 'us'; they were the people who disagree with us, and with whom we disagree; and the more vital to Luke and his Christian friends the point of disagreement the more intense the feeling between the two sides was bound to be. That there was strong feeling between Jews and Christians in the first century is amply attested by such a passage as 1 Thess. ii.15f, and it is not at all surprising that Luke should narrate incidents that illustrate the various points in Paul's summary. The story of arrests, incarcerations, and punishments contained in Acts iii–v appears in both B and D. In both texts Stephen is stoned. D is unfortunately not extant in Acts ix so that we do not know of any difference there may have been in its account of Saul the persecutor, but the pattern of the converted Saul's missionary work is expressed in both texts in the same words at xiii.46: Behold, we turn to the Gentiles. At the corresponding point in the story of Paul's work in Corinth (xviii.6) there is a difference between B and D. Where the former has *ἀπὸ τοῦ νῦν εἰς τὰ ἔθνη πορεύσομαι*, the latter reads *ἀφ' ὑμῶν*[1] *νῦν εἰς τὰ ἔθνη πορεύομαι*. This variant may be taken to heighten the anti-Judaic tone of the passage;[2] in fact it represents no more than the application of the Western editor's rather wooden common sense. It was simply not true (according to Acts) that from this point onwards Paul gave up his mission to the Jews and evangelized Gentiles only. 'I am now (in Corinth) leaving you Jews for the Gentiles' made good sense, whereas the B reading suggested what the Western editor knew (from Acts itself) to be false. It is hard to see any significance in the D variant at xxii.21 (*ἐξαποστέλλω* for *ἀποστελῶ*), and the Jewish reaction is the same in both texts; unfortunately at xxviii.28 D is not extant.

Thus there is a strong vein of anti-Judaism in Acts, and a corres-

[1] A few letters are missing here in D, but d's *a bobis* (sic) is clear.

[2] It is so taken by Epp, *The Theological Tendency*; see p. 87.

ponding interest in the spread of the Gospel to the Gentile world. It was inevitable that this should be so, and even more inevitable that a Christian work should make much of the central Christian figure, affirming that Jesus of Nazareth was the Jewish Messiah, and the Lord of all men; at ii.36 there is only slight verbal variation between B and D, of no theological significance, in the assertion that God had made the Jesus whom the Jews had crucified both *κύριος* and *χριστός*. It would, moreover, have been difficult for Luke to write Acts without devoting a good deal of attention to the apostles. In i.21f B and D are agreed, with insignificant variations,[1] that it is necessary to appoint, in the place of Judas and so as to bring the number of the apostles up to twelve, one who had accompanied Jesus through the whole of his ministry and could act as a witness of the resurrection. In both texts Peter and John act as leaders of the new community in its trials. When the rest of the church is scattered (viii.1) the apostles remain in Jerusalem. Peter obeys the commission to preach to the Gentile Cornelius in chapter x. When in chapter xv a dispute arises it is the apostles and elders who assemble to discuss and settle it (xv.6, both B and D). Later in the book it is Paul who assumes the centre of the stage. Whether Luke regarded him as an apostle is a notorious problem, and it is worth noting that at xiv.14 D omits the word; this however does not really affect the issue, since whatever terminology is used Luke undoubtedly regarded Paul as the great Christian leader and evangelist, and portrays him as such. It is hard to see how, even if the last chapters of Acts in D had not perished, more could have been made of him than is done in the familiar text. This is confirmed by the other authorities for the Western Text.

Finally, the interest Luke shows in the Holy Spirit needs no demonstration here; it is one of the most frequently observed features of both the Third Gospel and Acts. It may suffice to quote the familiar, and often repeated, comment of Bengel on Acts i.1: . . . *non tam apostolorum, quam Spiritus sancti Acta describens.*

Whether one reads Acts in the Old Uncial, the Western, or the Antiochian text there appears an interest in the apostles and Paul as the leaders and representatives of the true people of God, as well as an interest in Peter, Stephen, Philip, and Paul in their own right, and an opposition to the Jews and their leaders as the adversaries of this true people and true leadership. Both the Third Gospel and Acts glorify and proclaim Jesus of Nazareth as Jewish Messiah and universal Lord, whom Jews and Gentiles conspired to kill but God raised from the dead; and the author is convinced not only that those about whom he

[1] D's singular *ἐστησεν* in i.23 is interesting, and may indicate an interest in Peter.

wrote often manifested the signs of inspiration but that every significant step in the story was directed by the Holy Spirit. To draw attention to these facts is not to throw doubt upon all the evidence collected by those (notably Dr Epp) who have maintained some special interest, especially an anti-Jewish interest, in D. There are places where the D text shows a greater animosity against Jews, a greater readiness to blame them rather than the Gentiles for the attack on Jesus and subsequent attacks on the apostles. In these places however the tendency with which we have to do is not a specially anti-Jewish tendency but a tendency to emphasize whatever is to be found in the underlying text. This may be demonstrated as follows.

In the first place, there are numerous passages in Acts where the effect of the D reading is simply to increase interest, to heighten tension, to make descriptions more vivid, in a word, to brighten the colours of Luke's narrative, where no theological, ecclesiastical, racial, or any other such interest is involved. Examples are numerous. Thus at x.25, as Peter was approaching Caesarea, one of the servants (D reports) ran ahead to inform Cornelius of his arrival. It can hardly be said that this adds to the glorification of the apostle, who in any case is about to be greeted with a reverence he immediately abjures.[1] The long expansion at xi.2 serves no purpose beyond that of filling out the narrative with some circumstantial detail.[2] In xiv.10 the cure of the lame man at Lystra is made more vivid: *εὐθέως, παραχρῆμα* he leapt up and walked.[3] At xvi.9f small additions fill out the story of Paul's vision. At xviii.21 it is not enough for Paul to tell the Ephesians that he must now leave them but will return; he explains that he must keep a feast.[4] In xviii.27 D has a much more detailed account of Apollos' move from Ephesus to Corinth,[5] and at xix.1 mentions the overruling of Paul's desire to go to Jerusalem.[6] At xix.9 is the famous Western addition that notes

[1] Note Peter's refusal to be treated as a *θεῖος ἀνήρ*.

[2] Epp, *The Theological Tendency* (pp. 104–7) argues that the effect of the D expansion is to 'minimize the significance of the Judaizing problem as well as any urgent concern about it on the part of both the Jerusalem church and Peter himself' (p. 106). Peter is in no hurry to go. This misses the fact that in the B text the dispute does not arise till Peter reaches Jerusalem; there is no pressure on him to go.

[3] Epp may be right in saying that D enhances the parallelism between xiv.10 and iii.6 so as to place Peter and Paul on the same level, but it is gratuitous, as far as these passages are concerned, to add that the two 'represent the new faith over against the Jewish leaders' (p. 163).

[4] A Judaizing feature in the picture of Paul!

[5] Epp, *The Theological Tendency* (p. 118) finds an ecclesiastical interest here.

[6] Epp, *The Theological Tendency* (p. 117) rightly draws attention to the emphasis on the Holy Spirit.

that Paul's use of the school of Tyrannus was from the fifth hour to the tenth.[1] The story of Ephesus is rich in such material; at xix.28 we not only hear the shouts but see the movements of the rioters – *δραμόντες εἰς τὸ ἄμφοδον*. I have referred here only to passages where there is some significant variation or addition; again and again there are changes of word order, small substitutions, and the like, for which the only explanation (if we assume, as we should not always or necessarily do, that they are secondary readings) is that the editor did not feel closely bound to his exemplar and substituted the words – often synonyms, usually livelier synonyms – he preferred.

With these facts in mind we turn, secondly, to look at some of Dr Epp's chosen passages. First, the paragraph iii.13–18. We shall bear in mind that it is the way of D to present small verbal variations, and that these need have no special motivation beyond the desire to 'improve' the underlying text. The word *θεός* (iii.13) is repeated before the names of Isaac and Jacob: if there is any motive it is to make the sentence more impressive. After the name Jesus, Christ is added; this is best regarded as one of the many examples of the Western editor's habit of using the fullest forms of divine names – it would certainly be rash to suggest that Messiahship is in mind wherever *χριστός* appears in D. In the relative clause there is in D a possible Semitism;[2] if *ἀπηρνήσασθε* is to be coordinated with *παρεδώκατε*, *αὐτόν* must be regarded as a pronoun giving definiteness to the relative, as in both Hebrew and Aramaic. It is possible to separate the two verbs ('Whom you handed over . . . ; and you denied him . . .'), but this seems less probable. You handed him over (says D), *εἰς κρίσιν*; the addition is one justified by the trial narrative in Luke. B's simple *παρεδώκατε* must be translated either 'You betrayed' or 'You handed over (to death)'; neither of these seems to convey a more favourable thought than that the Jewish court passed Jesus on to the Roman. In verse 14 there follows the *ἠρνήσασθε* (B)–*ἐβαρύνατε* (D) variant, of which Dr Epp's explanation (above, p. 19) seems far less convincing than the simple suggestion that the writer of D, having just used *ἀπηρνήσασθε* (verse 13), thought a new word would be desirable.[3] Verse 16 contains, in the Old

[1] It is somewhat far-fetched to claim that Paul's lecture hour suggests the intensity of his desire to reach the Gentiles.

[2] See below, p. 27. The existence of Semitisms in D can hardly strengthen the case for anti-Jewish bias.

[3] For the equivalence of *ἀπαρνεῖσθαι* and *ἀρνεῖσθαι* Epp himself refers to H. Riesenfeld, 'The Meaning of the Verb *ἀρνεῖσθαι*' in *Coniectanea Neotestamentica* XI (in honorem Antonii Fridrichsen, 1947), pp. 207–19. There is something to be said for the belief that the variant arose through confusion of *k-p-r* and *k-b-d*, or *k-d-b* and *k-b-d*.

Uncial text, a notorious syntactical problem; D's addition of ἐπί before τῇ πίστει does little to resolve it, but the insertion of ὅτι before ἐστερέωσεν is so helpful that it is very unlikely that the word was inserted with any motive other than that of alleviating a difficult sentence. This brings us to verse 17, and a number of changes. ἄνδρες ἀδελφοί (instead of ἀδελφοί) introduces a form of address common in Acts (thirteen times). Dr Epp makes a good deal of the change from οἶδα to ἐπιστάμεθα. The change of verb is probably insignificant. οἴδατε was used in verse 16, and D (the Western editor) wanted a change. The alteration from singular to plural is more striking. It may be that the author of the variant remembered that John had been acting with Peter (iii.1, 11, etc.); more probably however Peter is made to speak on behalf of (not the apostles but) the whole Christian body: We Christians know ... This in turn will explain the introduction of ὑμεῖς, and once this was in the text the addition of μέν (a word which D omits in verse 13 in a very similar sentence) was natural in view of ὁ δὲ θεός in verse 18. There remains in verse 17 the addition of πονηρόν. Here we should probably recognize the measure of 'heightening' that the Western editor applies to all the constituents of the text before him. There is anti-Judaism in the text: let it (he says) stand out clearly. To some extent the Jews may be excused on the ground of ignorance, but the excuse must not lead the reader to forget that what they did was – πονηρόν.

The next passage to consider is xiii.27ff. The first thing to observe is that the construction and sense of the text of B are alike obscure. The main difficulties are as follows. (1) It seems that the participle ἀγνοήσαντες must govern both τοῦτον and τὰς φωνάς, although two different kinds of 'not knowing' are implied. (2) τοῦτον is also governed by κρείναντες and τὰς φωνάς by ἐπλήρωσαν. (3) It is said that the Jews found in Jesus οὐδεμίαν αἰτίαν θανάτου. In Luke xxii.4, 14, (15), 22 however Pilate repeatedly declares that he finds no αἴτιον in Jesus, but the Jews press for his death. Compare Mark xiv.64; also Acts ii.23; iii.13. Luke must mean (at xiii.28) that the Jews could find no valid charge. (4) The plain meaning of xiii.29, καθελόντες ἀπὸ τοῦ ξύλου ἔθηκαν αὐτὸν εἰς μνημεῖον, is that the Jewish authorities, who had brought about Jesus' death, removed his body from the cross and buried it. Contrast Luke xxiii.53 (Joseph καθελὼν ... ἔθηκεν αὐτὸν ἐν μνήματι ...). When we turn to D we find a conflate text[1] in which, however, though new

[1] See Ropes, *The Beginnings of Christianity*, pp. 261ff; 'the conflate and corrupt text of D' (p. 261). See also A. C. Clark, *The Acts of the Apostles* (Oxford, 1933), p. 81.

difficulties are introduced, difficulties (1) and (2) are dealt with. (3) is to some extent mitigated, but (4) remains, as it does in Ropes' reconstructed Western Text; it must be regarded as a divergent tradition, unless Joseph, a member of the Sanhedrin, is taken to represent his colleagues. What we have in D's omission of *ἀγνοήσαντες* is not the introduction of an anti-Jewish bias – there is plenty of anti-Jewish bias anyway – but part of an (inadequate) attempt to clear up a muddle.

This leaves xvii.30, where it is difficult to believe that the writer of D (the word *ταύτης* is not in e.g. Irenaeus and may not be part of the Western Text[1]) expected his reader, noticing the word *ταύτης*, to pick up the allusion to a different ignorance, that of the Jews, and to say to himself, I must remember that God's readiness to overlook Greek ignorance does not mean that he is prepared to overlook Jewish ignorance too.

Consideration of a few of Dr Epp's examples (and if space permitted similar observations could be made about many more, I believe most, of them) thus leads to the view that they are due not to a special anti-Jewish tendency in D but to a general tendency to explain and simplify, to emphasize and often to exaggerate, what is already to be found in other forms of the text. This may be confirmed, thirdly, by noting a few passages where Acts deals favourably with the Jews. These occur almost entirely in the early chapters; Luke seems to have thought that the Jews had their chance in the early days after the resurrection and neglected it – to the Gentiles' advantage. There are places where D seems to emphasize the pro-Jewish attitude.

At ii.33 Peter, making the offer of the Gospel to his Jewish countrymen, says that the Spirit has been poured out on them (*ὑμεῖν*), associating them with himself. At ii.38 D uses the regular baptismal formula, *εἰς ἄφεσιν ἁμαρτιῶν*, whereas B pins specific sins (of rejecting Jesus) upon the Jews: *εἰς ἄφεσιν ἁμαρτιῶν ὑμῶν*. In the next verse Peter again (according to D) associates his hearers with himself: *ἡμεῖν γάρ ἐστιν ἡ ἐπαγγελία καὶ τοῖς τέκνοις ἡμῶν*.[2] At iii.11 D strengthens the impression made by the miracle upon the (Jewish) beholders: *οἱ δὲ θαμβηθέντες ἔστησαν*. At iii.22 Peter again associates his hearers with himself and emphasizes the privileges of the Jews by saying (according to D) that Moses spoke *πρὸς τοὺς πατέρας ἡμῶν*, and predicted that the new prophet would arise from among *our* brothers; v.15 is worth noting not only because the healings it describes were performed in Jerusalem and

[1] Clark, *The Acts of the Apostles*, accepts it (p. 113), so far as I can see without discussion.

[2] Cf. xiii.26.

presumably for the benefit of Jews but also because it is a good illustration of the kind of reading found in D, which adds, after mention of Peter's shadow, *ἀπηλλάσσοντο γὰρ ἀπὸ πάσης ἀσθενίας ὡς εἶχεν ἕκαστος αὐτῶν*. The addition has the effect of underlining the blessing conferred on Jewish sufferers, but it is doubtful whether this was the intention; the reading is rather an example of D's (the Western editor's) unwillingness to leave anything to the imagination.[1] There is a group of readings worth noting in D's account of the intervention of Gamaliel in the Sanhedrin's debate about the course of action to be followed in regard to the apostles. At v.34 B represents Gamaliel as asking that 'the men', *τοὺς ἀνθρώπους*, be put outside while the case is discussed; in D they are *τοὺς ἀποστόλους*. It cannot be supposed that Gamaliel actually spoke of Peter and John as 'the apostles', but the effect of the variant is to make him appear more respectful. At v.38 Gamaliel warns his colleagues to let the apostles go, adding, according to D, *μὴ μιάναντες τὰς χεῖρας*. The modern English reader is likely to take this as a very disrespectful remark indeed: I wouldn't soil my hands on you. If this is what the text means it must certainly be taken as an example of D's heightening of Luke's anti-Jewish interest. This interpretation of the words, however, is not in accordance with the context, in which Gamaliel is urging the Council not to harm the apostles. To do so would – or might – mean that they would defile their hands with innocent blood; that is, the representative of Judaism is made to speak of the apostles as innocent men whom it would be a crime to injure.[2]

It would be a mistake to attempt, on the basis of the few observations in these pages, to prove too much. The main, perhaps the only, contention of this essay is that though scholars such as Menoud and Epp have rightly noted in D a tendency to anti-Judaism, and a few other related tendencies, these do not justify us in speaking of specific theological characteristics of the MS (or of the Western Text). The essential characteristic of the MS, or text, is to exaggerate existing tendencies. It is hard, however, even for the amateur textual critic to forbear from the $64,000 question of all textual criticism: Where and how did the Western Text originate? The question will not be answered, and the prize will not be won, here, but the following points seem worth noting.

(1) It is erroneous to charge the Western Text with a special tendency

[1] Cf. viii.1, where to 'all were scattered except the apostles' D adds 'who stayed in Jerusalem' – 'another glimpse of the obvious', as Bruce dryly remarks.

[2] Epp, *The Theological Tendency* (pp. 130f), sees here a 'high compliment to the apostolic office'. It is tempting to see here the expression *ṭimme' 'et hayyadaim*, an expression used of sacred books (e.g. Yadaim 3.2, 5), but it would be unwise to speculate on this basis.

to anti-Judaism. This interest, along with other characteristics, was found in the original text of Acts, and all were developed and exaggerated by the Western editor.

(2) To this observation may be added that Ehrhardt[1] found a Jewish tendency in D. He based this view only on the variants in xv.2, and the basis is slight; it is nevertheless worth considering.

(3) Another related point is that the Western Text has often been held to show more traces of Semitism than the Old Uncial Text. A discussion of this question would call for another paper, and I propose to offer no evidence here; only to say that though the Semitic character of D can be and has been exaggerated, and a number of supposed Semitisms can be explained away, there seems to me to be here and there a construction that has a definite Semitic turn.[2] It may be that in such places the Western Text is simply reproducing more accurately than the Old Uncial what Luke wrote; but at least Semitism was not so offensive to the editor that he felt he must remove it at all costs. We should recall also passages, notably iii.11 and xii.10, that suggest acquaintance with the topography of Jerusalem. The linguistic and topographical evidence is superficially, and perhaps more than superficially, discrepant with the theory of an anti-Jewish tendency.

(4) If the real tendency of the Western Text was to exaggerate, and to make stories more vivid and interesting, it is natural to compare it with the various apocryphal Acts, which also tell vivid and often supernatural stories, and tend to exaggerate whatever material may have been available to their authors. If we can determine the setting of the early apocryphal Acts we may be on the way to locating the Western Text of the canonical Acts. The apocryphal Acts present us with (from the viewpoint of the circles in which they were composed) brighter and better accounts of the apostles; so in a relatively innocent and undeveloped way does the Western Text of Luke's Acts. This theme however is not one that can be developed in this paper, since a survey of the Christian apocrypha would lead much too far afield.

[1] A. Ehrhardt, *The Apostolic Succession* (London, 1953), pp. 29f.

[2] See M. Black, *An Aramaic Approach to the Gospels and Acts* (Oxford, 1967), pp. 277–80; M. Wilcox, *The Semitisms of Acts* (Oxford, 1965), p. 185.

Ephesians i.1

ERNEST BEST

1. The disputed reading in Eph. i.1 forms a fascinating study in textual criticism. In the vast majority of cases the debate about disputed readings remains within the area of the immediate text but any decision in relation to Eph. i.1 interrelates with decisions which have to be made about the authorship of the letter and about its purpose, nature and content. In this study all we can hope to do is to determine the proper approach and isolate the factors which affect a final decision. It is not proposed to review the history of the discussion and reference will be made only to the major suggestions which have appeared. J. Schmid has given us an excellent review of the main positions up to about 1927 with comprehensive lists of those who have adhered to each.[1]

In respect of the letter itself there seem to be certain results which have been generally acceptable to commentators. We may describe these as the 'constants' of the discussion. Four 'constants' appear relevant to our problem:

(a) Paul is not or has not been personally known to the readers though they do know about him (i.15; iii.2; iv.20f).[2]

(b) The letter is not written to an individual Christian community but to a wider group (lack of personal details, etc.).

(c) It is not written to the universal church but to a limited group of communities (i.15ff; vi.21f).

[1] J. Schmid, *Der Epheserbrief des Apostels Paulus*, Biblische Studien, volume XXII, Heft 3/4 (Freiburg im Breisgau, 1928). More recent reviews will be found in E. Percy, *Die Probleme der Kolosser- und Epheserbriefe* (Lund, 1946), pp. 449–66; N. A. Dahl, 'Adresse und Proömium des Epheserbriefes', *TZ* 7 (1951), pp. 241–64; P. Dacquino, 'I destinatari della lettera agli Efesini', *Riv. Bib.*, 6 (1958), pp. 102–10; A. van Roon, *The Authenticity of Ephesians* (Suppl. *NT* 39), pp. 72–85; A. Lindemann, 'Bemerkungen zu den Adressaten und zum Anlass des Epheserbriefes', *ZNTW* 67 (1976), pp. 235–51.

[2] It may also be true that the actual writer of Ephesians, if he was not Paul, did not personally know those to whom he wrote.

(d) The letter is addressed largely, if not entirely, to Gentile Christians (ii.1ff, 11ff; iii.1f; iv.17).

Amongst the relevant 'variables', i.e. matters upon which scholarly opinion has not solidified, are the authorship, intention and nature of the letter (a genuine letter or a meditation, prayer, treatise, sermon made into a letter?). A variable which takes us beyond the letter itself is its possible identification with the letter mentioned in Col. iv.16 ('to the Laodiceans'). Different decisions in relation to the variables render certain solutions to the problem more or less attractive.

2. The manuscript evidence is easily set out.

P: *τοῖς ἁγίοις οὖσιν καὶ πιστοῖς* 𝔓[46]
B: *τοῖς ἁγίοις τοῖς οὖσιν καὶ πιστοῖς* ℵ* B* 424[c] 1739
A: *τοῖς ἁγίοις τοῖς* (om D) *οὖσιν ἐν Ἐφέσῳ καὶ πιστοῖς rell*

These are the only readings which require serious consideration; others, e.g. that with *πᾶσιν τοῖς οὖσιν*, can be safely eliminated. We shall refer to the three primary texts above as respectively the P, B and A text forms.

3. Patristic evidence.

3.1. It is clear that Origen neither read the reference to Ephesians in his text nor had a lacuna for he expounds the B text and has had to think up an explanation in order to escape its grammatical difficulties.[1] Basil[2] indicates that many if not all of the older manuscripts lack the reference 'in Ephesus'; in distinguishing between texts in this way he implies that some do have the words. The construction of Marcion's text from the references in Tertullian[3] is not undisputed. It is generally held that Tertullian's accusations relate to the superscription to the letter and not to the text itself; in that case Marcion cannot have had the A text; this would also imply that Tertullian did not have 'in Ephesus' in his text. It is however just possible that Tertullian accuses Marcion of differing from the true church's reading of the text. It is also unclear whether Marcion had a manuscript with 'to the Laodiceans' implying that he knew the letter under this name, or whether he altered an existing text 'to the Ephesians' into 'to the Laodiceans' and if so why he altered it. Was he dependent on tradition or, less probably, did he carry through an early piece of historical critical analysis and, observing that it was

[1] For Origen's discussion see especially J. A. F. Gregg, 'The Commentary of Origen upon the Epistle to the Ephesians', *JTS* 3 (1902), pp. 233–44, 398–420, 551–76 at p. 235.

[2] *Adv. Eunom.* ii.19.

[3] *Adv. Marc.* v.11.12; 17.1.

inappropriate for Paul to have written a letter in which he said he had not known the Ephesians personally when in fact he had visited them, made a guess on the basis of Col. iv.16?

3.2. As well as the question of reading there is, as a discussion of Tertullian shows, the question of the superscription. All the manuscripts, including those in the B and P tradition, have the title 'To the Ephesians'. How far back does this go? As soon as, or very shortly after a collection of Paul's letters was made, some identification would have been necessary for the individual letters in the collection. The problem here is not that of the use of the letter but its use as a letter to the Ephesians. Church Fathers whether or not they read 'in Ephesus' certainly knew the letter as 'to the Ephesians' (e.g. Irenaeus,[1] Clement of Alexandria,[2] Origen,[3] Tertullian,[4] Canon Muratori[5]). The much earlier letter of Ignatius to the Ephesians is important. Are there signs of the dependence of its address on our Ephesians, suggesting that Ignatius knew our Ephesians as addressed to the Ephesians and was playing on this knowledge in writing to them? With a greater recognition today of the influence of the liturgical tradition on early writing there is probably less reason to see Ignatius as dependent on Ephesians than both as dependent on that tradition.[6] We can probably then not trace back the recognition of the letter as 'to the Ephesians' earlier than Irenaeus, but that is not to say it was not so recognised earlier.

4. We now consider those solutions which accept one or other of the existing text forms.

4.1. The A text as the original reading. If this solution is accepted then because of (a) it is much easier to assume that Paul did not write the letter.[7] The A text has certain inherent difficulties. (i) The place name is awkwardly situated in that it appears to be especially associated with ἁγίοις and ἐν Χριστῷ Ἰησοῦ by implication with πιστοῖς. In Col. i.2, where we also have a double address, 'saints and faithful brothers', the

[1] *Adv. Haer.* v.2.2; 8.1; 14.3; 24.4.
[2] *Strom.* iv.8 (64.1 = *GCS* II, p. 277); *Paed.* i.5 (18.3 = *GCS* I, p. 100).
[3] See p. 30, n. 1 above.
[4] See p. 30, n. 3 above.
[5] The evidence of Canon Muratori is not important if it dates from the fourth century, cf. A. C. Sundberg, 'Canon Muratori: A Fourth Century List', *HTR* 66 (1973), pp. 1–41.
[6] Against the view that Ignatius knew our letter as addressed to the Ephesians is his statement that there are many letters of Paul in which he mentions the Ephesians (Ign. *Eph.* xii.2); a reference to our letter would have enabled him to make his point more strikingly.
[7] E. K. Simpson, *New International Commentary on the N.T.* (Grand Rapids, Mich., 1972), is one of the few who accept this reading and Pauline authorship.

geographical designation clearly applies to both halves of the address as does the final phrase 'in Christ'. In I Cor. i.2 the problem does not arise since those outside Corinth who are additionally addressed are introduced with a σύν phrase (cf. II Cor. i.1; Phil. i.1). (ii) (b) is not satisfied. (iii) If the account in Acts of Paul's visit to Ephesus reflects genuine tradition then the lack of personal reference to members of the community in Ephesus is surprising; (a) cannot be satisfied. (iv) If 'in Ephesus' was later omitted we should expect the scribe who did so to have also omitted *τοῖς οὖσιν*, for the B form of the text is very difficult to construe (see 4.2).

Assuming the A form of the text is original we require to account for the appearance of the B and P forms. The omission of 'in Ephesus' cannot be attributed to any of the ordinary scribal failures in sight or hearing but must have been deliberate. (i) A scribe observing that the writer of the letter had not visited the church to which he was writing and knowing that Paul had evangelised Ephesus may have thought it better to erase the reference to Ephesus than the attribution to Paul. This presupposes non-Pauline authorship. (ii) Ephesus as the destination of such an important letter may have been felt inappropriate in view of a subsequent failure on the part of the Ephesians to live up to the terms of the letter; such a failure might be deduced from Rev. ii.4f and the scribe believed he was fulfilling Rev. ii.5. (iii) It might have been felt that a letter dealing with a general subject and lacking personal reference should not be addressed to a particular congregation. (This argument has also been advanced to account for the G text of Romans.)

4.2. The B text as original. Such an assumption leaves a very difficult phrase to construe.

4.21. Origen[1] relates *τοῖς οὖσιν* to the singular participle with the article in the divine name as given in Exod. iii.14 and links this again with I Cor. i.28f. The saints are those who have been called out of non-existence into real existence because of their participation in the one to whom real existence belongs. This is very far fetched and lacks any parallel in NT thought: *καὶ πιστοῖς* comes in very oddly after it.

4.22. A number of commentators[2] translate 'to the saints who are (also) faithful in Christ Jesus'. It is doubtful if the Greek can easily be made to have this meaning.[3] It is also difficult to see what it means; almost by defi-

[1] See p. 30, n. 1 above.

[2] Most recently E. J. Goodspeed, *The Meaning of Ephesians* (Chicago, Ill., 1933), p. 18; M. Barth, Anchor Bible Commentary 34, volume 1 (Garden City, New York, 1974).

[3] Cf. G. Zuntz, *The Text of the Epistles* (London, 1953), p. 228, n. 1.

nition the saints are those who are faithful in Christ Jesus. πιστοί in this interpretation must be given the meaning 'faithful' rather than 'believers'.[1]

4.23. To avoid the difficulties of 4.22, attempts have been made to distinguish between the ἅγιοι and the πιστοί. G. B. Caird[2] has revived the attempt to refer the former to Jewish Christians and the latter to Gentile believers; presumably he would translate 'to those who are Jewish Christians and those who are also believers incorporate in Christ Jesus'.[3] He argues that οἱ ἅγιοι is sometimes used by Paul to refer to the Jewish Christians of Jerusalem (Rom. xv.25–31) and that it is used in this letter at ii.19 to refer to Jewish Christians. But where Paul uses the term in this way its meaning is clear from the context, and this meaning is not undisputed at ii.19;[4] certainly in other parts of the letter (i.18; iii.8; iii.18; iv.12; v.3) it refers to both Jewish and Gentile saints. It does not possess the exclusively Jewish Christian reference in any of the addresses of the other Pauline letters. This translation at i.1 might be easier to accept if the letter was not by Paul since it would then be unnecessary to argue for a variation in his normal usage of the word. This rendering conflicts with (d).

4.24. Lake and Cadbury[5] suggest understanding τοῖς οὖσιν as 'local', arguing that it has this sense in Acts v.17; xiii.1; xiv.13; xxviii.17, and translating 'to the local saints and believers in Jesus Christ'. Even if the participle of εἶναι can have this meaning in the passages in Acts[6] it is in each instance geographically anchored by the context; in Eph. i.1 it is impossible to know to what 'local' refers, and so it becomes meaningless. It is moreover not clear why only the ἅγιοι and not also the πιστοί are described as 'local'.

4.25. E. Mayser gives evidence to show that the participle of εἶναι with the article is often used almost redundantly in a kind of officialese (*Kanzleisprache*).[7] It is interesting at this point to go back and reread

1 Whether πιστοί should be translated 'faithful' or 'believers' is another of the variables; supporting evidence for either translation can be adduced.

2 G. B. Caird, *Paul's Letters from Prison* (Oxford, 1976), ad loc.; cf. J. C. Kirby, *Ephesians, Baptism and Pentecost* (London, 1968), pp. 170f; F. W. Beare, *Interpreters' Bible* x, (New York/Nashville, 1953), pp. 601f; W. G. Kümmel, *Introduction*, ET, 2nd edition (London, 1975), p. 355.

3 He does not offer an actual translation.

4 Some take it to refer to angels, cf. Gnilka, *Der Epheserbrief*, Herders theologischer Kommentar zum NT, x, 2 (Freiburg/Basel/Wien, 1971).

5 Lake and Cadbury, *The Beginnings of Christianity*, edited by F. Jackson and K. Lake volume IV (London, 1942), p. 56; see also A. T. Robertson, *Grammar*, 3rd edition (New York, 1919), p. 1107.

6 Lake and Cadbury are supported by N. Turner in J. H. Moulton, *Grammar*, III, p. 152.

7 E. Mayser, *Grammatik der griechischen Papyri aus der Ptolemäerzeit*, II 1, pp. 347f.

Origen who describes some phrase as redundant: *εἰ μὴ παρέλκει προσκείμενον τὸ τοῖς ἁγίοις τοῖς οὖσι.* Which words does he suppose to be redundant? Reading deep meaning into redundant words accords with his exegetical methods. Since he goes on to comment on *τοῖς οὖσι* it must be this phrase which he regards as redundant. Lightfoot[1] indeed suggested that we should read *τοῖς ἁγίοις τὸ τοῖς οὖσι* in Origen (the text of Cramer's *Catenae* is often uncertain); Gregg,[2] following J. A. Robinson, reads *τῷ τοῖς ἁγίοις τὸ τοῖς οὖσι* which is preferable. The difficulty still remains why the redundant phrase should be attached only to *ἁγίοις* and not also to *πιστοῖς*, yet a redundant phrase in Ephesians would not be out of keeping with the style.

4.26. It can be seen that the real difficulty commentators have with the B text is its meaning. If we begin with it then it is quite easy to explain the appearance of the P text: a scribe may have allowed his eye to stray and missed the second *τοῖς* due to the three successive *οις*, or else noticing the difficulty of understanding the B text he thought he could render it clearer with an emendation. The A text will have appeared because *οὖσιν* (or its singular equivalent) is normally followed by a place name in the Pauline addresses. This would account for the peculiar position of the geographical name in the A text, but it does not account for the appearance of Ephesus rather than some other place.

4.27. That difficulty exists for all views except 4.1. If the letter was first given the superscription 'To the Ephesians' it is easy to see why the name later entered the text. But how did it obtain this superscription? If we assume that it appeared at or about the time the letters were collected it is also reasonable to assume that this collection was made at a place where both Paul's acquaintanceship with Ephesus was unknown, and also Acts was unknown since the latter depicts a long visit of Paul to Ephesus. In such circumstances the attribution might have been a deduction from II Tim. iv.12 combined with Eph. vi.21f; this implies that II Timothy was recognised as a Pauline letter when the deduction was made; it would therefore have been included in the collection (yet it is generally held that the Pastorals were not part of the earliest *Corpus Paulinum*). Various other suggestions have been made for the attribution 'To the Ephesians' or 'in Ephesus'. A nameless circular letter was found at Ephesus or the original letter was preserved at Ephesus and so 'Ephesus' was attached to it; the Ephesian church imagined itself an important church which should have a letter of its own and so appropriated a nameless letter; the circular letter had been distributed from

[1] Lightfoot, *Biblical Essays* (London, 1893), p. 378, n. 1.

[2] See p. 30, n. 1, above.

Ephesus and so received that name;[1] when the Pauline letters were collected at Ephesus Ephesians was written as a general letter to introduce them;[2] a copy of a circular letter for churches in Asia but not intended for Ephesus was sent to Ephesus as the main church of the area and so eventually received its name. Schlier[3] suggests very tentatively that a copy of a circular letter was sent to Ephesus and therefore had the superscription 'To the Ephesians' on the outside to ensure its delivery; this presupposes the modern practice of redirecting an old letter in a fresh envelope with a new address; in those days the letter would have been taken by messenger and such an outside address would have been unnecessary. Kirby[4] believes the letter was written by one of the leaders of the church at Ephesus; a copy came to Corinth; there it required identification and the reference to Ephesus was inserted. The number and variety of suggestions and the inability of any one of them to gain general acceptance indicates the difficulty of the problem.

4.3. The P text as original.[5] This has never been seriously investigated.[6] It would be easier to accept if *οὖσιν* preceded *ἁγίοις* or followed the whole phrase, but as it stands it is still possible to translate it either as 'to those who are saints and believers in Christ Jesus' (treating *οὖσιν* as redundant 'officialese'; see 4.25)[7] or as 'to the local [see 4.24] saints and believers'. The former translation though it fits in with the verbose style of Ephesians conflicts with (c) since it suggests an unrestricted readership. The second provides a possible way of avoiding the great difficulty of the idea of a circular letter (see 5.1 and 5.2) if we suppose that Tychicus carried the letter round a number of churches; his presence within a particular community as he read the letter provided the necessary local anchorage (see 4.24). The lack of precise identification of the readership implied in either of these renderings is supported by the final

1 Cf. Schmid, *Der Epheserbrief des Apostels Paulus*, p. 128.

2 Cf. Goodspeed, *The Meaning of Ephesians*, pp. 10f.

3 H. Schlier, *Der Brief an die Epheser* (Düsseldorf, 1971), p. 32.

4 Kirby, *Ephesians, Baptism and Pentecost*, pp. 170f.

5 Since no special relation exists between 𝔓[46] and D (cf. Zuntz, *The Text of the Epistles*, pp. 41f) their combined evidence for this reading increases its probability.

6 So far as I am aware it has only been seriously suggested by J. Belser, *Der Epheserbrief des Apostels Paulus* (Freiburg, 1908), and he based his suggestion on the reading of D (he could not have known 𝔓[46]) and P. Benoit, DBS, volume VII, pp. 195–211, who says that this reading has been too little considered.

7 Blass–Debrunner, *Grammatik*, § 413. 3* consider this impossible unless accompanied by a qualifying phrase; this qualification could be 'in Christ Jesus'.

blessing. In the other letters of the Pauline corpus this is invariably of the form 'the grace of the Lord Jesus (Christ) be with you (your spirits) (all)', and the recipients are addressed in the second person without qualification. The concluding grace in Eph. vi.23f is not only much more elaborate but it is also couched in the third person and contains a qualification in vi.24 where grace is said to be 'with all who love the Lord Jesus Christ'. The use of the third person would harmonise with both suggested renderings, but the qualification would fit better with the first. The letter and the grace are only intended for those who acknowledge themselves as saints and believers.

If either of these suggestions is possible how did the A and B texts ever appear? It is almost impossible to imagine a scribe creating the B text out of the P in order to make it simpler; nor is there any way in which it could have been created accidentally. It is therefore necessary to assume that the A text appeared first. Codex Claromontanus may provide the missing link. If *οὖσιν* was understood by any scribe as 'local' it would be natural to add a place name directly after it to define it even without *τοῖς* preceding it; then the normal form of the Pauline address would force the introduction of *τοῖς* and the A text would come into existence. The B text would appear because some scribes remembered that MSS existed without a geographical designation. This suggestion does, at least, account for all the textual evidence.

5. We now turn to conjectural readings. All such readings have an initial disadvantage in that they add an extra stage to the development of the text.

5.1. The text contained a deliberate lacuna after *τοῖς οὖσιν*. This is a conjectural reading since no extant MS has such a lacuna. The lacuna was to be filled in by Tychicus as he read the letter to each particular church when he visited it or it was to be filled in by each church itself as the letter was passed from church to church, or else a number of copies were sent, each with a lacuna, and each church left to fill in its own name.

There are considerable difficulties with such a conjectural reading. (i) Roller's detailed examination of ancient letter writing suggests there is no evidence for the existence of letters in the contemporary world with such lacunae.[1] (ii) *ἐν* would always have been present;[2] no MS evidence

[1] Cf. O. Roller, *Das Formular der paulinischen Briefe*, *BWANT* IV, 6 (Stuttgart, 1933), pp. 199–212, 520–5. Only Zuntz, *The Text of the Epistles*, p. 228, n. 1, disagrees, but the evidence he produces is slender and dubious. (The reference he gives to *Mus. Helv.* should be 5 (1948), 218ff).

[2] Cf. Dahl, 'Adresse und Proömium des Epheserbriefes', pp. 243f.

exists for it except in connection with Ephesus (or, possibly, Laodicea). (iii) If the gap was to be filled up by each church why should copies without it continue to exist, for each church would make its own copy with its own name in it. (iv) Why should no memory of other churches, with the possible exception of Laodicea, remain in the manuscript evidence? (v) Why could Paul not have listed all the churches in the address instead of leaving a blank? He writes to the churches of Galatia. Could he not have written then to the churches of Asia or to those of the Lycus Valley or wherever the area was in which the alleged churches lay? 1 Peter is a round letter to the churches in a number of districts and each of the districts is listed (see 1.1). (vi) Why should strong evidence exist for the reading Ephesus since this was a church to which the letter was not addressed and therefore this name would not have been inserted in the lacuna? (This problem is less serious if the letter was not by Paul himself.) (vii) The alleged gap comes at the wrong point (see 4.1(i)).

The B text would arise quite easily from this conjectural text once a scribe forgot to leave the lacuna. The P form would presumably have been derived from the B form by the process suggested in 4.2. It is the appearance of the A form which it is difficult to envisage (see 4.2).

5.2. A number of identical letters were sent to different churches each carrying an individual name. This practice can be paralleled in the ancient world.[1] Yet this solution has also great difficulties. (i) the failure of any place name other than Ephesus to survive in the manuscript tradition since (unlike 5.1) the theory requires their presence; (ii) the existence of strong manuscript tradition relating the letter to Ephesus when many of the details of the letter itself are inappropriate to such a reference; (iii) the recognised simpler method in use among Christians of addressing churches as a group; (iv) the appearance of the name at the wrong point (see 4.2(i)).

It is exceedingly difficult to see how any of the known text forms arose out of this conjectural reading. Since Ephesus cannot have been one of the original churches which was addressed the A text can only have appeared through the deliberate alteration of an existing name into that of Ephesus. The B text could only have appeared through the deliberate omission of the name of a church; this does not explain why the name of the church was omitted and a difficult sentence to construe created.

5.3. The original reading was ἐν Λαοδικείᾳ. If we were sure that this was the text Marcion read then we should have considered it in §4 and not here. Marcion may have been making a guess but if he was not then he

[1] Cf. Roller, *Das Formular der paulinischen Briefe*, pp. 207ff, 603f. This solution is accepted by Dahl, 'Adresse und Proömium des Epheserbriefes'.

probably had only the superscription 'To the Laodiceans' and nothing in the text. The most popular form of this theory is that put forward by Harnack.[1] Since it has been frequently discussed we do not need to outline it, but shall briefly indicate its difficulties. (i) The letter referred to in Col. iv.16 appears to be a letter directed to one congregation and not a general letter like our Ephesians. (ii) Colossians contains much personal detail; why should a letter to neighbouring Laodicea be devoid of this? Epaphras gave Paul full information about Colossae; why did he not also give him full information about Laodicea? (iii) It seems more probable that Marcion was making an honest guess than that he was acting on information he possessed. (iv) The difficulty of Harnack's hypothesis is increased if we suppose that Paul is not the author of Ephesians. (v) A good case can also be made out for identifying the letter of Col. iv.16 with that to Philemon.[2]

It is not easy to see how the present text forms evolved from this supposed original reading. It may be that Ephesus was substituted for Laodicea on the grounds that the church in Laodicea proved a failure and its name deserved to be wiped out (Rev. iii.14–22) but this does not explain the substitution of Ephesus which itself is not too well spoken of in Rev. ii.1–7. We have then to suppose conditions in which the B text would arise and from it the P text. This involves a lengthy process. Alternatively the B text may have been created directly from the original text by the omission of 'in Laodicea'. We have seen the difficulty of this in 4.1 and it is a difficulty for all texts which originally possessed a name. The introduction of 'in Ephesus' would be a separate stage. Again this would be a lengthy process. In either case the P text would have been evolved from the B text.

5.4. The original place name was Colossae. Ochel[3] has suggested that Ephesians is a generalised Colossians intended to be used in a wider area and to replace Colossians, and originally put out as a letter to Colossae. Unfortunately canonical Colossians did not disappear and since two so similar letters addressed to the same church were unacceptable some scribe omitted the reference to Colossae. This clearly accounts for the relation between Colossians and Ephesians and for the more general nature of Ephesians. It is more acceptable if it is assumed Paul was not

[1] A. v. Harnack, 'Die Adresse des Epheserbriefes', SBA Hist.-philos. Kl., 1910, pp. 696–709.

[2] Cf. Goodspeed, *The Meaning of Ephesians*, pp. 6f.

[3] W. Ochel, *Die Annahme einer Bearbeitung des Kolosserbriefes im Epheserbrief in einer Analyse des Epheserbriefes untersucht* (Diss. Marburg, 1934). Unfortunately I have not yet been able to consult this and depend on others for information about it.

the author of Ephesians. But it has difficulties. (i) The complex situation which must be supposed for the production of Ephesians is only a hypothesis. (ii) The relation between Ephesians and Colossians can be accounted for in other ways. (iii) The omission of *ἐν Κολοσσαῖς* left the difficult text with *τοῖς οὖσιν*. (iv) The theory does not account adequately for the insertion of 'in Ephesus'.

5.5. Schmid[1] conjectured *τοῖς ἁγίοις καὶ πιστοῖς ἐν Χριστῷ Ἰησοῦ*. This permits an understanding of the letter as a general letter, yet it could still have been written to a limited readership for II Peter and Jude are simpler in their general addresses yet have limited readership. The A text appeared because the latter was circulated from Ephesus and 'to the Ephesians', at first used as a superscription, eventually entered the text. Its awkward position allowed it to be recognised as an insertion. The inconsistency between the letter as it existed and a letter to Ephesus, which Paul had not visited, was then observed and the reference to Ephesus omitted.[2] Hence the B text. This conjecture involves a long and complicated process of textual development. It does not satisfactorily explain the reference to the peculiar position of the place name. If II Peter and Jude are taken as parallels to the type of universal letter addressed to a limited readership then this might suggest Ephesians comes from a date nearer to that of these other two letters. It does not satisfactorily explain why the name Ephesus was introduced.

5.6. A. van Roon[3] conjectures an original *τοῖς ἁγίοις τοῖς οὖσιν ἐν Ἱεραπόλει καὶ ἐν Λαοδικείᾳ, πιστοῖς ἐν Χριστῷ Ἰησοῦ*. This conflicts with none of the constants. He supports this by associating Col. ii.1 and iv.13 so that ii.1b refers to the Christians of Hierapolis and the *ἀγών* of ii.1a has the same reference as the prayers of Eph. i.16, 17–23 and iii.16ff. When the two place names were omitted (to create an ecumenical letter) the *καί* which united them was retained; this explains its position in the B text. However it is exceedingly difficult to see why the *καί* should be left when the two place names were removed. Though van Roon does

1 J. Schmid, *Der Epheserbrief des Apostels Paulus*, pp. 125ff; cf. M. Goguel, 'Esquisse d'une solution nouvelle du problème de l'épître aux Éphésiens', *RHR* 111 (1935), pp. 254ff, and 112 (1936), pp. 73ff at p. 254, n. 1; Dacquino, 'I destinatari della lettera agli Efesini'. This also seems to be the reading adopted by Kirby, *Ephesians, Baptism and Pentecost*, p. 170, as original, though, curiously, he assumes that the 'saints' are Jewish Christians and the 'faithful' are Gentile Christians (cf. Caird, *Paul's Letters from Prison*, see 4.24).

2 Kirby, *Ephesians, Baptism and Pentecost*, p. 170, believes the reference to Ephesus was removed when the letter came back from Corinth (see 4.28) to Ephesus.

3 van Roon, *The Authenticity of Ephesians*, pp. 80ff.

not comment on it his conjecture accounts for the peculiar position of the geographical reference (see 4.1(i)) in the A text. It fails however to account for the disappearance of the original names and the appearance of Ephesus; it is not sufficient to say that it was omitted to create an ecumenical letter (cf. Rom i.7 and the omission of 'Rome' in G) for clearly the person who inserted 'in Ephesus' was unaware of an alleged tendency of the early church to universalise the letters of Paul. It also does not explain why Hierapolis is not mentioned in Col. ii.1 (ii.1b would be a very roundabout way of referring to it) or why the Colossians should not have sent to Hierapolis (iv.16) for a copy of the letter.

5.7. Santer[1] conjectures *τοῖς ἁγίοις καὶ πιστοῖς*[2] *τοῖς οὖσιν ἐν Χριστῷ Ἰησοῦ* and supposes '*καὶ πιστοῖς* was omitted through haplography, put in the margin by a corrector, and then inserted in the wrong place thus producing' the B text. As he notes *τοῖς οὖσιν ἐν Χριστῷ Ἰησοῦ* is not found in any other Pauline address but he offers two parallels; neither is as close as he suggests: in 1 Thess. ii.14 the participle is more correctly linked to *ἐν τῇ Ἰουδαίᾳ*[3] and in Rom. xvi.11 it could go with *ἀσπάσασθε* and it is in any case uncertain if Paul uses *ἐν Χριστῷ Ἰησοῦ* in the same way as he uses *ἐν Κυρίῳ*. In the position Santer puts it *τοῖς οὖσιν* would be unnecessary according to normal Pauline usage; e.g. II Cor. xii.2; Rom. viii.1; Phil. i.14; iv.21; Rom. xvi.7, 8. If Santer's conjecture were acceptable it would probably be better, as he suggests, to assume non-Pauline authorship. However the later we place the date of the writing the less time we allow for the two extra variations in the text which have to appear before the process leading to the B, A and P texts begins. Why, moreover, should the second corrector insert the reference at the wrong point, showing an insensitivity to Greek?

5.8. Readings which presuppose a misreading of, or damage to, the original text. Many conjectures have been made, but probably only two are worthy of mention, the first because of its intrinsic value and the second because it is recent.

5.81. Ewald[4] conjectured *τοῖς ἀγαπητοῖς οὖσι καὶ πιστοῖς* and assumed that the corner of the manuscript was damaged and the letters *απη* were lost; *ιοις* was then surmised to replace them. However the use of

[1] M. Santer, 'The Text of Ephesians i.1', *NTS* 15 (1968/9), pp. 247f.

[2] Although Santer does not note it the linking of two almost synonymous nouns or adjectives is in the style of Ephesians: cf. i.4, 8, 17; ii.1, 19; iii.10, 12; v.27; vi. 4, 5.

[3] Cf. B. Rigaux, *Les Épîtres aux Thessaloniciens*, Études Bibliques (Paris/Gembloux, 1956).

[4] P. Ewald, *An die Epheser, Kolosser und Philemon*, Kommentar zum NT, 2nd edition (Leipzig, 1910), pp. 15f.

ἀγαπητοί is unusual in the address of a Pauline letter; only Rom. i.7 incorporates the word. Ewald's solution implies that the original letter had no direct address to a town or area and so may be held to accord with its general nature. It is however difficult to see how any one should create such a difficult text as the B form by the surmise Ewald supposes. It is then necessary to account for the appearances of the A form and the P form. All this requires a very complex and lengthy procedure.

5.82. Batey[1] conjectures as the original reading *τοῖς ἁγίοις τοῖς Ἀσίας*. A scribe mistook *Ἀσίας* for *οὔσαις* which he then changed to the masculine *οὖσιν*. This is far fetched and as in 5.81 it has to be followed by a very complex process leading to the present text forms.

6. Few conclusions can be drawn other than that there is as yet no satisfactory solution. Certainly decisions taken on other grounds in respect of the variables eliminate some solutions, but not the same ones for every interpreter. It is difficult to conceive of the letter as existing in the Pauline corpus without some designation distinguishing it from other letters, but this designation need not have been in the text. The attachment of the name 'Ephesians' to the letter must therefore have been as early as the first collection of the letters which contained Ephesians. For this reason, if for no other, a process of development of text forms which contains as few steps as possible is essential, and this suggests one of the existing text forms, or if not, one which only adds one more step to the process; the more steps required the earlier the letter must be placed; complex theories therefore go best with Pauline authorship. While it might not settle the issue it would provide an important clue to it if we could determine why the name 'Ephesians' was originally attached to the letter. A full scale study of this is required.

[1] R. Batey, 'The Destination of Ephesians', *JBL* 82 (1963), p. 101.

Matthew vi.22f and ancient Greek theories of vision

HANS DIETER BETZ

The debate between Judaism and Hellenism not only predates Christianity, but has also influenced the early Christian literature at its oldest level of tradition. The Q-logion about the eye as the lamp of the body (Matt. vi.22–3; Luke xi.34–6),[1] puzzling as this saying doubtless is, shows evidence of the intellectual struggle between Judaism and Hellenism.

A. Jülicher[2] correctly observed that the passage looks harmless but is in fact one of the most difficult to interpret in the entire Gospel tradition. And J. Amstutz[3] perceptively remarked that the more work is done on the logion the more obscure it becomes. Even as early as 1912 P. Fiebig[4] had proposed a moratorium on further attempts to explain the riddle of Matt. vi.22f and par. New Testament scholarship surely ignored the moratorium, but no one has yet succeeded in satisfactorily explaining the mysterious word of Jesus. Although no exhaustive survey of recent studies can be provided here, the general situation may best be exemplified by the study of E. Sjöberg.[5] He goes to great lengths to recover the presumed Aramaic original of the logion, but in the end he seems himself to feel the inconclusive nature of the evidence. In an addition after the proof-reading he gives credit to J. Munck for having called his attention to Plato's *Timaeus* 45B–46A. It is indeed in this direction that one must look for a solution to the problem.[6]

[1] Cf. also the Coptic Gospel of Thomas, logion 24.

[2] A. Jülicher, *Die Gleichnisreden Jesu*, II (Tübingen, 1910[3]), p. 98.

[3] J. Amstutz, *ΑΠΛΟΤΗΣ. Eine begriffsgeschichtliche Studie zum jüdisch-christlichen Griechisch* (Bonn, 1968), p. 96.

[4] P. Fiebig, *Die Gleichnisreden Jesu* (Tübingen, 1912), p. 151.

[5] E. Sjöberg, 'Das Licht in dir. Zur Deutung von Matth. 6,22f Par.', *Studia Theologica* V (1951), pp. 89–105.

[6] This suggestion can be found in part of the older literature, but it did not make its way into the commentaries. J. J. Wetstein, *Novum Testamentum Graecum*, I (Amsterdam, 1751), pp. 330f, quotes some pertinent passages from the Greek literature and concludes: *Comparat Christus animum corpori, &*

In the following pages a beginning of such an interpretation is attempted. Limited space requires that the paper be confined to the essential points of discussion and pieces of evidence. For the same reason, the discussion will be limited to Matt. vi.22f, because Luke xi.34–6, as well as the Coptic Gospel of Thomas, logion 24, represent quite different doctrines.

I. ON THE FORM AND COMPOSITION

Verse 22a *Ὁ λύχνος τοῦ σώματός ἐστιν ὁ ὀφθαλμός·*
Verse 22b *ἐὰν οὖν ᾖ ὁ ὀφθαλμός σου ἁπλοῦς,*
ὅλον τὸ σῶμά σου φωτεινὸν ἔσται·
Verse 23a *ἐὰν δὲ ὁ ὀφθαλμός σου πονηρὸς ᾖ,*
ὅλον τὸ σῶμά σου σκοτεινὸν ἔσται.
Verse 23b *εἰ οὖν τὸ φῶς τὸ ἐν σοὶ σκότος ἐστίν, τὸ σκότος πόσον.*

The logion is a four-liner, but its composition, structure, and form have not been analyzed convincingly. R. Bultmann[1] in his *Geschichte der synoptischen Tradition* presents a very cautious and tentative discussion. He treats Matt. vi.22f as a logion and puts it into the subsection called 'sachlich formulierte Grundsätze'. He saw that the logion is composed of several elements. Verse 22a could be the original unit, which was then to be interpreted by verses 22b–23a. But because of what Bultmann perceived as a poverty in content in Matt. vi.22a, the double-logion in verses 22b–23a may well have been the starter, and verse 22a as well as 23b later additions. Luke xi.34–6 he took to be a later expanded version. Although Bultmann's suggestions have been taken over by many scholars, they are nothing but possibilities, and none of them is even probable.

1. The introductory sentence verse 22a looks proverbial.[2] For that reason it may have been thought suitable as an introduction. It certainly later became a proverb together with many other sayings of the Sermon on the Mount. The logion itself, however, takes verse 22a more seriously,

judicium oculis, similitudine etiam apud Philosophos usitata. The matter was clearly stated by J. Lindblom, 'Det solliknande ögat', *Svensk Teologisk Kvartalskrift* 3 (1927), pp. 230–47; and by G. Rudberg, *Hellas och Nya Testamentet* (Stockholm, 1929), pp. 150f.

[1] R. Bultmann, *Geschichte der synoptischen Tradition* (Göttingen, 1971[4]), pp. 77, 91, 95.

[2] Cf. *Deutsches Sprichwörter-Lexikon*, edited by K. F. W. Wander, I, column 172, no. 87 (Darmstadt, 1964): 'Die Augen sind des Leibs Latern'. For a comprehensive treatment of the eye and its symbolism see W. Deonna, *Le symbolisme de l'œil* (Bern, 1965).

so that in the present composition it is regarded as a *definition* of the human eye and a description of its functioning. The following commentary shows that it is 'cited' only to be critically evaluated.

2. Verses 22b–23a is an antithetical *parallelismus membrorum*, connected with verse 22a by way of *chiasmus*. While verse 22a names *ὁ λύχνος* first and *ὁ ὀφθαλμός* second, the eye is discussed first in verses 22b–23a, and the lamp second in verse 23b. The introductory words *ἐὰν οὖν* (verse 22b), *ἐὰν δέ* (verse 23a), and *εἰ οὖν* (verse 23b) suggest that the statements function as a commentary, proceeding from the objective phenomena stated in the third person singular (verse 22a) to the parenetic second person singular in verses 22b–23b. The commentary itself has two parts, the interpretation of the eye as the organ of vision (verses 22b–23a), and the interpretation of the image of the lamp (verse 23b). The first part can be subdivided again into the description of the proper and the defective functioning of the eye.

3. The second part of the commentary (verse 23b) interprets how the image of the lamp should be correctly understood. The light burning in the lamp is now identified as *τὸ φῶς τὸ ἐν σοί*. This identification as well as the form of the oxymoron[1] is evidence that we have definitely moved from a physiological to a moral level of thought. The oxymoron introduces the paradoxical possibility that 'the light within you' may well be 'darkness', and it concludes with an exclamation of surprise: *τὸ σκότος πόσον*. Of course, this exclamation is a rhetorical device, making inescapably clear that no time is to be wasted on trivialities and absurdities, but that matters of ultimate human concern are at stake.

4. It should be noted that this compositional structure has a parallel in one of the main sources for Greek theories of cognition, Theophrastus' *De sensibus*.[2] Theophrastus begins his essay by reporting on the theories of cognition proposed by earlier philosophers. Then he criticizes these theories by pointing out their inner consequences and resulting faults, which cause greater dilemmas than those they were intended to explain. The whole procedure of report, critique, and dilemma is, of course, informed and shaped not only by the sources but also by Theophrastus' own theory. Compared with Theophrastus' work, Matt. vi.22f is obviously extremely short. It looks like a condensation into a *mashal* of what in an elaborated form would be a treatise. At any rate, the formal structure of Matt. vi.22f seems to be as follows:

[1] See A. Jülicher, *Gleichnisreden*, II, p. 99.

[2] Theophrastus, *De sensibus*, edited by G. M. Stratton, *Theophrastus and the Greek Physiological Psychology Before Aristotle* (London and New York, 1917). See also the parallel composition in Epictetus, *Diss.* III.3.20–2.

Verse 22a	I. Definition of the human eye
Verses 22b–23b	II. Physiological and parenetical commentary
Verses 22b–23a	1. Interpretation of the eye as the organ of vision
Verse 22b	a. The condition for proper vision
	(1) the condition of the eye is *ἁπλοῦς*
	(2) the expected positive result
Verse 23a	b. The condition for defective vision
	(1) the condition of the eye is *πονηρός*
	(2) the expected negative result
Verse 23b	2. Interpretation of the image of the lamp
	a. Assumption of a paradoxical possibility
	b. An exclamation of surprise

II. THE THEME

In terms of the thematic content of Matt. vi.22f, we enter into the territory of the ancient theories of sense perception, especially vision. This territory is very diversified and includes fields of research such as theory of elementary cognition, theory of light and color, physiology of the eye, therapy of the eye. None of these fields can of course be adequately treated here, but only the main points of contact can be mentioned.[1]

1. The *style of definition* with regard to the human eye is found as early as Pythagoras who, according to anonymous Pythagoreans, called the eyes 'gates of the sun'.[2] This image reminds us of mythological notions, as when sun and moon are considered to be the eyes of a cosmic deity, or the human eyes to correspond to sun and moon. The interpretation of Pythagoras' saying is not clear.[3] Are the eyes 'gates of the sun'

[1] On this subject matter see especially the following studies: J. I. Beare, *Greek Theories of Elementary Cognition from Alcmaeon to Aristotle* (Oxford, 1906); A. E. Haas, 'Antike Lichttheorien', *Archiv für Geschichte der Philosophie* XX (1907), pp. 345–86; H. Lackenbacher, 'Beiträge zur antiken Optik', *Wiener Studien* XXXV (1913), pp. 34–61; R. Bultmann, 'Zur Geschichte der Lichtsymbolik im Altertum', *Philologus* XCVII (1948), pp. 1–36, reprinted in his *Exegetica* (Tübingen, 1967), pp. 323–55; W. Luther, 'Wahrheit, Licht und Erkenntnis in der griechischen Philosophie bis Demokrit', *Archiv für Begriffsgeschichte* X (1966), pp. 2–240. Especially important are W. Beierwaltes, *Lux intelligibilis. Untersuchung zur Lichtmetaphysik der Griechen* (München, 1957); D. Bremer, 'Licht als universales Darstellungsmedium; Materialien und Bibliographie', *Archiv für Begriffsgeschichte* 18 (1974), pp. 185–206, where a good bibliography is included (pp. 197–206).

[2] H. Diels and W. Kranz, *Die Fragmente der Vorsokratiker*, 6th edition, reprinted (Zürich and Berlin, 1964), 58 B 1a (I, 450, 13). The work will henceforth be referred to as Diels–Kranz.

[3] See on this problem Beierwaltes, *Lux intelligibilis*, pp. 31–3.

in the sense that the sunlight enters through them into the body? Or is the sun the image for the inner 'light of the soul', which again can be identical with the *νοῦς*? Or are several meanings combined as in another saying of the philosopher: *μὴ λέγειν ἄνευ φωτός*?[1] At any rate, Pythagorean tradition also contained the dualism of *φῶς* and *σκότος*, which according to some sources goes back to a Chaldean named Zaratas.[2] Furthermore, the Pythagoreans seem to have introduced the separation of *σῶμα* and *ψυχή*,[3] a dualism also presupposed in Matt. vi.22f. There the concept of *σῶμα* comes close to that of *σῶμα/σῆμα*, but *ψυχή* is not mentioned. Instead, Matt. vi.23 has *τὸ φῶς τὸ ἐν σοί*, a concept which even in Jewish thought is not unknown and is often identified with that of the soul.[4]

Two sayings of Heraclitus are important for the study of Matt. vi.22f. Perhaps the preference for the eye rather than the ear is proverbial in origin: *ὀφθαλμοὶ γὰρ τῶν ὤτων ἀκριβέστεροι μάρτυρες*.[5]

Another saying, critical of the eye and ear as organs of sense perception, is intentionally obscure: *κακοὶ μάρτυρες ἀνθρώποισιν ὀφθαλμοὶ καὶ ὦτα βαρβάρους ψυχὰς ἐχόντων*.[6] The phrase 'barbarian souls' is difficult to understand. According to Diels–Kranz these are souls who like barbarians cannot properly understand the information given by the senses. Heraclitus would then be saying that he does not doubt the value of sense perception *per se*,[7] but he contends that those who do not use the organs with *φρόνησις* cannot interpret what they have perceived.[8] The failure lies in the fact that they do not possess the *λόγος*.[9] On the whole, however, G. S. Kirk is correct in his exposition of Heraclitus: 'His criticism of men is based upon the fact that the truth is there to be observed, is common to all, but they cannot see it: apprehension of the Logos is no mystical process but the result of using eyes, ears, and common sense.'[10] There can be no doubt that although Matt. vi.22f does not mention the ear, it gives preference to the eye. This is similar to the

1 Iamblichus, *Vita Pyth.* 84 (Leipzig, 1937), p. 48.
2 Hippolytus, *Refut.* 1.2.12.
3 Cf. Diels–Kranz, 58 B 1a (1, 450, 5). See also W. Burkert, *Weisheit und Wissenschaft* (Nürnberg, 1962), p. 98.
4 Cf. H. Strack and P. Billerbeck, *Kommentar zum Neuen Testament aus Talmud und Midrasch* (München, 1926), 1, pp. 432f.
5 Diels–Kranz, 22 B 101a (1, 173, 15f). See M. Marcovich, *Heraclitus* (Venezuela, 1967), pp. 23f; Deonna, *Le symbolisme de l'œil*, pp. 1ff.
6 Diels–Kranz, 22 B 107 (1, 175, 1f). See Marcovich, *Heraclitus*, pp. 45–8.
7 Diels–Kranz, 22 B 55 (1, 162, 11f).
8 Diels–Kranz, 22 B 17 (1, 155, 6–8).
9 Diels–Kranz, 22 B 72 (1, 167, 9–11).
10 G. S. Kirk, *Heraclitus: The Cosmic Fragments* (Cambridge, 1954), p. 376.

idea that the eye alone is not capable of recognizing the truth, but that another factor must enter into the process of vision.

2. The *dualism of light and darkness* is pre-eminent in the cosmology and epistemology of Parmenides.[1] In his thought light and darkness are metaphors for 'truth' versus 'untruth', 'knowledge' versus 'ignorance', and 'being' versus 'non-being'. These principles also determine the process of vision.[2] Darkness is to the highest degree the nature of the corpse, which has no capacity for cognition.[3] If, however, the human mind is illuminated by light, cognition of being can take place. Consequently, the organ of cognition is no longer the eye, which is devalued,[4] but thought.[5] Also in Matt. vi.22f the eye and the capacity to see are distinguished, and in the final analysis the capacity to see depends on another factor not named in Matt. vi.23, which qualifies both 'the light within you' and the eye.

3. The *comparison of the eye* to a lamp we find first in Empedocles' poem *Περὶ φύσεως*.[6] Empedocles compared the process of vision to a man who wishes to go out in a winter night and who because of the darkness outside equips himself with stormlamps. When Aphrodite[7] created the human eye it was a kind of lamp she constructed: the eternal fire was enwrapped in fine membranes and thin veils behind the pupil. Within the eye water floated around the fire, but the eye lets the light pass from the inside out because it is so much finer.[8] Empedocles, therefore, assumed a fire-light within the eye behind the pupil. Like a lantern this light shines through the eye and thus facilitates the process of vision.[9]

At this point we note a clear difference between Empedocles and Matt. vi.22f: both use the term ὁ λύχνος, but in Matt. vi.22f the light is not in the eye, but somewhere else in the body. This difference is no doubt intended and not simply accidental.

4. The philosophers of the following periods continued to build their own theories of cognition and sense perception, but the foundations laid by the Presocratics remained decisive presuppositions. Theophrastus, who has transmitted to us important doxographical material in his *De sensibus*, has also attempted to sort things out historically. Basically, he

1 See Beierwaltes, *Lux intelligibilis*, pp. 34–6.
2 Cf. Diels–Kranz, 28 B 9 (I, 240ff).
3 Diels–Kranz, 28 A 46 (I, 226, 10ff).
4 Cf. the expression ἄσκοπον ὄμμα in Diels–Kranz, 28 B 7 (I, 234, 34).
5 Diels–Kranz, 28 B 4 (I, 232, 7); 28 B 7 (I, 235, 1).
6 Diels–Kranz, 31 B 84 (I, 342, 4–9).
7 Cf. Diels–Kranz, 31 B 85, 86, 95 (I, 343 and 345).
8 Diels–Kranz, 31 B 84 (I, 342, 10–14).
9 The fiery nature of the eye was observed earlier by the physician Alcmaeon, 24 A 5 (I, 212, 5). See also Beare, *Greek Theories*, pp. 16ff.

finds, there are two conceptions of the process of cognition.[1] Parmenides, Empedocles, and Plato share the principle of 'similarity' (τῷ ὁμοίῳ), while Anaxagoras and Heraclitus start from the principle of 'contrast' (τῷ ἐναντίῳ). The first group assumes that the agent of cognition is located within beings and that cognition, especially vision, occurs by way of an 'effluence' (ἀπόρροια) from within the body towards the objects outside, where they meet with entities akin to them in nature. The other group proceeds from the theory that opposites attract one another. This principle also underlies Democritus' theory of 'air-imprints',[2] by which he tried to explain why, if one looks into the eye, one perceives in the pupil a reduced 'appearance' (ἔμφασις) of the world outside, including perhaps the observer. Employing Empedocles' notion of 'effluence', Democritus thinks that the 'appearances' occur in this way: the objects seen send out atoms which produce 'air-imprints' (ἀποτύπωσις) when they hit the air. The medium of the air then transports these 'air-imprints' into the eye, a process which is facilitated by the sun. The fire-atoms of the sunlight compress the air, so that the 'imprints' can be received, and the light guides the 'air-imprints' through channels into the eye. After they have passed to the pupil, the 'appearances' occur and are then transmitted to the rest of the body, including the soul which, according to Democritus, is part of the body and a material entity.

The conditions for vision are established, if the physiology of the eye meets the needs of the passage of the 'appearances'. The external membranes must be thin and dense, the inner parts spongy and free from fat and meaty tissue, the veins must serve to pass the 'appearances' on into the body, etc.[3] Complicated as Democritus' ideas about vision and perturbance of vision certainly are, the conditions for vision or disturbance of vision are always physiological in nature. The same is true for Epicurus and his famous theory of 'images' (εἴδωλα).[4] These 'images' are constantly produced and emitted by the objects seen. Separating from them they float into the eye. Since this theory was also promoted later by Epicurean philosophers, among them especially Lucretius,[5]

[1] Theophrastus, *De sensibus* § 1–2, p. 66.

[2] On Democritus' theory I follow W. Burkert, 'Air-Imprints or Eidola: Democritus' Aetiology of Vision', *Illinois Classical Studies* II (1977), pp. 97–109, where further literature is also listed.

[3] Cf. Diels–Kranz, 68 A 135 (II, 114, 28–115, 3; 116, 3–4).

[4] See C. Bailey, *The Greek Atomists and Epicurus* (Oxford, 1928), pp. 406ff; Burkert, 'Air-Imprints', pp. 103ff.

[5] Lucretius, *De rer. nat.* IV, ll. 311–52, edited by H. Diels (Berlin, 1923–4). Cf. also Epicurus' saying: ἀλλὰ καὶ πηρωθεὶς τὰς ὄψεις (ὁ σοφὸς) καταξιοῖ αὑτὸν τοῦ βίου. (Fragment 15, edited by H. Usener, *Epicurea* (Leipzig, 1887), p. 96).

we may assume that it was rather widely known in the New Testament era.

Looking again at Matt. vi.22f, one will have to conclude that the passage, by intention or accident, implicitly rejects the atomistic and Epicurean theories of vision, while approving of the Empedoclean and Platonic tradition at least to the extent that vision occurs through light passing from the inside out.

5. The theory of cognition and, as part of it, of vision, is the topic of discussion especially in Plato's *Republic*, books VI and VII, and *Timaeus.* Notably, Plato uses the form of parable to explain the matter, the Parable of the Sun (*Rep.* VI. 507B–509C), the Parable of the Parallel Lines (*Rep.* VI. 510B–511B), and the Parable of the Cave (*Rep.* VII. 514A–518B).[1]

In connection with the Parable of the Sun Plato first calls to mind the difference between the phenomena and the ideas: 'And the class of things [viz. phenomena] we can say can be seen but not thought, while the ideas can be thought but not seen.'[2] Next, 'vision' (ἡ ὄψις) is the topic of consideration. Vision is, according to Plato, to be regarded as a higher sense compared with the others because it needs a third element without which it cannot function, light: 'Though vision may be in the eyes and its possessor may try to use it, and though colour be present, yet without the presence of a third thing specifically and naturally adapted to this purpose, you are aware that vision will see nothing and the colours will remain invisible.'[3] The origin and cause of this light is the god Helios, and therefore the eye can rightly be named 'the most sunlike of all the instruments of sense'.[4] But vision is identical neither with the eye nor with the sun; Helios is the 'cause' (αἴτιος)[5] of vision, and the eye receives 'the power which it possesses as an influx, as it were, dispensed from the sun'.[6] Then (508C) the discussion turns from the visible world to the world of thought. Here Plato discusses first the phenomena of the disturbance of vision.

We see normally as long as we direct our eyes toward objects illuminated by the light of day; but 'when the eyes are no longer turned upon objects upon whose colours the light of day falls but that of the dim luminaries of night, their edge is blunted and they appear almost blind, as if pure vision did not dwell in them'.[7] These observations are then applied to the ways in which the soul perceives the truth: 'When it is firmly fixed on the domain where truth and reality shine resplendent it

[1] See Beierwaltes, *Lux intelligibilis*, pp. 37ff.

[2] Plato, *Rep.* VI. 507B; text and translation are according to the Loeb Classical Library edition by P. Shorey, Plato, *The Republic*, volume II (London and Cambridge, Mass., 1935).

[3] Plato, *Rep*, VI. 507D/E.

[4] *Ibid.*, 508B.

[5] *Ibid.*

[6] *Ibid.*

[7] *Ibid.*, 508C.

apprehends and knows them and appears to possess reason; but when it inclines to that region which is mingled with darkness, the world of becoming and passing away, it opines only and its edge is blunted, and it shifts its opinions hither and thither, and again seems as if it lacked reason.'[1] This is the result as far as insight into the truth is concerned: 'This reality, then, that gives their truth to the objects of knowledge and the power of knowing to the knower, you must say is the idea of good, and you must conceive it as being the cause of knowledge, and of truth in so far as known. Yet fair as they both are, knowledge and truth, in supposing it to be something fairer still than these you will think rightly of it. But as for knowledge and truth, even as in our illustration it is right to deem light and vision sunlike, but never to think that they are the sun, so here it is right to consider these two their counterparts, as being like the good or boniform, but to think that either of them is the good is not right. Still higher honour belongs to the possession and habit of the good.'[2]

The problem of the disturbance of vision is given special consideration in the Parable of the Cave. Plato distinguishes between two kinds of disturbances of the eye: the one when a person comes out of the light into darkness, and the other when a person changes from darkness to light.[3] What this means for philosophy is explained by the parable. The cave-dwellers who have never seen anything else but the shadows on the wall can only take those shadows for reality itself. If, however, one of the cave-dwellers were 'freed from his fetters and compelled to stand up suddenly and turn his head around and walk and to lift up his eyes to the light',[4] he would only feel pain in his eyes because of the dazzle and glitter of the light and see nothing. Even 'if someone told him that what he had seen before was all a cheat and an illusion, but that now, being nearer to reality and turned toward more real things, he saw more truly, . . .'[5] he would turn back to the cave and to those objects of vision which he is able to discern. Plato's solution to the problem is gradual adjustment to the light, so that at its end cognition of reality can really occur.

The second kind of disturbance of vision happens when the same man, now accustomed to live in the light, returns to the darkness of the cave. Of course, his vision of things has now completely changed, and 'if he recalled to mind his first habitation and what passed for wisdom there, and his fellow-bondsmen, do you not think that he would count himself happy in the change and pity them?'[6] Such a man would no doubt lose

[1] *Ibid.*, 508D.
[2] *Ibid.*, 508E–509A.
[3] *Ibid.*, VII. 518A.
[4] *Ibid.*, 515C.
[5] *Ibid.*, 515D.
[6] *Ibid.*, 516C.

all interest in returning to the cave. But if one imagines he would indeed return he would have the problem of disturbed sight again. At this point Plato describes the situation of the philosopher, obviously with the destiny of Socrates in mind. 'Now if he should be required to contend with these perpetual prisoners in "evaluating" these shadows while his vision was still dim and before his eyes were accustomed to the dark – and this time required for habituation would not be very short – would he not provoke laughter, and would it not be said of him that he had returned from his journey aloft with his eyes ruined and that it was not worth while even to attempt the ascent? And if it were possible to lay hands on and to kill the man who tried to release them and lead them up, would they not kill him?'[1]

As Plato points out in the following interpretation of the parable, he intended to speak about 'the soul's ascension to the intelligible region'.[2] The goal is to see the idea of good and to accept it as 'the cause for all things of all that is right and beautiful, giving birth in the visible world to light, and the author of light and itself in the intelligible world being the authentic source of truth and reason, and that anyone who is to act wisely in private or public must have caught sight of this.'[3]

Based upon this assessment Plato outlines the task of the philosopher: '. . . whenever he saw a soul perturbed and unable to discern something, he would not laugh unthinkingly, but would observe whether coming from a brighter life its vision was obscured by the unfamiliar darkness, or whether the passage from the deeper dark of ignorance into a more luminous world and the greater brightness had dazzled its vision. And so he would deem the one happy in its experience and way of life and pity the other, and if it pleased him to laugh at it, his laughter would be less laughable than that at the expense of the soul that had come down from the light above.'[4]

This situation is for Plato also the starting point of *paideia*. Education, he emphasizes, cannot 'put true knowledge into a soul that does not possess it, as if they were inserting vision into blind eyes'.[5] Rather, education corresponds to the turning around of the liberated man in the cave; it is the 'art of changing around' the soul: 'not an art of producing vision in it, but on the assumption that it possesses vision but does not rightly direct it and does not look where it should, an art of bringing this about'.[6] The capacity of vision itself is never lost, and so 'the excellence of thought, it seems, is certainly of a more divine quality, a thing that

[1] *Ibid.*, 516E–517A.
[2] *Ibid.*, 517B.
[3] *Ibid.*, 517C.
[4] *Ibid.*, 518A.
[5] *Ibid.*, 518C.
[6] *Ibid.*, 518D.

never loses its potency . . .'.[1] It is only the use of the faculty which must be converted, from the useless and harmful to a useful and beneficent. Plato at this point inserts an interesting illustration: 'Have you never observed in those who are popularly spoken of as bad, but smart men, how keen is the vision of the little soul, how quick it is to discern the things that interest it, a proof that it is not a poor vision which it has, but one forcibly enlisted in the service of evil, so that the sharper its sight the more mischief it accomplishes?'[2]

Apart from the *Republic*, the eye and the processes of vision are also treated *in extenso* in the *Timaeus*.[3] A detailed comparison between the two works cannot be presented in this paper, but a few points may be brought out. In the *Timaeus* Plato makes use of Empedocles' idea of the fire in the eye and he calls the eyes 'fire-bearing eyes' (*φωσφόρα ὄμματα*). Vision involves three kinds of light: (1) the daylight dispersed by the sun in the air; (2) the light contained in the eye-ball and flowing out of it toward the objects seen; (3) the light that is part of the colours of the objects. Vision takes place through a cooperation of all these lights, a process later called *συναύγεια*.[4] 'Accordingly, whenever there is daylight round about, the visual current issues forth, like to like, and coalesces with it and is formed into a single homogeneous body in a direct line with the eyes, in whatever quarter the stream issuing from within strikes upon any object it encounters outside. So the whole, because of its homogeneity, is similarly affected and passes on the motions of anything it comes in contact with or that comes into contact with it, throughout the whole body, to the soul, and thus causes the sensation of vision.'[5] Disturbance of vision happens, e.g. at night, because then the eternal fire is cut off, so that the internal fire, when it issues, meets with something that is unlike it, and therefore vision is prohibited.[6]

6. This survey has covered at least superficially the major theoretical presuppositions of Greek philosophy, insofar as they are needed for the interpretation of Matt. vi.22f. It is, of course, understood that even after Plato these basic conceptions were constantly reproduced, criticized and modified in many different ways. Jewish thinking, which had for a long time paid an extraordinary amount of attention to the eye,[7] entered

1 *Ibid.*, 518E.
2 *Ibid.*, 519A.
3 Plato, *Tim.* 45Aff. See F. M. Cornford, *Plato's Cosmology* (London, 1937), pp. 151ff.
4 See on this concept Beare, *Greek Theories*, p. 45.
5 *Tim.* 45C–D, translation of Cornford, p. 153.
6 *Ibid.*, 45D.
7 See the large collection of references in A. Rosenzweig, *Das Auge in Bibel und Talmud* (Berlin, 1892); also W. Michaelis, '*ὀφθαλμός*', *Theological Dictionary of the New Testament* v, pp. 375ff.

into this debate only hesitatingly. Philo, however, takes over the whole Platonic tradition, most likely in a middle-Platonic version: it is not the eyes that see, but the νοῦς sees through them.[1] In a long section on the faculty of vision in *De Abrahamo* 150–66 Philo follows the doctrines of the *Timaeus*, but he strongly emphasizes that the faculty of vision is under the influence of the πάθη, a Stoic concept.[2]

III. THE CONCEPT OF VISION IN MATT. vi.22f

After having surveyed Greek theories of vision, it should now become evident that Matt. vi.22f contains quite different ideas on the subject. The introductory thesis (verse 22a) which may have been taken over from the proverbial or wisdom tradition is granted only qualified approval. The commentary (verses 22b–23b) treats it rather critically, and this critique seems justified because the image of the 'lamp of the body' leaves unexplained what relationship we are to assume to exist between the 'lamp' and the 'body'. Is τοῦ σώματος a *genitivus objectivus* or *subjectivus* ?

In effect the commentary verses 22b–23b rejects the concept that the eye itself sees. The eye, we are informed, not only facilitates vision, but may also prohibit it. The philosophers who, as we learnt in the previous section, also investigated the phenomena and causes of defective vision focused almost entirely upon the physiological conditions of the eye. At this point, Matt. vi.22f presents its own corrective point of view, suggesting that merely physiological considerations cannot decide whether or not the eye is capable of seeing.

To make this point clear, a quite peculiar pair of contrasting terms is introduced: ἁπλοῦς and πονηρός. The wide-ranging discussions which have developed around this word-pair cannot to any adequate degree be evaluated here.[3] The terms leave it unclear whether they are to be taken

[1] Philo, *De post. Caini* 126. Cf. Epicharmus, Diels–Kranz 23 B 12 (I, 200, 16); Cicero, *Tusc.* I, 20. 46. On Philo see M. Freudenthal, *Die Erkenntnislehre Philos von Alexandria* (Berlin, 1891); H. Schmidt, *Die Anthropologie Philons von Alexandreia* (Würzburg, 1933), pp. 75–9; F. N. Klein, *Die Lichtterminologie bei Philon von Alexandrien und in den hermetischen Schriften* (Leiden, 1962).

[2] On the doctrine of *pathos* in Philo, see Schmidt, *Die Anthropologie Philons von Alexandreia*, pp. 86ff.

[3] On this difficult concept see the investigations by C. Edlund, *Das Auge der Einfalt* (Copenhagen, 1952); R. Vischer, *Das einfache Leben. Wort- und motivgeschichtliche Untersuchungen zu einem Wertbegriff der antiken Literatur* (Göttingen, 1965); J. Amstutz, *ΑΠΛΟΤΗΣ. Eine begriffsgeschichtliche Studie zum jüdisch-christlichen Griechisch* (Bonn, 1968). See also H. Bacht, 'Einfalt', *Reallexikon für Antike und Christentum* IV (1959), pp. 821–40.

in the physiological ('healthy' versus 'sick') or ethical sense ('simple, sincere, generous' versus 'evil, wicked'). Perhaps this ambiguity is intended. Naturally, the hearer will think first of the physiological facts, but will then be moved to the ethical level of meaning. As a term describing the physiology of the eye, ἁπλοῦς is certainly unusual, while as ethical terms both ἁπλοῦς and πονηρός are quite common.[1] At any rate, the introduction of ethical terms opens up the completely new possibility that the ethical disposition of a person determines whether or not the eyes function properly. It appears that the merely physiological explanations are polemically replaced by ethical considerations. From a Jewish ethical point of view, the entire approach of Greek philosophical tradition is called into question. Although the terms ἁπλοῦς and πονηρός are derived from Greek ethical language, the concern which they express is typically Jewish.

If the eye itself does not contain the light, where is it located? Verse 23b introduces another familiar concept, the 'light within', the *lumen internum*.[2] But this concept, too, is immediately subjected to radical criticism. Contrary to what we would expect, the *lumen internum* is not connected with the 'soul', and we look in vain for concepts like the 'eye of the soul', the 'intelligible light', or the νοῦς. Instead, we are told, the 'light within you' may even become 'darkness'. This suggestion is flatly directed against the Greek philosophical tradition, according to which the *lumen internum* is divine in nature and can never be turned into its opposite, 'darkness'. In other words, this suggestion must be another correction of the Platonic–Stoic anthropology, and it follows from the first correction. If the eye is affected by human sinfulness, the same must be true for the 'inner light', because nothing human is exempt from sin. In conclusion: If even the *lumen internum* is subject to sin and, on that account, can turn into its opposite, it can no longer be regarded as the *ultima ratio* upon which man can rely in his battle against the 'desires' caused by the senses. The eye is not the real cause of sin, but the *lumen internum* itself when it has turned into darkness. This result, then, finds its dramatic expression in the exclamative τὸ σκότος πόσον.

What does this result mean for the introductory definition verse 22a? Is it accepted or rejected? At the end, after having heard the critical commentary verses 22b–23b, we are able to reaffirm the definition. Indeed, if the *lumen internum* shines, the eye is the lamp of the body. It

[1] Cf. especially Test. Iss. iii. 4 (β–γ, S[1]), edited by Charles: πορευόμενος ἐν ἁπλότητι ὀφθαλμῶν. iv. 6: μὴ ἐπιδεχόμενος ὀφθαλμοὺς πονηροὺς ἀπὸ τῆς πλάνης τοῦ κόσμου.

[2] See Beierwaltes, *Lux intelligibilis*, p. 42, n. 3; H. Conzelmann, 'φῶς', *Theological Dictionary of the New Testament* IX, especially pp. 334f.

can then illuminate the body, qualify the eye as ἁπλοῦς and thus make it function properly.

Where, however, does the parenetical edge of the logion lie? It appears that having heard and understood the logion the thoughtful and conscientious person will be worried: What if my inner light is darkness? How can it be made bright again? The logion is so designed as to provoke this concern, but it does not answer it. It leaves the concerned hearer alone and restless, and this open-ended situation seems to be the parenetical goal of the passage.

The relationship to the Fourth Gospel shared by the author of 1 John and by his opponents

RAYMOND E. BROWN

The relation of the First Epistle of John to the Gospel of John remains a disputed subject among scholars. Obvious similarities of vocabulary, grammar, and thought suggest that the two works came from the same milieu, whether we call it community, school or circle. What is not clear is whether the Epistle and Gospel share the same theological outlook (even if one work is more developed than the other) or the one writing is meant to correct or modify the other. The solution to that problem might be facilitated if scholars could agree on whether the same author wrote both works; but that is also a matter of dispute, both as regards style and content. As for dating, only a minority gives priority to the Epistle.

Comparison has been made more complicated by complex theories of the authorship of the Fourth Gospel, e.g. any theory which supposes both an evangelist (who may have revised his own first edition) and a redactor. The Epistle might be later than the work of the evangelist but before or contemporary with the work of the redactor. Indeed, the author of the Epistle might be the redactor rather than the evangelist. Theorizing can reach Byzantine complexity if one follows Bultmann in positing a source, an author, and a redactor for the Epistle as well.

What seems clear is that the adversaries of the Epistle are not the same as the adversaries of the Gospel (namely, the followers of John the Baptist, 'the Jews', and Jews who believed in Jesus but did not confess him publicly). The Epistle rails against Christians who, though they claim to know God (ii.4), acknowledge neither 'Jesus Christ come in the flesh' (iv.2) nor the sinfulness of their own lives (i.10). To correct them the author reiterates the commandment of God: 'We are to believe in the name of His Son, Jesus Christ, and we are to love one another just as God gave us the command' (iii.23). Although these opponents have certain features known to us from second-century Christian debates, no one has satisfactorily identified them with the systems of Cerinthus, the Docetists, or the Gnostics, as criticized by the early church fathers.[1]

In the introduction to the Anchor Bible commentary on the Epistles of John, at which I am now at work, I shall have to wrestle with these disputed questions, whether or not I come up with new or decisive answers. Here I wish to test *one tentative hypothesis*, advancing all the arguments I have already uncovered favoring it, but knowing that there are further arguments to be discovered, as well as objections against it. My hypothesis is this: *Both the adversaries in 1 John and the author knew the Johannine proclamation of Christianity and professed to accept it.* Notice that I have been cautious in speaking of 'the Johannine proclamation of Christianity', for I am not committing myself as to whether the final form of the Fourth Gospel had made its appearance. I am saying that, whether or not they had read the written Gospel, both the author and his opponents knew Johannine thought and expression as it has come to us in that Gospel. Thus, the adversaries were no outsiders but the offspring of Johannine thought itself,[2] and virtually every distinctive position they held had some basis in the Gospel of John. The author of the Epistle could not simply deny the echoes of the Johannine proclamation which furnished his adversaries with their slogans, for that proclamation was truth for him (and his community) as well. Rather he had to argue that the adversaries' *interpretation* of the proclamation was false and not taught from the beginning. His slogan in correcting his opponents is stated immediately after the prologue: 'This is the Gospel that we have heard from Jesus Christ' (i.5),[3] a slogan implying that any other interpretation is a dangerous novelty.

Stressing again the inchoative character of this essay, I shall divide my treatment topically rather than proceeding verse by verse. I recog-

[1] R. Schnackenburg, *Die Johannesbriefe*, HThK 13, 3rd edition (Freiburg, 1965), pp. 20–2, points out correctly that the ideas of some of the opponents of Ignatius of Antioch resemble the ideas of the opponents of 1 John.

[2] Malformed offspring from the viewpoint of the author of 1 John. Theoretically one might argue that the opponents were the true representatives of Johannine thought and that the author of 1 John is bringing into the community an alien corrective (somewhat in the sense of Bultmann's Ecclesiastical Redactor). The canonization of the Epistle means that the author of the Epistle was thought to speak for Christian faith; it does not make clear whether his true teaching results from correcting dangerous tendencies attested in the Fourth Gospel, or from preserving the correct implications of the Gospel from distortion.

[3] The designation εὐαγγέλιον never occurs in John or in the Epistles; but I suggest that ἀγγελία (1 John i.5; iii.11) deserves the translation 'Gospel' and was the Johannine word for the message of and about Jesus handed down from the beginning. What is not clear is whether this ἀγγελία had already been written down as the Fourth Gospel.

nize a double difficulty in reconstructing the views of the opponents. First, we must view them mirror-wise through the polemic affirmations of the author of the Epistle, as he refutes the claims that 'someone' might make. Second, we are not certain that his every affirmation was polemically oriented; at times he may simply have been affirming Christian faith without any reference to the views of his opponents. While I stress uncertainty about the views of the opponents, I propose a question that is valid nonetheless: If they did hold views that are contradictory to the affirmations of the author of 1 John, could they have reached such views from reading or hearing the message known to us from the Gospel of John?

I. CHRISTOLOGY

In the years 1975 through 1977 three reconstructions of Johannine community history, based on an analysis of the Gospel, were offered by the late Georg Richter, by J. Louis Martyn, and by me.[1] These analyses differed on several points, but all agree that the Johannine community originated among Jews who believed that Jesus had fulfilled Jewish expectations (whether of the Messiah or of the prophet-like-Moses). Only in a second stage of community life was there developed that remarkably high Christological evaluation of Jesus known to us from the Fourth Gospel.[2] The traditional title 'Son of God' was understood to mean that Jesus was a pre-existent divine figure (John i.1) who could speak of his own existence before creation (xvii.5) and who had come down from heaven into a world in which he was a stranger, rejected by his own (i.11).[3] Here below he acted according to what he had seen beforehand with the Father (v.19); indeed he and the heavenly Father were one (x.30), so that whoever saw him saw the Father

[1] G. Richter, 'Präsentische und futurische Eschatologie im 4. Evangelium', in *Gegenwart und kommendes Reich: Schülergabe Anton Vögtle zum 65. Geburtstag*, edited by P. Fiedler and D. Zeller (Stuttgart, 1975), pp. 117–52; see English summary by A. J. Mattill, *Theol. Stud.* 38 (1977), pp. 294–315. J. L. Martyn, 'Glimpses into the History of the Johannine Community', a lecture given at Louvain in 1975 and published in *L'Évangile de Jean: Sources, rédaction, théologie*, edited by M. de Jonge, BETL 44 (Gembloux, 1977), pp. 149–75. (This will be republished in a collection of Johannine essays by Martyn (1978).) R. E. Brown, 'Johannine Ecclesiology – The Community's Origins', *Interpretation* 31 (1977), pp. 379–93.

[2] Richter and I would agree that this development was catalyzed by the entrance into the community of another group of Christians, whose identity I find revealed in John iv.1–42 – a mixed group consisting of Jewish Christians who held anti-Temple views and of their Samaritan converts.

[3] See W. Meeks, 'The Man from Heaven in Johannine Sectarianism', *JBL* 91 (1972), pp. 44–72.

(xiv.9), and the designation 'God' could be applied to him (i.1; xx.28). This Christology seems to have been higher than that of most of the other Christian communities attested in the NT books.[1]

Such a Christology provoked bitter reaction among many Jews who had never accepted Jesus but had hitherto tolerated Christians, for it appeared to infringe upon monotheism. In the Fourth Gospel the struggles of Jesus with 'the Jews' are not only very sharp but also have their own tone: they are concerned primarily not with Jesus' violation of the Law but with his divine claims. 'Not only was he breaking the Sabbath; worse still, he was speaking of God as his own Father, thus making himself God's equal' (v.18). The presence in the Christian spectrum of a community making claims such as those found in the Fourth Gospel led to expulsions from the synagogue on christological grounds (ix.22);[2] and this expulsion tended to increase the sense of estrangement of the Johannine Christians, in imitation of their master, the stranger from above. If he was the light that had come into the world in judgment upon the darkness (iii.19), they were sons of light surrounded by darkness. If he did not belong to this world, neither did they (xvii.14). Indeed, they were alienated even from other Christians, e.g. from Jews who believed in Jesus but not in his divinity (viii.31–59).[3]

Finally, I suggest, the estrangement led to a division within the Johannine community itself, as some Johannine Christians pressed the implications of the Christology to an even 'higher' plane. Let me illustrate how this may have happened by interpreting the information

[1] Mark identifies Jesus as the Son of God at his baptism; Matthew and Luke identify him as the Son of God at his conception, since he was conceived without human father by the power of God's Spirit; but no Synoptic Gospel proposes pre-existence. It is not clear that Phil. ii.7 refers to pre-existence. 1 Cor. viii.6 speaks of 'Jesus Christ, through whom are all things', and Col. i.15 designates Jesus as 'the first-born of all creation'; but neither text makes it clear that Jesus was not created. After all, divine wisdom, 'the fashioner of all things' (Wis. vii.22) could say: 'The Lord created me at the beginning of His work' (Prov. viii.22). In the NT only John i.1–3 makes it clear that *before creation* the Word was.

[2] This is well treated in the important work of J. L. Martyn, *History and Theology in the Fourth Gospel* (New York, 1968), which will soon be republished in a new edition by Abingdon.

[3] In an article published in *JBL* 97 (1978), pp. 5–22, entitled, '"Other Sheep Not of This Fold" – The Johannine Perspective on Christian Diversity in the Late First Century', I have suggested that John vii.5 ('Not even his brothers believed in him') reflects a Johannine judgment on Jewish Christians in churches claiming James the brother of the Lord as founding father or patron. Alongside Christology, sacramental issues may have been at the root of the dispute between the Johannine community and such Jewish Christians, e.g. John vi.60–6 which describes disciples who had followed Jesus from the synagogue (vi.59) only to break away over the Eucharist.

in the Fourth Gospel in a way that suggests that Jesus' humanity had no real importance. (Of course, I am not suggesting that this is the correct interpretation of the Gospel, but only one way in which it could have been read or heard by a segment of the Johannine community.) The Johannine Jesus proclaimed, 'I do not belong to the world' (xvii.14). True, in the hymn that became the prologue of the Gospel, we hear that 'the Word became flesh and made his dwelling among us' (i.14ab), but that took place only that we might see his glory (i.14c), a glory that shone transparently through his career in the world (ii.11), so that even his opponents understood that he was acting like God (v.18; x.33). In Johannine tradition the earthly Jesus knew all things, so that it was not out of necessity that he asked even the simplest information (vi.5–6), nor could he have made a mistake in the choice of Judas.[1] He could not pray to God seeking a change in the divine will (xi.42; xii.27), precisely because he and the Father were one (x.30). Nor could he be a victim in his passion since he totally controlled his own destiny (x.17–18).[2] Even in the trial before Pilate, the powerful representative of Rome was powerless before Jesus and actually afraid of him as Son of God (xix.8, 11).

The salvific import of such a Christology is illustrated in xvii.3: 'Eternal life consists in this: that they know you, the one true God, and Jesus Christ, the one whom you sent.' As the glorious Word passing among men but not subject to human frailty, Jesus has brought eternal life; and one needs to know that in order to receive eternal life. But eternal life may be seen as dependent simply on the presence of the Word in the world, not on his death. The human career of Jesus may be seen merely as the occasion of God's communicating life rather than as an integral redemptive element. The important factor may be: 'They knew in truth that I came forth from you, and they believed that you sent me' (xvii.8). The Johannine Jesus does not lay down his life *to take away sin* but to protect his sheep (x.11, 15); and he takes his life up again and returns to his Father to prepare a place to which he may take his own (xiv.3), leaving the world behind (xvii.24). True, the Gospel begins with a proclamation of Jesus as 'the Lamb of God who takes away the world's sin' (i.29), but that need not be understood as accomplished by a redemptive death. The next verses describe the Lamb of God as the pre-existent one who needs to be recognized; and it is well

1 From the first mention of Judas (vi.70–1), Jesus has chosen him knowing that he would betray.

2 R. E. Brown, 'The Passion According to John', *Worship* 49 (1975), pp. 126–34. For a strong emphasis on the element of glory in Johannine Christology, see E. Käsemann, *The Testament of Jesus* (Philadelphia, 1968).

known that scholars are divided on whether 'Lamb of God' refers to the paschal lamb whose blood was shed or to some heavenly, apocalyptic figure.

Turning to the adversaries in 1 John, I am suggesting that they may have interpreted the common Johannine Gospel tradition (*ἀγγελία*) much in the manner described above. Theirs was a Christology so high that it really 'annulled' the humanity of Jesus.[1] They believed in the eternal Word and they believed that through this Word they knew God (1 John ii.4: 'I know Him'); but for them human existence was only a stage in the career of the Word and no intrinsic component. I do not think they were advanced Docetists. For them, the flesh in 'the Word became flesh' was real but unimportant: not the flesh but the glory of Jesus was the life-giving factor. I do not think they were followers of Cerinthus for whom the divine principle came upon the man Jesus at the baptism and left just before the crucifixion. There is little in the Johannine tradition to support such a view. Rather for the adversaries of 1 John the death was simply part of the return of the Word to God who had spoken that Word; it was important because it showed that the Word could not remain in the world any more than his followers are destined to remain in the world. Other Christians might regard the death as the lowest point in the career of the servant (Phil. ii.8), or as the moment when Jesus learned obedience through suffering (Heb. v.8), or as the moment of total abandonment and dependence upon God (Mk. xv.34). But the adversaries of 1 John could argue that this was not the picture of the death of Jesus in the Johannine tradition. In that tradition the death was an ascension and a pentecost in which Jesus, totally in control, did not give up the Spirit but handed it over to his followers (xiii.1; xix.30).

How does the author of 1 John refute such adversaries? He cannot attack the tradition which for him as well as his opponents constitutes 'Gospel'. (Nor seemingly can he appeal to the Synoptic tradition for a corrective; either it is not known to the community or it does not have the same authority as the Johannine tradition.) Rather he must challenge his opponents' interpretation of the tradition. He cannot deny pre-existence, for example, but he can shift the stress to the career of the Word-made-flesh. A comparison of the prologue of the Epistle with the prologue of the Gospel is instructive: terms like *ἀρχή*, *λόγος*, and *ζωή* appear also in the prologue of the Epistle but with the emphasis shifted toward the earthly ministry of Jesus. The *ἀρχή* is now the

[1] With Schnackenburg, Bultmann, and others, I am tempted to regard the correct reading of 1 John iv.3 as *πᾶν πνεῦμα ὃ λύει τὸν Ἰησοῦν* to be translated: 'Everyone who annuls [negates the importance of] Jesus reflects a spirit which does not belong to God.'

beginning of that ministry,[1] for 'what was from the beginning' is parallel to 'what we have heard, what we have seen with our own eyes, what we looked at, and what we felt with our own hands' (I John i.1). Indeed, that set of 'we have' clauses makes an interesting contrast to the 'we have seen his glory' of John i.14 – the author of the Epistle is refuting an over-emphasis on the glory by an emphasis on the observable and tangible character of the ministry. The Gospel prologue proclaimed the pre-existence of a Word in whom there was life; the Epistle prologue moves on quickly to the human manifestation of that life: 'We proclaim to you this eternal life such as it was in the Father's presence and has been *revealed to us*' (I John i.2). The λόγος is now 'the word of life of which we are speaking' (i.1). By making himself part of the 'we' and 'us' which are so prominent in the Epistle prologue, the author makes his emphasis on the tangible career of Jesus part of the common testimony in the Johannine community, and nothing personal. 'What we have seen and heard we proclaim in turn to you, so that you may be joined in communion with us' (i.3). He has anticipated and blocked the charge of his opponents: 'That is your personal interpretation of the Gospel.'

Another significant shift from the Gospel to the Epistle concerns πιστεύειν and ὁμολογεῖν. The ninety-eight uses of πιστεύειν in the Gospel yield an average of about five times a chapter, contrasted with an average of two times a chapter in the Epistle (total: nine times; πίστις once). On the other hand, while ὁμολογεῖν appears only three times in the whole Gospel, it is used six times in the Epistle. Like the author of the Epistle the opponents can say they believe that Jesus Christ is the one sent by God (John xvii.3), but the author wants to test them by demanding public acknowledgment or *confession* that Jesus Christ has come in the flesh (I John iv.2; II John 7). As Bonnard[2] has pointed out, when the author demands a confession that 'Jesus is the Son of God' (I John iv.15; cf. v.13), he is not placing stress on the identity of Jesus but on the identity of God's Son: that Son is really Jesus and none other. The opponents have no difficulty with the general

1 The use of ἀρχή in I John i.1 should be studied in the light of ii.7, 24 and iii.11 where it refers not to a pre-creation beginning but to the beginning of the ministry of Jesus as handed down in the tradition. (Although some would argue for a reference to incarnation in i.1, the rest of the Epistle's prologue stresses the public part of Jesus' career.) That the Genesis background of the term is neither denied nor forgotten is clear from iii.8, but that is not the author's main interest.

2 I am indebted here to the excellent article of P. Bonnard, 'La première épître de Jean est-elle johannique?', in *L'Évangile de Jean* (cited on p. 59, n. 1 above), pp. 301–5.

idea of God's Son; but since they do not think that God's Son was affected or changed by his mortal career, they see no special significance in the fact that God's Son was Jesus who lived a specific kind of life and died a specific death. The author is striking out against such an attitude in iv.10: 'In this, then, does love consist: not that we have loved God but that He loved us and sent His Son as an expiation for our sins.' The kind of death that Jesus died, the author insists, is significant and salvific; and he uses the blood of Jesus as a symbol for that: 'The blood of Jesus, His Son, cleanses us from all sin.' If the graphic detail that blood and water flowed from Jesus' body on the cross was a well-known part of the Johannine tradition,[1] the opponents of 1 John may not have understood such a scene in terms of the salvific death of Jesus. For them it may have been a sign that Jesus' death was not the decisive moment; that Jesus gave life to his community was symbolized on the cross both before and after his death (John xix.25–7, 34). But 1 John v.7 stresses that the shedding of blood was salvific: 'Jesus Christ – he is the one who came by water and blood, not in water only, but in water and in blood.' Most commentators agree that the author is referring symbolically to the perimeters of the ministry of Jesus, his baptism and his death.[2] Without those perimeters one does not truly believe that Jesus is the Son of God (v.5). Only the Jesus Christ who came by water and blood is 'the true God and eternal life' (v.21).

II. ETHICS

I have never agreed with Bultmann that the Johannine Jesus is a revealer without a revelation.[3] Nevertheless, the very fact that Bultmann can make such a claim indicates the extent to which the christological question dominates the Johannine proclamation. The Fourth Gospel is relatively deficient on other topics when compared with the Synoptic tradition. Matthew can gather the ethical demands of Jesus into the Sermon on the Mount – the eschatological law code of the Messiah –

[1] Many attribute the passage to a redactor, but that does not mean that the tradition is necessarily late. In xxi.18, 22 the redactor reports ancient sayings from the Johannine tradition which are now so obscure that he has to interpret them.

[2] If the Fourth Gospel might be interpreted in a way that would put little emphasis on physical death, so also it could be interpreted (by the opponents of the Epistle) so as to discount the baptism of Jesus. It is the only Gospel that does not describe the baptism, and i.33 interprets the baptism as a revelation about God's pre-existent Son.

[3] R. Bultmann, *Theology of the New Testament*, II (New York, 1955), p. 66: 'The Reveaeler of God reveals nothing but that he is a revealer.' See also pp. 62–3, and my critique in 'The Kerygma of the Gospel according to John', *Interpretation* 21 (1967), pp. 387–400, esp. 392ff.

but no such collection is found in John. The opponents of the Epistle may have had their ethical outlook shaped by the lack of specific directions in the Johannine tradition. Presumably in their theology the earthly life of the Christian would have had no more pertinence to salvation than had the earthly life of Jesus; neither they nor he belonged to this world. Their claims to spiritual attainment were not of an ethical nature but stemmed from a relationship to God based on acceptance of Jesus as God's Word: they knew God (1 John ii.4); they remained or abode in Him (ii.6); they were in light (ii.9).

Once again the author is handicapped in refuting his opponents. After all the Johannine Jesus speaks of knowing God (xiv.7; xvii.3, 25–6), of remaining or being in Him (xvii.21–2), and of being in light (iii.21; viii.12; xii.35–6). Thus the author must challenge such claims on the basis of an ethical criterion: it is possible to know God and remain in Him and be in the light, but only if one lives righteously. Yet how can he justify such a criterion when there is no body of ethical maxims in the Johannine tradition as it is known to us from the Gospel?[1]

He adopts two procedures to attain his goal. Firstly, he calls upon the general example of Jesus' earthly life as a model for the life of the Christians, an argument that is in harmony with the difference between his Christology and that of his opponents. The author of 1 John calls upon the members of the community to walk *just as* Christ walked (ii.6), to make themselves pure *just as* Christ is pure (iii.3), to act justly and be just (δίκαιος) *just as* Christ is just (iii.7). This 'just as' (καθώς) ethic may place emphasis on the model of Jesus' career; but it is vague in details, precisely because the Johannine Gospel tradition of that career does not offer the specifics for comparison.[2] And so, secondly, the author calls upon the principal ethical maxim known to

[1] The failure once again to call upon the Synoptic tradition suggests very strongly that such material was simply not 'Gospel' (ἀγγελία) for the Johannine community. This reinforces the view that dominated in Johannine research from the 1940s to the 1970s that the Gospel of John was written in independence of the Synoptics, and is an argument against the thesis gaining ground among Synoptic specialists (e.g. Norman Perrin, Frans Neirynck) that John drew heavily upon the Synoptic Gospels.

[2] The vague comparisons that he does make can be approximated in the Fourth Gospel: (1) 'As Christ walked'. The verb περιπατεῖν occurs in John more than in any other Gospel and with a special ethical sense. Since 1 John, in urging the readers to walk just as Christ walked, is warning them against the opponents who 'walk in the dark', compare John viii.12; xi.9–10; xii.35. (2) 'Makes himself pure even as Christ is pure'. The closest parallel is John xvii.19: 'It is for them [those given him by God] that I consecrate myself in order that they too may be consecrated in truth.' (3) 'The person who acts justly is truly just, even as Christ is just.' Cf. John v.30: 'My judgment is just.'

us from the Johannine tradition – indeed, virtually the only ethical maxim – the commandment to love one another (John xiii.34–5; xv.12–13, 17). The author of I John makes this a very important theme in his battle against his opponents (ii.9–11; iii.10–24; iv.7–v.4), and he stresses that love of brethren constitutes an old commandment which his readers have had from the beginning (ii.7). This reflects his contention that his opponents are neglecting an established aspect of the community tradition stemming from the earthly Jesus. In iii.11 he says: 'For this is the Gospel [ἀγγελία] that you heard from the beginning: we should love one another'; and in iv.9–10 the death of Christ as an expiation for our sins is invoked as an example for this brotherly love (see also iii.16 and compare John iii.16).

If I am right that, in appealing especially to love of brethren as a criterion, the author is calling upon the limited Johannine ethical tradition to correct his opponents, is this not proof that the opponents were not interested in that tradition as we know it in the Fourth Gospel? If they hated their brethren as the author charges (ii.11; iii.10, 12; iv.20), they were going against the specific commands of the Johannine Jesus mentioned above. *But did the opponents say that they hated their brethren?* Or was their attitude exactly the same as that of the author of the Epistle, namely, one of intense dislike for those who in his judgment had distorted the Christian tradition, on the grounds that such pseudo-Christians were no longer children of God (or brethren) but children of the devil (iii.7–12)?

Here we touch upon the great anomaly of the First Epistle. No more eloquent voice is raised in the NT for love within the Christian brotherhood and sisterhood, but that same voice is extremely bitter in condemning opponents who had been members of his community and were so no longer (I John ii.19). They are demonic, Antichrists, false prophets, and serve as the embodiment of eschatological lawlessness or iniquity (ἀνομία: ii.18, 22; iv.1–6; iii.4–5). Although the members of the community are exhorted to love one another, the way they should treat dissenters is illustrated by II John 10–11: 'If anyone comes to you who does not bring this teaching [Jesus Christ as coming in the flesh – verse 7], do not receive him into your house – do not even greet him, for whoever greets him shares the evil he does.' I suspect that the opponents of I John had exactly the same attitude toward the author and his followers, even though they too may have cited Jesus' command to love one another.[1] They could do this in good conscience

[1] We are not certain that Diotrephes, the opponent of III John 9, was a false teacher of the type attacked in I John. Nevertheless, his way of opposing the

because in the judgment of each party the others were no longer 'brethren', but had gone out into the world as false prophets.

In other words, we are once again seeing the development of tendencies present in the Johannine proclamation of Christianity. Just as Johannine Christology known to us in the Fourth Gospel could become heady when worked out to the '*n*th' degree, so also dualistic tendencies present in that proclamation could become dangerous when transplanted into inner-Christian debate. The Matthean Jesus says, 'Love your enemies and pray for those who persecute you' (Matt. v.44), but there is no such maxim in the Johannine tradition. The command to love is not in terms of love of neighbor (as in Matt. xix.19) but in terms of loving *one another* (John xiii.34–5; xv.12, 17); and John xv.13–15 allows that to be interpreted in terms of those who are disciples of Christ and obey his commandments. The attitude of the Johannine Jesus who did not pray for the world (xvii.9) is easily translated in the Epistle into a refusal to pray for Christians whose sin is deadly (1 John v.16).

Indeed, when we compare the Gospel and First Epistle, we see that the dualistic language (love/hate; light/darkness; truth/falsehood; from above/from below; of God/of the devil), once employed by Jesus in his attack on the world or on 'the Jews', has been shifted over to an attack on Christians with whom the author disagrees. (And if I am right, it is probably also being used by his opponents in their attack on him.) Already the Gospel dualism had its dangers, for it nourished Christians of later centuries in their false contention that only those who believe in Jesus can be saved. As used in the Epistle, the dualism has served to fuel Christians who feel justified in hating other Christians for the love of God.[1] Let me illustrate this terminological shift. In the Gospel Jesus assures his followers that they do not walk in darkness (viii.12; xii.46), for 'darkness' is the realm of those who do not accept Jesus (i.5; iii.19–21; xii.35). But in the Epistle those who do not meet the author's moral standard, even though they claim to be followers of Christ, are said to walk in darkness (1 John ii.9–11). In the Gospel the Paraclete

author of III John is interesting: he refuses to receive those whom that author calls 'brethren' and expels from the church their supporters. This is the same treatment that the author of 1 John ii.19 and of II John 10–11 thinks of for his opponents.

1 It is true that the author never says he hates his opponents, although his equation of them with the children of the devil certainly points in that direction. And undoubtedly he would say that if they left their evil ways and came back to the true community of Christ, he would love them. But would not the opponents say the same of him? I should stress too that extreme hostility toward erroneous teachers is not peculiar in the NT to the Johannine writings (Titus i.16 is quite close to 1 John ii.4; see also Acts xx.29–30).

proves the *world* wrong about justice (John xvi.8, 10). In the Epistle the opponents claim to be just (1 John iii.7); but the author offers a criterion to prove who is really just (iii.7–8; ii.29), with the clear implication that his opponents do not meet that criterion. In a bitter passage of Gospel dialogue, Jesus attacks Jews who believe in him inadequately by telling them that they belong to the devil, their father, who is a murderer and liar (John viii.44). In the Epistle, at the very moment when the author is speaking about the need for love, he uses this same terminology for his opponents (1 John iii.10–15; also ii.22). The Gospel (xii.39–40) applies Isa. vi.10 to 'the Jews' – God has blinded their eyes – but the Epistle (ii.11) applies it to the opponents who hate the Johannine brethren: 'The darkness has blinded their eyes.' Certainly the ethical battle in the Epistle is fought with the same terminological weapons as employed in the Gospel.

I have tested the patience of the editors by stretching to the limit the space allotment for articles in this Festschrift in honor of a scholar whose work I greatly admire. A fuller treatment[1] would require a detailed discussion of eschatology and pneumatology. By way of anticipation I remark that the adversaries may have latched on to Johannine-realized eschatology, according to which they had already been judged favorably and given the gift of eternal life; and they may have used this eschatology to support the thesis that ethical behavior makes no real difference. The failure of the author to crush his opponents by authority (such as the appeal to the teaching bishops in the Pastorals: 1 Tim. i.3; Titus i.9) may reflect a situation bound by the Johannine tradition (known to his opponents) wherein the Spirit/Paraclete is *the* teacher and the Spirit is possessed by each follower of Jesus. The most he can do is to seek a criterion for discerning the Spirit of God (1 John iv.1–6).

This preliminary investigation suggests that there is much to recommend an identification of the opponents of 1 John as a radical group of Johannine Christians who had developed certain tendencies of the Johannine tradition to an extreme. As a whole, Johannine Christians are often portrayed as more radical than many other first-century Christians. That some of them would reject their own extremists teaches us something about diversity and its limits in Christianity.

[1] I shall have the opportunity to do this in the Shaffer Lectures at Yale University in February 1978. I hope to combine the work mentioned on p. 59, n. 1 and p. 60, n.3 with the Shaffer Lectures to produce a history of the Johannine community stretching through the pre-Gospel, Gospel, and Epistle stages, entitled *The Community of the Beloved Disciple* (1979).

The Gospel text of Marius Victorinus

F. F. BRUCE

Gaius Marius Victorinus Afer (*c*.300–*c*.370), rhetorician and Neoplatonist, was converted to Christianity about 355 and devoted a good part of his time thereafter to theological writing. He seems to have thrown himself immediately into the Arian controversy, expounding Nicene orthodoxy in Neoplatonic categories, and later (perhaps after Julian's educational rescript in 362 obliged him to relinquish his public professorship of rhetoric at Rome) he composed commentaries on the Epistles to the Galatians, Ephesians and Philippians.

Only in recent years have critical editions of his theological works become available: his contributions to the Arian controversy (his exchange of letters with the Arian Candidus, his four books *Against Arius*, with an appendix *De homoousio recipiendo*, and his three *Hymns on the Trinity*) have been edited by P. Henry, S.J. and P. Hadot for the *Corpus Scriptorum Ecclesiasticorum Latinorum* (volume 83, part 1, Vienna, 1971) and by A. Locher for the *Bibliotheca Teubneriana* (Leipzig, 1976),[1] and his Pauline commentaries by A. Locher for the *Bibliotheca Teubneriana* (Leipzig, 1972). For the anti-Arian works I have made use of a rotograph copy of the tenth-century Berlin MS Phillips 1684, designated A in the critical editions. References to Victorinus's works are given below by treatise, book and chapter, together with the column in the Migne edition (PL viii).

Victorinus's Latin biblical text is generally 'European' in character, of the type current in Italy at the time when he was writing; he did not become a Christian until long after he left his native Africa for Rome, and only a few 'African' readings are found among his quotations.

1 Scholarly translations have also been made available recently: C. Marius Victorinus: *Traités théologiques sur la Trinité*, edited by P. Henry, Introduction, traduction et notes par P. Hadot, tomes 1 et 2, Sources chrétiennes, nos. 68, 69 (Paris, 1960); *Christlicher Platonismus: Die theologischen Schriften des Marius Victorinus*, übersetzt von P. Hadot und U. Brenke, eingeleitet und erläutert von P. Hadot (Zürich, 1967).

A detailed study of his biblical text does not throw much light on the history of the Latin Bible. He frequently appears to quote from memory, sometimes substituting a word or construction which he regards as better Latin, and sometimes giving an independent rendering when he is dissatisfied with the current version of a text crucial to his argument. Occasionally, as though despairing of finding any adequate Latin equivalent for a Greek word or phrase, he quotes the untranslated Greek. He tends to quote frequently recurring texts in a variety of forms, probably from a love of stylistic variation. He often gives a paraphrase rather than a strict translation.

A few of his quotations have more theological than textual interest. His interest in the adjective *homoousios* alerts him to occurrences of *ousia* and its compounds (as also to occurrences of *hypostasis* and similar terms) and leads him to see christological significance in texts where it has not usually been suspected.

For example, the petition for daily bread in the Lord's Prayer (Matt. vi.11) is quoted once in the form *da panem nobis ἐπιούσιον, hodiernum* (*Ar*. i.30.1063B). The context makes it clear that the current renderings of the Latin versions at this place are felt to be quite inadequate. The bread in question is the body of Christ, the bread of life; the adjective ἐπιούσιος means *ex ipsa aut in ipsa substantia* – just, Victorinus adds, as in Tit. ii.14 λαὸν περιούσιον means *populum . . . circa substantiam, hoc est circa uitam consistentem populum*. Elsewhere he coins his own rendering of ἐπιούσιον in the petition: *panem nostrum consubstantialem da nobis hodie* (*Ar*. i.59.1085C). He justifies the use of *consubstantialis* in *Ar*. ii.8.1094C: 'This is the meaning of δὸς ἡμῖν ἐπιούσιον ἄρτον, namely, life from the same substance. If what we receive is the body of Christ, and Christ himself is our life, we ask for ἐπιούσιον ἄρτον, since divinity dwells bodily in Christ.[1] The Greek gospel therefore has ἐπιούσιον, which is derived from "substance", that is to say God's substance; the Latins, either failing to understand this or being unable to express it, could not say this and so put down merely *cotidianum*, not ἐπιούσιον.' It may be wondered if Victorinus's rendering in any way influenced Jerome's *panem supersubstantialem*.

A new interpretation is placed upon the parable of the prodigal son, when the father's dividing his living (βίος) or substance (οὐσία) between his sons is allegorized. On the literal level the reference is to his fortune and patrimony. 'But if this is to be understood of God, ὑπόστασις here also will mean all his power and virtue. This is what is "wasted" by the one son who departs from God. For he who "takes a journey" from

[1] Cf. Col. ii.9.

God has neither the Spirit of God nor light nor Christ: left to himself he wastes the substance of God' (*Ar.* ii.6.1093B–C).[1] It is probably a simple lapse of memory that makes Victorinus replace *οὐσία* in Luke xv.12f by *ὑπόστασις*, but he has made it plain a few lines earlier that the two words are for him synonymous.

It is naturally in the Fourth Gospel that Victorinus finds the richest quarry for anti-Arian texts. The opening words of the Johannine prologue are repeatedly quoted, and that in a variety of wording. 'He almost exhausts the prepositions', wrote William Sanday, 'in his attempts to translate *ὁ λόγος ἦν πρὸς τὸν θεόν*: "circa Deum", "apud Deum", "juxta Deum", are all used in turn.'[2] He prefers to retain the Greek *λόγος* in quoting the prologue, no doubt regarding the customary Latin equivalents as inadequate.

The frequency with which Victorinus cites this prologue reminds us how Augustine, after quoting John i.1–5, remarks that 'a certain Platonist [i.e. Neoplatonist], as we were accustomed to hear from the holy elder Simplicianus, later bishop of Milan, used to say that these opening words of the Gospel according to John should be written in letters of gold and set up in the most prominent positions in all the churches'.[3] The 'Platonist' may well have been Victorinus, since it was from Simplicianus that Augustine heard the story of Victorinus's conversion shortly before his own conversion (A.D. 386).[4]

'In principio erat *λόγος*, et *λόγος* erat circa deum', says Victorinus in his letter to Candidus, and goes on immediately to quote verse 18: *unigenitus filius, qui est in gremio patris*. Then he asks, 'How do you take or understand these words? The Romans render *πρὸς τὸν θεόν* as *apud deum*, as though to say "wholly within", that is in the existence of God; and this is true. For in "being" action is also present. The *λόγος* is in God and so is the Son in the Father. "Being" itself is the cause of action, for that in which action is present must itself first exist . . . If therefore "being" itself is the cause of action, action is begotten by "being". The Father is "being"; the Son therefore is action' (*Ad Candidum* 20.1030C–1031A). This is a relatively simple instance of Victorinus's tendency to neoplatonize the sense of scripture.

1 He gives a similar meaning to the Old Latin rendering of Jer. xxiii.18, 22 (*quia quis stetit in substantia domini, et uidit uerbum eius? . . . si stetissent in substantia mea et audissent uerba mea*), interpreting both *substantia* (LXX *ὑπόστασις*) and *uerbum* (LXX *λόγος*) christologically (*Ar.* i.30.1063B–C, 59. 1085B, ii.3.1091C–D, 5. 1093A, 12.1097D, iv.4.1115C; *De homoousio recipiendo* 2.1138C).

2 *Old Latin Biblical Texts* II (Oxford, 1886), p. lxxxv.

3 *Ciu. dei* x.29.

4 *Conf.* viii.3ff.

In his punctuation of John i.3f he follows the general ante-Nicene precedent, for example: *per quem facta sunt omnia et sine quo factum est nihil* (*Ar.* iv.21.1128C); *quod est factum, in ipso uita est, et uita erat lumen hominum* (*Ar.* i.4.1042B).

John i.9 is rendered: *erat lumen quod est uerum, quod inluminat omnem hominem uenientem in mundum* (*Ar.* i.4.1042B). We note that *lumen* is followed by *quod est*, Victorinus's characteristic equivalent for the Greek *τό* before *ἀληθινόν*. His choice of *lumen* rather than *lux* as the rendering of *φῶς* agrees with several Old Latin MSS (a f q r) and with Cyprian and Augustine. In common with the other Latin translators he construes *ἐρχόμενον* with *ἄνθρωπον* and not with *φῶς*. In the same context he goes on to cite the first two clauses of John i.10: *in mundo erat et mundus per ipsum factus est* (*Ar.* i.4.1042B–C). The last clause of this verse is elsewhere cited along with the first clause of verse 11, the original sequence of the two clauses being transposed: *in sua uenit et mundus eum non agnouit* (*Ar.* iii.14.1109D) – a fairly clear instance of quotation from memory.

In John i.14, as in verse 1, he retains *λόγος* untranslated: *et λόγος caro factus est* (*Ar.* i.45.1075C, 56.1083C, 58.1085A; cf. ii.1.1088D).

He quotes John i.18 some eight times, with several variations in wording. It appears in full in *Ad Candidum* 16.1029B: *deum nullus uidit aliquando: unigenitus filius, qui est in gremio patris, ipse enarrauit*. The more usual rendering of the first clause is *deum nemo uidit umquam* (*Ar.* i.4.1042C, etc.); once the order of words is changed to *deum nemo umquam uidit* (*Ar.* iv.8.1119C). In *Ar.* iv.33.1137B *unigenitus filius* is amplified to *unigenitus solus filius*. In two places (*Ar.* iv.8.1119C, 33.1137B) *unigenitus filius* is preceded by *nisi* (as in a b e ff_2 l r Augustine). The adjective clause *qui est in gremio patris* is once reproduced in the paraphrastic form *qui de sinu eius exiuit* (*Ar.* iv.8.1119C); here the sense of the present text is combined with that of John xvi.28a.

Victorinus discusses the rival merits of *gremium* and *sinus* as the equivalent of *κόλπος* in John i.18 as follows: '*deum nemo uidit umquam, nisi unigenitus solus filius qui est in sinu patris*: we shall do better to say *gremio*. The Greeks have *ἐν κόλπῳ*, that is *in gremio*. But either this word or that signifies that the Son is both begotten, that is, he is external to the Father, and yet also with the Father, as it is said, *qui est in sinu patris*. The diligent and faithful seeker will understand that this is so in all the readings' (*Ar.* iv.33.1137B). His statement that the Greek has *ἐν κόλπῳ* may be put down to a slip of memory.

Other Johannine citations from Victorinus are now given more summarily.

i.20 *non sum christus* (*Ar*. i.5.1042D).

i.23 *uox exclamantis in deserto: dirigite uiam domini* (*Ar*. i.56.1083A).

iii.3 *nisi quis renatus fuerit, non potest regnum dei tenere* (*In Eph*. iv.9.1273D). The reading *tenere* is free rendering.

iii.5 *uti renascatur homo per spiritum et aquam* (*In Eph*. iii.1f.1262C).

iii.6 *quod ex carne nascitur caro est, quod autem ex spiritu nascitur spiritus est* (*In Eph*. iv.9.1273D). Here and in other places where this text is partially quoted (*Ar*. iv.6.1117C, 9.1119D, 14.1123B) Victorinus has the present *nascitur* in place of the perfect *natum est*.

iii.8 *spirat enim ubi uult* (*Ar*. iii.14.1109B).

iii.13 *nullus ascendit in caelum, nisi qui de caelo descendit* (*Ar*. i.5.1042C). (This text is paraphrased in *In Eph*. iv.9.1273D).

iii.15f *ut qui credit in ipsum non pereat . . . sed habeat* spem, *uitam aeternam* (*Ar*. i.5.1042C–D).

iii.16 *unde filium suum unigenitum tradidit . . . ut omnis qui credit in ipsum non pereat, sed habeat uitam aeternam* (*Ar*. i.5.1042D).

iii.17 *non enim misit deus filium, ut iudicet mundum, sed ut saluet mundum* (*Ar*. i.5.1042D). For the active instead of the passive verb in the last clause, cf. John xii.47.

iii.19 *quoniam lumen uenit in mundum* (*Ar*. i.5.1042D).

iii.31 *qui desuper uenit, supra omnes est.* Et rursus: *de caelo ueniens* (*Ar*. i.5.1043A).

iv.10 *si scires donum dei, et quis est qui dicit tibi, Da mihi bibere, tu magis petisses eum et dedisset tibi aquam uiuam* (*Ar*. iv.6.1117B).

iv.10, 13 *tu ab eo peteres et tibi daret aquam uiuentem.* Et rursus: *omnis qui biberit ex aqua ista, iterum sitiet; qui autem biberit ex ista aqua quam ego dabo ipsi non sitiet in omni saeculo, sed aqua quam ipsi dabo efficietur in ipso fons aquae scatentis in uitam aeternam* (*Ar*. i.5.1043A; for verse 13 cf., with variants, *Ar*. iv.6.1117C).

iv.24 *spiritus deus est, et adorantes eum in spiritu et ueritate adorare oportet* (*Ar*. iv.4.1115D).

v.17 *pater meus usque nunc operatur* (*Ar*. i.5.1043A).

v.19 *Amen, amen dico uobis: non potest filius a semetipso facere aliquid, si non uiderit patrem facientem; quae enim ille facit, eadem et filius facit* (*Ar*. iii.2.1099C).

v.20 *pater enim amat filium* (*Ar*. i.6.1043B).

v.21 *sicut enim pater suscitat mortuos et uiuificat, sic et filius quos uult uiuificat* (*Ar*. iv.31.1135C).

v.26 *sicuti enim pater uitam habet in semetipso, sic dedit et filio uitam habere in semetipso* (*Ar*. iii.10.1106B). A text cited ten times by Victorinus with variations (cf. *Ar*. i.6.1043B, 41.1071C–D, 51.1079C; ii.7.1094A; iii.3.1100B, 6.1103A–B; iv.14.1123B, 1123C, 30.1134D.

v.30 *iustum meum iudicium est, quia non quaero* facere *uoluntatem meam, sed eius qui me misit* (*Ar*. iii.10.1106C).

v.38 *et λόγον eius non habebitis in uobis manentem, quoniam quem misit ille, ipsi uos non creditis* (*Ar*. i.6.1043B–C). The future *habebitis* appears also in a.

v.40 *non uultis ad me uenire, ut uitam habeatis* (*Ar*. iii.10.1106C).

vi.32f *pater meus dat uobis panem de caelo uerum*. Quod Christus non ab homine homo: *panis enim ex deo est, qui descendit de caelo*. Quod uita: *et uitam dans mundo* (*Ar*. i.6.1043C).

vi.35 *ego sum panis uitae* (*Ar*. i.6.1043C).

vi.37 *quem mittit ad me pater, iste ad me uenit* (*Ar*. i.43.1074A; cf. the paraphrase in *Ar*. iii.10.1106C: *omne quod mihi datum est a patre apud me habeo*, influenced partly by xvii. 12).

vi.38 *non meam sed patris facio uoluntatem* (*Ar*. iv.31.1135B). A paraphrase, but note *patris*, appearing also in a b d ff_2 r.

vi.39f *quae est*, inquit, *uoluntas patris qui me misit? ut ex eo quod mihi dedit nihil perdam, sed resurgere faciam id ipsum postrema die. haec enim uoluntas est patris mei, ut omnis qui uidet filium et in ipsum credit, habeat uitam aeternam, et in die nouissima resurgat* (*Ar*. iii.10.1106D–1107A). A rather free and rhetorical quotation).

vi.46 *non uidit patrem aliquis, nisi qui est a patre* (*Ar*. i.6.1043C). The substitution of *a patre* for *a deo* is peculiar among Latin renderings, but agrees with **א**.

vi.50, 58 *hic est panis qui de caelo descendit* (*Ar*. iv.7.1118A; cf. ii.8.1094B).

vi.51 *panis uitae sum ego: qui istum manducat, uiuet in saeculum* (*Ar*. i.7.1044A).

vi.53f *nisi acceperitis corpus filii hominis, sicut panem uitae, et biberitis sanguinem eius, non habebitis uitam in uobis: qui autem edet carnem eius et bibet eius sanguinem, habet uitam aeternam* (*Ar*. iv.7.1118A). Note *acceperitis* with a, d (λάβητε D), *corpus* with a, the additional *sicut panem uitae* with a. One may compare the Western addition to verse 56: *nisi acceperitis corpus filii hominis, sicut panem uitae, non habetis uitam in eo* (d, in agreement with D; similarly a ff_2).

vi.57f *sicut misit me uiuens pater . . . et ego uiuo propter patrem . . . et qui accipit me, et ille uiuet propter me. hic est panis de caelo descendens, non sicuti patres uestri manducauerunt et mortui sunt: manducans istum panem uiuet in omne saeculum* (*Ar.* i.6.1043C–D). The first two clauses of verse 57 are quoted repeatedly, with minor variations (cf. *Ar.* i.7.1043D, 15.1049A, 42.1073B; ii.7.1094A; iii.10.1106B; iv.7.1117D, 14.1123A).

vi.62 *si igitur uideritis filium hominis ascendentem ubi fuit prius* (*Ar.* i.7.1044A). With *si igitur* cf. Vg *si ergo*; another citation of the text (*Ar.* iv.7.1118B) has *quid si* (found also in b d q). For *fuit prius* (found also in b) the citation in *Ar.* iv.7.1118B has *primum fuit* (cf. *erat primum* q and *fuit primum* r).

vi.63 *spiritus est qui uiuificat* (*Ar.* iv.4.1115D; in *Ar.* i.19.1052B and iv.9.1119D it is quoted in the form *spiritus autem uiuificat*).

vi.68f *post quem ibimus? uerbum uitae aeternae habes: et nos credidimus et cognouimus quod tu es christus filius dei* (*Ar.* iii.10.1107A). We note the unique *post*, the singular *uerbum* with Cyprian, the perfect *credidimus* with a b d f q Vg, *christus filius dei* with f Vg. The passage from *uerbum uitae aeternae* to *filius dei* is cited in *Ar.* i.7.1044A with the present *credimus* (with c e ff_2 1 r δ aur. Tert. Cypr. Vg. codd.), followed by *in te* (cf. *te* d), and *quoniam* for *quod* (so a b q).

vii.29 *ego scio ipsum, quod ab ipso sum* (*Ar.* i.7.1044A).

vii.37f *Iesus stabat et clamabat, si quis est qui sitit, ueniat et bibat. qui credit in me, quemadmodum dicit scriptura, flumina ex uentre ipsius manant aquae uiuentis* (*Ar.* i.8.1044B). In rendering ὕδατος ζῶντος by *aquae uiuentis* Victorinus shows his predilection for Latin participles as the equivalent of Greek participles; cf. John iii.31 (*ueniens*); iv.10 (*uiuentem*); iv.24 (*adorantes*); vi.33 (*dans*); vi.58 (*descendens . . . manducans*). Jesus' proclamation is cited in *Ar.* iv.6.1117B as follows: *qui sitit, ueniat ad me et bibat. qui credit in me, sicut dixit scriptura, flumina de uentre eius fluent aquae uiuae* (*qui sitit* agrees with a).

vii.39 *hoc autem dixit de spiritu, quem futuri erant accipere credentes in ipsum: nondum enim spiritus erat datus, quia Iesus nondum erat glorificatus* (*Ar.* i.8.1044C). The periphrasis *futuri erant accipere* – 'a rendering to attract attention'[1] – appears to be Victorinus's preferred construction to render Greek ἔμελλον λαμβάνειν.

viii.12 *ego sum lumen mundi* (*Ar.* i.8.1044C). We have noted already Victorinus's preference of *lumen* (so here e r) over *lux* (cf. i.4, etc.).

viii.16, 29 *non sum solus, quoniam pater mecum est* (*Ar.* i.14.1048C).

[1] W. Sanday, *Old Latin Biblical Texts* II, p. lxxxv.

The former clause, from viii.16, is combined with the latter clause, derived (in general sense, at least) from viii.29 – evidently a memory quotation.

viii.19 *me si sciretis, sciretis patrem meum. neque me scitis neque patrem meum* (*Ar.* iii.11.1107A). The two sentences are transposed; they are cited in their proper order in *Ar.* iii.11.1107B: *quia non scitis me, nec patrem: si sciretis me, sciretis et patrem meum.*

viii.26 item *qui me misit uerus est, et ego quae audiui ab ipso ea loquor* (*Ar.* iii.11.1107B).

viii.51 *amen amen dico uobis: si quis uerbum meum custodierit, mortem non uidebit* (*Ar.* iii.11.1107C). We note *uerbum* with a b d e q r, *custodierit* with d e Hier.

viii.55 *noui enim patrem, et uerbum eius custodio* (*Ar.* iii.11.1107C). We note *noui* with a e q, *uerbum* with a b d e l q r, and *custodio* with b q.

viii.56 *Abraham pater uester laetabatur ut uideret diem meum, et uidit et gauisus est* (*Ar.* i.8.1044D). We note *laetabatur* with b l (r). An abbreviated quotation of the text occurs in *Ar.* iv.32.1136C: *Abraham uidit diem meum, et gauisus est.*

viii.58 *ante Abraham ego sum* (*Ar.* i.8.1044D). This is the common Old Latin reading, as against Vg *antequam Abraham fieret ego sum.* In *Ar.* i.10.1045C the MS reading is *ante Adam ego sum.* Locher follows Galland in emending *Adam* to *Abraham*, but Victorinus may have altered the wording deliberately, meaning 'not only before Abraham, but even before Adam'.

ix.5 *cum sum in mundo, lumen sum mundi* (*Ar.* i.8.1044D). More interesting than the text of its citation is the use to which Victorinus puts it: he introduces it with the words, 'That he was not a human being' (*quod non homo*), and continues: 'But who gave sight to the blind man ? A human being ? Impossible.' So far was he from grasping the Nicene faith which he had undertaken to defend. (Cf. vi. 32f above.)

ix.31 *peccantes ⟨deus⟩ non audit* (*Ar.* i.7.1043D). *deus* om A.

ix.35ff *tu credis in filium dei? respondit ille: quis est, domine, ut credam in eum? dixit ipsi Iesus: et uidisti eum et qui loquitur tecum ipse est* (*Ar.* i.8.1045A). Close to Vg which, however, has *et dixit* after *respondit ille* and *ei* in place of *ipsi.*

x.9 *ego sum ianua* (*Ar.* iv.31.1135C). The rendering *ianua* (contrast *ostium* Vg) appears in several Old Latin witnesses (a b ff_2 q etc.).

x.17f *propterea me pater amat, et ego pono animam meam ut iterum sumam eam. nemo illam a me tollit; sed ego eam pono a me ipso: licentiam habeo ponere eam, et licentiam habeo sumere eam* (*Ar.* iii.11.1107C).

x.28 *ego do uitam in aeternum* (*Ar.* iv.31.1135C). A free citation.

x.30 *ego et pater unum sumus* (*Ar.* i.8.1045A, 9.1045A, 13.1047C, 29.1062A; iii.17.1113B; iv.10.1120D; *In Eph.* v.2.1283A).

xi.25 ipse saluator dicit: *ego sum resurrectio*, quod ipse *uita* (*Ar.* i.10.1045C).

xi.27 Martha dicit: *quoniam tu es Christus, filius dei, qui in mundum uenisti* (*Ar.* i.10.1045C). Wordsworth and White mistakenly cite Victorinus for *uiui* after *dei*.

xi.41 *pater, gratias tibi ago quod me audisti* (*Ar.* i.10.1045D).

xi.52 *qui dispersi sunt filii* (*Ar.* i.10.1045D). 'We are not only Gentiles', says Victorinus, 'but also "the children . . . who are scattered abroad".'

xii.27 *pater, salua me ex ista hora* (*Ar.* i.10.1045D).

xii.28 *et glorificaui, et rursus glorifico* (*Ar.* i.10.1046A).

xii.30 *non propter me uenit haec uox, sed propter uos* (*Ar.* i.10.1046A).

xii.34ff *nos audiuimus a lege, quoniam christus manet in aeternum: et quomodo dicis tu, quod filium hominis oportet altificari? quis est filius hominis? Dixit ipsis Iesus: adhuc paululum tempus lumen in uobis est*. Et deinde: *quamdiu lumen habetis, creditis in lumen, ut filii luminis efficiamini* (*Ar.* i.11.1046A–B). The vocabulary of this citation deviates sufficiently from that of our other Latin witnesses to suggest that in some degree Victorinus is making an independent translation from the Greek: this would also account for the indicative *creditis* against the imperative *credite* of other witnesses, as an alternative rendering of πιστεύετε.

There is a wealth of quotation from the upper-room discourse of John xiv–xvi (especially the paraclete passages) and from the high-priestly prayer of John xvii – enough to provide subject matter for a separate article. We therefore pass over these chapters for the present and conclude with three citations or allusions from the end of the Gospel of John.

xviii.37 *in istud natus sum, et in istud ueni in mundum* (*Ar.* i.15.1049B).

xx.1ff Sed contra dictum quod *nocte quae sabbatum sequitur apparuerit Mariae, tangi noluerit, priusquam iret ad patrem. Nuntiauit Maria discipulis. Eadem nocte ad ipsos uenit, ostendens manus et latus*, utique tangi iam non prohibens. *Post, Thomas palpauit, tetigit, ipso quidem hortante, quia ille desperabat*, quod significat sanctificatum iam fuisse (*Ar.* iii.15.1110B–C). This allusion to part of the resurrection narrative of John xx is intended to explain why Jesus forbade Mary Magdalene to touch him (xx.17) but not more than a few days later invited Thomas to do so (xx.27). Victorinus' explanation is that in the interval he had to go to the Father (by an interior process, not by a geographical ascension) for the sanctification of the human life which he had recovered from Hades (as distinct from the divine life which was eternally his as the Logos).

xx.22 *insufflauit* christus *et dixit: accipite spiritum sanctum* (*Ar.* i.15.1049B).

The freedom with which Victorinus quotes the Gospel text means that a study of his citations throws more light on his own thought than on the precise wording of the text which was accessible to him. But this collection of citations, such as it is, is offered with profound admiration to a scholar, colleague and friend whom I have known and esteemed since our student days in Scotland half a century ago.

0230 (= PSI 1306) and the fourth-century Greek–Latin edition of the letters of Paul

NILS ALSTRUP DAHL

In 1953 Giovanni, Cardinal Mercati published a tiny parchment fragment, not greater than *c.* 13.5 × 2.5 cm. The hair side (recto) contains the text of Eph. vi.5b–6 in Latin, the flesh side (verso) Eph. vi.11b–12a in Greek. The fragment was found near Antinoë in Egypt and published, as no. 1306, among the *Papiri Greci e Latini* edited by the Società Italiana per la ricerca dei Papiri greci e latini in Egitto, volume XIII (Firenze, 1953), 87–97. In the list of Greek New Testament manuscripts the fragment has received the signum 0230; in the Beuron edition of the *Vetus Latina*, the Latin text is no. 85.

In comparison with other manuscripts discovered in the last generation, the small fragment seems to be insignificant, especially since it does not contain any variant readings of real importance for New Testament textual criticism. Yet Cardinal Mercati rightly claimed that the interest of the fragment is out of proportion to its size. On the basis of paleography, he was able to date the manuscript to the early fifth or the late fourth century. In its original form, the manuscript is likely to have contained the whole Pauline Corpus, with the Greek and Latin texts in parallel columns. It is, therefore, the earliest example of a Greek–Latin biblical bilingual. The Egyptian provenience adds to its significance. It is quite likely that the manuscript was written and used in the same area in which the fragment was found.[1]

Since its foundation by Hadrian, Antinoë had been a center of Roman military and civil administration in Egypt. The city with its surroundings also became one of the centers of early Christian monasticism.[2] In

[1] As the editor points out, pp. 91 and 94, the form of the Greek letter Mu betrays that the scribe was accustomed to the Coptic alphabet. On pp. 92f he leaves open the possibility that the Latin column was written by another scribe.

[2] On Antinoë or Antinoopolis, see esp. H. Leclerq in DALC I.2 (1907), pp. 2326–59. Palladius, who was in exile there in A.D. 408–12, tells that about 1,200 hermits lived in the surroundings and that there were twelve

the fourth and fifth centuries the use of the Latin language was increasing in Egypt, both in general and among Christians.[1] We also have information to the effect that men and women, who had retired from the world, could best support themselves by copying manuscripts. By doing so, they could follow the prescription of the apostle and work with their own hands, without any interruption of their monastic life.[2] Thus, our fragment adds a small piece of evidence that fits into the general picture of the cultural and religious history of the time and the area.

The importance of the fragment would be greatly increased if 0230 could be demonstrated to have a family relationship to the major Greek–Latin bilingual manuscripts of the Pauline letters. In his edition, Cardinal Mercati paid some attention to these manuscripts, but he did not pursue the question of whether or not 0230 might go back to the same archetype as the other Pauline bilinguals. I have myself long been of the opinion that a close family relationship does exist, without ever stating my reasons in a printed publication.[3] In direct contradiction to this,

convents of women, see *Historia Lausiaca* 58–9, edited by Butler, TS vi.2, Cambridge, 1904, pp. 151–3. Several Latin papyri found at Antinoë have been edited in C. H. Roberts or J. W. Barns/H. Zilliacus, editors, *The Antinoopolis Papyri*, i–iii (London, 1950–67), and/or R. Cavenaile, editor, *Corpus Papyrorum Latinorum* (Wiesbaden, 1958). They include two fragments of Virgil (P. Antin. 29–30, CPL 15, 17), one of Juvenal (CPL 37), two other literary texts (P. Antin. 154–5), two Greek–Latin legal fragments (P. Antin. 152–3, fifth–sixth century), a Latin alphabet (CPL 58), and a small number of other texts) (CPL 72, 78 (?), 135, 181). The most interesting Christian text is fragments of a Gothic–Latin bilingual with some verses from Luke xxiii–xxiv, P. Giessen 15, edited by P. Glaue/H. Helm, *ZNTW* 11 (1910), pp. 1–38 (= *Vetus Latina* 36; CPL 53; fifth or sixth century). Another fragment has been supposed to contain a hagiographic text, or a version of Esther (P. Antin. 14; CPL 54; fifth century).

[1] Among the literary papyri collected in CPL, nos. 1–47, only 12–14 are dated before A.D. 300; 27–9 are from the fourth–fifth century, 3 from the sixth; one small fragment is not dated, and nos. 8 and 16 are from sixth century Palestine. Virgil seems to have been the most popular Latin author in fourth–fifth century Egypt, see CPL 1–7, 9–15, 17. The data indicate that in Egypt the need for Latin biblical texts reached its peak around A.D. 400, the time when our Pauline bilingual originated. On the use of Latin among Christians in Egypt, see also G. Bardy, *La question des langues dans l'Église ancienne* (Paris, 1948), pp. 143–6.

[2] Mercati, *Papiri Greci e Latini*, p. 96, reports a touching story about the poor brother Symeon who mastered no craft except copying Latin books. An old hermit helped him to support himself for a whole year by copying the Latin Apostolus, which the hermit wanted an alleged brother in the army to read for his edification; see John Cassian, *De institutis coenobiorum*, v.38 (*CSEL* 17, pp. 110–12). For other references to writing hermits, see John Cassian, *ibid.*, iv.12, pp. 54f; *Historia Lausiaca* 38 (on Euagrios Pontikos) and 13, 32, 35 (Butler 120, 36, 96, 133); *S. Melaniae Iunioris Acta Graeca*, edited by Delehaye, *Analecta Bollandiana* 22 (1903), 23, 26, 36.

[3] Unpublished papers read at the Annual Meeting of the Society for Biblical

H. J. Frede, the editor of the Pauline Epistles in the Beuron *Vetus Latina*, has repeatedly denied that any such relationship exists.[1] The problem is important enough to deserve a detailed discussion.

The major Pauline bilinguals are known to all students of the Greek New Testament, mainly because they are the chief witnesses to the 'Western text' of the letters of Paul. In two annual 'programs' of a German *Gymnasium*, Peter Corssen published the fundamental study of the relationship between these manuscripts, some 90 years ago.[2] I need only give the basic data, as I can refer to the works of Frede, who has not only summarized the results of Corssen and his successors but also added fresh insights of his own.[3] As Corssen already recognized, there are two streams of textual transmission which both go back to the same source. The chief representative of the first line is Codex Claromontanus (D^{Paul} = 06 = a 1026 von Soden; in Latin d = 75).[4] This manuscript was written in southern Italy, in the fifth, rather than the sixth, century. The manuscript was worked over by several correctors, none of whom were later than the sixth century. The main correctors were more interested in the Greek than in the Latin text. Their general tendency was to eliminate singular readings and thus to normalize the text(s) according to current standards.[5]

Subsidiary representatives of this line are all copies of Codex Claromontanus, made in the eighth, ninth, or tenth century, in Corbie or its

Literature in 1961 and at a meeting of the section for humanities of Det Norske Videnskabs-Akademi i Oslo in 1963. I stated my opinion but not my reasons in an article on 'The Particularity of the Pauline Epistles as a Problem in the Ancient Church', in *Neotestamentica et Patristica: Freundesgabe O. Cullmann*, edited by W. C. van Unnik (Leiden, 1962), p. 207.

1 See Frede, *Altlateinische Paulus-Handschriften*, Vetus Latina: Aus der Geschichte der lateinischen Bibel, 4 (Freiburg, 1964), p. 100; *Ein neuer Paulustext mit Kommentar*, same series as above, 7.1 (Freiburg, 1973), p. 83. These publications will be quoted as *Paulus-Handschriften* and *Paulustext*.

2 P. Corssen, *Epistularum Paulinarum codices Graece et Latine scriptos Augiensem, Boernerianum, Claromontanum examinavit inter se comparavit ad communem originem revocavit*, I–II, Programme des Gymnasiums Jever (Kiel, 1887 and 1889). Cf. 'Zur Überlieferungsgeschichte des Römerbriefs', *ZNTW* 10 (1911), pp. 1–46, esp. pp. 2–8.

3 Frede, *Paulus-Handschriften*, pp. 15–101; *Paulustext*, pp. 76–83. See also *Vetus Latina* 24/1, *Epistula ad Ephesios*, edited by Erzabtei Beuron (Freiburg, 1962–4), 11*–13*; 25/1, *Epistula ad Thessalonicenses* (Freiburg, 1975ff), 23*–27*. Cf. also E. Nellesen, *Untersuchungen zur altlateinischen Überlieferung des Ersten Thessalonikerbriefes*, BBB 22 (Bonn, 1965), pp. 28–33.

4 I have used the standard editions, C. Tischendorf, *Codex Claromontanus* (Leipzig, 1852); A. Reichardt, *Der Codex Boernerianus . . . in Lichtdruck nachgebildet* (Leipzig, 1909); F. H. Scrivener, *An Exact Transcript of Codex Augiensis* (Cambridge/London, 1859). In 1968 I had the opportunity to consult Codex Claromontanus at the Bibliothèque Nationale in Paris.

5 See Frede, *Paulus-Handschriften*, pp. 20–33.

environs. One of them has been well preserved; 176 of 188 leaves remain of Codex Sangermanensis (E^{Paul} = D^{abs1} = a 1031; in Latin e = 76). The scribe copied sometimes the original text and sometimes the corrections in Claromontanus, most often both.[1] Some fragments, with text from Eph. i–ii, have been preserved of another copy, Codex Waldeccensis (D^{abs2}, in Latin 83). In general, this manuscript reproduces the corrected text of Claromontanus.[2] A lectionary fragment in Leningrad, with text from Eph. ii.19–22, is also a descendant of the corrected text of Claromontanus.[3] An eleventh-century catalogue from Corbie attests the existence of a bilingual Paul manuscript which has been lost. Frede conjectures that it was another copy of Claromontanus.[4]

The other stream of transmission is represented by two manuscripts, Codex Boernerianus (G^{Paul} = 012 = a 1028; in Latin g = 77) and Codex Augiensis (F^{Paul} = 010 = a 1029; in Latin f = 78). Scholars have long recognized that these two manuscripts were closely related, but only Frede has been able to figure out the exact nature of that relationship. His solution is elegant, simple, and fully convincing. In the ninth century, an ancient but defective bilingual manuscript, since Corssen called 'X', was brought from Italy to the Benedictine monastery in St Gallen, where there was a revival of Greek studies but no available Greek copy of Paul's letters. In order to prepare for a Greek text with interlinear Latin translation, an Irish monk, possibly Moengal, edited the ancient exemplar, marking the division between words, adding alternative Latin translations etc. To this purpose the editor made use of various tools, including a local St Gallen version of the Old Latin translation, a variant of Frede's text type 'I'. The scribe who carried out the plan copied the text with much care but little knowledge of Greek. He sometimes failed to understand the editorial notes.[5]

Somewhat later, the ancient exemplar 'X' came from St Gallen to the

[1] *Ibid.*, pp. 34–42. Sangermanensis does not always follow the colometry in Claromontanus, as I was able to observe on a microfilm at the *Vetus Latina* Institut in Beuron, in 1961.

[2] See V. Schultze, *Codex Waldeccensis* (Dw Paul) (München, 1904); Frede, *Paulus-Handschriften*, pp. 47–8.

[3] Frede, *Paulus-Handschriften*, pp. 46–7.

[4] *Ibid.*, pp. 44–5.

[5] Frede, *Paulus-Handschriften*, pp. 50–77. The 'I text' is a fluid type of text, represented by the manuscripts *Vetus Latina* 61 (Book of Armagh, formerly Vulgate MS D) and 86 (Monza i 2/9, edited by Frede, *Paulus-Handschriften*), by the commentaries of Marius Victorinus, Ambrosiaster, and Pelagius (B text only), and by Ambrose and other fathers. Its main characteristics are changes in the Latin vocabulary and, more occasionally, corrections after the Greek text. See Frede, *Paulus-Handschriften*, pp. 137–50; *Vetus Latina* 24/1, pp. 33*–35*, with references to earlier studies of the author.

sister monastery at Reichenau, where it was copied a second time. The scribe at Reichenau, however, wrote the Latin and Greek texts in separate columns. He revised the Latin text, more or less carefully, according to a local form of the Vulgate, but retained some of the alternative translations which he, like the editor of the exemplar, placed above the Greek words. As a consequence, the Greek text is the same in the St Gallen copy, our Boernerianus, and in the Reichenau copy, Augiensis. Exceptions are due to scribal errors or to corrections after the Latin in Augiensis. The Latin texts, by contrast, have many common elements but are far from identical. Both are mixed texts, but not of the same type.[1]

Corssen already recognized that both branches of Pauline bilinguals go back to a common fourth-century archetype, which he called 'Z'. For reasons which will become apparent later in this article, I am inclined to think of this archetype as a very carefully planned and executed edition of which the existing manuscripts are but degenerated descendants. The editor made use of an already existing Latin version which he adapted to the Greek text in order to make the sense lines of the two columns correspond exactly to each other.[2] For the Greek column, he used a manuscript with a text of a type that in the fourth century was already obsolete in most parts of Christendom. It was similar to but not identical with the Greek text from which the Latin translation had originally been made. It would seem that some discrepancies between the Greek and the Latin texts in the Pauline bilinguals go back to the original edition.

In the course of transmission, both the Greek and/or the Latin texts were corrected. In most cases, the one or the other was made to conform more closely to the predominant text used in the environment, but even some secondary harmonization between the two columns seems to have occurred. In spite of such complications, however, the original text of the bilingual edition can be recovered with a remarkably high degree of probability.[3] The Greek text was already at an early date corrected in

[1] This conclusion is drawn on the basis of Frede's data, esp. *Paulus-Handschriften*, pp. 80–7. I have myself done some work with the text of Ephesians and of Rom. xi.33–xv.13.

[2] Since A. Souter, 'The Original Home of Codex Claromontanus', *JTS* 6 (1905), pp. 240–3, it has been recognized that Lucifer used a text similar to that of Claromontanus (d), but one which was not drawn from the bilingual edition. Cf. Frede, *Paulus-Handschriften*, pp. 92 n. 2, 93, 96f. Recently, Frede has been able to identify a manuscript which contains a text very similar to the text adapted for use in the bilingual edition (Budapest, National Library, Cod. lat. med. aevi 1 = 89 *Vetus Latina*). See Frede, *Paulustext*, *passim.*

[3] Nellesen's investigation of 1 Thessalonians (p. 81, n. 3 above) includes a reconstruction of the Greek as well as the Latin column, on pp. 115–28. For corrections, cf. Frede, *Paulustext*, pp. 81–2. Nellesen's assumption that the colometric system was the same in the bilingual archetype as in Claromontanus is

both branches of the transmission. In many cases, Boernerianus and Augiensis have retained the original reading. By contrast, the text that has undergone the least amount of change is the Latin of Claromontanus, obviously because this codex and its immediate predecessor(s) originated in an area where Greek was the predominant language. The consequence of this is that where the Greek of Boernerianus and Augiensis (G F) and the Latin of Claromontanus (d) coincide, the combination of G and d almost certainly represents the original text of the two columns of the common archetype. In several cases it is even likely that the Latin of Claromontanus (d) alone has preserved the original text of the bilingual archetype and that the Greek column originally had a corresponding text.[1]

The Greek–Latin bilinguals, D and G/F, are not only our most important witnesses to the 'Western text', and, in Frede's words, a 'museum of textual history', preserving a number of otherwise obsolete variant readings. They also have a more general interest for the study of textual history. I know of no other case in which so many important New Testament manuscripts can be traced back to one common archetype and thus form a family of manuscripts in the strictest sense of this term. It is therefore all the more important to observe the great textual variation within this family. Codex Claromontanus, in its original form, and the lost manuscript 'X', the exemplar from which Boernerianus and Augiensis derive, must still have had Greek and Latin texts of the same type, in spite of a number of variant readings. But if we also take into consideration the corrections in Claromontanus (D^c and d^c), the descendants of this codex, and the Latin texts of Boernerianus and Augiensis (g f), the one family of manuscripts includes several types of mixed texts.

The Pauline bilinguals provide a school example from which we can gain two insights: (1) We should make a strict distinction between families of manuscripts and types of texts. (2) The extreme complexity of New Testament textual history is due to the activity of editors and correctors, much more than to the errors or whims of scribes. There are other reasons for these assumptions, but a school example may be a useful reminder. Both insights must be kept in mind when we now return to the fragment 0230 and the question of its relationship to the major Pauline bilinguals.

The facsimiles make it quite clear that 0230 derives from a codex that

questionable, see below p. 93. The D-line in Frede's edition of the Pauline letters, *Vetus Latina*, is important for the Latin text of the bilingual original.

[1] H. J. Vogels, 'Der Codex Claromontanus der Paulinischen Briefe', in H. G. Wood, editor, *Amicitiae Corolla: A volume of Essays presented to J. R. Harris* (London, 1933), pp. 274–99. Cf. Frede, *Paulustext*, p. 81.

was more similar to Claromontanus than to Boernerianus or Augiensis. The following reproduction of the text of the fragment and corresponding passages in Claromontanus will give an impression of similarities and differences.

Eph. vi.5b–6a

0230 recto

INSIMPLICITATE] CORDISVESTRAESICV[TXPO
NONADOCVLVM SERVIENTES
QVASIHOMINIBVS PLACENTES
SEDQVASISERVIXPI

Claromontanus

ΕΝΑΠΛΟΤΗΤΙ	INSIMPLICITATE
ΤΗΣΚΑΡΔΙΑΣΥΜΩΝ	CORDISVESTRIS
ΩΣΤΩΧΩ	SICVTXPO
ΜΗΚΑΤΟΦΘΑΛΜΟΔΟΥΛΙΑΝ	NONADOCVLVM SERVIENTES
ΩΣΑΝΘΡΩΠΑΡΕΣΚΟΙ	QVASIHOMINIBVS PLACENTES
ΑΛΛΩΣΔΟΥΛΟΙΧΥ	SEDVTSERVIXPI

Ephesians vi.11b–12a

0230 verso

ΠΡΟΣΤ]ΟΔΥΝΑΣΘΑΙΥΜΑΣ[ΣΤΗΝΑΙ
ΠΡΟΣΤ]ΑΣΜΕΘΟΔΕΙΑΣΤΟΥΔΕΙΑΒΟΛΟΥ
ΟΤΙΟΥΚΕΣΤΙΝΗΜΙΝΗΠΑΛΗ
ΠΡΟΣΑΙΜΑΚΑ]ΙΣΑΡΚΑ

Claromontanus

ΕΙΣΤΟΔΥΝΑΣΘΑΙΣΤΗ ΝΑΙΥΜΑΣ	VTPOSSITISSTARE
ΠΡΟΣΤΑΣΜΕΘΟΔΙΑΣ	ADVERSVMREMEDIVM
ΤΟΥΔΙΑΒΟΛΟΥ	DIABOLI
ΟΤΙΟΥΚΕΣΤΙΝΥΜΙΝ	QVIANONESTVOBIS
ΗΠΑΛΗ	COLLVCTATIO
	ADVERSVS SANGVINEM
ΠΡΟΣΑΙΜΑΚΑΙΣΑΡΚΑ	ETCARNEM

In 0230 as in Claromontanus the text is written in sense lines, without any distinction between cola and commata or, to use roughly corresponding English terms, between clauses and phrases. The only difference is that four lines in 0230 correspond to six lines in Claromontanus, both in Latin and in Greek. The first Latin line of 0230 recto is written as three lines in Claromontanus, while the second and third lines of the Greek verso correspond to two lines each. In general, the length of the lines in Claromontanus varies a great deal, and that does not seem to have been the case in the codex of which 0230 is a fragment.

In spite of the similarity of design, 0230 has no striking textual affinity to Claromontanus. A comparison of the text must take account of the whole textual history of the major bilinguals and of other representative witnesses as well. I list the variants according to the lines in 0230, beginning with the Greek text on the verso.[1]

Eph. 6.11b–12a, Greek, 0230 verso:

Line 1: *προς*, (0230 ?) $\mathfrak{P}^{46}$ S B A P pm.; *εις* D E G F
υμας στηναι, 0230 with G F and S B 1739 P pm.; *στηναι υμας*, D E; *στηναι* (om. *υμας*), $\mathfrak{P}^{46}$ K.

Line 2: *μεθοδειας*, 0230 with D^c B^c P al.; *μεθοδιας* D* G F with $\mathfrak{P}^{46}$ S B* A pm.
δειαβολον, 0230; *διαβολον*, D G F pm.

Line 3: *ημιν*, 0230 with D^c E and S A 1739 I K P pm., Clement; cf. nobis, g* with 61 (= Vulgate D, Book of Armagh) al. Vg; *υμιν* D* G F with $\mathfrak{P}^{46}$ B al., cf. vobis, d e g^c (first hand ?) f 86 89 Lucifer.

Line 4: No variant. But cf. *carnem et sanguinem*, 89 Lucifer latt. pl.; *sanguinem et carnem*, d g.

In comparison with D G F, the four preserved Greek lines of 0230 contain four variant readings. As the lost part of the first line is likely to have contained five, rather than four letters, Cardinal Mercati was

[1] I have consulted separate editions of $\mathfrak{P}^{46}$, S (= Sinaiticus), B, A, and P, as well as of the bilinguals D/d, G/g and F/f (see p. 81, n. 4) and of the Latin manuscripts 86 and 89 (see p. 82, n. 5; p. 83, n. 2). I have found it most practical to retain the sigla d, g and f for the Latin texts of the bilinguals but to use the Beuron *Vetus Latina* numbers 86 and 89 for the Monza and Budapest manuscripts edited by Frede. For the text of 1739 I am dependent upon the collation in K. Lake and S. New, editors, *Six Collations of New Testament Manuscripts* (*HTS* 17, Cambridge, Mass., 1932). Other information is taken over from the critical editions of the Greek New Testament by Tischendorf, von Soden, Nestle–Aland, and the United Bible Societies, and, for the Latin text, from the Beuron *Vetus Latina* and/or Wordsworth and White.

probably correct in restoring *προς το* . . . If so, 0230 had the common text at this point, in contrast to the bilingual edition which had *εις το*, attested by D E G F but, apparently, by no other manuscript. Of the other variants, two are purely orthographical. While *δειαβολου* is an itacistic error, the spelling *μεθοδειας* was also preferred by the correctors of Vaticanus and Claromontanus. In line 3 the fragment agrees with D^c^ and most manuscripts over against the bilingual edition (D* G F) and the earliest Egyptian manuscripts (𝔓⁴⁶ B). At the end of the first line, the word order *υμας στηναι* is supported by G and F. Since this is the common text, the variant *στηναι υμας* in D and E could more easily go back to the bilingual archetype. But it is equally possible, and I would think more likely, that the archetype had the same text as 𝔓⁴⁶, without the personal pronoun. The Latin, of course, has no pronoun. The text of D would then be a less and the text of 'X' (= G F) a more successful correction, intended to make the obsolete text of the bilingual edition conform to the common Greek text.[1]

Apart from the scribal error *δειαβολου*, the text of 0230 is identical with that of P (= 025 = a 3, ninth century). In other words, the Greek fragment has a normal Egyptian text from the time around A.D. 400. The fragment contains no ancient variant characteristic of the bilingual edition, nor any variant peculiar to 𝔓⁴⁶ and/or B. But we should also observe that three of the variants in 0230 are attested within the family of bilingual manuscripts, either by G F (line 1 end) or by D^c^ and E (lines 2–3).[2] This fact does not prove anything about common ancestry, but these variants do illustrate how the original text of the bilingual edition was corrected during the process of transmission. Before we draw any conclusion, we must also consider the Latin text of the fragment.

Eph. vi.5b–6a, Latin, 0230 recto:

Line 1: *cordis+vestrae*, 0230; *vestris*, d; *vestri*, e g f rell.

Lines 2–3: No variants.

Line 4: *quasi servi*, 0230 with g, Cyprian, Test. III.72, pc.; *ut servi* d 61 86 89 al., Vg.; *sicut servi*, f pc.

[1] 𝔓⁴⁶ (and/or B) has several ancient variant readings in common with the bilinguals. There are several examples in Ephesians: iii.3, *οτι* om. 𝔓⁴⁶ B G d; v.19 *πνευματικαις* om. 𝔓⁴⁶ B d; vi.16 end, *τα* om . 𝔓⁴⁶ B D* G; ii.4, *αυτου* om. 𝔓⁴⁶ D* G; *ελεησεν* 𝔓⁴⁶ d ½g; iii.20 *υπερ* om. 𝔓⁴⁶ D G; v.20 *πατρι και θεω* 𝔓⁴⁶ D G; vi.1 *εν κυριω* om. B D* G. Cf. ii.15 *κοινον* 𝔓⁴⁶ G (error ?). For examples from other letters, see G. Zuntz, *The Text of the Epistles* (London, 1953), 87, 90–107, 117–23.

[2] The alterations in Eph. vi.11b and vi.12a were both made by the corrector of Claromontanus which Tischendorf named D*** and which Frede, *Paulus-Handschriften*, pp. 29f, assigns to the sixth century and considers an early witness to the Byzantine text.

The first of these two variants simply proves that the scribe of 0230 was not strong in Latin, just like the scribe of Claromontanus who made another grammatical error at the same point. Apart from this error, the Latin text of 0230 is identical with the interlinear version in Boernerianus (g). The second *quasi* in g and 0230 goes back to the ancient version which was used by Cyprian but later became obsolete. The reading can hardly have been known at St Gallen in the ninth century if it was not present in the ancient exemplar 'X'. It is therefore likely that the *sicut* of f and the *ut* of d are due to correctors, while the *quasi* of g (and 0230) represents the text of the bilingual archetype.[1]

The textual evidence is so slim that it remains inconclusive. The Greek text of 0230 is a normal Egyptian text and would, therefore, seem to favor Frede's opinion that there is no connection between 0230 and the major Pauline bilinguals. But three of the variants in the Greek text occur elsewhere as corrections of the ancient bilingual text, and the conjectured *προς* in 0230 can very well be due to a correction of the same type. The Latin text of 0230 is slightly in favor of a connection between the fragment and the other bilinguals, but it is not conclusive either. If considerable parts of the manuscript had been preserved, one would expect that some characteristic variants of the fourth-century bilingual edition had escaped the notice of the corrector(s), if 0230 were one of its descendants. The total absence of any such variants would then be a strong argument against any family relationship. But the preserved fragment is so brief that no decision can be reached on textual grounds. The actual data are fully compatible with what we might expect from a member of the family of bilingual manuscripts prepared for use in Egypt: the Greek text has been corrected to conform with the current standard, whereas the Latin, less current in Egypt, has been left unchanged. But textual investigations can only prove that this is one possible explanation, not that it is the true one.

Further study of the layout of the manuscript, from which 0230 derives, holds more promise of leading to a definitive result. We have already observed a striking similarity between 0230 and Claromontanus in the use of sense lines and have to try to find out how far the similarity extends. Both Claromontanus and 0230 have the Greek text in the left and the Latin in the right column. Claromontanus has the two columns on opposite pages. Cardinal Mercati assumed that 0230 had two columns, Greek and Latin, on each page. Some of his arguments, how-

[1] In *Vetus Latina* 24/1, p. 270, Frede himself prints *quasi . . . sed quasi . . .* in the D-line of Eph. vi.6. This is likely to be correct, even though the Budapest manuscript (89) has *quasi . . . sed ut . . . .*

ever, have little or no value, and the result is not entirely convincing. No trace of a second column exists. The question of whether there were one or two columns on each page depends upon the interpretation of horizontal and vertical ruling lines that delineate the space intended for writing. The lines were scratched on the verso but are clearly visible on both sides, even in reproduction.

The beginning of the Greek and the end of the Latin lines have been lost, but it is easy to figure out that the breadth of the room intended for writing must have been *c.* 132 mm, as stated by Cardinal Mercati.[1] The Cardinal made no attempt to calculate the height of the columns, but an approximate calculation is possible. The distance between the horizontal ruling lines alternates between *c.* 3 mm, the size of average letters, and *c.* 4 mm, the intervals between the lines of the text. The text intervening between the end of the Latin and the beginning of the Greek portion of 0230, i.e. Eph. vi.6b–11a, occupies 24 lines in Codex Claromontanus. If we assume a constant proportion of 2 lines in 0230 to 3 lines in Claromontanus, as in the preserved fragment, the same text would have occupied 16 lines in 0230. This figure is probably very nearly correct. Attempts to write the intervening text in sense lines, similar to those in 0230, have convinced me that one would at least need 15 and could at the utmost use 20 lines. With the 4 preserved lines added, 0230 must therefore have had between 19 and 24 lines. A likely figure would be 21, the same number of lines as in Claromontanus. Considering the distance between the horizontal lines, we can draw the conclusion that the height of the columns must have been *c.* 160, certainly not more than 200 mm.

Leaves with one column 132 mm wide and, approximately, 160 mm high would fit a normal size parchment codex, whereas leaves with two such columns would be unusual, the breadth being considerably greater than the height. Cardinal Mercati estimated that the total breadth would have been *c.* 27 cm text, with addition of margins on both sides. But this figure is too small, as it leaves too little room between the two columns. There are two vertical ruling lines, at a distance of 6–7 mm, placed near the beginning of the recto, and at the end of the verso, of the fragment. But these lines cannot possibly have marked the middle of the page, as the learned Cardinal seems to have assumed.[2] If there were

[1] Mercati, *Papiri Greci e Latini*, p. 90. See also Table 6 at the end of PSI volume XIII for a reproduction of no. 1306 (= 0230).

[2] I have not been able to find the reasons for this assumption. The Latin text begins at the first vertical line on the recto and the longest Greek line (line 3 with 28 letters) extends to the first vertical line on the verso (= the second line on the recto). But these facts do not tell anything about whether there was a second column or where it began. The observations, that there is no evidence

indeed two columns on both sides of the leaf, the vertical lines can only have marked the beginning of the second, Latin, column on the recto and the limit of the space allotted for the first, Greek, column on the recto. We can safely assume that the beginning of the Greek (and the end of the Latin) text was delineated by similar ruling lines. If there were two columns a page, there must have been four pairs of parallel lines, and there must have been a distance of *c.* 20 mm or more between the end of the first and the beginning of the second column.[1] The total space delineated for writing must therefore have been *c.* 29 cm plus margins on both sides.

On the basis of these calculations, I am inclined to think that the 0230 codex had the same arrangement as Claromontanus, with the Greek and Latin columns written on opposite pages. The fact that the preserved fragment has four lines of one column almost intact, with no trace of a second column, is itself in favor of this assumption. The only difficulty is that the horizontal lines would then be extended into the margin, beyond the space designed for writing. To the left of the page, initial letters at the beginning of a new section may have been placed outside the delineated space. The designer could also have anticipated the possibility that some of the sense lines might be too long to fit between the vertical lines, whose main function was to mark the beginning and not the end of the lines of text. Yet the extension of the horizontal lines remains a fact which may favor Mercati's assumption that the horizontal ruling lines continued through two columns of text.[2]

The probability of a family relation between 0230 and Claromontanus would increase if both codices had the Greek and the Latin texts on

that the parchment sheet was folded or that a second sheet was attached (Mercati, *Papiri Greci e Latini*, pp. 89–90) are equally irrelevant. On p. 95 the Cardinal states that he first thought that he could see traces of two letters after the end of the fourth Greek line on the verso and assumed that they were illegible remnants of the beginning of the second, Latin column. My guess is that he never really abandoned this idea although he later detected that there was no evidence for it. On the facsimile (PSI XIII, plate 6), I have not been able to detect any traces of the alleged letters. If they were written a bit below the ruling line ('un pò sotto del solco della riga'), they would represent a marginal gloss rather than a second column.

1 The Greek text corresponding to the first Latin line on the recto must have contained 30 or 31 letters, depending upon whether the genitive of the name of Christ was abbreviated $\overline{XY}$ (as in D) or $\overline{XPY}$ (as in G and the Latin text of 0230 and d). If the preserved pair of ruling lines had marked the middle of the page, the Greek text on the recto would have reached to the point where the Latin text begins and should, definitely, have been visible on the fragment.

2 On pricking and ruling of manuscripts, see e.g. B. Metzger, *The Text of the New Testament* (New York/London, 1964), p. 8. I regret that I have not had time for a comparative study of various systems for pricking and ruling.

opposite pages, possibly with 21 lines. But these may remain open questions.[1] What I have been driving at is another point. If the vertical ruling lines were designed to delineate one single column, as they certainly were, it becomes a problem why there are two parallel lines rather than one single line. On the recto of 0230 all Latin lines of text begin at the first vertical line, and we have every reason to think that the lost beginning of the Greek text was arranged in the same way. As initial letters of new sections had to be placed before this line, we have to ask: What is the function of the second vertical line? It would only have a function if some lines of text were to be indented and were to begin at the second ruling line. These indented lines cannot have contained minor sense units (commata), since the colometry in 0230 does not make any distinction between cola and commata. But what kind of lines were then to be indented? Codex Claromontanus provides the answer, and I can see no other answer that would make sense. The lines to be indented were quotations from the Old Testament. In Claromontanus, quotations are not only indented but also written with red ink, as are the opening lines of each letter. For lack of evidence, we cannot tell whether or not the similarity between 0230 and Claromontanus extended to the use of red ink. But the small, vertical lines not more than 2.5 cm long on the parchment of 0230, indicating the indenting of biblical quotations, are the conclusive link in the circumstantial evidence that indicates, beyond reasonable doubt, that the fragment derives from a codex that belonged to the same family as Claromontanus.

In Boernerianus and Augiensis the layout is different, and that would also seem to have been the case in 'X', the exemplar from which they both derive. Apparently, even this manuscript was written in sense lines, but in a colometric system that was less like that of Claromontanus and 0230 than like that of Codex Euthalianus (H^{Paul} = 0230 = a 1022) and of Codex Amiatinus and other Vulgate manuscripts. That is, the cola were treated as the important units, with little or no attention paid to the subdivision of the cola into smaller units (commata).[2] Thus it would

[1] It is quite possible that both the exemplar 'X' and the bilingual archetype 'Z' had two columns on each page, with the Greek to the left. Augiensis has the Latin text on both sides and the Greek in the inner columns of the opened book, but this is likely to be an innovation, just as the interlinear translation in Boernerianus. Codex Sangermanensis (E = $D^{abs\ 1}$) has two columns with the Greek on the left side of the pages. As we shall see, it may be more important that the preserved leaves of a Gothic–Latin bilingual have the Gothic column on the left and the Latin on the right side of the pages. On the archetype 'Z', cf. Frede, *Vetus Latina*, 25/1, p. 26.

[2] The demarcation of new cola in 'X' is indicated by big coloured letters in Boernerianus (G). Such big letters occur less frequently in Augiensis, but in the Latin column of this codex (f) a point, mostly placed slightly higher than

seem that the kinship between 0230 and Claromontanus is not simply due to their common descent from the fourth-century bilingual edition. They even belong to the same branch of the family of bilingual manuscripts, even though the family features in 0230 are only recognizable in the editorial design, not in the character of the text.

When the family relationship has been recognized, the difference between Claromontanus and 0230 calls for an explanation. In 0230 the length of the lines varies from 35 to 16 letters in Latin and from 28 to 16 in the Greek text. In the corresponding lines in Claromontanus the variation is from 23 to 8 letters in Latin and from 23 to 5 in Greek. The difference is not so much that the lines in 0230 are longer as that the variation is much greater in Claromontanus, which also has some lines with more than 30 letters. By comparison, the arrangement in 0230 did not only save space and parchment. It also resulted in more regular subdivisions of the text and more beautiful pages. If any of the two arrangements of the text is dependent upon the other, the more irregular arrangement in Claromontanus is likely to be the earlier one. It is, however, conceivable that the combination of similarity and difference is due to different executions of a common design, an editor being responsible for the design and two scribes for the differences in execution. In order to leave time for textual corrections, especially in the Greek of 0230, we would then have to assume that the common colometric system did not originate much later than the original bilingual edition itself, perhaps in the mid-fourth century.

What calls for an explanation is the very irregular colometry in

a regular period, indicates the beginning of a new colon. By and large, the two manners of demarcation attest the same length of the cola. This means that the common exemplar 'X' exhibited a colometric arrangement of the text. In some cases, G and/or f indicate a division of the text into lines of the same length as we find in Claromontanus (D/d). Nellesen, *Untersuchungen*, 37 and 51f, gives some examples (1 Thess. v.4–8 in G, f and D/d; 1 Thess. i.4–5, iii.3–4 in G and D). Similar, even if somewhat less striking, cases occur e.g. Eph. ii.5, 8; iv.4–6, 11, 25–6, 31 (f); v.4–5, 14, 18. Such instances, however, are much too infrequent to allow for the conclusion that the colometric display was by and large the same in 'X' as in D/d. In the great majority of cases, the big letters and/or the punctuation in G and f make it clear that the main colometric unit in 'X' was the colon, not the type of short sense lines which we find in Claromontanus (and 0230). The cases in which sense units in 'X', indicated by G and f, coincide with the lines in D can easily be explained. Some cola were very short, and in other cases a big letter in G and a period in f marks a division between commata and not between cola. I am not able to say how far such 'errors' are due to the scribes and how far they go back to the exemplar 'X'. The indications are that the colometry in 'X' was similar to that of Codex Amiatinus and other Latin codices, in which the cola may or may not be subdivided into regular commata. In *Vetus Latina* 89 a similar colometry is indicated by periods in a continuous text.

Claromontanus. In a study of this codex, H. Vogels was able to show that attention to colometric irregularities could be used to reconstruct the prehistory of the text and to recover the original text of the bilingual archetype. In several cases, alteration of text is the cause of the overlong lines in Codex Claromontanus.[1] But this explanation does not account for all, and so far as I can see, not even for the majority of cases. More often, the variation in the length of lines is better explained on the assumption that Claromontanus derives from an archetype in which only one small unit, a comma, was written on each line. A scribe, probably not the scribe of Claromontanus but one of his predecessors, sometimes retained the very short lines; in other cases he wrote two or, occasionally, three lines as one. The scribe from whose work 0230 is derived proceeded with more consistency. Apparently he tried to give the lines a fairly equal length and combined short lines whenever that could be done in the space available without doing violence to natural sense units.

In order to proceed, and to substantiate the explanation which I have just given, it would be necessary to draw further materials into the discussion. In his fundamental study of the Pauline bilinguals, Corssen drew attention to the similarity between Claromontanus and the fragments of a Gothic–Latin bilingual manuscript which is preserved in the Codex Carolinus at Wolfenbüttel. The Latin column is known as Guelferbytanus (gue = 79).[2] The length of the lines in Claromontanus and Guelferbytanus coincides so often that there must be some connection, especially since the colometric similarities between these two manuscripts have little in common with the system used in manuscripts like Euthalianus (H^{Paul}) and Amiatinus (A^{Vg}).[3]

1 Cf. Vogels, 'Der Codex Claromontanus der Paulinischen Briefe' (p. 84, n. 1, above).

2 The manuscript was written in the fifth century, probably in the Ostrogoth kingdom in Italy. It contains four leaves with text from Rom. xi.33–xii.5; xii.17–xiii.5; xiv.9–20; xv.3–13. See H. Henning, *Der Wulfila der Bibliotheca Augusta zu Wolfenbüttel* (Hamburg, 1913), with 8 plates of the palimpsest. The Latin text (gue = 79) was edited by Tischendorf, *Anecdota sacra et profana* (Leipzig, 1855), pp. 155–8 and, with exact colometry and critical apparatus, by P. Alban Dold, 'Die Provenienz der altlateinischen Römerbrieftexte in den gotisch-lateinischen Fragmenten des Codex Carolinus zu Wolfenbüttel', in *Aus der Welt des Buches: Festgabe ... Georg Leyh, Zentralblatt für Bibliothekswesen*, Beiheft 75 (Leipzig, 1950), pp. 13–29. W. Streitberg, *Die gotische Bibel* (1908, 5th edition, Darmstadt, 1965) prints both the Gothic and the Latin text, without attention to the colometry. For a detailed investigation, see G. W. S. Friedrichsen, *The Gothic Version of the Epistles* (London, 1939), pp. 49–61, 116–23. My own comments point to questions in need of further study.

3 A page from codex H (= 015) is reproduced on Plate XXXII in W. H. P. Hatch, *The Principal Uncial Manuscripts of the New Testament* (Chicago, 1959). See

A detailed comparison between d and gue confirms Corssen's insight. The four preserved leaves of the Gothic–Latin bilingual have two columns, Gothic and Latin, each with 27 lines on the page. Four lines have been lost but can easily be reconstructed. Of the 216 lines in gue, more than 100, almost 50 per cent, are identical with lines in d except for minor textual variations. In more than 30 per cent of the lines, the relation is 2:1. Mostly, two lines in gue are written as one in d, but in three cases it is the other way round.[1] The remaining difference in the length of lines can easily be explained as due to one or more of three causes: (1) Three short sense units have been written on two lines, with the second line beginning at different points in the two codices. (2) Due to scribal errors, one word has been misplaced, at the end of one line instead of at the beginning of the next. (3) The difference in colometry is due to alteration of the text, usually in gue.[2]

Unfortunately, Corssen was not able to make full use of the clue which he held in his hand. The reason for this was that he relied upon Tischendorf's edition of gue, an edition which reproduced the individual lines but paid no attention to the distinction between the beginning of a new colon and indented commata in the Gothic–Latin bilingual. Facsimiles show that the parchment was very carefully prepared for colometric writing of the bilingual text. On each leaf there are four sets of three parallel vertical ruling lines, marking the beginning of new

also the reconstructed pages in J. A. Robinson, *Euthaliana*, TS III.3 (Cambridge, 1895), pp. 48–65. The editions of the Vulgate by Wordsworth and White and by R. Weber give a good impression of the colometry in Codex Amiatinus. The Gothic manuscripts of the Pauline letters, codices Ambrosiani A and B, likewise display a colometry that neglects subdivisions of the cola, see Friedrichsen, *The Gothic Version of the Epistles*, pp. 90–116. Parts of cod. Ambr. A are written in sense lines, but mostly the colometry is indicated by punctuation. Friedrichsen thinks that the two codices go back 'to a different continuous colometric original' (p. 123), but cod. A at least may have been copied from an exemplar which had a typographic display of lines.

[1] The three cases are Rom. xii.3, *sed sapere/ ad prudentiam*; xiv.14 *scio et confido/ in domino*; xiv.15 *iam non secundum caritatem/ ambulas.* The text is that of gue; / marks the beginning of a new line in d. A page with 21 lines in d contains more or less exactly the same amount of text as a page with 27 lines in gue. This could be more than a coincidence. The irregular colometry in Claromontanus would be explained if, at some stage in the process of transmission, the content of pages with 27 lines was condensed to fit pages with 21 lines. (I owe this suggestion to Corssen, whose basic work is not accessible to me at the time of writing.)

[2] Three lines are written as two in Rom. xi.36b where gue divides *ipsi gloria/ in saecula amen* and d *ipsi gloria in saecula/ amen.* Similar cases occur Rom. xiii.3a, 3b, xiv.15a. In d one word is misplaced in Rom. xii.5a; xiv.14c, 15c; cf. also Rom. xv.16 in gue, *et patrem domini/ nostri Iesu Christi.* Textual difference accounts for the difference in colometry in Rom. xi.34b; xii.5b; xiii.1a, 4d. I refrain from treating more complicated cases here.

sections, cola, and commata in two columns on both sides. Old Testament quotations are marked by a sign (>) in the margin. This means that the divergent colometric systems in Claromontanus, 0230 and the common exemplar of Boernerianus and Augiensis can all be explained as simplifications of an ingenious arrangement of the text similar to the layout of the Gothic–Latin fragments. In other words, it is likely that the Gothic–Latin edition, of which a fragmentary copy has been preserved, was modelled upon a Greek–Latin bilingual and gives a better impression of the editorial design of the fourth-century archetype than does any of the preserved manuscripts with Greek and Latin texts.

Possibly the original edition had an even more sophisticated arrangement of the text, with Old Testament quotations marked, not by quotation marks, as in Guelferbytanus and Boernerianus, but by being indented further to the right and/or written with red ink as in Claromontanus. This means that the parchment sheets would have to be very carefully prepared with 3–5 parallel vertical ruling lines on both sides of each column. It is very easy to understand that later editors and scribes simplified the complicated system. In any case, the original design for the bilingual edition presupposes a high standard of craftsmanship and can only have originated at a major center of book production. I guess that it was produced in Rome, at a time when Greek was still used in the liturgy even though Latin was the common language spoken by Christians in the city.[1]

My theory would have to be checked and, if possible, verified by an investigation of the text(s) in the Latin–Gothic fragment. Frede has denied that there is any close relationship between the text in gue or the Gothic version and the text(s) of the major Pauline bilinguals. He is certainly right that gue does not, on the whole, represent the same type of text as the Greek–Latin bilinguals (his D text) but, rather, a more fluid

[1] At an early stage of my research, I played with the idea that the bilingual edition of the Pauline letters might have been produced at the Christian library of Caesarea, the place where Origen's Hexapla originated, as did the colometric writing of Paul's letters attested by cod. H (015) and the Euthalian apparatus. I have abandoned that idea, considering the text of the edition and its use, possibly first for liturgical reading and later, certainly, for purposes of study. It remains possible that bible editions produced at Caesarea, or Alexandria, provided models for the creator of the fourth century bilingual edition of Paul. Profane analogies are also likely to have existed, see esp. CPL 8 (P. Colt 1), at the beginning the text of, later only a glossary to the Aeneid, and CPL 279 (P. Bon. 5), a handbook with model letters. I have found no clear indications that Greek–Latin editions of the Gospels and Acts, or Greek–Coptic manuscripts of Paul, were arranged according to the same ingenious system as the Gothic–Latin and the original Greek–Latin editions of Paul.

type of text that was current in northern Italy (his I type).[1] Even the undeniable Latin influence upon the Gothic text in the Pauline epistles may be due to other sources than Greek–Latin bilinguals.[2] But our investigation of 0230 has demonstrated that textual differences do not disprove a family relationship between manuscripts.

One can imagine the possibility that a Greek–Latin bilingual provided the inspiration and the model for the person who first planned a Gothic–Latin or, possibly, a Greek–Gothic–Latin edition, even if the editor took his Latin as well as his Gothic text from other sources. I think, however, that some textual and colometric peculiarities in gue make it more likely that some genealogical relationship exists between the Latin text of gue and that of the Greek–Latin bilinguals.[3] One would then have to assume that the text had been thoroughly revised, on more than one occasion, both to conform with a current form of the Latin version and to conform with the Gothic text.[4] In order to make this assumption

[1] See the materials collected by Dold, 'Provenienz', pp. 23–9, and the conclusions drawn by Frede, *Paulus-Handschriften*, pp. 100f, and *Paulustext*, p. 117.

[2] On the influence of Latin versions and commentaries (esp. Ambrosiaster) upon the Gothic text of Paul, see esp. Friedrichsen, *The Gothic Version of the Epistles*, pp. 172–231 and 260ff. Cod. Ambr. A and B and Guelferbytanus are likely to have a remote common ancestor which would seem to have been a Gothic–Latin bilingual or, possibly, a Greek–Gothic–Latin trilingual. The originators of this edition used existing Gothic and Latin versions but would seem to have taken account of the Greek text of the Greek–Latin bilinguals.

[3] Colometric irregularities in Guelferbytanus, Rom. xii.5 and xiii.1, are best explained on the assumption that an ancestor manuscript had the same text as d g and 89. A number of variants which gue shares with d, g and 89 are likely to represent an early layer of the text. In cases of disagreement between these manuscripts, however, gue follows the independent text of 89 against the bilinguals d and g as often as it follows d and g against 89. In most, but not in all, such cases, the Latin of gue coincides with the Gothic text. Under these circumstances it is very hard to decide on textual grounds whether the elements of the D-type of text in gue stem from the Latin column of a Greek–Latin bilingual or from a separate Latin manuscript with the same type of text. There are, however, some instances in favor of the former alternative:
Rom. xii.3, *et nolite*: *et* om. d* gue with goth and 1739 and its allies 424** and 1908. Here both D and G/F are likely to have a corrected text, whereas d* and both columns in Guelferbytanus have preserved the original text of the bilingual edition.
Rom. xii.20, *sed si*: *sed* om. f g gue (d^c) with goth and D* F G. xii.20b, *si*: *et si* d gue with goth and D*. The two variants are interrelated; Claromontanus and Guelferbytanus have preserved the text of 'Z'. The textual evidence does not provide any definite proof, but the data are fully compatible with the assumption that the text of gue is a thoroughly revised offshoot of the Latin text of the Greek–Latin bilingual edition.

[4] We may distinguish between various components in the text of gue: (1) relics of an ancient text, similar to that of d g and 89 and, probably, either derived from or influenced by the Latin text of a Greek–Latin bilingual; (2) alterations of Latin vocabulary and word order, as in the I-type of text; (3)

more than a loose conjecture, it would be necessary to undertake a minute investigation which would have to extend to the Gothic version as well as to the Greek and Latin texts.

The investigation would also have to take account of some evidence for the history of the Latin text which has no certain connection with the bilinguals. H. J. Vogels has demonstrated that two manuscripts of the Ambrosiaster commentary are witnesses to a text which is not that of Ambrosiaster but closely akin to the text used by Rufinus in his translation of Origen's commentary on the Epistle to the Romans.[1] G. Bardy has suggested that Rufinus made use of a Greek–Latin bilingual for the lemma in the Latin version of this commentary.[2] If Bardy were right, we would have evidence for an ongoing revision of the Latin column in Greek–Latin bilinguals. For several variant readings, we would also be able to identify the connecting link between the Latin of d and g and the Latin of gue. In order to move from suggestive possibilities to probability one would have to engage in detailed and extensive investigations. The laborious work would only be meaningful in conjunction with an attempt to reconstruct the colometry as well as the text of the original fourth-century bilingual edition. I am inclined to think that the task can be accomplished but will certainly not have time for it until well after my retirement, if ever.

My study of Pauline bilinguals has not only illustrated the necessity of making a clear-cut distinction between types of texts and families of manuscripts, it has also convinced me that neither the use of computers

corrections after the Greek; (4) an incomplete adaptation to the Gothic text; (5) scribal errors and other alterations within the transmission of the Gothic–Latin bilinguals.

1 See H. J. Vogels, *Untersuchungen zum Text paulinischer Briefe bei Rufin und Ambrosiaster*, BBB 9 (Bonn, 1950). The two manuscripts are Amiens, Bibl. Munic. 87 (Amst A) and Wien, Nationalbibl., Lat. 743 (Amst W). The texts have several variants in common with the Vulgate, by which they may have been influenced. But they, most often Rufinus, do also have variants in common with gue. Some of these variants have little, if any, attestation elsewhere, see Rom. xii.20 *sitierit*; xv.4 *praescribta* (*-pta*). There is no clear evidence for any Vulgate influence in gue.

2 See G. Bardy, 'Le texte de l'épître aux Romains dans le commentaire d'Origène–Rufin', *RB* n.s. 17 (1920), pp. 229–41. Bardy's conclusion, which was anticipated by Westcott and Turner, is based upon Rufinus' references to the Greek text, not upon the character of the text. If the conjecture holds good, and textual evidence would seem to support it, the bilingual edition had a somewhat greater influence than Frede is willing to concede in *Paulus-Handschriften*, pp. 82f. As Amiens 87 (Amst A) was written in Corbie in the eighth or ninth century, we can even speculate that the lost bilingual which existed in Corbie in the eleventh century may have been a revised version like the one which Rufinus used, and not a copy of Claromontanus, as Frede thinks, *Paulus-Handschriften*, pp. 39–45.

and statistical methods nor an eclecticism based upon stylistic and linguistic criteria can ever substitute for careful examination of the most important manuscripts and their prehistory. I have also found that early editions of biblical texts is a neglected field of study, probably because of the separation of textual criticism from the history of the New Testament canon, and of both these disciplines from the history of book production, illumination, prologues, colometrical writing, and Bible editions in general.[1] Bilingual manuscripts have to be studied as such, not simply as textual witnesses, and this is only one example among many in this area. I hope that this preliminary report of my own efforts in the area will be of some interest to my friend and colleague Matthew Black, who for so many years has been the editor of *New Testament Studies* and before that the treasurer of Studiorum Novi Testamenti Societas, and whose contributions to New Testament studies have included textual criticism, ancient translations and many other fields.

[1] Even the *Cambridge History of the Bible*, I (Cambridge, 1970), does not overcome the dichotomy between history of the text and history of the Canon. A model for the kind of work which ought to be done is Bonifatius Fischer, 'Bibelausgaben des frühen Mittelalters', in *Settimane di studio del Centro italiano di studi sull'alto medioevo*, x, *La Bibbia nell'alto medioevo* (Spoleto, 1963), pp. 519–600 and 685–704. Only very preliminary studies seem to exist for the early period, see e.g. Charles Willard, *The Euthalian Apparatus* (Diss. Yale, 1970) and my own essay, 'Bibelutgaver i oldkirken', in *Kirkens arv – kirkens fremtid*: Festskrift J. Smemo (Oslo, 1968), pp. 133–51.

The Beloved Disciple and the date of the Gospel of John

M. DE JONGE

INTRODUCTION

Much has been written lately on the passages dealing with the Beloved Disciple in the Fourth Gospel. For the purpose of the present paper two studies are of primary importance. First, R. Schnackenburg's Exkurs 18 'Der Jünger den Jesus liebte' at the end of the third volume of his great commentary on the Gospel of John,[1] in which he gives a good survey of the problems involved and the solutions suggested in recent literature. Secondly, H. Thyen's long article 'Entwicklungen innerhalb der johanneischen Theologie und Kirche im Spiegel von Joh. 21 und der Lieblingsjüngertexte des Evangeliums',[2] in which he discusses the function of the passages on the Beloved Disciple in the present Gospel which, for him, is the result of a thorough redaction of an earlier *Grundschrift*. The historical circumstances behind this redactional process and the possible role of the historical figure behind the Beloved Disciple in the 'Johannine' communities are reconstructed with great ingenuity.

In this paper I intend to concentrate on a limited number of problems. First, I shall say something on the function of the Beloved Disciple in the passages dealing with him. Next, some suggestions will be given on the place of those passages in the Gospel as a whole. Finally, I shall discuss the implications of the (tentative) conclusions reached in the first two sections for the establishment of the date of the Fourth Gospel. Here I shall enter into a discussion with J. A. T. Robinson, who in his recent provocative book *Redating The New Testament*,[3] tries to defend a pre-70 date.

1 R. Schnackenburg, *Das Johannesevangelium*, III, Kommentar zu Kap. 13–21, Herders Theol. Komm. z. N.T. IV, 3 (Freiburg–Basel–Wien, 1975), pp. 449–64.

2 It is a contribution to M. de Jonge *et alii*, *L'Évangile de Jean*. Sources, rédaction, théologie, BETL XLIV (Gembloux/Leuven, 1977), pp. 259–99.

3 John A. T. Robinson, *Redating the New Testament* (London, 1976), esp. pp. 254–311.

THE FUNCTION OF THE BELOVED DISCIPLE[1]

In John xxi.15–25 two things stand out very clearly. First of all the parallel between Simon Peter and the Beloved Disciple, secondly the attempt of the group responsible for verse 24 to give the right interpretation of the word of Jesus concerning the Beloved Disciple in verse 22 and to ward off a wrong interpretation current among 'the brothers' (verse 23).

In verses 15–17 Simon Peter is installed as shepherd of the flock of Jesus, the Good Shepherd, to whom, in turn, the Father has entrusted the care of his children (x.1–18, 27–30; xvii.9–10).

Three times Simon is instructed by the risen Lord to tend his sheep, just as in the Passion story he denied the Lord three times. There is a clear reference to the story of the denial (xviii.15–18, 25–7) and particularly to Jesus' announcement of that denial in xiii. 36–8, which speaks of it in the context of Peter's following of Jesus and his desire to lay down his life for his master. These two themes now recur in verses 18–19 with such a clear emphasis that we may reasonably ask whether the person who wrote xiii.36–8 did not envisage a return at a later stage in his story to what had been announced here rather enigmatically.[2] In any case verses 18–19 state clearly that Peter's following will include his death as a martyr, to the glory of God. There is, I think, little doubt that the intended readers knew of Peter's special position in the church and were aware of the fact that he had died as a martyr.

Peter's way of following is directly connected, and to some extent contrasted, with the following of the Beloved Disciple. We should note the explicit reference to xiii.21–30, the first time this disciple is mentioned in this Gospel, and also the use of the present participle *ἀκολοθοῦντα*. The Beloved Disciple continues to follow Jesus, that is: continues to be his disciple (cf. viii.12; x.4, 5, 27), without being faced with the necessity to lay down his life for his master. About him Jesus says: 'If I wish him to remain until I come, what is that to you? Follow *you* me!' This word underlines the expectation of Jesus' (second) coming, clearly present in 1 John (ii.28; iii.2; iv.17) but by no means absent in the Gospel (xiv.3, xvii.24–5).[3] Important here is the

[1] I am taking up here and expanding a number of remarks made on the final pages of chapter VIII 'Variety and Development in Johannine Christology' in my *Jesus: Stranger from Heaven and Son of God.* Jesus Christ and the Christians in Johannine Perspective, SBL Sources for Biblical Study 11 (Missoula, Mo., 1977), pp. 193–221.

[2] Compare R. Schnackenburg, *Das Johannesevangelium*, p. 431.

[3] On this difficult question see chapter VII 'Eschatology and Ethics in the Fourth Gospel' on pp. 169–91 of my *Jesus: Stranger from Heaven and Son of God* (see n. 1 above), particularly pp. 174f: 'One cannot speak of a parousia in the

use of the verb *μένειν*, which in the Farewell Discourses as well as in the First Epistle is used repeatedly in connection with the communion of the (true) disciples with the Son and the Father.[1] This word denotes a complex reality, but in the Christian community indicated as 'the brothers' (see xx.17 and I and II John) it was taken to mean 'to remain alive', and this interpretation is in need of correction.

Verse 23 states emphatically that Jesus did not say to Peter that the other disciple was not to die, but it does not tell us what Jesus really meant. Some exegetes have emphasized the 'if' in Jesus' words of verse 22, literally repeated in verse 23, but it can hardly have been the authors' intention to underline that Jesus indicated a possibility, not a reality. The risen Lord who knew what would happen to Peter was surely able to predict the fate of the Beloved Disciple.[2]

After the negative statement of verse 23 a positive interpretation is given in verse 24, and it is not too rash to assume that some such interpretation had become necessary because the disciple who was known as the Beloved Disciple had, in fact, died. In answer to the obvious embarrassment among 'the brothers' the 'we' group of verse 24 points out that this disciple is the one who 'is bearing witness to these things' and who 'has written these things'. The present participle *ὁ μαρτυρῶν* may be connected with the perfect *μεμαρτύρηκεν* in xix.35, another passage dealing with the Beloved Disciple, which also emphasizes the reliability of the testimony concerned. The 'remaining' of the disciple is explained as his continuing witness in the gospel which he has written. Opinions may differ as to whether *ὁ γράψας* should be interpreted as a causative (cf. xix.22) or not; the important thing is, however, that the 'we' who wrote verse 24[3] regard this anonymous Beloved Disciple as the author of the Gospel[4] and claim his authority for it, the

sense of an appearing of Christ upon earth in a way recognizable to all, but of a consummation. All attention is concentrated on the fate of the community in a world that is hostile but is already in principle conquered; the world has no future, in contrast to the community which lives for the final and definitive "being in the Lord".'

1 See, again, chapter VII in my *Jesus: Stranger from Heaven and Son of God*, particularly pp. 177–84.

2 See especially H. Thyen's discussion of the passage, 'Entwicklungen', pp. 270–3.

3 Schnackenburg, *Das Johannesevangelium*, p. 447, rightly thinks that 'we' refers to the actual 'editors' of the Gospel as well as to the (Johannine) community of all true believers. He rightly points to parallels in the First Epistle. See also chapter X 'Who are "We" ' in M. de Jonge, *Jesus: Inspiring and Disturbing Presence*, translated by J. E. Steely (Nashville–New York, 1974), pp. 148–66.

4 In verse 24 as an editorial remark at the end of the present Gospel *ταῦτα* can hardly refer to anything else but the contents of the book.

authority of an eye-witness and a direct follower of Jesus. His name is not mentioned; his identity was known to 'the brothers' who, if not identical with, are at least in direct communication with the intended readers of the Gospel.

The Beloved Disciple is the crown-witness 'about these things' – and this is also clear in the other passages devoted to him. In the immediately preceding story xxi.1–14 it is he who recognizes the stranger who stands at the shore and tells Simon Peter and his companions to cast the net on the right side of the ship – with the result that they cannot haul it in because of the great quantity of fish. The important feature to note is that Peter does not go into action before the Beloved Disciple has told him: 'It is the Lord' (verse 7). Peter, whose installation as shepherd is of supreme importance for the church and is by no means denied or belittled in John xxi, is dependent on the insight and the word of the Beloved Disciple. This disciple is the first to see the implication of what has just happened and to recognize the Lord.

There is a clear parallel between this story and that in xx.2–10 about the visit of Peter and the Beloved Disciple to the tomb on the first Easter morning. Many features of the story call for comment, but I only want to stress that the Beloved Disciple, in contrast with Peter, 'saw and believed' (verse 8). The editorial comment on verse 9 tells us that 'they (Peter and the Beloved Disciple, or the disciples in general always including the Beloved Disciple) did not yet know the scriptures which showed that he must rise from the dead'. It is in line with similar comments earlier in the Gospel (ii.22; xii.16) which make clear that the true interpretation of the events, and of words in scripture pointing to these events, was only granted to Jesus' disciples after his resurrection. When the Beloved Disciple saw the empty grave with the linen wrappings and the napkin he could not rely on the right knowledge of scripture, yet he believed on account of what he 'saw'. In this he was ahead of Peter, and of the other disciples. We should note, however, that we do not hear that the Beloved Disciple informs Peter. It is also remarkable that the visit of the two disciples to the tomb has no effect whatever on subsequent events. I shall return to this later.

In the very first story mentioning the Beloved Disciple we meet him again together with Peter. The fact that we are told that at the meal he lies *ἐν τῷ κόλπῳ τοῦ Ἰησοῦ* with a clear reference to the relation between Jesus as the only Son and the Father in i.18 is highly significant. The disciple introduced here in the story and, in fact, in the Gospel as a whole,[1]

[1] There have been repeated attempts to prove that the anonymous companion of Andrew in i.35–42 should be identified with the Beloved Disciple. The

is one whom Jesus loved and trusted completely. The readers of the Gospel may know that the one who 'wrote these things' is absolutely trustworthy, and that he has 'inside knowledge'. Simon Peter tells him to ask Jesus about the identity of the traitor, whose betrayal has just been announced (verse 24). Jesus' announcement in verse 21 comes as a climax after his words in verse 7 and in verses 18–19, and this is the intention of the person responsible for the present form of chapter xiii, as the introductory passage xiii.1–3 clearly shows. In xiii.21–30 the Beloved Disciple is allowed to know that Judas will betray his master. Judas leaves the meal after having received the piece of bread given by Jesus (which, as it were, makes the way free for Satan to enter into Judas; see verse 27 in connection with verses 2–3), but none of the (other) disciples really understood what Jesus meant when he said to Judas: 'What you are going to do, do quickly', or why Judas went away. The Beloved Disciple does not share his knowledge with his fellow disciples, nor does he answer Simon Peter's explicit request.

In the Passion story the Beloved Disciple is mentioned three times. His identification with the 'other disciple' in xviii.15–18 is disputed, but F. Neirynck, in a very full and detailed article,[1] has shown that the close similarity of this passage with xx.3–10 is a strong argument in favour of this identification. We should note that Peter is again dependent on this disciple. The Beloved Disciple does not reappear in the story until xix.25–7 in a very short and cryptic episode, which can easily be (and in fact has been[2]) over-interpreted. In any case the Beloved Disciple is an eye-witness of Jesus' death at the cross. Immediately before 'the end' (*τετέλεσται* verses 28, 30 with an emphasis on achievement, accomplishment!) Jesus speaks to his mother and this disciple. As in xiii.21–30 the Beloved Disciple has a special place among the disciples. He succeeds Jesus as son of his mother, he is 'brother of Jesus' (xx.17) in a very special way. There may also be a third element in the story. The only other occurrence of the mother of Jesus is in the Cana story (ii.1–11). There also Jesus addresses her as *γύναι* when he

latest can be found in H. Thyen, 'Entwicklungen', pp. 274–5. I remain unconvinced. Just as xix.39 and vii.50 in editorial remarks on Nicodemus clearly refer back to the first time he is mentioned explicitly (iii.1ff), so also xxi.20 refers back to xiii.21–30 where the Beloved Disciple is mentioned explicitly; an (at the most) implicit reference to him in chapter i would have no clear function in the Gospel. Thyen's theory that the author wishes to introduce the Beloved Disciple as a true witness from the very beginning (p. 292) remains a hypothesis.

[1] 'The "Other Disciple" in Jn. 18, 15–16' in *Ephem. Theol. Lov.* 51 (1975), pp. 113–41.

[2] See e.g. the short survey of interpretations given by Schnackenburg, *Das Johannesevangelium*, pp. 325–8.

tells her that his 'hour' has not yet come (verse 4). This 'hour' has now arrived and consequently we are told in xix.27: 'From that hour the disciple took her into his home.' In chapter ii the mother of Jesus, notwithstanding her son's rebuttal, tells the servants that they should do whatever Jesus orders them – and a sign takes place although Jesus' hour has not come yet. After that crucial moment she is referred to the Beloved Disciple, like the readers of the Gospel and, in fact, all believers. He will disclose the true meaning of what Jesus did and said during his earthly life, and explain the importance of 'the hour' for those who believe in him after his departure from the earth and return to the Father.[1]

There is no indication here of a special relation between the Beloved Disciple and Peter. The same is true of xix.35–6 where the Beloved Disciple is not mentioned explicitly but certainly indicated as the clear parallel with xxi.24 shows. Again, he appears as the eye-witness of Jesus' death and he is able to testify that it was a real death: he saw blood and water flowing from Jesus' side after one of the soldiers had stabbed it with a lance. Here the anti-docetic element is very evident. Whether there are further overtones (e.g. sacramental ones, see 1 John v.6–8) remains a matter of dispute.[2]

In the picture given above a few points stand out clearly:

1. For the 'we' in xxi.24 who represent and address the Johannine communities the Beloved Disciple is the authority *par excellence*, because he was the disciple *par excellence*.

2. In the period after Jesus' departure to the Father the Christian community, represented by Simon Peter, its shepherd (xxi.7, 15–17), and Mary (xix.27) is dependent on his insight into the true meaning of Jesus' coming to the world and his departure to the Father.

3. As Jesus' most intimate disciple and eye-witness he is allowed to know by whom Jesus will be betrayed (xiii.13–21) and to understand the meaning of the empty tomb (xx.2–10). He witnesses Jesus' suffering and death and because he saw blood and water coming out of Jesus' side he is able to state beyond any doubt that Jesus died a real death.

[1] See also H. Thyen, 'Entwicklungen', pp. 281–6, who also supposes an anti-docetic element. The story would emphasize that Jesus really had a mother. This is, however, by no means evident.

[2] See Schnackenburg, *Das Johannesevangelium*, pp. 340f, and Thyen, 'Entwicklungen', pp. 286–8, who both refer to G. Richter, 'Blut und Wasser aus der durchbohrten Seite Jesu (Joh. 19, 34b)', *MThZ* 21 (1970), pp. 1–21.

4. Before the 'hour' the knowledge and the insight of the Beloved Disciple are not imparted to his fellow disciples and do not influence their actions, notwithstanding the fact that not only in chapter xxi but also in chapters xiii, xviii and xx the Beloved Disciple appears together with Simon Peter.

THE PLACE OF THE PASSAGES ABOUT THE BELOVED DISCIPLE IN THE GOSPEL

The Beloved Disciple occupies a central place in the present Gospel. From chapter xxi we may conclude that at some time after his death, when the Gospel received its final form, his authority was invoked for the traditions incorporated in it. He remains anonymous for us, but was not so for the original readers who knew him and revered him as an 'apostolic' eye-witness.

In this respect the situation with regard to the Gospel is not very different from that in the First Epistle (see the emphasis on the reliable knowledge of eye-witnesses in 1 John i.1–4). There is also a clear connection between the emphasis on the real death and bodily resurrection of Jesus in the passages about the Beloved Disciple and the anti-docetic thrust in the christology of the First (and Second) Epistle.[1] H. Thyen thinks one may even go one step further and connect the emphasis on the Beloved Disciple's knowledge of Judas' unfaithfulness and treason in John xiii with the difficulties presupposed in the Epistles (including the third).[2] This hypothesis, however, cannot be substantiated.

Now, if the Gospel in its final form, with the passages dealing with the Beloved Disciple as integral and essential parts in it, agrees at a number of points with the First Epistle, is there any evidence for an earlier redaction of the Gospel in which these passages did not yet appear, and the Beloved Disciple was not yet treated as the central authority for the traditions incorporated in it? After all, everyone beginning the study of the Gospel knows the theory that chapter xxi has to be regarded as an appendix to the Gospel, and if that chapter,

1 See the conclusion in *Jesus: Stranger from Heaven and Son of God*, chapter VIII, 'Variety and Development in Johannine Christology' (see p. 100, n. 1, above), pp. 209f: 'Our conclusion must, therefore, be that the present Gospel . . . also reacts to difficulties within the Johannine communities and people who have left them. What is a major christological issue in the First and Second Epistles is a minor one in the Gospel, but the necessity of 'anti-docetic emphasis' is (already) there.'

2 Thyen, 'Entwicklungen', pp. 296–9.

so essential for the picture given above, was added later perhaps also the other passages about the Beloved Disciple may not have belonged to the Gospel at an earlier stage.

Here we may refer to H. Thyen's study and Th. Lorenzen's book *Der Lieblingsjünger im Johannesevangelium* with the sub-title 'Eine redaktionsgeschichtliche Studie'.[1] Even R. Schnackenburg, who is very cautious in matters of sources and redaction(s), adds a short final section 4 to his excursus on the Beloved Disciple entitled 'Rückblick auf die Entstehungsgeschichte des vierten Evangeliums',[2] in which he supposes a long process of growth for the Fourth Gospel during which traditions of diverse provenance were incorporated, plus a final (but congenial) redaction of the work of the evangelist. Earlier in his excursus[3] he leaves the possibility open that all Beloved Disciple passages were added at the stage of that redaction. In his opinion this cannot be proved in xiii.23–6, and also xix.26–7 and xx.2–10 can be explained more easily if we assume that the evangelist himself used and redacted an already existing Passion and Easter story.

The difficulty is that any theory about the place of the passages on the Beloved Disciple in the history of the Fourth Gospel is immediately bound up with hypotheses concerning that history as a whole. Many theories about sources used in the Gospel have been advanced and different redactions have been assumed. Of course, this is all linked up with the views of the various authors on the doctrinal developments during the obviously stormy history of the Johannine communities for which (the successive forms of) the Gospel was (were) written and to which the Epistles were addressed. Elsewhere[4] I have tried to sketch some major solutions and expressed some sympathy for Thyen's approach in the study which has already been referred to many times and in earlier articles from his hand,[5] which are consistently redaction-critical and start where every scholar should start: the present Gospel as a literary product with a (more or less) consistent theology of its own. So he regards chapter xxi as a well-edited epilogue to the Gospel rather than as an appendix incorporating a number of odd pieces of information and some theologoumena only relevant at a later stage of redaction. In this he is clearly right, but in other instances I cannot

[1] SBS 55 (Stuttgart, 1971).

[2] Schnackenburg, *Das Johannesevangelium*, pp. 463f.

[3] *Ibid.*, pp. 455f.

[4] M. de Jonge, *Jesus: Stranger from Heaven and Son of God* (see p. 100, n. 1, above), pp. 193–200.

[5] Particularly in a series of articles 'Aus der Literatur zum Johannesevangelium' in *Theologische Rundschau* 39 (1974), pp. 1–69, 222–52, 289–330 (to be continued).

possibly follow him, particularly where he tries to distinguish between redaction and source material, much of which in his view already belonged to a '*Grundschrift*' with certain theological tendencies of its own.

But even if we treat supposedly 'redactional' and supposedly 'traditional' elements as integral parts of a new and complete literary entity which has to be read and studied on its own, and regard attempts to dissect pericopes in order to assign sentences and clauses to various sources, traditions and redactional layers as impossible and not always relevant, some tentative arguments may be adduced in favour of the theory that the pericopes concerning the Beloved Disciple were incorporated into the Gospel at a time when other elements giving a story coherent in itself had already been assembled. It remains very remarkable that before chapter xxi the Beloved Disciple does not really function in the drama of the Passion and resurrection which unfolds itself. This is, no doubt, intentional because his real function is bound up with the time after 'the hour' when his inside information and deep insight guarantee exact knowledge of the facts and their right interpretation. The passages xix.26–7, xxi.7 and xxi.24, each in its own way, make that clear. Yet the lack of real communication between the Beloved Disciple and his fellow disciples, particularly Peter, before chapter xxi is strange. The Beloved Disciple keeps all information and explanation to himself; the readers (after 'the hour') benefit from his knowledge, but none of the people who participated in the events do so.

In xiii.23 the very designation 'the disciple whom Jesus loved' comes unexpectedly after the categorical statement about Jesus' supreme love for (all) his disciples in xiii.1 (cf. xv.9–10); nowhere else in the Farewell Discourses is this disciple singled out. There is also a certain tension between the statement in xvi.32 addressed to all disciples present 'the *hour* is coming, has indeed already come, when you are all to be scattered, each *to his home*, leaving me alone' and xix.27 where 'the disciple whom Jesus loved' does *not* leave Jesus alone in his last moments on earth, and 'from that *hour*' takes his mother '*into his home*'. I. de la Potterie is right where he speaks of an intended antithetical parallelism between the two verses;[1] yet we cannot deny that xvi.32 in its context does not leave much room for an exceptional position of one of the disciples later on.

Also in chapter xx the Beloved Disciple's insight, expressed in

1 'Das Wort Jesu, "Siehe, deine Mutter" und die Annahme der Mutter durch den Jünger (Joh 19, 27b)' in Joachim Gnilka, editor, *Neues Testament und Kirche*, Festschrift für R. Schnackenburg (Freiburg–Basel–Wien, 1974), pp. 191–219, esp. pp. 208–14.

verse 8, does not play any part in the subsequent development of events. The Lord reveals himself to Mary Magdalene and uses her as a messenger to his 'brothers' (verses 11–18). He sends the disciples out into the world and gives them the Spirit (verses 19–23). These pericopes are of crucial importance in the structure of the Gospel and essential for the understanding of Johannine 'hermeneutics', as I have tried to show elsewhere.[1] This also applies to the Thomas story in verses 24–9 leading over to the so-called first ending of the Gospel in verses 30–1. Considering this, it is strange that the drama unfolds itself regardless of the episode recorded in verses 2–9, which only serves to emphasize the superior insight of the Beloved Disciple as only becoming effective at the stage reached in chapter xxi.

These phenomena may (but need not) point to the later addition of passages dealing with the Beloved Disciple to an already available, more or less coherent story. But whether they were added by a redactor to an already complete gospel or by an evangelist to a Passion and resurrection story in front of him, whether there was a Gospel before the present one or only a *Grundschrift*, and which parts of the present passages were already found in the Gospel, *Grundschrift* or Passion and resurrection story and which not, we shall never be able to decide with absolute certainty on the basis of the available evidence.

THE IMPLICATIONS FOR THE ESTABLISHMENT OF THE DATE OF THE GOSPEL

For the establishment of the date of the Fourth Gospel the problem of the delineation of the various stages in its prehistory is of minor importance. We ask for the date of the final redaction, when the Gospel received its present form and contents – apart from a number of passages which are text-critically uncertain.

Now, if we ask what can be gleaned from the analysis of the passages on the Beloved Disciple for a solution of the problem of the date of the Gospel, we can mention the following points:

a. The Gospel brings together traditions current (in whatever form and assembled in whatever earlier collections) in certain circles in early Christianity which, for the sake of convenience, we call the Johannine communities. The editors responsible for the publication of the Gospel invoke the authority of 'the Disciple whom Jesus

[1] M. de Jonge, *Jesus: Stranger from Heaven and Son of God* (see p. 100, n. 1, above), chapter 1, 'The Fourth Gospel: The Book of the Disciples', esp. pp. 1–7.

loved', as an intimate follower of Jesus, to whom special information and insight were given in view of his acting as a trustworthy witness and a reliable interpreter for the Christian community after the Son's departure to the Father.

b. The editors published their work after the death of the Beloved Disciple, probably in order to preserve and to protect what was handed down as important and authoritative tradition in the community, and claim the authority of this deceased disciple for it. This took place in a period of internal crisis (see *d* below).

c. The Beloved Disciple is known to the editors and the readers; in fact during his lifetime he has been a man of great authority in the communities. There is evidently no reason to disclose his identity to people outside, although he is often mentioned besides Simon Peter whom everybody knows. H. Thyen is right, I think, when he emphasizes that this makes it unlikely that the Beloved Disciple was one of the disciples who, in the early Christian tradition, were known by name. There is no indication in the Gospel that the later identification of this disciple as John the son of Zebedee is right.[1]

d. The expectation of the return of Jesus Christ to his followers is an important aspect of the life of the communities. Therefore the death of the Beloved Disciple has created uncertainty and confusion in the light of a word of Jesus about him which circulated in Johannine circles. Also in the First Epistle we find *Naherwartung*, obviously directly connected with the assumption that the activity of false prophets and heretical Christians outside and inside the communities points to the coming of the Antichrist (ii.18!). Also the anti-docetic emphasis in the passages connected with the Beloved Disciple presupposes the situation addressed in the First Epistle.

Both the First Epistle and the Gospel try to counter false ideas and schismatic tendencies resulting from them through an appeal to remain in close community with the eye-witnesses who know what they are talking about and are able to interpret what they have witnessed.[2]

e. There is, however, a difference in emphasis between the Gospel and the First (and Second) Epistle as far as Christology is concerned. What is central in the First Epistle remains peripheral in the Gospel, for which debates between 'the Jews' and followers of Jesus Christ

1 Thyen, 'Entwicklungen', p. 295. For further arguments see Schnackenburg, *Das Johannesevangelium*, pp. 458–60.

2 On these questions see, again, 'Variety and Development in Johannine Christology' mentioned on p. 100, n. 1, above and also my commentary on the Johannine Epistles, *De Brieven van Johannes* (Nijkerk, 1968, 1973²).

outside the synagogue about the authority of Jesus are of primary importance. There are indications that the period of internal crisis reflected in the Epistles and in the passages on the Beloved Disciple (and some other texts) in the Gospel came after the period of debates between Jews and Christians. This means that the Gospel reflects a rather long history of development of ideas within communities faced with several problems: the break with the synagogue and ongoing debates with 'the Jews'; discussions with Christians who had a different Christology, and a schism in their own circles.[1]

Do these considerations help us to fix a date for the Gospel? There seem to be two possible ways of approach. First, at the time of the publication of the Gospel Peter's death as a martyr was an established and well-known fact. If there is, as many scholars think,[2] no need to doubt the traditional connection between Peter's martyrdom and Nero's persecution of the Christians after the great fire of Rome in A.D. 64, this presents us with a *terminus a quo* of, say, A.D. 66. Unfortunately we do not know when the Beloved Disciple died. We cannot connect xxi.24 with Irenaeus' statement that the apostle John remained (*παραμείναντος*) with the Church of Ephesus until the time of Trajan,[3] and conclude that he must have died as an old man a considerable time after Peter's death.

J. A. T. Robinson, who rightly objects to the use of xxi.20–5 as an argument in favour of a late date of the Gospel, goes to another extreme, however, when he tries to prove that this passage points to a pre-70 date.[4] He writes: 'The present participle *μαρτυρῶν* ("attests") suggests, until proved otherwise, that the disciple in question is still alive.' And the misinterpretation of the 'until I come' in Jesus' word about the Beloved Disciple shows that 'the latter 60s of the first century (not unnaturally in the light of what was happening both in Rome and in Jerusalem) saw a quickening of the expectation that the end could not now long be delayed'. After all James had died in 62, Peter and Paul in 65+ and only John 'remained'. The epilogue was not written to

[1] On the matter mentioned here see my publications mentioned on p. 109, n. 2, above, and chapter IV 'Jewish Expectations about the "Messiah" according to the Fourth Gospel' in *Jesus: Stranger from Heaven and Son of God*, particularly pp. 97–102. This chapter was originally published in *NTS* 19 (1972–3), pp. 246–70.

[2] See e.g. the full discussion in O. Cullmann, *Petrus. Jünger, Apostel, Märtyrer*, Siebenstern Taschenbuch 90/91 (München–Hamburg, 1967 = 1960²), Teil I, Kapitel 3.

[3] *Adv. Haer.* III, 3, 4.

[4] Robinson, *Redating the New Testament*, pp. 278–82; the following quotations are found on p. 279 and on p. 281.

correct idle speculation about a disciple who would not die before the coming of the Lord, but to damp false hopes of an apocalyptic intervention.

All this is very ingenious, but hardly capable of proof. Robinson does less than justice to a number of recent expositions of xxi.20–5 and for his traditional identification of the Beloved Disciple with John the son of Zebedee he adduces surprisingly few arguments from the Gospel itself.[1] He also fails to make clear why *Naherwartung* in Johannine circles could not flare up in any crisis situation, and should particularly be connected with the late sixties of the first century.

The points mentioned above under *a*, *b* and *c* do not provide us with a certain date. They do not compel us to date the Gospel in the period between 90 and 100,[2] but certainly do not provide any clues for a date before 70.

Our next question should be: Do the arguments advanced under *d* and *e* bring us any further? The conflict reflected in the Johannine Epistles cannot be dated with any certainty, nor are we told where it occurred.[3] If the Gospel in its present form at least partly addresses itself to the situation reflected in the Epistles we shall have to date it at about the same time as the Epistles. Yet the Epistles 'are intelligible on the assumption that their readers, who have evidently been their writer's pastoral charge from "the beginning" (ii.7, 24; iii.11; II John 6), have been nurtured in "Johannine Christianity"' as Robinson rightly remarks.[4] And the Gospel itself reflects also the complex history of the

[1] Pp. 298–311 of Robinson's book are devoted to the question of the identity of the author of the Gospel. On the basis of a number of data about John in other books of the NT the author sets out to prove that 'the evidence for the person we are seeking . . . points suspiciously towards the kind of man that John, son of Zebedee, might have been'.

[2] 'The span 90–100 is agreed by Catholic and Protestant, by conservative and radical, by those who defend apostolic authorship and those who reject it, by those who believe that John used the synoptists and those who do not. It includes virtually all those who have written commentaries on the gospel, not to mention other interpreters' (Robinson, *Redating the New Testament*, p. 261).

[3] Robinson devotes pp. 284–91 of his book to the Epistles of John. In his opinion (already expressed in his 'The Destination and Purpose of the Johannine Epistles' in *Twelve New Testament Studies*, *SBTh* 34 (London, 1962), pp. 126–38) they are addressed to Jewish Christians in Asia Minor. He now dates them in the early 60s, emphasizing their links with Jude and II Peter which are dated equally early.

[4] Robinson, *Redating the New Testament*, p. 289. I agree with Robinson that the readers must have been acquainted with much of the teaching incorporated in the Gospel, but do not accept his conclusion: 'If then the epistles do come from the early 60s we are back at any rate to the early 50s for some form of the gospel message' (p. 291).

Johannine communities before the crisis mentioned in the Epistles broke out. This history cannot be reconstructed in detail, but one point stands out clearly: the Christian communities to which the Gospel is directed live apart from the synagogue and no longer try to convert 'the Jews'. Elsewhere I have tried to show that the fact that the Jewish interlocutors remain vague and that there is no real *discussion* with the Jews on Christological issues shows that the Gospel gives theological reflection on the real issues in the debate between Christians and Jews rather than provides arguments in an acute struggle. There are, perhaps, still occasional debates, but no real discussion, no hope of persuading 'the Jews', who are organized in their own communities. Moreover the Gospel also criticizes other Christian attempts to answer Jewish objections.[1] W. A. Meeks has well summed up my position as follows: 'Representative people (disciples; ordinary people: the crowd, Jewish leaders, Samaritans) express representative beliefs and raise representative objections. Further they are "representative" not in the sense that they sum up typical beliefs of actual Jews in Jesus' time or even towards the end of the first century when the gospel was written, but in the sense that they represent the *Johannine* conception of the Jewish beliefs that are obstacles to Christian faith, in a form which can serve as a foil to the gospel's refutation by irony.'[2] Elsewhere he formulates as follows: 'The Fourth Gospel is most anti-Jewish just at the points it is most Jewish' and, after a discussion of the complex use of the term 'the Jews' in the Fourth Gospel, he concludes: 'At the time of composition the Johannine community is separate from "the Jews" and no longer expects "Jews" to convert. The Johannine letters show no sign of any further direct involvement with Judaism.'[3]

If this was the situation at the time of the writing of the Gospel, when did it occur? J. L. Martyn who more than anyone else has tried to reconstruct the various stages in the history of the Johannine community[4] has rightly devoted much attention to the parallels between the passages dealing with exclusion from the synagogue (particularly ix.22; xii.42

[1] See de Jonge, *Jesus: Stranger from Heaven and Son of God*, chapter IV' mentioned p. 110, n. 1, above, particularly pp. 96–102.

[2] In his excellent survey-article ' "Am I a Jew?". Johannine Christianity and Judaism' in J. Neusner, editor, *Christianity, Judaism and Other Greco-Roman Cults* I, Festschrift for M. Smith (Leiden, 1975), pp. 163–85; see p. 172.

[3] See p. 182.

[4] See J. L. Martyn, *History and Theology in the Fourth Gospel* (New York and Evanston, 1968); 'Source Criticism and Religionsgeschichte in the Fourth Gospel' in D. G. Miller, editor, *Jesus and Man's Hope* I (Pittsburgh, 1971), pp. 247–73, and also 'Glimpses into the History of the Johannine Community' in M. de Jonge *et alii*, *L'Évangile de Jean* (see p. 99, n. 2, above), pp. 149–75.

and xvi.1–4), similar passages in Acts and the rabbinic references to the *Birkath ha-Minim*. He is of the opinion that 'the Fourth Gospel affords us a picture of a Jewish community which has been (recently ?) shaken by the introduction of a newly formulated means for detecting those Jews who want to hold a dual allegiance to Moses and to Jesus as Messiah. Even against the will of some of the synagogue leaders, the Heretic Benediction is now employed in order formally and irretrievably to separate the church from the synagogue.'[1] This would lead to a date after A.D. 85, but we may rightly ask whether Martyn does not want to prove too much. After all we do not know where the Johannine communities were situated[2] and how representative their relations with the Jews of their region were for the general relations between 'Judaism' and 'Christianity' of the time. Nor do we know about the relations between the Jews of the region and Rabban Gamliel and the Academy at Jamnia. Yet we may say that if we look for parallels we have to look here; Robinson's criticism of Martyn's views, which leads to the conclusion that the circumstances reflected in the Gospel of John have to be compared with the records in Acts about the attitude of the Jews to Paul in various places, does not only do no justice to Martyn's careful assessment of the evidence but also overlooks the fact that the Gospel as a whole, though thoroughly Jewish, speaks about 'the Jews' from the outside. Nor can we with Robinson simply refer to Paul's use of 'the Jews' in 1 Thess ii.14f and conclude from this that the use of that term in the Gospel leaves room for an early date.[3]

In conclusion we shall have to say that the points mentioned under *d* and *e* also do not allow us to come to a final decision with regard to the date of the Gospel. An early date (before 70) cannot be demonstrated and is, as such, far less likely than a later one. But exactly how much time was needed for the developments reflected in the Gospel to lead to a definite break with the Jews and to the internal struggles in the communities, we simply do not know. To date the Gospel convincingly we shall have to look for other arguments.[4]

1 J. L. Martyn, *History and Theology in the Fourth Gospel*, pp. 22–41. The quotation is from pp. 40–1.

2 The case for Ephesus, or Asia Minor in general, is not at all strong. Robinson's arguments for the theory that the Gospel 'was an appeal to the Greek-speaking *diaspora* Judaism of Asia Minor' (Robinson, *Redating the New Testament*, p. 292, referring back to his 'The Destination and Purpose of St John's Gospel' in *Twelve New Testament Studies*, pp. 107–25) are not strong either. To deal with this question would, however, require another article.

3 Robinson, *Redating the New Testament*, pp. 272–4.

4 The most promising approach may well be a new study of the literary dependence of the Fourth Gospel on the Synoptics. In his paper 'John and the

Synoptics, on pp. 73–106 of M. de Jonge *et alii*, *L'Évangile de Jean* (see p. 99, n. 2 above), F. Neirynck has reopened a debate which in Robinson's opinion (Robinson, *Redating the New Testament*, p. 262) had already been won by those who think that 'John' is dependent on 'Synoptic' material rather than on the Synoptic Gospels. Even if this dependence cannot be proved in all cases where parallels occur, a few clear instances are sufficient to prove the case. The fact that the Fourth Gospel contains much reliable historical material (see C. H. Dodd, *Historical Tradition in the Fourth Gospel* (Cambridge, 1963)) does not in itself point to an early date (see Robinson, *Redating the New Testament*, pp. 263–7). And the absence of references to the destruction of the Temple and the city of Jerusalem (Robinson, *Redating the New Testament*, pp. 275–8) simply provides us with an inconclusive argument from silence – as Robinson himself admits. His attempt to build a better case on the present ἐστιν in v.2 is hardly convincing.

De quoi est-il besoin (Lc x.42)?

JACQUES DUPONT

Les données de la tradition textuelle sont connues, et nous n'avons pas l'intention d'ajouter ici des témoignages nouveaux à ceux que fournit l'apparat du *Greek New Testament*. On trouve là neuf formes du texte de Lc x.41–2; elles peuvent aisément se ramener à quatre formes principales. D'abord deux formes contrastées dans lesquelles, à Marthe qui s'agite 'pour beaucoup de choses' (περὶ πολλά), Jésus déclare qu'il n'est besoin que 'd'une seule chose' (ἑνός), ou qu'il n'est besoin que de 'peu de choses' (ὀλίγων). Ensuite une forme longue que nous pouvons appeler graduelle, passant de 'beaucoup de choses' à 'peu de choses', pour aboutir à 'une seule chose'. On trouve enfin des formes courtes qui ne contiennent aucune de ces précisions: ni le reproche de s'agiter pour 'beaucoup de choses', ni l'observation sur 'une seule chose' ou 'peu de choses'.

Les critiques restent partagés. S'il est vrai que la première forme contrastée (πολλά–ἑνός) l'emporte le plus souvent aujourd'hui,[1] les éditeurs du *Greek New Testament* ne lui accordent que la note C ('considerable degree of doubt'). En 1968, dans les *New Testament Studies*, une lance a encore été rompue par M. Augsten en faveur de l'autre leçon contrastée.[2] La forme longue, qui était celle du *Textus receptus*, garde ses partisans: qu'il suffise de mentionner, pour la France, la Bible de Jérusalem et celle d'Osty dénonçant comme mutilées et altérées les leçons contrastées,[3] alors que la *Traduction Œcuménique de la Bible* opte résolument en faveur de l'antithèse πολλά–ἑνός.[4] Les

[1] Il n'y a pas lieu de répéter ici tout ce qui a été fort bien dit par A. Baker, 'One Thing Necessary', *CBQ* 27 (1965), pp. 127–37. Dans la même ligne, bonne étude de B. Prete, 'Il "logion" di Gesù: "una sola cosa è necessaria" (Lc. x.42)', dans le volume du même auteur: *Storia e teologia nel vangelo di Luca*, Agnitio Mysterii, 3 (Bologna, 1973), pp. 71–103.

[2] M. Augsten, 'Lukanische Miszelle', *NTS* 14 (1967–8), pp. 581–3.

[3] *La Bible de Jérusalem*, nouvelle édition (Paris, 1973), p. 1499, note b; E. Osty–J. Trinquet, *Le Nouveau Testament*, Livre de Vie (Paris, 1974), p. 178.

[4] *Traduction Œcuménique de la Bible, Nouveau Testament* (Paris, 1972), p. 231, note t.

partisans de la leçon courte se font plus rares, mais T. W. Manson et G. B. Caird ne sont pas tellement éloignés de nous.[1]

Parmi les critères qui font pencher la balance dans un sens ou dans l'autre, il y a d'abord celui de la largeur de l'éventail représenté par les témoins d'un texte. On se contente parfois de ce critère pour écarter la seconde leçon contrastée, *ὀλίγων*; la prudence s'impose cependant, car elle semble ancienne (Origène), et la leçon longue pourrait en dériver et donc en attester indirectement la diffusion.[2] C'est par ce même critère que certains écartent la leçon courte, dont les témoins sont exclusivement 'occidentaux'; ici encore il faut éviter un jugement précipité, car il s'agit d'une 'non-interpolation': la tendance à l'amplification qui se constate dans la tradition occidentale invite à ne pas prendre à la légère les 'omissions' que l'on y découvre parfois.[3]

En fait, le critère qui joue le rôle majeur dans la discussion est celui de la *lectio difficilior*: il faut attribuer la priorité à la leçon dont la difficulté permet de comprendre la naissance de leçons plus faciles. Le principe est incontestable, mais on ne peut que rester perplexe devant les applications qui en sont faites en faveur de chacune des leçons qui se présentent à nous. Dans l'état actuel de la discussion, ce principe s'avère pratiquement inopérant.

A. Baker[4] suggère une autre voie en se demandant si la réponse que Jésus fait à Marthe ne s'inspire pas d'un thème traditionnel. Il cite la recommandation de Ben Sira invitant à ne pas entreprendre beaucoup d'affaires (xi. 10), ou la pieuse aspiration du psalmiste qui ne désire qu'une seule chose, habiter dans la maison du Seigneur (Ps xxvi (xxvii). 4). Avouons que nous ne trouvons pas cela très éclairant.

Le même Baker estime qu'il serait utile de confronter ce passage avec les habitudes stylistiques de Luc.[5] Il n'entreprend malheureusement pas ce travail. Voici quelques observations à ce sujet. Au verset 41, la double appellation 'Marthe, Marthe' est conforme au style de Luc, comme l'a remarqué R. Morgenthaler.[6] En revanche, on ne conçoit pas que Luc continue immédiatement 'Marie a choisi . . .', comme dans la leçon la plus courte;[7] Lc xxii.31 évite une maladresse de ce genre.

[1] T. W. Manson, *The Sayings of Jesus* (London, 1949), p. 264; G. B. Caird, *The Gospel of St Luke*, The Pelican Gospel Commentaries (Harmondsworth, 1963), p. 150.

[2] Voir M. Augsten, 'Lukanische Miszelle', *NTS* 14.

[3] Voir B. Prete, *Storia e teologia nel vangelo di Luca*, pp. 75s.

[4] A. Baker, 'One Thing Necessary', p. 136.

[5] *Ibid.*

[6] R. Morgenthaler, *Die lukanische Geschichtsschreibung als Zeugnis. Gestalt und Gehalt der Kunst des Lukas*, I, ATANT 14 (Zürich, 1948), pp. 17s.

[7] D'accord avec M. Augsten, 'Lukanische Miszelle', *NTS* 14, p. 581.

L'hendiadys μεριμνᾷς καὶ θορυβάζῃ est typiquement lucanien.[1] Il semble assez normal que πολλά ait ὀλίγα comme antithèse: ce sont les deux termes qui s'opposent naturellement[2] (*lectio facilior*?). Luc oppose aussi πολλοί à οὐδείς (Lc iv.25s, 27; xiv.16 et 24): ce n'est pas encore l'antithèse πολλά–ἕν, mais on n'en est pas loin.[3] Quant à la forme longue et à la manière dont elle ajoute ἤ ἑνός en finale, il semble qu'on peut dire que, sans être caractéristique du style de Luc, cette construction ne lui est pas étrangère (cfr Lc ix.25; xii.14, 47; xiv.3, 12; xvii.7; xx.22; xxi.15). Ce rapide examen désavantage nettement la leçon courte, mais il ne fournit pas d'argument permettant de trancher entre les deux leçons contrastées, ou entre elles et la leçon longue.

On s'est interrogé sur la possibilité d'un rapport entre le passage qui nous occupe et 1 Cor vii.32–5:[4] le rapprochement jouerait en faveur de l'antithèse πολλά–ἕν; mais peut-on en tirer un argument concluant ? Luc lui-même fournit un excellent parallèle en Act vi.2–4:[5] les apôtres estiment qu'ils ne doivent pas délaisser (καταλείπω: cfr Lc x.40) la parole de Dieu pour servir (διακονέω: cfr Lc x.40) aux tables; d'autres seront donc préposés à cette χρεία (cfr Lc x.42), de manière à ce que les apôtres puissent se consacrer à la prière et au service de la parole. La priorité que les Actes donnent au service de la parole sur le service de la table correspond naturellement à la priorité que notre passage accorde à l'écoute de la parole du Seigneur sur les soins multiples du service de la table. Mais le parallèle, éclairant pour le sens général du texte qui nous occupe, l'est moins pour sa formulation précise.

Voilà déjà quelques chemins. L'établissement d'un texte ne peut négliger aucune voie d'approche. Nous avons cependant l'impression que, dans le cas présent, il y aurait un chemin plus direct, et qu'on n'en

1 Voir R. Morgenthaler, *Geschichtsschreibung*, pp. 28s, liste d'expressions doubles que l'auteur appelle 'Tautologien'. Notons plus particulièrement Lc ii.8; xix.10; xxi.15; xxiv.15.

2 Voir Lc vii.47 (bis); x.2; xii.47–8; xiii.23–4; Act xvii.4, 12.

3 Voir aussi Lc xii.6–7.

4 Voir surtout F. Puzo, 'Marta y María. Nota exegética a Lc 10, 38–42 y 1 Cor 7, 29–35', *Estudios Eccles.*, 34 (1960), pp. 851–7; B. Gerhardsson, *Memory and Manuscript. Oral Tradition and Written Transmission in Rabbinic Judaism and Early Christianity* (ASNTU xxii) (Uppsala, 1961), p. 314; G. Bouwman, *Das dritte Evangelium. Einübung in die formgeschichtliche Methode* (Düsseldorf, 1968), pp. 110s; I. de la Potterie, 'Le titre κύριος appliqué à Jésus dans l'évangile de Luc', *Mélanges Bibliques B. Rigaux* (Gembloux, 1970), pp. 117–46 (131s).

5 Voir surtout Bo Reicke, *Diakonie, Festfreude und Zelos in Verbindung mit der altchristlichen Agapenfeier*, Upps. Univ. Årsskrift 1951:5 (Uppsala–Wiesbaden, 1951), pp. 28–31; B. Gerhardsson, *Memory and Manuscript*, pp. 240s; A. George, 'L'accueil du Seigneur: Lc 10, 38–42', *Seizième dimanche ordinaire*, Ass. Seign., 47 (Paris, 1970), pp. 75–85 (82).

tire pas le parti qu'on pourrait en tirer. Puisque nous avons affaire à une réponse que Jésus fait à Marthe, il semble tout naturel de penser que les termes de cette réponse ont été préparés par ceux de la question. S'il y a quelque incertitude sur la formulation exacte des versets 41–2, n'est-ce pas d'abord au verset 40 qu'il convient de demander un éclaircissement ?

Dans ce que Marthe dit à Jésus, au verset 40, il y a deux choses. D'abord une question, qui est en même temps un reproche: 'Cela ne t'intéresse pas . . . ?' (*οὐ μέλει σοι . . .;*).[1] Ensuite une proposition impérative, liée à la question par un 'donc': 'Dis-lui donc . . .' (*εἰπὲ οὖν . . .*); Marthe indique à Jésus la manière de réparer son inattention. Les versets 41–2 répondent aux deux points, Luc ayant d'ailleurs soin d'éviter toute rigidité dans le parallélisme. Au reproche interrogatif 'Tu ne te soucies pas ?' correspond (après la double interpellation 'Marthe, Marthe!', parallèle au 'Seigneur!' du verset 40) l'expression double: 'Tu t'inquiètes et t'agites . . .';[2] le reproche est ainsi retourné contre Marthe. Liée à cette réponse par un 'car', la seconde partie du verset 42, *Μαριὰμ γάρ*, explique pourquoi Jésus ne dira pas à Marie ce que Marthe aurait voulu qu'il dise.

L'intérêt que nous portons ici à la première partie de la réponse de Jésus doit attirer notre attention sur la première partie du discours de Marthe. En fait, un procédé de répétition montre que la question posée par Marthe ne peut pas être séparée de la notice qui introduit cette question: le verbe *διακονεῖν* qui termine la question fait évidemment écho au substantif *διακονίαν* qui achève l'introduction narrative. Il saute alors aux yeux que la première partie du verset 40 tend à mettre en valeur les deux termes d'une antithèse: d'une part, Marthe s'affaire *περὶ πολλὴν διακονίαν*; d'autre part sa sœur la laisse *μόνην . . . διακονεῖν*. Souligné par l'emploi des termes *διακονία* et *διακονέω*, le contraste se situe tout entier entre les deux adjectifs *πολλήν* et *μόνην*. C'est précisément du contraste entre ces deux termes que résulte l'injustice d'une situation dont Marthe se sent la victime: alors qu'il y a *tant* à faire, elle reste *seule* à le faire.

Si l'on admet que Luc sait composer un récit, il semble naturel de supposer que le contraste souligné dans la première partie du verset 40 prépare le lecteur à saisir la portée de la réponse de Jésus, et plus précisément sans doute la présence d'un contraste dans cette réponse. Assurément, le contraste eût été plus clair si la réponse de Jésus avait

[1] Très désinvolte, cette formulation avait été gommée en Lc viii.24 (diff. Mc iv.38). Luc n'éprouve pas le même scrupule ici (voir encore Act xviii.17).

[2] On reste sur le registre psychologique des préoccupations.

répété les termes caractéristiques du verset 40, *διακονία* et *διακονεῖν*. On comprend sans trop de peine que le reproche adressé par Jésus à Marthe ne pouvait pas viser directement son 'service'; seules, son inquiétude et son agitation sont mises en cause. Ce glissement ne doit pas empêcher de reconnaître que l'antithèse *πολλήν–μόνην* du verset 40 prépare naturellement le contraste *πολλά–ἑνός*, auquel la critique textuelle tend actuellement à donner la préférence dans les versets 41–2. Il n'est peut-être pas inutile de se rendre compte que le parallélisme structurel qui caractérise la composition des versets 40 et 41–2 joue en faveur de cette lecture.

D'autres considérations devraient intervenir; nous pensons qu'elles confirmeraient le résultat auquel conduit l'examen de la structure du dialogue entre Marthe et Jésus. Notons d'abord que la manière dont le problème est posé au verset 40 éclaire le sens de l'expression 'il est besoin' (*ἔστιν χρεία*). Th. Zahn l'avait déjà fort bien souligné:[1] en fonction du verset 40, il ne s'agit pas de ce dont Jésus a besoin (c'est-à-dire de ce qui lui 'suffit', *ἀρκεῖ*), mais du jugement à porter sur la tâche qui s'impose en ce moment: qu'est-ce qui est vraiment nécessaire? L'activité déployée par Marthe a-t-elle une importance si grande qu'elle devrait empêcher Marie de rester à écouter la parole du Seigneur? Si, en fait, 'il est besoin' qualifie l'attitude de Marie, qui ne s'occupe manifestement que 'd'une seule chose',[2] on voit mal le sens que pourrait prendre ici *ὀλίγων*: cette leçon, qui s'intéresse aux besoins de Jésus, ne correspond pas au problème réellement posé.

Il conviendrait également de tenir compte du rapport naturel qui doit exister entre les deux parties du verset 42. Jésus explique pourquoi il ne dira pas à Marie d'aller aider sa sœur: il estime que 'Marie a choisi la bonne part', *τὴν ἀγαθὴν μερίδα*. Cette 'part' est présentée comme unique, la seule qui soit vraiment bonne (ou la meilleure). La manière dont on en parle correspond à l'idée qu'une seule chose importe, mieux qu'à une mention de 'peu de choses'.

Nos observations n'aboutissent à aucun résultat révolutionnaire. En invitant à se demander si la leçon choisie par les éditeurs du *Greek*

[1] Th. Zahn, *Das Evangelium des Lucas*, KNT III (Leipzig, 1913), p. 440.

[2] C'est ce qu'exprime très heureusement au verset 39 la construction du participe aoriste suivi d'un indicatif imparfait: Marie s'est assise, une fois pour toutes, et elle écoute, une action qui dure dans le temps. On reconnaît là une finesse de style qui caractérise l'écriture de Luc et n'est pas sans portée pour la question qui nous occupe. Luc introduit la même construction en corrigeant Marc dans Lc iv.39, 40; v.28; viii.29, 41; ix.11, 31; xviii.36; xix.28; xx.14; xxii.41, 55, 59; xxiii.39. Voir aussi Lc i.22; ii.38; iv.30; v.2–3; vii.4; xv.28; xix.1; xxiv.15, 30. Nous avons relevé dans les Actes 55 exemples de cette construction.

New Testament ne doit être acceptée qu'avec un 'considerable degree of doubt', elles pourront illustrer, et confirmer peut-être, le commentaire de ce choix qui a été publié par B. M. Metzger au nom de ces mêmes éditeurs.[1]

[1] B. M. Metzger, *A Textual Commentary on the Greek New Testament* (London–New York), 1971, pp. 153s. A noter que les questions de ponctuation ne font pas l'objet d'un examen critique. Pour peu qu'on se rende compte que la déclaration de Lc iv.43 fait écho au texte d'Isaïe cité au verset 18, il est clair qu'il faut construire ici *εὐαγγελίσασθαι πτωχοῖς ἀπέσταλκέν με* sans introduire une virgule entre l'infinitif et le verbe dont il dépend. C'est vérifier d'une autre manière que l'établissement d'un texte ne peut pas se désintéresser du contexte.

Aramaic Kepha' and Peter's name in the New Testament

JOSEPH A. FITZMYER S.J.

Among the many problems surrounding the figure of Peter in the New Testament are the meaning of his name and the significance attached to the change of it.[1] Some of them involve the relation between Symeon and Simon as used of him; some of them the relation between Cephas and Peter. In this sort of discussion it is surprising how little attention has been paid to a striking occurrence of the Aramaic name *Kephā'*, and I should like to draw the attention of New Testament scholars to it. It is the sort of topic that has interested Professor Matthew Black during most of his scholarly career, and it is, therefore, a fitting topic to discuss in a volume that honors him at an important stage in his career. May these few lines about Cephas be taken, then, as a mark of lasting esteem.

At the outset we may be permitted to set the context for this discussion of Peter's name by recalling the various names that are given to him and the problems they raise. In this way we shall be able to see better the relation to them of the Aramaic material to be discussed.

First of all, we may recall that he is given the name Symeon or Simon.[2] The Semitic form of the name, Symeon or *Šimĕʿōn*, is reflected in the Greek of Acts xv.14 – at least so it is intended in the Lucan text as we have it. James refers thus to Peter, who has just spoken in xv.7–11. This is the only time that Peter is so named in Luke–Acts; elsewhere he is always referred to as Simon, a similar-sounding Greek name (*Simōn*),[3]

[1] Modestly tucked away in an otherwise informative article on *Πέτρος* in Bauer–Arndt–Gingrich, *A Greek–English Lexicon of the New Testament and Other Early Christian Literature* (Chicago, 1957), p. 660 is the admission: 'Not all the problems connected w. the conferring of the name Cephas-Peter upon Simon . . . have yet been solved'.

[2] *Ibid.*, pp. 758, 785.

[3] Luke iv.38; v.3, 4, 5, 8, 10; xxii.31; xxiv.34.

or as Peter (*Petros*),[1] or as Simon[2] Peter. The use of Symeon in xv.14 for Peter is striking and has given rise to one of the classic problems in that chapter (often used as an important piece of evidence that Luke is here depending on a source – which he may not have completely understood).[3] The name Symeon is likewise attested for him in some MSS of II Pet. i.1, but even there it is not uniformly attested.[4] In any case, the use of both Symeon and Simon reflects the well-known custom among Jews of that time of giving the name of a famous patriarch or personage of the Old Testament to a male child along with a similar-sounding Greek/Roman name. This use of Symeon can be compared with Luke ii.25, 34; iii.30 and with the names of Joseph or Jacob. The Old Testament background for Symeon is undoubtedly to be sought in Gen. xxix.33. Used of this disciple of Jesus, it stands in contrast to that of other disciples like Philip or Andrew.

Second, in addition to the use of Symeon/Simon for him, the New Testament has recorded the recollection of Jesus having changed Simon's name: 'Simon, whom he surnamed Peter' (Mark iii.16; cf. Matt. iv.18; x.2; Luke vi.14; Acts x.5). This change of name is preserved in an even more explicit way in the Gospels of Matthew and John. In the Matthean form of the episode at Caesarea Philippi, after Simon has stated, 'You are the Christ, the Son of the living God', Jesus says to him, 'Blessed are you Simon, son of Jonah! . . . I tell you,

[1] Luke viii.45, 51; ix.20, 28, 32, 33; xii.41; xviii.28; xxii.8, 34, 54, 55, 58, 60, 61; Acts i.13, 15; ii.14, 37, 38; iii.1, 3, 4, 6, 11, 12; iv. 8, 13, 19; v.3, 8, 9, 15, 29; viii.14, 20; ix.32, 34, 38, 39, 40; x.5, 9, 13, 14, 17, 19, 21, 25, 26, 34, 44, 45, 46; xi.2, 4, 7; xii.3, 5, 6, 7, 11, 14, 16, 18; xv.7.

[2] Luke v.8; cf., in addition to Acts x.5 cited in note 1 above, x.18, 32; xi.13.

[3] To some commentators it has seemed that the Jewish-Christian James would naturally use the Semitic form Symeon in speaking of Peter; so O. Cullmann, *Peter: Disciple, Apostle, Martyr: A Historical and Theological Study*, 2nd edition (Philadelphia, 1962), p. 19, n. 3. Others, aware of the compilatory nature of Acts xv, raise the question whether verses 13–29 may not have been derived by Luke from a source which was different from that from which he derived the information in verses 4–12. In this hypothesis, the name Symeon may have referred to another person (e.g. Symeon Niger of Acts xiii.1; see S. Giet, 'L'Assemblée apostolique et le décret de Jérusalem: Qui était Siméon ?', *RSR* 39 (1951), pp. 203–20; cf. *The Jerome Biblical Commentary*, §46:32–4; §45:72–7). In any case, as the text of Acts stands today, Symeon is to be understood as referring to Peter (for Luke has undoubtedly 'telescoped' accounts of two originally separate and distinct Jerusalem decisions).

[4] See B. M. Metzger, *A Textual Commentary on the Greek New Testament* (London/New York, 1971), p. 699: 'The weight of external support for the two readings is almost equally divided.' 'The Committee was agreed that transcriptionally it is more likely that *Σίμων* is a correction of *Συμεών* than vice versa . . .'

you are Peter, and on this rock I will build my church' (Matt. xvi.17–18, RSV): *σὺ εἶ Πέτρος, καὶ ἐπὶ ταύτῃ τῇ πέτρᾳ οἰκοδομήσω....* In the Johannine Gospel, Andrew finds his brother Simon and brings him to Jesus, who says to him, '"So you are Simon the son of John ? You shall be called Cephas" (which means Peter)' (i.42, RSV): *Σὺ εἶ Σίμων ὁ υἱὸς Ἰωάννου; σὺ κληθήσῃ Κηφᾶς ὃ ἑρμηνεύεται Πέτρος*). Cephas is not used again in the Fourth Gospel, where the Greek name Peter rather prevails. Aside from the translation of Cephas that is given in i.42, which removes any hesitation about the way in which one part of the early church understood the change of the name from Simon to Cephas, little is otherwise told in the Johannine Gospel about the significance of the change. A significance of the new name is found in the Matthean passage – at least if one grants that there is a wordplay involved and that the underlying Aramaic substratum involved a similar wordplay.

Reasons for the change of Simon's name have often been proposed. Today we smile at the relation seen between Greek *Κηφᾶς* and Latin *caput* by some patristic writers, who assumed a connection between *Κηφᾶς* and *κεφαλή*. Thus Optatus of Milevis once wrote (*c.* A.D. 370): '... omnium apostolorum caput, Petrus, unde et Cephas est appellatus ...'[1] How much was made of this connection and its unsophisticated medieval exploitation need not detain us here.[2] In a similar way we may treat the theorizing about the alleged tendency of Jews at the turn of the Christian era to avoid the use of the Hebrew name Symeon or the Greek name Simon either because it was supposedly forbidden to them by the Roman occupiers of Palestine on account of its hyper-patriotic associations with famous bygone military figures or because it was regarded as too sacred a name for normal use by nationalistic Jews.[3] Such speculation has had to yield to the fact that Symeon/Simon was among the most widely used names for Palestinian male children of the period.[4] Such an avoidance of the name is scarcely the reason for the change from Simon to Cephas/Peter.

Much more frequently the reason for the change of the name has

1 *CSEL* 26.36, edited by C. Ziwsa (1893). Similarly, Isidore of Seville, *Etym.* 7.9,3; W. M. Lindsay, *Isidori hispalensis episcopi Etymologiarum sive originum libri xx*, 2 volumes (Oxford, 1957); PL 82.287.

2 See Y. M.-J. Congar, 'Cephas–Céphalè–Caput', *Revue du moyen âge latin* 8 (1952), pp. 5–42; cf. J. A. Burgess, *History of the Exegesis of Matthew 16: 17–19 from 1781 to 1965* (Ann Arbor, Mich., 1976), pp. 58–9, 89.

3 See C. Roth, 'Simon-Peter', *HTR* 54 (1961), pp. 91–7.

4 See my reply to C. Roth, 'The Name Simon', *HTR* 56 (1963), pp. 1–5, with further discussion in *HTR* 57 (1964), 60–1. It has all been reprinted in my *Essays on the Semitic Background of the New Testament* (London, 1971; paperback edition, Missoula, Montana, 1974), pp. 104–12.

been explained by relating it to the change of names of rather prominent persons in the Old Testament in view of roles that they were to play in the history of the people of Israel: Abram/Abraham (Gen. xvii.5); Jacob/Israel (Gen. xxxii.28); etc. Against such a background the wordplay of Matt. xvi.18b has been understood. It is not my purpose to rehearse here all the details of the long debate over that wordplay – whether 'this rock' refers to the faith of Peter, to the confession of Peter, to Peter himself, or to Jesus.[1] There are rather some aspects of the question that have, in my opinion, been somewhat neglected and some philological evidence that should be brought to bear on the names Cephas and Peter.

I. THE NAME *Κηφᾶς*

The name *Κηφᾶς* is found in the New Testament, outside of the Johannine passage (i.42), only in the Pauline writings (Gal. i.18; ii.9, 11, 14; 1 Cor. i.12; iii.22; ix.5; xv.5).[2] Paul, however, never uses of him the name Simon/Symeon, and he uses *Πέτρος* of him only in Gal. ii.7–8, in a context in which *Κηφᾶς* otherwise predominates.

Either on the basis of the early church's interpretation of *Κηφᾶς* as *Πέτρος* (in John i.42) or for other reasons, modern commentators usually identify the Cephas of Galatians with Peter. However, there has always been a small group of commentators who have sought to identify the Cephas of Galatians i–ii with someone other than Simon Peter. Eusebius quotes the fifth book of the *Hypotyposes* of Clement of Alexandria to the effect that the 'Cephas concerning whom Paul says "and when Cephas came to Antioch I withstood him to the face" [Gal. ii.11] was one of the seventy disciples, who had the same name as the apostle Peter'.[3] More sophisticated reasons for hesitating about the identity of Cephas and Peter in Galatians have been found in modern times.[4] In antiquity it was often a question of the supposed relative positions of Peter and Paul in the church; in recent times it is the peculiar shift from Cephas

[1] For a recent survey of these opinions, see J. A. Burgess, *A History of the Exegesis* (p. 123, n. 2 above), *passim*.

[2] The name Cephas further appears in *I Clem.* 47.3. The antiquity of the name is established by the Pauline use of it. One can only speculate about his seeming preference for it.

[3] *Hist. eccl.* 1.12.2; GCS 2/1.82.

[4] See K. Lake, 'Simon, Cephas, Peter', *HTR* 14 (1921), pp. 95–7; A. M. Völlmecke, *Jahrbuch des Missionshauses St Gabriel* 2 (1925), pp. 69–104; 3 (1926), pp. 31–75; D. W. Riddle, 'The Cephas–Peter Problem, and a Possible Solution', *JBL* 59 (1940), pp. 169–80; N. Huffman, 'Emmaus among the Resurrection Narratives', *JBL* 64 (1945), pp. 205–26, esp. pp. 205–6, n. 1; C. M. Henze, 'Cephas seu Kephas non est Simon Petrus!', *Divus Thomas*, 35 (1958), pp. 63–7; J. Herrera, 'Cephas seu Kephas est Simon Petrus', *ibid.*, pp. 481–4.

to Peter. Though the majority of modern commentators agree that Cephas and Peter are the same person in Galatians i–ii, the shift has been explained by postulating that Paul is 'quoting an official document'[1] in verses 7–8, whereas he has elsewhere used the name that he preferred for him. Another aspect of the problem is that whereas the manuscript tradition is constant in 1 Corinthians in reading *Κηφᾶς*, there is fluctuation between *Κηφᾶς* and *Πέτρος* in the manuscripts of Galatians.[2] In any case, though we take note of this minority opinion about the identity of Cephas and Peter in Galatians i–ii, we cannot consider it seriously.

The translation of *Κηφᾶς* by *Πέτρος* in John i.42 and the wordplay in Matt. xvi.18 between *Πέτρος* and *πέτρα* have been explained from time immemorial by an appeal to the Aramaic background of the name Cephas. *Κηφᾶς* is regarded as a Grecized form of the Aramaic word *kephā'*, assimilating it to masculine nouns of the first declension (cf. *'Ιούδας, -ου*).[3] The Hebrew noun *kēph* is found in Jer. iv.29; Job xxx.6; Sir. xi.14. To illustrate the Aramaic use, one has often appealed to later rabbinic writings, Syriac, and Christian Palestinian Aramaic.[4] However, there is now some better Aramaic evidence that can be used, coming from earlier or contemporary sources.

The common noun *kephā'* appears twice in the targum of Job from Qumran Cave 11. A fragmentary phrase containing it is preserved in 11QtgJob 32:1: *y'ly kp'*, 'wild goats of the crag', translating Hebrew *ya'ălê sela'* (Job xxxix.1), 'mountain goats' (RSV).[5] It also occurs in

1 O. Cullmann, '*Πέτρος*', TDNT 6 (1968), p. 100, n. 6; O. Cullmann, *Peter*, p. 20. Cf. G. Klein, 'Galater 2, 6–9 und die Geschichte der Jerusalemer Urgemeinde', *ZTK* 57 (1960), pp. 275–95, esp. p. 283; reprinted in *Rekonstruktion und Interpretation: Gesammelte Aufsätze zum Neuen Testament* (Munich, 1969), pp. 99–128 (mit einem Nachtrag), esp. pp. 106–7.

2 *The Greek New Testament*, edited by K. Aland *et al.* (London–New York, 1966) makes no mention of this fluctuation, probably considering it not serious enough to note. According to E. Nestle's *apparatus criticus*, *Πέτρον* is read in i.18 by ℜ, D, G, *pl*, latt. sy^h; in ii. 9 $\mathfrak{P}^{46}$ reads *'Ιάκωβος καὶ Πέτρος*, but MSS D, G, it, Marcion, Origen, and Ambrosiaster invert the order of these names; in ii.11 *Πέτρος* is read by ℜ, D, G, *pm*, s^h, Marcion; in ii.14 *Πέτρῳ* is read by the same MSS as in i.19. – Cf. J. T. Clemons, 'Some Questions on the Syriac Support for Variant Greek Readings', *NT* 10 (1968), pp. 26–30.

3 See BDF §53(1).

4 See, e.g. A. Dell, 'Matthäus 16, 17–19', *ZNTW* 15 (1914), pp. 1–49, esp. pp. 14–17. For an interesting comparison of the nuances of *kephā'* in Syriac as a translation of Greek *petros, petra, lithos* or Hebrew *'eben, sela'*, and *ṣûr*, see G. Gander, 'Le sens de mots: *Πέτρος–πέτρα/KIPHÂ–KIPHÂ/*כיפא–כיפא dans Matthieu xvi : 18a', *RTP* 29 (1941), pp. 5–29; but some of his reasoning is a bit strange.

5 See J. P. M. van der Ploeg and A. S. van der Woude, *Le targum de Job de la grotte xi de Qumran*, Koninklijke nederlandse Akademie van Wetenschappen (Leiden, 1971), p. 74.

11QtgJob 33:9: [*b*]*kp*' *yškwn wyqnn* [ ],[1] '[On] the crag it (i.e. the black eagle[2]) dwells, and it nests [ ]', translating Hebrew *sela' yiškōn* (Job xxxix.28), '(On) the rock he dwells' (RSV).

It is further found several times in the newly published texts of Aramaic Enoch from Qumran Cave 4: [*w'mr' s*]*lq lr*['*š k*]*p ḥd rm*, '[and the sheep] climbed to the sum[mit of] a certain high [cr]ag' (4QEn^e 4 iii 19 [=1 Enoch 89:29]);[3] [*b*]*tnyn' wslq lr'š kp' dn*, 'climbed up [again for] a second time to the summit of that crag' (4QEn^c 4:3 [=1 Enoch 89:32]);[4] [*wlm*]*drk* '*l* '*prh w*['']*l* [*kp*]*yh l' tškḥwn mn* [*ḥmth*], 'and you are not able to tread upon the dirt or upon the [roc]ks on account [of the heat' (4QEn^a 1 ii 8 [=1 Enoch 4]).[5] In all of these passages the word seems to have the sense of a 'rock' or a 'crag', part of a mountainous or hilly region. Coming from Aramaic texts that originated in Palestine in pre-Christian times, this evidence is obviously valuable.

But does *kp*' occur in pre-Christian writings as a proper name? T. Zahn, in his commentary on Matt. xvi.18, implied that the word was so used, but he provided no examples of it.[6] O. Cullmann, who notes Zahn's lack of documentation, has stated that *kp*' 'is not, as one might suppose, attested as a proper name in Aram.'[7] Indeed, this lack of attestation of *kp*' as a proper name has been seen as one of the major problems in viewing the occurrence of *Πέτρος* and *πέτρα* in Matt. xvi.18

[1] *Ibid.*, p. 76.

[2] On the 'black eagle', see my remarks in 'The Contribution of Qumran Aramaic to the Study of the New Testament', *NTS* 20 (1973–4), pp. 382–407, esp. p. 396.

[3] See J. T. Milik, *The Books of Enoch: Aramaic Fragments of Qumran Cave 4* (with the collaboration of Matthew Black) (Oxford, 1976), pp. 243–4. Note the use of the adjective *rm*, 'high', here.

[4] *Ibid.*, pp. 204–5.

[5] *Ibid.*, pp. 146–7. Here [*kp*]*yh*, 'rocks', is in parallelism with '*prh*, 'dirt'. The preposition '*l* is interesting here, as a background for the Matthean *epi*. (One should also note the meaning of the verb *tškḥwn* here, 'you are able'; for the problem on which it bears, see my commentary on *The Genesis Apocryphon of Qumran Cave 1*, BibOr 18A; 2nd edition (Rome, 1971), p. 150.)

[6] *Das Evangelium des Matthäus*, Kommentar zum Neuen Testament, 1, 4th edition (Leipzig, 1922), p. 540.

[7] '*Πετρος, Κηφᾶς*', TDNT 6 (1969), p. 100, n. 6. Cf. R. E. Brown, *The Gospel According to John* (*i–xii*): *Introduction, Translation, and Notes*, AB 29 (Garden City, N.J., 1966), p. 76: 'Neither *Petros* in Greek nor *Kēphâ* in Aramaic is a normal proper name; rather it is a nickname . . .' Brown has a similar statement in his article on 'Peter' in *Supplementary Volume of the Interpreter's Dictionary of the Bible* (Nashville/New York, 1976), p. 654. See further J. Schmid, 'Petrus "der Fels" und die Petrusgestalt der Urgemeinde', *Begegnung der Christen: Studien evangelischer und katholischer Theologen* (edited by M. Roesle and O. Cullmann (Stuttgart; Frankfurt, 1959), pp. 347–59, esp. pp. 356–7; H. Rheinfelder, 'Philologische Erwägungen zu Matth 16, 18', *BZ* 24 (1938–9), pp. 139–63, esp. p. 153, n. 1; H. Clavier, '*Πέτρος καὶ πέτρα*', *Neutestamentliche Studien für Rudolf Bultmann*, BZNW 21 (Berlin, 1954), pp. 94–109, esp. p. 106; J. Lowe, *Saint Peter* (New York/Oxford, 1956), p. 7.

as a play on words. In answering an objection which O. Immisch[1] had brought against his interpretation of Matt. xvi.17–19,[2] A. Dell argued that Jesus could not have used the wordplay, because it could not have been a translation from an Aramaic *Vorlage*, since that would imply that *kp'* was a proper name. 'Nun ist aber *kyp'* kein Eigenname.'[3] And in John i.42, argued Dell, *Πέτρος* is a translation of *Κηφᾶς*, not of a proper name, but of a description (*Bezeichnung*). The main thrust of Dell's argument, then, is that since *kp'* is unknown as a proper name, there could be no wordplay involved.

Now, aside from the fact that, as we noted above, Paul uses the grecized form of *kp'* properly as a name for Peter – which reflects a very early Christian use of it as a proper name (certainly prior to the composition of Matthew) – there does exist an instance of the Aramaic name which should be introduced into the discussion.

Though the text in which it appears has been known since 1953, when it was first published, it has scarcely been noticed; as far as I know, it has not been introduced into the discussion of the *Κηφᾶς/Πέτρος* problem. However, *kp'* does occur as a proper name in an Aramaic text from Elephantine (BMAP 8:10), dated to the eighth year of Darius the King (=Darius II, 424–402 B.C.), hence to 416 B.C.[4] The name is found in a list of witnesses to a document in which a certain Zakkur gives or transfers a slave, named Yedaniah, to a certain Uriah. Nine lines of the document spell out the details of the transfer, and the last three give the names of the witnesses, the first of which runs as follows:

> 10 *śhdy' bgw 'trmlky br qlqln, snkšr br šbty; śhd, 'qb br kp'*
> Witnesses hereto (are): 'Atarmalki, son of QLQLN; Sinkishir, son of Shabbetai; witness: 'Aqab, son of Kepha'.

The Uriah to whom the slave is given is identified in the text as an 'Aramean of Syene' (*'rmy zy swn*). This is not the place to discuss in detail the meaning of *'rmy* over against *yhwdy* as designations of Jewish

1 'Matthäus 16, 18: Laienbemerkungen zu der Untersuchung Dells', *ZNTW* xv, 1914, pp. 1ff, *ZNTW* 17 (1916), pp. 18–26.

2 'Matthäus 16, 17–18', *ZNTW* 15 (1914), pp. 1–49. On the value of Dell's interpretation, see R. Bultmann, 'Die Frage nach dem messianischen Bewusstsein Jesu und das Petrus-Bekenntnis', *ZNTW* 19 (1919–20), pp. 165–74, esp. p. 170, n. 2.

3 'Zur Erklärung von Matthäus 16, 17–19', *ZNTW* 17 (1916), p. 27–32.

4 E. G. Kraeling, *The Brooklyn Museum Aramaic Papyri: New Documents of the Fifth Century B.C. from the Jewish Colony at Elephantine* (New Haven, 1953; reprinted, New York, 1969), pp. 224–31 (+pl. VIII). The text is actually dated to the 6th of Tishri (by the Babylonian calendar = 22 October) and to the 22nd of Paoni (by the Egyptian calendar = 22 September), but there seems to be an error in the text. See Kraeling's note, p. 228.

individuals in Elephantine texts.[1] Suffice it to say that many Jews and persons with Jewish names figured in the fifth-century military colony on the island of Elephantine and in the town of Syene (=modern Assuan), on the east bank of the Nile opposite the island, and have been given these gentilic designations in the papyri discovered there. The persons mentioned in these Aramaic texts bore not only Northwest Semitic names (Hebrew, Aramaic, or Phoenician), but also Babylonian, Egyptian, and Persian names. Indeed, there was a mixture of these names too, even within families, as other names in line 10 attest: Sin-kishir, a Babylonian name for a son of Shabbetai, an (almost certainly) Hebrew name (used of a Jew in Ezra x.15; Neh viii.7; xi.16).

This mixture of names in the Elephantine texts raises a question about the patronymic in BMAP 8:10. The *br* that precedes it makes it clear that *kp*ʾ is a proper name; so it can no longer be maintained that the name is unattested. But is it clearly an Aramaic name, one that would underlie Κηφᾶς in the New Testament? When E. G. Kraeling first published this Elephantine text, he translated the name of the last witness on line 10 simply as "ʿAḳab b. *Kp*ʾ", setting the transliterated consonants of the patronymic in italics, as he did elsewhere for names about which he was uncertain or for which he had no real explanation.[2] His note on 8:10 explains the son's name thus:

> the perf. (or part.) of the same verb that appears in the impf. in *y*ʿ*qb*, Jacob. In both cases we have hypocoristica – the full name must have been something like ʿ*qbyh* (on a third century B.C. inscription from Alexandria; see *RES*, 2. No. 79) or ʿ*qbnbw*, Aqab-Nebo, in *AP* 54:10 . . .[3]

Concerning the patronymic, Kraeling wrote:

> The name *kp*ʾ must also have a deity for a subject; J.A. *kp*ʾ, 'overthrows.' Or may one compare *kf*ʾ, Ranke, *ÄP*, 344:15 ?'[4]

That the name *kp*ʾ is a hypocoristicon is most probable, even though we have no clear instance of a fuller form of the name. That it has anything to do with *kp*ʾ, 'overthrow', is quite problematic, in my opinion, since that root more properly means 'to bend, curve'.

[1] See B. Porten, *Archives from Elephantine: The Life of an Ancient Jewish Military Colony* (Berkeley–Los Angeles, 1968), pp. 3–27 (and the literature cited there); P. Grelot, *Documents araméens d'Égypte: Introduction, traduction, présentation*, Littératures anciennes du Proche-Orient (Paris, 1972), pp. 33–47.

[2] E. G. Kraeling, *The Brooklyn Museum Aramaic Papyri*, p. 227.

[3] *Ibid.*, p. 230.

[4] *Ibid.*; H. Ranke (*Die ägyptischen Personennamen* (Glückstadt, 1935), pp. 1, 344) gives as the meaning of *kf*ʾ' '"der Hintere" (?)'.

The name *kp'* resembles other proper names which end in *aleph* in Aramaic documents from Egypt, such as *Bs'* (BMAP 11:2), *Ṣḥ'* (*AP* 18:4), *Pms'* (*AP* 73:13), *Ky'* (*AP* 2:19), *Tb'* (*RES* 1794:18), etc. The problem is to suggest real Egyptian equivalents for such short names in these Aramaic texts. In a name like *Ḥrtb'* (CIS 138B:3) an Egyptian equivalent has been suggested, *Ḥr-(n)i-tꜣibꜣ-t* (=Greek *Artbōs*), where the *aleph* of the Aramaic form may reflect a real *aleph* in an Egyptian word, *bꜣ.t*, 'tree': 'Horus of the tree'. But in some of the short names there are also variants, such as *Kyh* (*RES* 1297:2), or *Ṣḥẖ* which suggest that the final *aleph* of the Aramaic form is a vowel letter. In the last instance, the name *Ṣḥ'* is usually explained as Egyptian,[1] but it is in reality an Aramaized form, and the Akkadian transcription of it as *Ṣi-ḫa-a* argues in favor of the final *aleph* as a vowel letter. Compare also *Pms'* (*AP* 73:13) and *Pmsy* (*AP* 44:7). All of this may not be making out an air-tight case, but it does at least suggest that the best explanation for *kp'* is that it is not an Egyptian name, but rather an Aramaic name. In that case, the best explanation is that it represents *Kephā'*.

It has, at any rate, been so interpreted by no less an authority in things Aramaic than W. Baumgartner. He listed it under the Hebrew word *kēph*, 'Fels', in *Hebräisches und aramäisches Lexikon zum Alten Testament*,[2] identifying it as a masculine proper name and equating it, without further question, with '*Κηφᾶς* NT'. P. Grelot similarly toyed with the equation of the BMAP form and the New Testament name,[3] but he was obviously hesitant about it, since he mentions two other explanations: a hypocoristicon derived from *kpp*, 'bend, bow down' (yet he gives no plausible fuller form of the name with which it could be compared); or the Egyptian *kfꜣ* (an explanation that he simply

[1] See further my article, 'A Re-Study of an Elephantine Aramaic Marriage Contract (*AP* 15)', *Near Eastern Studies in Honor of William Foxwell Albright*, edited by H. Goedicke (Baltimore, 1971), pp. 137–68, esp. p. 147. What is said there about *Ṣḥ'* being 'Egyptian' needs the more proper nuance that is now being stated here. I am indebted to Professor Thomas O. Lambdin, of Harvard University, for advice on this matter of Egyptian names appearing in Aramaic texts, especially for the treatment of the *aleph* in the short names. The formulation of the matter given above, however, is my own; and I alone am responsible for any possibly unfortunate formulations.

[2] W. Baumgartner, *Hebräisches und aramäisches Lexikon zum Alten Testament*, 2 (Leiden, 1974), pp. 468. I am indebted to J. A. Burgess for calling this reference to my attention.

[3] P. Grelot, *Documents araméens d'Égypte*, p. 476. Strangely enough, Grelot writes the New Testament form with ϵ instead of with η. The spelling [*K*]*ephas* (with a short *e*) turns up in the Coptic *Acts of Peter and the Twelve Apostles* 1:2, M. Krause and P. Labib, *Gnostische und hermetische Schriften aus Codex II und Codex VI* (Glückstadt, 1971), p. 107.

borrows from Kraeling). But, as Baumgartner has rightly seen, the only plausible explanation of the BMAP name is that it is an Aramaic name, related to Hebrew *kēph* and the Aramaic common noun *kephāʾ*.

If one has to justify the existence of such an Aramaic name in the fifth century B.C., the best explanation of it would be that it is a hypocoristicon which has lost some theophoric element. In itself, it would be no more enigmatic as a name than the Hebrew *Ṣûr*, 'Rock', borne by one of the sons of Jeiel and Maacah of Gibeon (1 Chron. viii.30; ix.36) and by one of the kings or leaders of the Midianites (Num. xxv.15; xxxi.8; Josh xiii.21).[1] This name is rendered in the RSV as Zur, but it is a hypocoristicon of such names as *Ṣûrîʾēl* (Num. iii.35) or *Ṣûrîšadday* (Num. i.6; ii.12).

The least one can say is that *kpʾ* is not unknown as a proper name and that Peter is not the first person to have borne it. That it was otherwise in use among Jews of Palestine remains, of course, still to be shown. But the existence of it as a proper name at least makes more plausible the suggestion that a wordplay in Aramaic was involved. On the other hand, it may take away some of the uniqueness of the name which was often seen in the conferral of it on a disciple by Jesus.

The Aramaic substratum of Matt. xvi.17–18 (at least for those phrases mentioned at the beginning of this paper) might have been something like the following:[2]

> *ʿantāh hūʾ mĕšîaḥ, bĕreh dī ĕʾlāhāʾ ḥayyāʾ . . . ṭūbayk, Šimʿōn bar Yōnāh . . . ʾantāh hūʾ Kephāʾ weʿal kephāʾ dēn ʾebnêh . . .*

The wordplay that emerges from such an Aramaic substratum of the Matthean verse could be the key to the role that Simon is to play: He or some aspect of him is to be a crag/rock in the building of the *ἐκκλησία*. The further connotations of this image can be explored by others.

One further aspect of the philological consideration of the Matthean verse needs to be explored, viz. the relation of Aramaic *kpʾ* to Greek *Πέτρος*. But this brings us to the second part of this paper.

II. THE GREEK NAME *Πέτρος*

The problem that confronts one is to explain why there is in the Mat-

[1] Note that Koehler–Baumgartner, *Lexicon in Veteris Testamenti libros* (Leiden, 1958), p. 800, even compares Hebrew *Ṣûr*, the proper name, with Aramaic *kypʾ*.

[2] If I attempt to retrovert the words of Matt. xvi.18 here, I am implying only the pre-Matthean existence of such a tradition in Aramaic.

thean passage a translation of the Aramaic substratum, which is claimed to have the same word *kp'* twice, by two Greek words, *Πέτρος* and *πέτρα*. In John i.42 *Πέτρος* is given as the equivalent of Aramaic *Kephā'* (grecized as *Κηφᾶς*); this is quite understandable. But if the underlying Aramaic of Matt. xvi.18 had *kephā'* twice, then we should expect *σὺ εἶ Πέτρος καὶ ἐπὶ τούτῳ τῷ πέτρῳ οἰκοδομήσω*.... Because of this problem, two different conclusions have been drawn: (1) A. Dell has concluded that verse 18 cannot be a translation of an underlying Aramaic saying ('kein Jesuswort'), but must rather be the creation of Greek-speaking Christians.[1] (2) P. E. Hughes, in studying the pair *Πέτρος/πέτρα*, 'for which a suitable Semitic equivalent is not available', infers rather that 'Jesus actually spoke in Greek on this occasion'.[2] It is hard to imagine two more radically opposed conclusions!

But part of the problem comes from the nature of the languages involved. Both *πέτρος* and *πέτρα* are quite at home in the Greek language from its earliest periods; and though the words were at times used with slightly different nuances, it is clear that 'they are often used interchangeably'.[3] On the other hand, G. Gander has shown how Hebrew *'eben*, *sela'*, and *ṣûr* are all rendered by *kephā'* in Syriac.[4] So perhaps we are dealing with an Aramaic term that was used with different nuances. When translated into Greek, the masculine form *πέτρος* would suggest itself as a designation for Simon, and a literary variant, the feminine form, for the aspect of him that was to be played upon.

Part of the problem here is that *Πέτρος* has not turned up yet in Greek as a proper name prior to its occurrence for Simon in the New Testament. The impression has been given that it does indeed occur. The first two occurrences of *Πέτρος* in D. Foraboschi's *Onomasticon alterum papyrologicum*[5] would suggest that there is a contemporary extrabiblical occurrence or a nearly contemporary one: in SB 6191,[6] which Foraboschi

1 A. Dell, 'Zur Erklärung', pp. 29–30.

2 P. E. Hughes, 'The Languages Spoken by Jesus', *New Dimensions in New Testament Study*, edited by R. N. Longenecker and M. C. Tenney (Grand Rapids, Mich., 1974), pp. 127–43, esp. p. 141. I am extremely sceptical about the preservation of any Greek sayings of Jesus.

3 '*Πέτρα*', TDNT 6 (1968), p. 95.

4 G. Gander, 'Le sens des mots' (see p. 125, n. 4 above), pp. 15–16.

5 *Onomasticon alterum papyrologicum: Supplemento al Namenbuch di F. Preisigke*, Testi e documenti per lo studio dell'antichità, xvi, serie papirologica, ii (Milano–Varese, 1967–71), fasc. 4, p. 256. I am indebted to my colleague, Francis T. Gignac, S.J., for help in checking these Greek texts, and especially for this reference to Foraboschi.

6 See F. Preisigke and F. Bilabel, *Sammelbuch griechischer Urkunden aus Ägypten* (Berlin/Leipzig, 1926), p. 28.

dates to the first century;[1] and in *Papyrus Oxyrhynchus* 2235, which Foraboschi dates to the second century.[2]

But neither of these references is accurate. The text in SB 6191 is most likely late Roman or Byzantine. It is listed under '*christliche Grabsteine*' and comes from Antinoe.[3] So Foraboschi's date for it in the first century A.D. is erroneous. Similarly, his second-century date for *Pap. Oxy.* 2235 is not correct; the editor of the text says of it, '*Circa A.D.* 346'.[4] The list of occurrences of the name *Πέτρος* in F. Preisigke's *Namenbuch*[5] contains no names that are clearly pre-Christian. In Christian usage after the New Testament the name *Πέτρος* is, of course, often found. It is even found as the name of a pagan in Damascius, *Vita Isidori* 170 (fifth–sixth centuries A.D.), and as the name of the *praeses Arabiae* (A.D. 278–9), Petrus Aurelius.[6]

These, then, are the philological considerations that I have thought worth reconsidering in the matter of the names, Cephas/Peter. Even if what is presented here stands up under further scrutiny, we should still have to admit that 'not all the problems connected w. the conferring of the name Cephas–Peter upon Simon . . . have yet been solved'.[7]

[1] Foraboschi, *Onomasticon alterum*, p. 256.

[2] *Ibid.* Cf. E. Lobel *et al.*, *The Oxyrhynchus Papyri, Part XIX* (London, 1948), p. 101.

[3] F. Preisigke and F. Bilabel, *Sammelbuch* (see p. 131, n. 6 above), p. 28. Cf. G. Lefebvre, 'Égypte chrétienne', *ASAE* 15 (1915), pp. 113–39, esp. pp. 131–2 (§839). Lines 4–6 date the inscription to 'the month of Pachon, 16th (day), beginning of the 13th indiction'.

[4] E. Lobel *et al.*, *The Oxyrhynchus Papyri, Part XIX* (see n. 2 above), p. 101.

[5] F. Preisigke, *Namenbuch* (Heidelberg, 1922; reprinted, Amsterdam, 1967), p. 321.

[6] The attempts to cite *Πέτρον* as a reading in one manuscript of Josephus (*Ant.* 18.6.3 §156) have long been recognized to be useless. The best reading there is *Πρῶτον*.

The name *Πέτρος* is not found in such lists as those given in the following places: F. Bechtel, *Die historischen Personennamen des Griechischen bis zur Kaiserzeit* (Halle, 1917; reprinted Hildesheim, 1964) (should be on pp. 370–1); L. Robert, *Noms indigènes dans l'Asie Mineure gréco-romaine: Première partie*, Bibliothèque archéologique et historique de l'Institut français d'archéologie d'Istanbul, 13 (Paris, 1963) (should be on p. 563). The entry on *Πέτρος* in W. Pape and G. Benseler, *Wörterbuch der griechischen Eigennamen* (Braunschweig, 1911; reprinted, Graz, 1959), pp. 1187–8, gives only Christian names, or those of pagans of the Christian period.

[7] See p. 121, n. 1 above.

Das Gleichnis von der ausgestreuten Saat und seine Deutung (Mk iv.3–8, 14–20)

FERDINAND HAHN

I

Die Gleichnisrede in Mk iv hat eine zentrale Funktion innerhalb des ältesten Evangeliums. Für den Verfasser geht es dabei um eine grundsätzliche Aussage über Jesu Verkündigung. Das Kapitel bildet die Mitte des ersten Teiles, der von i.14–viii.26 reicht und vor allem die Zuwendung Jesu zu dem Volk, das keinen Hirten hat, beinhaltet (vi.34). Die Gleichnisrede korrespondiert auf Grund ihrer Stellung im Aufbau der einzigen anderen großen Redekomposition des Markusevangeliums, der eschatologischen Unterweisung in c. xiii, die in der Mitte des Schlußteils xi.1–xvi.8 steht. Der zweite Teil des Evangeliums viii.27–x.52 ist vornehmlich der Jüngerbelehrung gewidmet, die nicht mit größeren Reden, sondern mit Hilfe kürzerer Spruchsammlungen und einzelner Aussagen in Verbindung mit Taten Jesu gestaltet ist.

Die literarkritische Analyse des Kapitels Mk iv ist im einzelnen schwierig.[1] Es ist eine alte Streitfrage, ob der Evangelist hier eine regelrechte Gleichnisrede übernommen oder eine lockere Sammlung verwendet oder ob er eventuell sogar verstreutes Gut aufgegriffen hat.[2] Eindeutig ist jedenfalls, daß das Gleichnis Mk iv.3–8 zusammen mit seiner Deutung in iv.14–20 dem Verfasser bereits vorgegeben war. Denn die sprachliche und inhaltliche Untersuchung von Mk iv.14–20 erweist, worauf zurückzukommen ist, daß keine typisch markinischen Elemente vorliegen, so sehr der Evangelist diese Gleichnisdeutung innerhalb seiner Gesamtkonzeption verwerten konnte. Die ausgesprochen paränetische Tendenz ist unverkennbar. Neben der eschatologi-

[1] Es sei hier nur verwiesen auf J. Jeremias, *Die Gleichnisse Jesu* (Göttingen, 1970[8]), S.9ff, und auf R. Pesch, *Das Markusevangelium I*, HThK II/1 (Freiburg i.B., 1976), S.225ff.

[2] Die Parallelüberlieferung in ThEv 9 bietet zur Entscheidung dieser Frage keine Hilfe und kann außer Betracht bleiben.

schen Orientierung der Gleichniserzählung Mk iv.3–8 bietet Mk iv.14–20 eine Applikation an die Glieder der Gemeinde.

Für den Evangelisten liegt der entscheidende Angelpunkt zum Verständnis der Gleichnisse in den Rahmenstücken Mk iv.1f, 10–13, 33f. Nicht nur die drei übernommenen Gleichniserzählungen iv.3–8, 26–9, 30–2, sondern auch die zu der iv.10 beginnenden Jüngerunterweisung gehörende Spruchgruppe in iv.21–5 will von den Rahmenstücken, vor allem von iv.11f her verstanden und erklärt sein. Damit rückt Mk die Gleichnisrede zugleich in den Zusammenhang mit der christologischen Thematik seines Evangeliums.

Was in diesem Beitrag zu Ehren des hochverdienten Kollegen, der sich in seinen umfangreichen und viele Gebiete erfassenden exegetischen Forschungen auch mit Fragen der Gleichnisauslegung befaßt hat,[1] untersucht werden soll, ist lediglich das Verhältnis von Mk iv.3–8 zu iv.14–20. Hier bestehen Probleme, die eine erneute Erörterung verdienen, während die von Mk iv.11f ausgehende Gesamtinterpretation des Gleichniskapitels seitens des Evangelisten nur im größeren Zusammenhang der markinischen Christologie behandelt werden könnte.

II

Sieht man von der griechischen Sprache und Ausdrucksweise ab, so ist in Mk iv.3–8 mit einem echten Jesusgleichnis zu rechnen,[2] an das die im Neuen Testament mehrfach begegnende Formel 'Wer Ohren hat zu hören, der höre' in iv.9 angeschlossen wurde.[3] A. Jülicher hat diesen Text in seinem grundlegenden Werk über Jesu Gleichnisreden den 'Parabeln' zugeordnet,[4] obwohl der Vorgang des Säens etwas Alltägliches und sich regelmäßig Wiederholendes ist, was eher seine eigene Näherbestimmung der 'Gleichnisse' (im engeren Sinn) kennzeichnet. G. Dalman hat darüber hinaus gezeigt, daß die Verhaltensweise des Sämanns nicht Ungeschick ist, sondern der früheren Technik der Feldbestellung in Palästina entspricht.[5] Aber es geht hier, was Jülicher mit guten Gründen berücksichtigt hat, zugleich um etwas

[1] M. Black, 'The Parables as Allegory', *BJRL* 42 (1959/60), S.273–87.

[2] Das ist in der neueren Forschung so gut wie allgemein anerkannt.

[3] Dazu verweise ich auf meinen Aufsatz: 'Die Sendschreiben der Johannesapokalypse', in: *Tradition und Glaube,* Festschrift für K. G. Kuhn (Göttingen, 1971), S.357–94, dort S.377ff.

[4] A. Jülicher, *Die Gleichnisreden Jesu,* II (Tübingen, 1898; Neudruck 1976), S.514–38.

[5] G. Dalman, 'Viererlei Acker', in: *Palästina-Jahrbuch 22* (1926), S.120–32; dazu ferner J. Jeremias, 'Palästinakundliches zum Gleichnis vom Säemann', *NTS* 13 (1966–7), S.48–53; ders., *Gleichnisse,* S.7ff.

Besonderes. Was ist das Besondere? Zweifellos das, wovon am Ende berichtet wird: der unwahrscheinlich große Ertrag – trotz des scheinbaren Mißerfolgs, von dem zuvor die Rede ist. Im Blick auf das Gleichnis insgesamt ist es allerdings abwegig, von Mißerfolg zu sprechen, wie das etwa J. Schniewind getan hat.[1] Das zeigt sich vor allem daran, daß der Schluß des Gleichnisses jeden in Palästina gewohnten Ertrag eines Feldes übersteigt. Mag ein sieben- bis zehnfacher Ertrag das Normale gewesen sein, ein dreißigfacher, sechzigfacher oder gar hundertfacher Ertrag ist unvorstellbar gewesen. Hier schlägt, worauf schon P. Fiebig und nach ihm vor allem J. Jeremias aufmerksam gemacht hat, die gemeinte Sache durch das Bild durch.[2]

Damit sind Grundfragen der Gleichnisauslegung und speziell dieses Gleichnisses berührt. Was zunächst die Struktur des Textes Mk iv.3–8 betrifft, so ist entgegen einer verbreiteten Auslegung nicht das Verhältnis 3:1, sondern das Verhältnis 3:3 maßgebend. Dies läßt sich durch eine philologische, gerade auch im griechischen Text des Markusevangeliums noch feststellbare Beobachtung stützen: es wird in iv.4 *ὃ μέν* gesagt, in iv.5 und iv.7 *καὶ ἄλλο*, während es dann in iv.8 *καὶ ἄλλα* heißt. Die meist wenig beachtete Unterscheidung von Singular und Plural ist offensichtlich sehr bewußt erfolgt, und in iv.3f, 4–6, 7 ist ebenso wie in iv.8 um der Konkretheit der Anschauung willen jeweils nur ein einzelnes Samenkorn mit seinem Halm und seiner Ähre in den Blick gefaßt.[3] Dies ist bei Matthäus, der regelmäßig den Plural gebraucht, und bei Lukas, der durchgängig den Singular verwendet, verwischt worden. Wie in den drei ersten Fällen geht es somit auch in iv.8 um drei einzelne Samenkörner und ihren dreißig- bzw. sechzig- oder hundertfachen Ertrag. In diesem Sinne wird im Schlußvers formuliert: *ἓν τριάκοντα καὶ ἓν ἑξήκοντα καὶ ἓν ἑκατόν*, wobei das dreimalige *ἕν* dem aramäischen חַד korrespondiert, wie der Jubilar in seinem grundlegenden Werk über den aramäischen Hintergrund der Evangelien und der Apostelgeschichte nachgewiesen hat.[4]

[1] J. Schniewind, *Das Evangelium nach Markus*, NTD 1 (Göttingen, 1949[5]), S.73f.

[2] P. Fiebig, *Die Gleichnisreden Jesu im Lichte der rabbinischen Gleichnisse des neutestamentlichen Zeitalters* (Tübingen, 1912), bes. S.127ff; Jeremias, *Gleichnisse*, S.16f, 149f.

[3] Diese Eigenart der Gleichniserzählung wird meist übersehen. So erklärt z. B. V. Taylor, *The Gospel according to St Mark* (London, 1952), S.252, *ὃ μέν* in iv.4 mit 'a part', *ἄλλο* in iv.5 und 7 mit 'another portion', während er dann überraschenderweise zu iv.8 sagt: '*ἄλλα* is used of the individual seeds'. Ebenso C. E. B. Cranfield, *The Gospel according to St Mark* (Cambridge, 1966[3]), S.149f.

[4] M. Black, *An Aramaic Approach to the Gospels and Acts* (Oxford, 1967[3]), S.90. Das dreimalige *ἕν* darf zudem als ursprünglicher Text angesehen werden (so auch das Greek New Testament).

Von hier aus ist festzustellen, daß der ausgestreute Same im Zentrum des Gleichnisses steht. Vom Samen und seinen Widerfahrnissen soll hier erzählt werden.[1] Die Bedingungen des jeweiligen Ackerlandes sind dem zu- und untergeordnet, der Sämann tritt demgegenüber völlig zurück.

Hinsichtlich der Gleichnisgestalt läßt zumindest der Schluß erkennen, daß die konsequente Trennung von Bild und Sache, wie sie Jülicher im Anschluß an die aristotelische Gleichnistheorie vorgenommen hat,[2] nicht haltbar ist.[3] Ob allerdings eine Unterscheidung von Bild und Sache überhaupt aufgegeben werden muß, wie E. Jüngel meint,[4] ist äußerst fraglich. Doch die innere Verklammerung von Bild und Sache ist in neutestamentlichen Gleichnissen zweifellos größer, als dies bei einer aus griechischen Prämissen abgeleiteten Gleichnistheorie der Fall ist, ohne daß damit die Unterscheidung von Gleichnis und Allegorie aufgegeben werden darf.[5]

Aber nicht erst am Ende des Gleichnisses von der ausgestreuten Saat zeigt sich die enge Verwobenheit von Bild und Sache. In der ganzen Erzählung geht es um das Geschick von einzelnen Samenkörnern. Auch wenn zu *ὃ μέν*, *καὶ ἄλλο* und *καὶ ἄλλα* als Bezugswort weder *τὸ σπέρμα* noch das Partizip *τὸ σπειρόμενον* in den Text aufgenommen ist, so ist doch der geschilderte Same ebenso wie die in iv.8 vorausgesetzte Ernte ein 'stehendes Bild' für Gottes wunderbares Handeln und seine Zukunft. Der von Schniewind eingeführte Terminus 'stehendes Bild'[6] will besagen, daß es nicht einfach wie bei einer Metapher um einen von vornherein übertragenen Gebrauch geht, wohl aber, daß innerhalb der Bildhälfte bei einzelnen Aussagen noch andere Bezüge und Dimensionen erkennbar werden.[7]

Hinzu kommt, daß die Gleichnisse Jesu keine allgemeinen religiösen

[1] Zu den verschiedenen Bezeichnungen des Gleichnisses vgl. Chr. Dietzfelbinger, 'Das Gleichnis vom ausgestreuten Samen', in: *Der Ruf Jesu und die Antwort der Gemeinde*, Festschrift für J. Jeremias (Göttingen, 1970), S.80–93, dort S.81ff. Er selbst betont mit Recht, daß das 'Schicksal des ausgestreuten Samens' die 'Mitte des Gleichnisgeschehens' sei.

[2] A. Jülicher, *Die Gleichnisreden Jesu*, I (Tübingen, 1899[2]; Neudruck, 1976), S.25ff, 69ff.

[3] Außer auf Jeremias, *Gleichnisse*, S.14ff, sei hierzu verwiesen auf T. W. Manson, *The Teaching of Jesus* (Cambridge, 1935[2]), S.57ff.

[4] E. Jüngel, *Paulus und Jesus* (Tübingen, 1932[4]), S.87ff, 130ff.

[5] Vgl. auch D. O. Via, *Die Gleichnisse Jesu*, BEvTh 57 (München, 1970), S.16ff.

[6] Schniewind, *Markus*, S.76f.

[7] Pesch, *Markusevangelium*, S.228ff, der eine Vielzahl von metaphorischen Elementen bzw. 'allegorischen Fingerzeigen' (S.234) annimmt, überschätzt deren Bedeutung. Er geht jedoch davon aus, daß das Gleichnis von vornherein auf die allegorische Deutung hin angelegt sei (S.229).

Wahrheiten zum Ausdruck bringen wollen, wie A. Jülicher annahm. Sie stehen, was vor allem C. H. Dodd betont hat, im Rahmen der eschatologischen Botschaft Jesu und haben ihrerseits eine unmittelbar eschatologische Intention.[1] Im Unterschied zu J. Jeremias wird man aber in Bezug auf Mk iv.3–8 und verwandte Gleichnisse sagen müssen, daß nicht der bloße 'Kontrast' von geringem Anfang und herrlichem Ende kennzeichnend ist,[2] sondern, wie gerade die Wachstumsgleichnisse erkennen lassen, die wunderbare, von Gott selbst bewirkte Dynamik, die vom bereits geschehenen Anfang zu dem großartigen Ende hinführt.[3] Hierauf hat N. A. Dahl mit seinem Beitrag zu dieser Gruppe von Gleichnissen mit Recht hingewiesen.[4]

Das tertium comparationis, nach dem unter allen Umständen gefragt werden muß, obwohl es dabei nicht ausschließlich um ein isoliertes Einzelmotiv gehen darf, ist eben jenes mit dem Ausstreuen des Samenkorns beginnende Geschehen, das trotz mancher widriger Umstände auf die Ernte hindrängt und einen reichen Ertrag mit sich bringen wird. Es geht also um eine Bewegung, die von diesem Anfang zu einem damit zusammengehörenden Ende führt, und die 'stehenden Bilder' Same und Ernte lassen sichtbar werden – ganz unabhängig von einer Einleitungsformel, die hier selbst in der redaktionellen Fassung fehlen kann – welcher Sachzusammenhang bei dieser Gleichniserzählung vor Augen steht.[5] Es geht um Gottes eschatologisches Handeln, das sich gegenwärtig in Welt und Geschichte ereignet und das trotz äußerer Widerstände zu einem herrlichen Ziel, der Vollendung des göttlichen Heils, hinführen wird. Weil es das eschatologische Gotteshandeln ist, erschließt es Zukunft und führt auf das Zukünftige hin. Das Gleichnis steht somit ganz im Zusammenhang und Dienst der

1 C. H. Dodd, *The Parables of the Kingdom* (London, 1936²), S.11ff.

2 Jeremias, *Gleichnisse*, S.145ff, 149f.

3 Das Bild vom Samen und dessen Keimen und Wachsen wird in biblischer Tradition niemals im modernen Sinn eines 'organischen' Vorgangs verstanden; vielmehr verweist es dort auf Gottes Eingreifen und wunderbares Handeln (vgl. z. B. 1 Kor xv.35ff).

4 N. A. Dahl, 'The Parables of Growth', *StTh* 5 (1951–2), S.132–66. Vgl. aber auch Black, 'The Parables as Allegory', S.278; er bezieht sich auf die eschatologische Interpretation des Gleichnisses und fährt dann fort: 'There is no need to deny this modern insight: it seems at the same time necessary, however, to recall that the bulk of the parable appears to be describing *not* the miraculous rise of the Kingdom under the symbol of the harvest, but the kind of reception the *mission* of the kingdom got.'

5 Abzulehnen ist die Auffassung von R. Bultmann, *Die Geschichte der synoptischen Tradition* (Göttingen, 1931² = 1970⁸) (mit Ergänzungsheft), S.216, daß der ursprüngliche Sinn des Gleichnisses unerkennbar geworden sei. E. Linnemann, *Die Gleichnisse Jesu* (Göttingen, 1961), S.123, urteilt ebenso und verzichtet deshalb auf eine Interpretation abgesehen von der Gleichnisdeutung.

Botschaft von der Gottesherrschaft. Es ist von Jesus selbst bezogen worden auf das sich durchsetzende Handeln Gottes zur Rettung der Menschen, nicht aber speziell auf das von ihm verkündigte Wort[1] oder gar auf seine Person.[2] Hier gilt, ohne daß der Satz verallgemeinert werden darf: die Gottesherrschaft kommt 'in den Gleichnissen Jesu als Gleichnis zur Sprache'.[3] Denn Wesen und Wirklichkeit der Gottesherrschaft ließen sich am unmittelbarsten und verständlichsten durch die Gleichnisrede verdeutlichen.[4]

III

Beurteilt man das Gleichnis von der ausgestreuten Saat so, wie eben dargelegt, ergeben sich etliche Konsequenzen für die genaue Bestimmung der Gleichnisdeutung in Mk iv.14–20. Trotz seiner gegenüber dem Gleichnis eigenständigen Tendenz und der unbestreitbar nachösterlichen Entstehung steht diese Deutung dem zugrundeliegenden Gleichnistext doch etwas näher, als in der neueren Exegese vielfach angenommen worden ist.[5]

Die Unterschiede sind natürlich deutlich: geht es iv.3–8 um Anbruch und Vollendung der Gottesherrschaft, so hier um das Wort, durch das die Gottesherrschaft angekündigt wird. Nicht die eschatologische Thematik steht im Vordergrund, sondern, wie eingangs schon erwähnt, das paränetische Anliegen; deshalb wird zum rechten Hören angehalten und vor falschem, leichtfertigem Tun gewarnt. Anders ausgedrückt: es geht nicht um die grundlegende Heilsverkündigung, sondern

[1] So neuerdings wieder Pesch, *Markusevangelium*, S.231ff. Vgl. z. B. auch A. M. Hunter, *Interpreting the Parables* (London, 1964²), S.46f.

[2] Die von Dietzfelbinger, 'Das Gleichnis vom ausgestreuten Samen', S.90ff, versuchte Deutung im Blick auf Jesu Sendung und Tod ist eine Überinterpretation, die nicht einmal durch Mk iv.14–20 gestützt wird. Daß Jesus derjenige ist, durch den sich der Anbruch der Gottesherrschaft ereignet, ist zwar unbestritten, wird aber hier ebensowenig wie in anderen Worten Jesu über die Gottesherrschaft thematisiert. Erst die nachösterliche Gemeinde hat dann auch den Zusammenhang von Jesu Person und der Verwirklichung des Heils expliziert, nicht jedoch in alle überkommenen Texte eingetragen.

[3] So Jüngel, *Paulus und Jesus*, S.173.

[4] Zur neueren Auslegung vgl. Dietzfelbinger, 'Das Gleichnis vom ausgestreuten Samen', S.83ff; R. Bultmann, 'Die Interpretation von Mk 4, 3–9 seit Jülicher', in: *Jesus und Paulus*, Festschrift für W. G. Kümmel (Göttingen, 1975), S.30–4.

[5] In jüngster Zeit wird bisweilen auch die umgekehrte Tendenz sichtbar, nämlich wegen der engen Zusammengehörigkeit von Gleichnis und Deutung beide für gleich ursprünglich zu halten; so B. Gerhardsson, 'The Parable of the Sower and its Interpretation', *NTS* 14 (1967–8), S.165–93. Auf die Frage eines Bezuges der Parabel auf die jüdische Auslegungstradition des Schᵉma gehe ich hier nicht ein.

um den rechten Umgang mit dem Gehörten im alltäglichen Leben der Jünger Jesu. Hat also iv.3–8 eine missionarische Intention, so ist iv.14–20 auf die Zurüstung und Stärkung der Gemeinde ausgerichtet. Auch Begrifflichkeit und sprachlicher Stil zeigen, wie eingehend J. Jeremias nachgewiesen hat, daß hier die nachösterliche Situation der Gemeinde vorausgesetzt ist.[1] Im übrigen ist bereits in dieser Deutung die für das Gleichnis selbst kennzeichnende Struktur 3:3 zugunsten des Verhältnisses 3:1 aufgegeben.

Seit Jülicher hat die exegetische Arbeit immer wieder festgestellt, in Mk iv.14–20 handle es sich um eine Umprägung des Gleichnisses in eine Allegorie.[2] Doch es ist sehr genau zu prüfen, was hier eigentlich vorliegt. Die Allegorie war der damaligen Zeit vertraut und zumindest von der sekundär an einen Text herangetragenen Allegorese wurde nicht nur im antiken Heidentum, sondern auch im hellenistischen Judentum und in der alten Kirche reichlich Gebrauch gemacht. Im Neuen Testament ist man in dieser Hinsicht zurückhaltender gewesen, obwohl sich auch hier allegorisierende Elemente in Einzelfällen nachweisen lassen.[3] Entscheidend für die urchristliche Tradition ist etwas anderes: der Übergang von der Gleichnisrede zur allegorisierenden Rede war allein schon wegen der fast regelmäßigen Verwendung stehender Bilder durchaus fließend.

Speziell in Mk iv.14–20 liegt keineswegs eine durchgängige Übertragung aller Einzelmotive vor.[4] Weder das Aufpicken durch die Vögel noch das Versengt- und Ersticktwerden des Samens wird gedeutet, das Fehlen tiefer Erde bleibt unübertragen, ebenso das Aufgehen und Wachsen des Samens in iv.8 oder die Zahlen am Ende des Gleichnisses; vor allem bleibt der Sämann ungedeutet.[5] Die ausschlaggebende inhaltliche Festlegung liegt darin, daß der Same auf den *λόγος*, das verkündigte Wort, bezogen wird. Da *ὁ λόγος* terminus technicus der Missionssprache ist,[6] erhält in diesem Zusammenhang das beibehaltene *σπείρειν* einen prägnanten Sinn[7] und die Bedeutung eines ‘stehenden

[1] Jeremias, *Gleichnisse*, S.75ff. Vgl. auch Taylor, *Mark*, S.258, 261. Eine gute Übersicht über Gründe und Gegengründe findet sich bei Cranfield, *Mark*, S.158ff.

[2] Interessanterweise hat Jülicher, *Gleichnisreden*, II, S.532ff, in dieser Hinsicht bei Mk iv.14–20 sehr vorsichtig geurteilt.

[3] Hierhin gehören z. B. Gal iv.21ff; 1 Kor x.4b.

[4] Die Deutung der Unkrautparabel in Mt xiii.36–43 ist in dieser Hinsicht viel konsequenter.

[5] Auf diese Tatbestände hat schon Jülicher, *Gleichnisreden*, II, S.534, verwiesen.

[6] Innerhalb des Markusevangeliums ist zu verweisen auf i.45; ii.2; iv.33. Aus der Briefliteratur seien nur 1 Thess i.6 und Gal vi.6 erwähnt.

[7] Vgl. die zumindest ähnliche Verwendung des Wortes in 1 Kor ix.11.

Bildes'.[1] Alle anderen Motive, soweit sie überhaupt gedeutet werden, sind auf dieses Ausstreuen des Wortes bezogen.

Bei der Deutung des Samens auf das verkündigte Wort kommt es dann allerdings auch zu bemerkenswerten Verschiebungen. Im Gleichnis geht es um den ausgestreuten und im Ackerboden keimenden und wachsenden Samen. Dabei spielt die Beschaffenheit des Bodens zwar eine gewisse Rolle, aber in der Auslegung gewinnt nun der Ackerboden eine verstärkte und selbständige Bedeutung. Statt des Samens, der auf den Weg, das Steinige, unter die Dornen oder auf den guten Boden fällt, wird hier von denen gesprochen, die ihrerseits am Wege, auf dem Steinigen, unter den Dornen bzw. auf gutem Boden sind und das ausgestreute Wort hören und annehmen, zum Teil aber auch nach einiger Zeit wieder preisgeben.[2] In iv.15a wird das Bild vom Säen insofern noch korrekt beibehalten, als hier formuliert ist: *οὗτοι δέ εἰσιν οἱ παρὰ τὴν ὁδόν, ὅπου σπείρεται ὁ λόγος* (vgl. iv.15fin.). In iv.16, 18, 20 ist das Bild dann aber wesentlich verschoben, wenn nicht mehr vom Ausstreuen des Wortes, sondern von den hörenden Menschen als den auf den Weg, das Steinige, unter die Dornen und auf das gute Land 'Ausgesäten' (*οἱ σπειρόμενοι* bzw. *οἱ σπαρέντες*) gesprochen wird.[3] Dieser Verschiebung entspricht, daß statt vom 'Fallen' des Samens jetzt vom 'Hören' (*ἀκούειν*) bzw. 'Annehmen' (*λαμβάνειν, παραδέχεσθαι*) die Rede ist.

Nach der bisherigen Untersuchung ist also festzustellen, daß neben ungedeuteten Motiven zunächst der Begriff *ὁ λόγος* als Deutekategorie eingeführt und in Verbindung mit *σπείρειν* an die Stelle des Samenkorns gesetzt worden ist. Dies hat am Anfang noch zu keiner Veränderung des Bildes geführt. Dagegen hat die Einführung des Korrelatbegriffs *ἀκούειν* (bzw. *λαμβάνειν* oder *παραδέχεσθαι*) jene Verschiebung der Bildmotive nach sich gezogen.[4]

[1] Bis zu einem gewissen Grad gilt dies natürlich auch für *ὁ σπείρων*. Aber daß der Sämann ungedeutet bleibt, besagt für diese Gleichnisauslegung, daß es unwesentlich ist, wer das Wort ausstreut. Vgl. A. E. J. Rawlinson, *The Gospel according to St Mark* (London, 1925), S.53: 'The "sower" is in no specific sense our Lord; he is any preacher of the Gospel.'

[2] Matthäus und Lukas haben diese Inkongruenz empfunden und in je verschiedener Weise behoben.

[3] Daß die Veränderung nicht unbemerkt blieb, zeigt das in Mk. iv.16 aufgenommene *ὁμοίως*. Jeremias, *Gleichnisse*, S.77, erklärt den Sachverhalt damit, daß zwei verschiedene Gedanken aufgenommen seien: einerseits der Vergleich des göttlichen Wortes mit Gottes Saat (IV Esra ix.31), andererseits der Vergleich der Menschen mit Gottes Pflanzung (IV Esra viii.41 u. ö.). Aber damit ist lediglich auf die Ermöglichung der Verschiebung, nicht auf deren eigentlichen Grund hingewiesen.

[4] Die von E. Biser, *Die Gleichnisse Jesu* (München, 1965), S.51ff, stark betonte 'Rolle des Hörers' und die Bedeutung des Hörens als 'Vernehmen' gilt zweifellos für die Gleichnisdeutung, nicht aber für das ursprüngliche Jesusgleichnis.

Um nun im einzelnen zu beschreiben, wie es nach anfänglichem Hören einerseits zu Abfall, andererseits zu reichem Fruchtbringen kommt, werden Einzelmotive der Gleichniserzählung allegorisierend ausgedeutet, so die Vögel in iv.15 auf den Satan, der mangelnde Boden in iv.16f auf die Wurzellosigkeit bei Drangsal und Verfolgung, die Dornen in iv.18f auf die weltlichen Sorgen, die verführerische Macht des Reichtums und sonstige begehrliche Wünsche. In iv.20 dagegen bleibt das *καρποφορεῖν – ἓν τριάκοντα καὶ ἓν ἑξήκοντα καὶ ἓν ἑκατόν* erhalten und gewinnt nun einen übertragenen Charakter, was beim sonstigen Gebrauch von *καρπός* und *καρποφορεῖν* im Urchristentum durchaus begreiflich ist.[1]

So liegt in Mk iv.14–20 ein Gebilde sui generis vor. Einerseits ist das Bemühen erkennbar, die Gleichnishandlung beizubehalten und in wichtigen Einzelzügen nicht auszudeuten. Andererseits wird das Bestreben deutlich, bestimmte Motive inhaltlich festzulegen. Aber es fehlen eben auch Verschiebungen und allegorisierende Tendenzen nicht.

Natürlich kann man die Frage stellen, ob nicht schon die Gleichsetzung des ausgestreuten Samens mit dem verkündigten Wort eine Allegorisierung sei. Das hängt von der exakten Definition des Begriffes 'Allegorie' ab. Dabei geht es keineswegs bloß um eine Ermessensfrage hinsichtlich terminologischer Kennzeichnung.[2] Denn Allegorisierung setzt die Uneigentlichkeit der Bildrede voraus, was in Mk iv.14–20 mit der Einführung von *ὁ λόγος* nicht intendiert ist. Das vorgegebene Gleichnis soll zwar in einem bestimmten Sinn festgelegt und unmißverständlich ausgedeutet werden.[3] Dabei werden weitere Deutekategorien aufgenommen, die zum Teil sogar das Bild etwas verändern. Dennoch dominiert die gleichnishafte Rede mit ihren stehenden Bildern, und die zweifellos vorhandenen allegorischen Elemente bleiben dem unter-

[1] Vgl. zu Mk iv.20 im besonderen noch H. W. Kuhn, *Ältere Sammlungen im Markusevangelium*, *StUNT* 8 (Göttingen, 1971), S.117ff, 120f.

[2] Es bestehen grundsätzliche Bedenken gegen eine allzu weite Fassung des Begriffs 'Allegorie', wie sie etwa bei A. H. McNeile, *The Gospel according to St Matthew* (London, 1915), S.186, vorliegt: 'When more than one truth is illustrated (in a parable) the picture approaches an allegory, and it is not always certain which details are intended to illustrate something, and which are merely part of the scenic framework. The tendency to allegorize every detail, seen notably in Philo, but also in Christian writers, e.g. Origen and Hilary, often led to strained, and even grotesque methods of interpretation' (zitiert bei Black, *Parables as Allegory*, S.287).

[3] C. F. D. Moule, 'Mark 4:1–20 yet once more', in: *Neotestamentica et Semitica*, Studies in Honour of M. Black (Edinburgh, 1969), S.95–113, spricht S.109 von einer 'multiple parable', die in Mk iv.14–20 expliziert werde, weswegen es nicht korrekt sei, dort von 'allegorisierender Applikation' zu sprechen.

geordnet. Gerade weil Bild und Sache nicht voneinander getrennt werden können, wie schon das Gleichnis selber zeigt, kann in dieser Gleichnisdeutung der Sachbezug stärker und deutlicher hervorgehoben werden. Sicher nähert sich die Deutung des Gleichnisses von der ausgestreuten Saat schon der Allegorie. Aber gerade weil die Grenzen zwischen Gleichnis, stehenden Bildern und Allegorie nicht so eindeutig festzulegen sind, bedarf es in jedem Einzelfall einer sehr präzisen Beschreibung des im Text vorliegenden Tatbestandes.

In Mk iv.14–20 hat sich inhaltlich die Erfahrung der ersten Christen niedergeschlagen, und dementsprechend wurde auch urkirchliche Terminologie verwendet. Der Akzent hat sich dabei vom Eschatologischen auf das Paränetische und auf den ekklesiologischen Aspekt verlagert.[1] Aber so wenig die zugrundeliegende Gleichniskonzeption zugunsten einer Allegorie einfach aufgegeben wäre, so wenig ist bei dem hier vorausgesetzten Verständnis des verkündigten und gehörten Wortes die eschatologische Dimension der ursprünglichen Gleichniserzählung ausgeschlossen. Gleichnis und Gleichnisdeutung bedingen sich insofern gegenseitig. Die Deutung, obwohl nicht gleichzeitig entstanden und in der Absicht durchaus verschieden, zieht die Linien der Gleichniserzählung weiter aus, um diese auf die Situation der Gemeinde nach Ostern anzuwenden.

[1] E. Schweizer, *Das Evangelium nach Markus*, NTD 1 (Göttingen, 1975[4]), S.48f verweist im besonderen darauf, daß die Jünger von Blindheit und Unglauben nicht ausgenommen sind.

Jesus and Josephus' 'messianic prophets'

DAVID HILL

In several of his writings on the Qumran Scrolls and Christian origins Matthew Black has referred approvingly to D. E. Nineham's view that one of the few approaches left to us to the complex problem of Christian beginnings is to seek 'to wring truth relevant to the history of Jesus from the increasing stock of the remains of the Judaism of his time'.[1] In this essay, by means of which I am privileged to thank him both for his outstanding contribution, as author and editor, to New Testament scholarship and for twenty-five years of warm personal friendship and encouragement, I wish to follow the approach Professor Black has commended, by seeking some information relevant to the search for the historical Jesus from a long available, but often and unwisely neglected, Jewish source, Josephus' reports about 'messianic prophets'[2] of the first half of the first century A.D.

I

Why have New Testament scholars – with a few distinguished exceptions – disregarded the comparative value of Josephus' accounts of these 'messianic prophets' for understanding Jesus' ministry? One reason may be distrust of Josephus' reliability as an historian. Admittedly, since he was writing for Greek readers, some allowance must be made for his desire to accommodate Jewish thought and customs to Greek ideas and institutions. Nevertheless Josephus' reputation as an accurate recorder of events has been enhanced by what is now known from Masada, and the *War* (written *c.* A.D. 75), being much more carefully composed than the *Antiquities* (*c.* A.D. 95), provides an account whose substantial reliability there is no reason to doubt. Whatever may be said about

[1] *JTS* XI (1960), p. 260.

[2] The phrase 'messianic prophets' is derived from R. Meyer, *TDNT* VI, p. 826. Josephus knows also of prophets among the Essenes (*War* ii.159) and the Pharisees (*Ant.* xvii.43ff).

Josephus' imperfections as an historian, it must be conceded that his main weakness was not discreditable, namely that he wrote with the intention of eulogizing his people. Deeply influenced though he was by the cultural milieu of Hellenism, Josephus wrote as a Jew and remained a Jew throughout – a fact which, though obvious from his concern about theocracy, is frequently overlooked.

A more important reason for the neglect of Josephus' records about first-century 'messianic prophets' is the widespread use of the 'criterion of dissimilarity' as the primary and authoritative principle by which to establish what is authentic in Jesus' ministry and, in particular, his teaching. If discerningly used, this criterion may give us a collection of sayings concerning whose genuineness we may be fairly confident, but those sayings will not necessarily represent the heart of Jesus' teaching or express his characteristic thought. Only a seriously distorted view of Jesus results from an emphasis upon what is peculiar, discontinuous and unique about him and his teaching. To say that 'we can only feel ourselves to be on safe ground where a tradition cannot be derived from a Jewish environment'[1] is to presuppose that Jesus' message and ministry owed nothing to the Jewish culture, tradition and movements of his time, a presupposition which fails to acknowledge the correctness of N. A. Dahl's assertion that 'the criterion of dissimilarity should only be used in conjunction with historical considerations of synchronic similarity and diachronic continuity'.[2] The simple fact that Jesus did not write down his proclamation nor request his disciples to preserve it in writing differentiates him from the prophet-like teacher at Qumran who was probably directly responsible for some of the writings of that community and from (later) Jewish apocalyptic prophets who wrote down their 'revelations': but Dahl's advice compels us to explore Jesus' relationship to other prophets,[3] whose messages required a similar 'oral' communication or visible authentication.

We turn therefore to consider Josephus' reports about 'messianic prophets' of the first half of the first Christian century. None of these figures is described as having explicitly claimed the status or title of Messiah: the term *Χριστός* appears only in the much-debated allusions to Jesus (*Ant.* xviii.63; xx.200), and *War* vi.312 is the only reference to

[1] H. Zahrnt, *The Historical Jesus* (London, 1963), p. 107.

[2] N. A. Dahl, *Jesus in the Memory of the Early Church* (Minneapolis, 1976), p. 172.

[3] The assumption that Jesus was a prophet hardly needs justification. The Gospels attest his recognition as such by others and imply its propriety to his self-understanding (Mk vi.4; Luke xiii.33). Less widely accepted, but still quite defensible, is the view that Jesus' eschatology was prophetic, rather than apocalyptic.

the Jewish expectation of a future, and presumably, messianic world ruler. But from Josephus' consistent silence (for apologetic reasons ?) about the messianic hopes of his people it cannot be concluded that the expectation of an ideal figure, sent by God (king, priest or prophet), played no part in the thought and actions of individuals and groups he describes. As M. de Jonge reminds us, '*Messianismus ohne Messias*' was a recognized phenomenon at the turn of the centuries[1]: consequently some of the leaders of rebellion against Rome – like Menahem who assumed royal apparel (*War* ii.444) or Judas ben Ezechias who espoused kingly ambitions (*Ant.* xvii.272) – may have been interpreted by their adherents as messianic aspirants. In other words, Josephus was unable to excise from his chronicle references to *implicit* messianism, a phenomenon associated with, among others in the first century, certain prophet-like figures.

We begin with Judas the Galilean who owes his place in history to his reaction to the census of Judaea by Quirinius in A.D. 6–7.[2] There is no need to set out again what Josephus tells us about this figure and the 'fourth philosophy' he founded, which, according to *War* ii.118, had nothing in common with the other three (Pharisees, Sadducees and Essenes), but, according to *Ant.* xviii.23, 'agreed in all other respects with the opinions of the Pharisees, except that they are convinced that God alone is their leader and master'. It was this deeply-held conviction that impelled Judas (assisted by a Pharisee named Saddouk[3]) to incite his countrymen to rebel against the assessment for taxation which was tantamount to an acknowledgment of Roman overlordship and therefore an act of disloyalty to God (*Ant.* xviii.4–5).

Judas is nowhere called by Josephus a 'brigand'. Two of his sons were crucified in A.D. 46 for revolutionary activities (*Ant.* xx.102), and a third, Menahem, was murdered in A.D. 66 as he entered the Temple to worship, followed by armed Zealots (*War* ii.444): but only if their father is identified with the Judas who seized arms from Herod's arsenal (in 4 B.C.) and who was the son of the Galilean arch-brigand, Ezechias, who was executed by Herod (*c.* 47 B.C.),[4] is there a *prima facie* case for sug-

[1] M. de Jonge, 'Josephus und die Zukunftserwartungen seines Volkes', *Josephus-Studien, Festschrift* for O. Michel (Göttingen, 1974), p. 216.

[2] Cf. M. Black, 'Judas of Galilee and Josephus's "Fourth Philosophy"', *Josephus-Studien*, pp. 45–54.

[3] Of this Pharisee we know nothing more: has he been introduced by Josephus in order to affirm the continuity of Judas' attitude with Pharisaic opposition to any method of acknowledging allegiance to Roman power (cf. *Ant.* xvii.42) ? On his possible priestly connections, see G. R. Driver, *The Judean Scrolls* (Oxford, 1965), pp. 226f and M. Black, *Josephus-Studien*, p. 52.

[4] Circumstantial evidence for the identification is presented by J. S. Kennard,

gesting that Judas the Galilean was actively involved in banditry. In *War* vii.254 Josephus states that the Sicarii ('dagger-men') came into or were in existence in A.D. 6 when Judas urged rebellion, yet, according to *War* ii.253–7, the Sicarii arose in A.D. 54 in the time of Felix's procuratorship. It is probable that the terrorists of the mid-fifties were called 'Sicarii' by the Romans (as a kind of nickname) and that the designation was taken over by Jews (including Josephus) and its reference extended so that it became a general name for insurgents, including those who had responded to Judas' incitement in A.D. 6. 'Zealots' is not used as a party-name till A.D. 66, but before that this typical Jewish-religious term *ζηλωταί* – with its ancient and honourable ancestry in the theology of zeal, inspired by Phineas and Elijah – was employed to designate various rebel groups who were at one in their aim, to free God's people (Israel) from the Roman yoke and to cleanse the holy land of all transgressors of the Law and traitors.[1] This is the religio-political inspiration for the activities of *all* those who resisted Roman occupation and oppression. With good reason Josephus describes Judas as a *σοφιστής*, that is, probably a teacher, learned in Torah, perhaps even a rabbi, who used his position to persuade, incite, arouse, urge or encourage – and these are the verbs Josephus consistently uses of his activity – his fellow Jews to rebel, on religious grounds, against the ominous signs of Roman domination. In short, Judas provided the credo on which active resistance was based, what Hengel calls 'eine theokratische Ideologie des Freiheitskampfes',[2] and which may legitimately be classed as prophetic, in affirming the sole and total lordship of God over his people – a radicalization of the first commandment – and in promising divine help to those who would rid the land of foreign or disloyal transgressors.

Josephus' association of Judas' 'philosophy' with Pharisaism seems well founded,[3] but concerning any messianic expectation among the

'Judas of Galilee and his Clan', *JQR* XXXVI (1945–6), pp. 281–6, but scholars appear to be fairly evenly divided on the question. It would have suited Josephus' purpose well to have made the identification clear, if it had been correct: in persuading the Romans of the loyalty of most Jews he could have suggested that the inspiration of the entire revolutionary agitation against Rome sprang from one Galilean family which maintained a kind of dynastic succession in brigandage for over a century.

[1] The best recent treatment of the relationship between the Sicarii and the Zealots is by M. Hengel, 'Zeloten und Sikarier', *Josephus-Studien*, pp. 175–96. Cf. also H. Merkel, 'Zealots', IDB (Supplementary volume: 1976), pp. 979–82.

[2] Hengel, *Josephus-Studien*, p. 180.

[3] They were at one in refusing to acknowledge Roman suzerainty, for when Herod (*c.* 7 B.C.) required the whole Jewish people to take an oath of allegiance to Augustus and to the king's government over 6,000 Pharisees refused

Pharisees (to be shared by Judas and his followers) Josephus is silent. The silence may be attributed to his accuracy[1] or his diplomacy in writing: but a strong hope for the coming of a 'political' messiah of David's line is witnessed to in Ps. Sol. xvii and xviii, and these are regarded by many as emanating from Pharisaic circles in the middle of the first century B.C. Did these hopes, if ever widespread, wane with changing circumstances and fail to become an integral part of Pharisaic doctrine? It is most unlikely that Judas the Galilean advanced messianic claims for himself, and it is improbable that his philosophy's 'almost unconquerable passion for freedom' (*Ant.* xviii.44) implied a hope for liberty under some messianic deliverer, since it accepted God alone as leader and lord. Judas was not a messianic pretender, but he could be described as a charismatic teacher who, standing in the line of prophets, not only affirmed and longed for God's absolute sovereignty over his holy people, but also expected and promised its imminent realization, assisted by violent, human action.

We may pass quickly over the report concerning a Samaritan who (*c.* A.D. 35) wanted to gather his people to Mount Gerizim in order to produce the sacred vessels traditionally hidden there by Moses (*Ant.* xviii.85ff). Obviously this miracle was intended to authenticate the man's claim to be the initiator of a new, ideal Mosaic age, of a messianic character, for the Samaritans believed that the *Ta'eb* (Messiah-Restorer) would reveal the hidden vessels. But the affair was swiftly and ruthlessly dealt with by the procurator Pilate.

Much more significant is the action and claim of Theudas (*Ant.* xx.97ff). During the procuratorship of C. Fadus (A.D. 44–6) this magician or deceiver (γόης) persuaded a large number to follow him to Jordan, for he claimed to be a προφήτης and asserted that, at his command, the waters would part and let them pass to the other side. The miracle by which this prophetic claimant would be accredited was to be an eschatological re-enactment of the crossing of the river under Joshua (Jos. iii.15ff) and was perhaps intended to be the first stage in a fresh conquest of the land and the capital for God and his people. But Fadus regarded the enterprise as politically dangerous, crushed it and eventually beheaded its leader. This pseudo-prophet Theudas is mentioned in Acts v.36 in a Lucan speech attributed to Gamaliel I and therefore having

to comply (*Ant.* xvii.42). There is no need to view Judas' 'philosophy' as a splinter-group or militant left-wing of Pharisaism.

[1] E. Rivkin, 'The Meaning of Messiah in Jewish Thought', *USQR* XXVI (1970–1), pp. 383–406, claims that the Pharisees never emphasized the messianic concept prior to A.D. 70, even when events occurred which lent themselves admirably to the affirmation of such a doctrine (pp. 394–5).

a putative date of at least a decade before the actual appearance of Theudas, who, in the speech, is mentioned as preceding Judas the Galilean. However we explain or reconcile the divergence between Acts v and Josephus' accounts,[1] what is of interest is that the followers of Jesus are compared with the supporters of Judas and Theudas, both of whom had, temporarily or sporadically, clashed with Roman political interests in Palestine. When Luke has Gamaliel say that Theudas 'claimed to be somebody (λέγων εἶναί τινα ἑαυτόν)' we may have an implicit witness to his messianic pretensions.

Under the procuratorship of Felix (A.D. 52–60) the Sicariot terrorist activities began (*War* ii.254ff), but a prophetic movement arose as well whose members almost certainly interacted with the guerrillas: at least their different brands of fanaticism produced a common effect, that of stirring up the people. The most notorious case was that of 'the Egyptian' (*War* ii.261; *Ant.* xx.169), a Jew who proclaimed himself a prophet and assembled in the wilderness a large band of supporters whom he intended to lead to the Mount of Olives, promising that at his command the walls of Jerusalem would fall and that they would enter the city and overpower the Roman force. Felix did not give the prophet time to stage his repeat performance of Joshua's miraculous capture of Jericho, but quickly quelled the rising. The Egyptian himself escaped and disappeared, but it is likely that the people believed this to be a miraculous deliverance and hoped for his return. Acts xxi.38 refers to this when Paul is mistaken for this Egyptian, who, Luke says, was the leader of 4,000 Sicarii. What the Egyptian and Theudas sought to accomplish to substantiate their claim seems to be the liberation of Israel. Since their claim of prophecy could be made only within the context of events heralding the messianic times (when the prophetic spirit was expected to be active again), we may justifiably suggest that these two individuals, at least, believed themselves to be involved in the imminent messianic release of the nation.[2]

Finally, we turn to the account of John the Baptist (*Ant.* xviii.116–19). Josephus' version of John's teaching and of the nature of his baptism – a rite of purification or consecration, and not for the remission of sins – may be adapted to Graeco-Roman taste, and the Gospels possibly strike a more authentic note: but it is not at all improbable that Josephus is right in asserting that John's imprisonment and death were due to Herod Antipas' fear that his popularity among the Jews might lead to

[1] For the main possibilities and a fresh suggestion (based on the reading of Codex Bezae) see M. Black, *Josephus-Studien*, pp. 48–9.

[2] Cf. Strack–Billerbeck, II, p. 480.

civil unrest.[1] The impact of John as a prophetic preacher was primarily religious, but, at a time when a large proportion of the Jews was unable to differentiate between religious and political hopes, John and his following could scarcely have avoided being regarded by the authorities as a potential source of political disturbance.

II

The prophets described above – some of them rightly deserving the epithet 'messianic' – were obviously convinced that the inauguration of the eschatological age of God's sovereignty would correspond to the early history of Israel (hence the wilderness and Moses/Joshua typologies), that the age of salvation was imminent, and that they were called to bring matters to a head. They were exponents of the imminent expectation of the *national* eschatology (*die Endzeit*). The similarities of many of the characteristics of these Palestinian prophets and their movements with features of primitive portions of the Synoptic (and perhaps the Johannine) tradition are patently clear: the working of miracles and signs, the wilderness setting, the gathering on the Mount of Olives, and possibly the rite of baptism. Should such similarities be excluded, on the principle of dissimilarity, in the attempt to discover the authentic setting of Jesus and his teaching? No: these similarities can and should be used in order to establish the appropriate context to which the eschatological prophecy of Jesus belongs. What is distinctive, as well as what is characteristic, in Jesus' ministry must be argued within this context, rather than (or, at least as much as) in comparison with the expectations of messianic figures in Jewish apocalyptic literature.

The limits of this essay allow us only to indicate briefly some of the consequences of such an exploration.

(1) Jesus' proclamation of the imminent coming of the Kingdom of God, the realization of the divine sovereignty in righteousness, would no longer appear as an unusual feature in his message, since it seems that it is similar to the convictions of Theudas, the Egyptian, John the Baptist and others: nevertheless, it is most surely historical, in spite of this similarity.

(2) If we had carried our examination of 'messianic prophets' a little further towards A.D. 70 we would have discovered that one of the most important elements in first-century messianism was the inevitable

[1] Is it a mere coincidence that the Fourth Gospel attributes an almost identical motive to the priestly plot against Jesus (John xi.47–50)?

destruction of the Temple (cf. *War* vi.301).[1] It is therefore not improbable that Jesus' decision to go to Jerusalem and his sayings about the Temple should be interpreted against this background. Aware of the guilt of Israel and its national apostasy, was he not also aware of its coming tragic dénouement, and, with prophetic insight, affirming the messianic scenario of the Holy Place in ruins (Mk xiii.1–2) ?[2] Not every reference to the destruction of the Temple necessitates a date *post eventum*.

(3) Several of Josephus' 'messianic prophets' worked, or promised to work, authenticating miracles or signs. Their activity is of considerable interest for investigations of the prophetic ideology in the Fourth Gospel and of the form and content of the postulated *Sēmeia*-source, but they have significance for the investigation of the historical Jesus as well. Having set out the evidence for charismatic, miracle-working figures in Judaism roughly contemporary with Jesus, including some of those described above, and having drawn attention in this connection to the expectation of the 'prophet like Moses', which is reflected in New Testament Christology, G. Vermes rightly regards these figures who raised hopes of God's deliverance of his people and performed remarkable deeds as relevant to the historical understanding of Jesus.[3] It is probable that we ought not to exclude altogether the possibility that some of Jesus' miracles and actions were intended and/or understood to be authenticating signs of his authoritative teaching and claim to be a charismatic prophet. This may be confirmed by Mk i.27 (after an exorcism): '"Here is a teaching that is new", they said, "and with authority behind it: he gives orders even to unclean spirits and they obey him"' (JerB). Prophetic authority is again the issue between Jesus and the priests, scribes and elders (Mk xi.27–33) after the cleansing of the Temple, a prophetic act symbolizing divine judgment.[4]

(4) If the religio-political situation in which the 'messianic prophets' were active forms the background of the events of the Gospel narrative, it is not without significance that Jesus and his movement emerged from Galilee, the home of staunch nationalism and an area whose orthodoxy was constantly suspect within the Jerusalemite religious establishment.

1 Cf. F. Dexinger, 'Ein "Messianisches Szenarium" als Gemeingut des Judentums in nachherodianischer Zeit ?', *Kairos* XVII (1975), pp. 249–78.

2 Cf. G. B. Caird, *Jesus and the Jewish Nation* (London, 1965), pp. 11f.

3 G. Vermes, *Jesus the Jew* (London, 1973), pp. 58–99.

4 The refusal by Jesus of the Pharisees' demand for 'a sign from heaven' (Mk viii.11–13) is, as in the temptation-narratives, a refusal to put God to the test: many authenticating signs (δυνάμεις) of Jesus' understanding of liberating power were in fact given to those able to recognize them; the Pharisees *demand* a proof of their own choosing.

We can hardly avoid the issue posed by Brandon:

> How far the career of Jesus, which brought him to his tragic end on Calvary, is to be regarded as an episode in that resistance movement to Roman suzerainty which was started by Judas of Galilee in A.D. 6, and which ended in A.D. 73 with the resolute refusal of the tortured Sicarii to acknowledge Caesar as Lord, is not easily to be estimated. Zealotism produced a long roll of martyrs for Israel's freedom, and there are some aspects of Jesus' career which would seem to entitle him to a place among them.[1]

Although Brandon argues forcefully for the close association of Jesus and revolutionary zealotism, the case ultimately fails to convince. There is more than enough in the Gospel tradition of Jesus' teaching (e.g. Matt. xxvi.52; Mk xii.16f) and attitude that is utterly contrary to the methods, spirit and aims of political zealotism to outweigh the few and ambiguous suggestions that Jesus embraced it.[2] Even though he may have been prosecuted and sentenced as a rebel, and even though some of his Galilean followers seem to have expected him to fulfil *their* nationalistic messianic and political aspirations (Mk xi.9f; Luke xix.37f; cf. also Acts i.6), Jesus was not a revolutionary zealot: but could he perhaps be claimed – on the basis of texts such as Matt. x.34; Luke xii.49 and xxii.53, and in the tradition of Qumran 'zealotry' derived from Exod. xxxii.27–9 and Deut. xiii.7–12 – as an apocalyptic zealot, proclaiming a spiritual warfare, not against the Romans, but against the forces of Belial and all his followers in heaven and on earth, even within families, a warfare whose final act is the Last Judgment upon a godless world? This view of O. Betz[3] has been taken up by Professor Black,[4] but since, in my view, Jesus' eschatology was prophetic rather than apocalyptic, it seems more likely that the 'zealotic' phrases that may be attributed, with reasonable certainty, to Jesus suggest that he was drawing upon the ancient and noble tradition of 'zeal' – which originally inspired men like Judas of Galilee before it became transmuted into a violent and political ideology – zeal for the sole and supreme sovereignty of God, for God's covenant (and that included his love, *hesed̲*) and God's word, with, as corollary, warning and threats against the unfaithfulness and unrighteousness of Israel: the fact that Mic. vii.6 stands behind Matt. x.34 may support this view. In short, Jesus, though no political zealot, affirmed

[1] S. G. F. Brandon, *Jesus and the Zealots* (Manchester, 1967), pp. 354f.
[2] E.g. Luke xii.36 probably alludes to prudential measures for self-defence.
[3] O. Betz, 'Jesu Heiliger Krieg', *NT* II (1957–8), pp. 116–37.
[4] M. Black, *Josephus-Studien*, p. 54, and *ET* LXXX (1969–70), pp. 115–18.

or reaffirmed the honoured 'theology of zeal' with prophetic fervour and expected to suffer the almost inevitable fate of the prophet – persecution and martyrdom (by stoning ?) – though, in fact, he was crucified as a pernicious revolutionary.

(5) Whether Jesus made a messianic claim for himself is almost impossibly difficult to decide. The evidence of the Passion narratives may permit us to say no more than that he reluctantly refused to disown the title when forced to give an answer to Pilate at his trial, and therefore allowed himself to be condemned for claiming to be Messiah. If this claim was interpreted by those who accused and sentenced him as tantamount to 'rebel leader', how was it understood by Jesus himself ? Most scholars who allow that Jesus made a messianic claim assume that his conception of Messiahship was deeply influenced by the Isaianic Servant-songs. But, even if the difficulties that surround this assumption are solved, is it not likely that Jesus drew into his conception of Messiahship elements from the political and religious atmosphere he breathed, elements from the Jewish tradition and from the revolutionary enthusiasm of his day which, perhaps, he never fully isolated or refined ? If Jesus really belonged to his first-century Jewish milieu, it seems impossible to deny this likelihood. This would not mean that he was or wanted to be the nationalistic Messiah of a revolutionary front: it would mean that his consciousness of a divinely appointed mission to Israel was deeply imbued with the theocratic ideal, with God's covenant-loyalty and the demand for righteousness. These were not the concerns solely of the revered heroes of the zealots' tradition (Elijah and Phineas) but of virtually all Old Testament prophets. And, it should be noted, from the point of view of nationalistic *self-interest* the prophets were traitors, and were often so regarded by many of their contemporaries. Perhaps the weakest point in Brandon's case for a Jesus who is hardly distinguishable from a zealot is his failure or unwillingness to see that Jesus restored prophetism and reaffirmed, with radical zeal, the concern of the prophet for national repentance, justice and faithfulness. In the true sense of the word these are 'political', even revolutionary issues, but they had been lost sight of in the fanaticism and violence of the resistance groups in rebellion against Rome. Collaboration or resistance were not the only courses open to Jews under Roman oppression: Pharisaic quietism was another possibility, and so was a revival of prophetic realism and independence, and it is along these latter lines that we may understand Jesus' messianic consciousness (if we dare use that phrase) in its first-century context.

(6) One of the two terms in the famous *Testimonium Flavianum* (*Ant.*

xviii.63–4) which even the majority of those who are otherwise sceptical of the historical value of the passage would treat as probably genuine is the description of Jesus as a σοφός [ἀνήρ], a 'wise man' (the other is 'teacher').[1] If this unusual characterization is a remnant of Josephus' original reference to Jesus, it is noteworthy that he does not use this term for any other 'messianic prophet' of this period: amongst them he is distinguished as a 'wise man'. Within the general frame of comparison we are exploiting does not this peculiar designation of Jesus (if genuine) open the way to a reconsideration of the wisdom-teaching of Jesus, i.e. a large part of very primitive sayings-material in the Synoptics, and also many of the injunctions preserved in Matt. v–vii which are, in fact, wisdom-sayings?[2] Since the vast majority of the wisdom-sayings in the Gospels seem to have many parallels in Jewish, Christian and even pagan tradition, we have become accustomed to accepting the conclusion that none of them can be claimed to be characteristic of Jesus' original proclamation. The 'criterion of dissimilarity' therefore eliminates the wisdom-sayings of the Sermon on the Mount (Matt. v.13f, 29f; vi.19f, 21, 24, 25–34; vii.1–6) and also such sayings as Mk iv.21–3; Matt. x.28ff; Luke xii.47f; xiv.7–14 and many others, including wisdom-parables such as Luke xii.16ff. A few wisdom-sayings are commonly considered authentic because they exhibit some eschatological features (e.g. Mk ii.21f; Luke xiv.28ff; Matt. xiii.44–8). But why must a wisdom-saying have a special eschatological twist or application in order to qualify as an original saying of Jesus?

We would not urge wholesale acceptance of the wisdom-materials as part of the teaching of the historical Jesus. But these materials do constitute a considerable portion of the Synoptic sayings-tradition: what is their origin? If wisdom-sayings which exhibit no particular eschatological features do not originate with Jesus himself, who introduced them into the tradition of his sayings? Among the prophetic sayings in the Gospel of Thomas a comparatively large number are Synoptic sayings which Bultmann and others assign to the historical Jesus: but few, if any, of the wisdom-sayings in that Gospel seem ever to be considered for that distinction. Since we have not yet developed any criteria which would enable us to write a history of the tradition of the wisdom-sayings, it remains difficult to trace their trajectory (or line of

[1] Cf. Excursus II (written by P. Winter) in *The History of the Jewish People in the Age of Jesus Christ*, I, revised edition (Edinburgh, 1973), pp. 428–41, especially p. 433; and even more recently, E. Bammel, 'Zum Testimonium Flavianum', *Josephus-Studien*, pp. 1–22, especially p. 18.

[2] Cf. H. Koester's observations in *Christology and a Modern Pilgrimage: A Discussion with Norman Perrin* (Claremont, 1971), pp. 128f.

development) from the Jewish wisdom movement, through their use in Jesus' teaching, to the early church and to the beginnings of Gnosticism. But that this trajectory existed has been shown by J. M. Robinson, primarily through an investigation of quotation formulae and general references to these sayings.[1] What still requires to be done is the tracing of the history of these sayings themselves and of their form and content. The relationship of the tradition of wisdom-sayings to the historical Jesus remains an open question. But when that question is faced and solved on its own terms, without being forced into a fixed schema of Jesus' eschatological teaching, the teaching of Jesus will almost certainly emerge as more complex and less unambiguous than many reconstructions suggest. An intriguing enterprise of investigation into a large part of the Synoptic tradition is suggested by taking seriously Josephus' peculiar characterization of Jesus as a 'wise man' among the 'messianic prophets' of the first half of the first century A.D.

To these six considerations others could, doubtlessly, be added; but this modest attempt to wring some suggestions relevant to the historical Jesus from Josephus' references to 'messianic prophets' has not, I trust, proved valueless: and I hope that the essay is not an offering too unworthy of the distinguished scholar honoured by this volume.

[1] J. M. Robinson, 'Logoi Sophon: on the Gattung of Q', in *The Future of our Religious Past* (London, 1971), pp. 84–130; and in *Trajectories through Early Christianity* (Philadelphia, 1971), pp. 71–113.

Is the Son of Man problem really insoluble?

M. D. HOOKER

Many years ago Principal Black, hearing that I was working on the problem of the meaning of the phrase 'the Son of Man', sought to deter me by issuing the simple warning: 'Don't!' I hope it will not seem inappropriate if, in spite of his warning, I now offer to him yet another article on this hoary problem. For in an earlier volume of essays published in his honour there appeared an article by A. J. B. Higgins entitled 'Is the Son of Man problem insoluble?'[1] which took issue with my own 'solution' to the problem.[2] Perhaps I may be forgiven, then, for failing once again to heed Principal Black's advice, and returning to a question which he, too, has found irresistible.

'Who is this Son of Man?' The most popular answer to this ancient question has been, in recent years, that he is an eschatological figure expected by Jesus as the vindicator of his message and mission, with whom he himself, after his death and resurrection, was identified by the early church.[3] This widely held belief is based upon three assumptions, all of which have recently come under attack.

Firstly, this interpretation of the evidence depends upon the conviction that there was already in existence, at the time of Jesus, a Jewish expectation of a heavenly Son of Man. It has been widely assumed that this belief was a commonplace of first-century Judaism, but the evidence for it is flimsy in the extreme; it is drawn mainly from the Gospels themselves (which offer us primarily a Christian reinterpretation of the phrase), from a messianic interpretation of the passage in Dan. vii

[1] A. J. B. Higgins, *Neotestamentica et Semitica*, edited by E. Earle Ellis and Max Wilcox (Edinburgh, 1969), pp. 70–87.

[2] M. D. Hooker, *The Son of Man in Mark* (London, 1967).

[3] Among many presentations of this view, see e.g. J. Knox, *The Death of Christ* (London, 1959), pp. 52–125; H. E. Tödt, *The Son of Man in the Synoptic Tradition* (London, 1963; ET of *Der Menschensohn in der synoptischen Überlieferung*, Gütersloh, 1959); F. Hahn, *The Titles of Jesus in Christology* (London, 1969; ET of *Christologische Hoheitstitel. Ihre Geschichte im frühen Christentum*, Göttingen, 1963), pp. 15–53.

which disagrees with the author's own interpretation of it, and above all from chapters xxxvii–lxxi of 1 Enoch, whose early dating is becoming more and more unlikely.[1] Although it seems probable that Daniel's vision was increasingly interpreted in terms of an individual 'messianic' figure, this is a long way from the suggestion that there was a widely-held expectation of a glorious, heavenly Son of Man in first-century Judaism.[2]

Secondly, the idea that Jesus proclaimed a coming Son of Man rests upon the assumption that he made no messianic claims for himself: sayings about the future role of the Son of Man, therefore, if they are authentic, must refer to someone else. Some scholars have, of course, challenged the basic assumption that Jesus made no messianic claims. More significant for our present discussion, however, is the fact that the argument rests on the assumption that 'the Son of Man' was a messianic title. If the phrase was not, after all, a messianic title, then its use by Jesus as a self-designation may well have been appropriate.

Thirdly, this theory is based upon what Dr Higgins described as 'the results of traditio-historical study, according to which the only authentic sayings are to be found among those referring to the eschatological functions of the Son of Man'.[3] These 'results', however, are based upon the previous two premises, and if these prove to be uncertain, so is the conclusion that only 'eschatological' sayings can be authentic.

In spite of its popularity, therefore, this solution has little firm evidence to support it. Moreover, it raises many problems: what was Jesus' understanding of his own function if he expected another figure in the future, and what was the relation between them? What is the relation between the coming Son of Man and the Kingdom of God, which Jesus also (separately) announced? Why did the church invent 'Son of Man' sayings which are totally different from those 'eschatological' sayings in their understanding of the function of the Son of Man?

1 See, most recently, *The Books of Enoch*, edited by J. Milik with the collaboration of Matthew Black (Oxford, 1976), pp. 89–98; Milik places the Similitudes very late, at the end of the third century A.D. Cf. also J. C. Hindley, 'Towards a Date for the Similitudes of Enoch. An Historical Approach', *NTS* XIV (1968), pp. 551–65, who suggests the early second century A.D. In a private communication Dr M. A. Knibb (editor of *The Ethiopic Book of Enoch* (Oxford, 1978)), tells me that he is inclined to date the Similitudes at the end of the first century A.D.

2 R. Leivestad, 'Exit the Apocalyptic Son of Man', *NTS* XVIII (1972), pp. 243–67; M. D. Hooker, *The Son of Man in Mark*, pp. 11–74; N. Perrin, *Rediscovering the teaching of Jesus* (London, 1967), pp. 164–73; Maurice Casey, 'The Use of the term "Son of Man" in the Similitudes of Enoch', *Journal for the Study of Judaism*, VII (1976), pp. 11–29.

3 A. J. B. Higgins, *Neotestamentica et Semitica*, p. 79.

It is, perhaps, not surprising if the rival theory set out by Dr Vermes in an appendix to the third edition of Principal Black's book *An Aramaic Approach to the Gospels and Acts*[1] has recently been gathering support. Dr Vermes argued that the Aramaic phrase *bar nāsh*(*ā*) could be used in first-century Palestinian Aramaic not only to mean 'a human being' and 'someone' but also as a circumlocution for 'I'. Some scholars have taken issue with Dr Vermes over the question of the date of the relevant material.[2] Even if we allow that his examples provide fair evidence for the time of Jesus, however, it is questionable whether, in the passages which he quotes, the phrase is really being used in place of the pronoun 'I', since in every case it would be more natural to substitute 'one' or 'a man'; the examples which he gives are in fact general statements which could refer to any man but which happen to refer to the speaker because he is known to be in the particular circumstances described.

Now this does not mean, of course, that the suggestion that Jesus used the phrase in accordance with this idiom must therefore be excluded: indeed, it has recently been argued that it is precisely this general application of the term which explains its use by Jesus.[3] Dr Vermes' solution runs into several difficulties, however. Firstly, we must explain how the phrase came to be carefully preserved in the oral tradition, mistranslated into Greek and then misunderstood to the extent that wholly inappropriate sayings (this time the eschatological ones) were created around it. If the phrase was a common expression for 'I' in Aramaic, then the use of the barbaric Greek phrase ὁ υἱὸς τοῦ ἀνθρώπου seems an inexplicable blunder; the fact that it was thought necessary to use this translationese suggests that there was already something a little unusual and special about the Aramaic phrase, even in an Aramaic-speaking community.

Secondly, if the phrase is simply a circumlocution for 'I', then the only sayings which can be accepted as original are presumably those which refer to his experiences of suffering and deprivation, such as

1 M. Black, *An Aramaic Approach to the Gospels and Acts* (Oxford, 1967), pp. 310–28. See also G. Vermes, *Jesus the Jew* (London, 1973).

2 E.g. J. A. Fitzmyer in a review of Matthew Black's book in *CBQ* xxx (1968), pp. 426f. Vermes cites material from the Palestinian Pentateuch Targum, the Palestinian Talmud and Genesis Rabba.

3 P. M. Casey, 'The Son of Man Problem', *ZNTW* LXVII (1976), pp. 147–54, who suggests that the sayings have two levels of meaning – the general statement and the statement about the speaker in particular. He lists twelve authentic sayings: Mark ii.10, 28; Matt. viii.20 = Luke ix.58; Matt. xi.19 = Luke vii.34; Matt. xii.32 = Luke xii.10; Luke xxii.48; Mark x.45; xiv.21a and b; Luke xii.8; Mark viii.38; Mark viii.31 (ix.31; x.33f).

Mk viii.31 and its parallels and Matt. viii.20 = Luke ix.58; taken in this sense, the phrase offers no explanation for claims to authority or hopes of future glory.[1] Nor is there anything in the phrase to explain the note of necessity which characterizes the Passion predictions, and this must be understood as part of the interpretation which has been introduced after the event. In other words, the original core of sayings is reduced to little more than 'the Son of Man has nowhere to lay his head' and 'the Son of Man expects to suffer'. This seems an insufficient explanation of the way in which the phrase came to be regarded as Jesus' characteristic self-designation, and a slender basis on which so many other Son of Man sayings came to be built.

If, on the other hand, these sayings about suffering and death are understood as general statements about mankind which apply to Jesus in particular, then either they are manifestly untrue ('a man has nowhere to lay his head') or they are so obvious as to be trite ('a man must die').

The understanding of the phrase as a simple periphrasis for 'I' fails, therefore, to explain why it should appear in the particular contexts where it is found, or be remembered as in any way distinctive of Jesus' speech. Nevertheless, Dr Vermes' evidence is important in demonstrating that the phrase was unlikely to have been understood by Jesus' hearers as a messianic title, and in suggesting that it would have been possible for him to use this phrase to refer to himself in contexts where this application was clear. His arguments therefore add strength to the view that there was no expectation of an eschatological Son of Man in first-century Palestine, and that Christians were misled by the literal Greek translation into assuming that it had been used by Jesus as a title. What still needs to be explained is why Jesus should have chosen to use this particular phrase (which, *pace* Dr Vermes, seems to have been rare, if not unknown, as a self-designation at this period) and whether he attached to it any particular meaning which might explain why it occurs in such varied sayings in the tradition.

A final piece of evidence which demonstrates how unlikely it is that the term 'the Son of Man' was in use as a messianic title in first-

[1] Vermes comments on the contexts where he argues for the circumlocutional use of *bar nāsh*(*ā*) as follows: 'In most instances the sentence contains an allusion to humiliation, danger, or death, but there are also examples where reference to the self in the third person is dictated by humility or modesty)' (in M. Black, *An Aramaic Approach to the Gospels and Acts*, p. 327). It might perhaps be argued that Jesus used the term for motives of modesty in speaking of power and glory, but this would not explain why he felt entitled to make such extraordinary claims to authority and honour.

century Judaism is the way in which the early church failed to employ it as a title for Jesus. It is true that some at least of the Son of Man sayings must have been created in the Christian community; but all of them are placed in the mouth of Jesus, and there is no evidence that 'the Son of Man' was used (as were 'Lord' and 'Christ') as a title to refer to Jesus. However much significance may have been poured into the phrase, it continued to be understood as a self-designation of Jesus, and was not taken over as a living messianic title by the community.

These two rival interpretations of the phrase 'the Son of Man' in the Gospels, one taking it as a messianic title, the other as a modest self-designation, appear to be incompatible. But since each of them succeeds in offering a satisfactory explanation of only half the evidence, it is arguable that their insights are complementary. The phrase cannot be a messianic title – yet the theory which interprets it as such at least offers a reason for its use; the view that it was an acceptable self-designation offers a possible explanation as to *how* Jesus could have used it of himself – but fails to explain *why* he should have employed a colourless phrase which has no particular function. Each theory is able to offer an interpretation of only part of the evidence: those who hold the messianic interpretation have to explain all but the eschatological sayings as the result of a misunderstanding in the Christian community, while Dr Vermes' interpretation reverses this procedure, and it is the eschatological sayings which are seen as the product of misunderstanding.

These two diametrically opposed approaches thus highlight the basic problem of the Son of Man passages in the Gospels – namely, the apparent incompatibility of the various types of Son of Man sayings found there. All explanations of the term have to solve the problem of the relationship between present and future sayings, and the tendency in recent scholarship has been to abandon attempts to reconcile them and to jettison one group as unauthentic. Yet the juxtaposition of ideas which seem to twentieth-century scholars incompatible may itself be the key to the problem: is it perhaps the phrase 'the Son of Man' itself which links together these disparate ideas?

I have argued previously that the division of the sayings into different groups, though sometimes convenient, can be a misleading exercise.[1] It is worth noting also that the labels which are given to these groups of sayings can be equally misleading. A saying such as Mk viii.31, e.g. is commonly described as 'a prediction of the Passion' or 'a suffering saying'. Yet this is to give the saying a particular slant by emphasizing only part of it: certainly the suffering is described in more detail than

[1] M. D. Hooker, *The Son of Man in Mark*, p. 80.

the resurrection, but it would be more accurate to label the saying as 'a prediction of death and resurrection' than as 'a Passion prediction'. The details of the Passion which have been included in these sayings are likely to have been added *ex eventu*; the idea that the sayings are primarily 'Passion predictions' is perhaps due to the use which Mark has made of them, as pointers towards the death of Jesus. In themselves, however, they are predictions of resurrection as well as of death, of vindication as well as of suffering.

Similarly, it is worthy of note that all the 'eschatological' sayings in Mark occur in contexts which refer to suffering, and ought therefore to be described as promises of vindication rather than as prophecies of the parousia of the Son of Man.[1] Just as the 'Passion predictions' combine the ideas of death and resurrection, so these 'eschatological' sayings hold together the persecution which belongs to the present era and the glorious vindication of the future.

It could be argued, of course, that the context of these sayings is due to Mark, just as it has been argued that the Passion predictions are creations of Mark. The other 'eschatological' sayings in Matthew and Luke are not found in this kind of context – indeed, as will be noted presently, their whole emphasis is somewhat different. However, the linking together of suffering and exaltation is found elsewhere in the New Testament tradition about the Son of Man – to such an extent, indeed, that Matthew Black has suggested that the oldest stratum of the Son of Man tradition may have referred to rejection and exaltation, rather than to death and resurrection.[2] In addition to the Johannine sayings (where the two ideas are combined by the play on the words 'glory' and 'lift up') and the one reference to the Son of Man outside the Gospels at Acts vii.56, he lists the quotation from Ps. viii in Heb. ii (where the argument points the contrast between humiliation and glory) and Phil. ii, which he considers to be dependent on tradition about the Son of Man. If this is correct, it would be in accord not only with the vision of the one like a Son of Man in Dan. vii, where a promise of future vindication is set in the context of the persecution presently being experienced by the author's readers, but with the wider background in Judaism of confident expectation that the suffering and righteous within Israel will be vindicated in the coming judgment.[3]

[1] *Ibid.*, pp. 180f.

[2] M. Black, 'The Son of Man Problem in Recent Research and Debate', *BJRL* XLV (1963), pp. 305–18.

[3] See the discussion in E. Schweizer, *Lordship and Discipleship* (London, 1960, ET of *Erniedrigung und Erhöhung bei Jesus und seinen Nachfolgern*, Zürich, 1955), pp. 22–31.

It is therefore arguable that the central problem of the Son of Man sayings – the incompatibility of the 'suffering' and 'eschatological' sayings – is an unreal one, and results from emphasizing one element in each saying at the expense of another, as well as one group of sayings over against the other. If this is so, however, it is a process which has already been begun by the evangelists. If they include different selections of sayings about the Son of Man, this process is likely to reflect their different interests and purposes; the extent to which each has created sayings or merely chosen them remains, of course, debatable.

Because Mark's references to the death and resurrection of the Son of Man have no real parallels in non-Markan material it has often been suggested that they are Markan creations. The standard response to this argument, that such prophecies have a place only in a 'Gospel', and not in a collection of Jesus' sayings, may well receive support from redactional critical work on the Gospels. If Mark is responsible for the inclusion of these sayings it is because for him the death of Jesus is central; whether because he is concerned to answer the question 'Why did the Messiah die?' or because he is anxious to encourage Christians facing persecution or because he is trying to correct the beliefs of those for whom he writes, these sayings are relevant to his theme. Unless it can be shown that the remaining New Testament evidence for the Son of Man's humiliation–exaltation is based solely upon Mark, it seems unlikely that the idea is a Markan creation, though the emphasis on this particular theme may be due to his interests.

Attention has less often been concentrated on the character of those sayings which are found in Matthew and Luke but not in Mark. Matthew takes over all the Markan sayings, and Luke the great majority, but each of them uses in addition a considerable number of non-Markan sayings. Those which speak of the suffering of the Son of Man[1] are similar to the Markan sayings and are usually held to be editorial.[2] The great increase is in sayings which refer to the future role of the Son of Man. Examination of these sayings shows that, almost without exception, they refer explicitly to this role as one of judgment; even the exceptions occur in passages which are concerned with judgment.[3] This feature does not normally excite comment, since it is widely assumed that judgment is the obvious characteristic of the Son of Man.

[1] Matt. xxvi.2; Luke xvii.25; xxii.48; xxiv.7.

[2] E.g. by A. J. B. Higgins, *Jesus and the Son of Man* (London, 1964), pp. 78–82, 99f.

[3] The sayings occur in Matt. x.23; xiii.41; xvi.28; xix.28; xxiv.30, 39; xxv.31; Luke xvii.22, 30; xviii.8; xxi.36; (Matt. x.32 =) Luke xii.8; (Matt. xii.40 =) Luke xi.30; Matt. xxiv.27, 37, 44 = Luke xvii.24, 26; xii.40.

Yet it is remarkable that the role of judge is never predicated of the Son of Man in Mark. The closest that any of the Markan sayings comes to ascribing this role to the Son of Man is Mk viii.38, where it is said that he will be ashamed of those who have been ashamed of following Jesus; the scene depicted here is one in which the Son of Man acknowledges Jesus' disciples and recognizes those who make up the elect community. It is possible that Mark understands the role of the Son of Man to be that of judge, but the language is more appropriate if the Son of Man is understood to be acknowledging his own before the judgment throne of God.[1] The role of witness is made explicit in the parallel saying in Q where the Son of Man acknowledges or denies men before the angels of God;[2] the Q form of the saying is probably more original than the one found in Mk viii.38,[3] but in both Matt. x and Luke xii it has been set in a context of future judgment, which suggests a shift of emphasis in its interpretation.[4] A similar shift is seen in the Matthaean version of Mk viii.38, which adds the words 'he will requite each according to what he has done'[5] to the Markan saying, and so indicates that the Son of Man himself is understood to be the judge; it is significant that Matthew also changes Mark's 'the kingdom of God coming in power' in the following verse to 'the Son of man coming in his kingdom' (Matt. xvi.28).

The Son of Man also appears in the role of head of the elect community in Mk xiii.26, where he is again said to come in power and glory: he sends angels throughout the world to gather the elect. It is natural for us to interpret this as a judgment scene – but nothing is in fact said about the Son of Man as judge. Insofar as the theme of judgment is present in Mk xiii at all, it appears in the description of the disasters which are going to come upon the world before the appearance of the Son of Man.[6] The coming of the Son of Man is the climax

[1] It is possible that the 'coming' in viii.38 is understood by Mark as a coming to God, though the phrase 'in the glory of his Father' suggests that he is thinking of a coming to earth (to gather those who belong to him). See the discussion in J. A. T. Robinson, *Jesus and His Coming* (London, 1957), pp. 53–6.

[2] Luke xii.8f. Luke's version of this saying, with its reference to the Son of Man and the angels of God, is more likely to be original than that found in Matt. x.32f, which uses 'I' and 'my Father'.

[3] Cf. T. F. Glasson, *The Second Advent*, 3rd edition (London, 1963), p. 68.

[4] F. Hahn assumes that Luke xii.8f 'refers to the function of the Son of man as judge' (*The Titles of Jesus*, p. 33), but H. E. Tödt is surely correct when he says that in this passage 'the Son of Man does not appear as a judge, but as the guarantor' (*The Son of Man in the Synoptic Tradition*, p. 56).

[5] A quotation from Ps. lxii.12 (LXX lxi.13).

[6] Once again, it may be asked whether the 'coming' of the Son of Man was originally understood, even here, as a coming to earth. It is probable that Mark was thinking of a 'parousia', but the saying could be interpreted as a

of the chapter – but it is described as a promise, and not as a threat; those who endure suffering and persecution as followers of Jesus may be confident that finally, when the Son of Man appears in power and glory, they will be acknowledged by him and receive a reward. The disciples are to watch – not for fear of impending disaster, but lest they fail to be ready to welcome their master. Once again, it is noticeable that Matthew has altered the significance of the saying about the Son of Man; instead of the parable of the absent householder (Mk xiii.34–7) he has followed the statement that no one knows the time of the end with a saying comparing the coming of the Son of Man to the coming of the flood, a warning that when disaster comes 'one will be taken and one left', and another parable about a householder which is totally different in emphasis from that in Mark, since this time what is unknown is the time of the thief's arrival (Matt. xxiv.37–44); an additional parable then describes the rewards and punishments meted out to his servants by a householder when he returns home unexpectedly (xxiv.45–51). Matthew has extended the time of tribulation, which in Mark belongs to the period before the coming of the Son of Man, and has interpreted that coming as itself a judgment on the wicked. Luke, too, has added a section warning his readers to be ready for a final day of judgment, on which they will be called upon to stand before the Son of Man (Luke xxii.34–6).

The third and final saying in Mark which refers to a future role for the Son of Man is that in xiv.62. This promises vindication for the Son of Man, who will be seen 'at the right hand of power and coming with the clouds of heaven'; the *ὄψεσθε* suggests that the vindication is imminent – an impression confirmed by Matthew's *ἀπ' ἄρτι* and Luke's *ἀπὸ τοῦ νῦν*. Commentators have tended to assume that the 'coming' of the Son of Man means a coming to earth, and Luke's omission of the phrase perhaps indicates that he also interpreted it in this way and left it out in order to solve the problem of an unfulfilled prophecy. Remarkably, Matthew has not only retained the phrase about coming with the clouds of heaven but has intensified the problem by adding the words *ἀπ' ἄρτι*: it seems that he has understood it as parallel to 'sitting at the right hand of power' – another way of speaking of a vindication which is to follow immediately, and which presumably takes place at the resurrection (cf. Matt. xxviii.18). There is no reference in any of the gospels to the idea of judgment, though this may be implied in the sitting at the right hand of God.

coming to God, and may have had that significance at an earlier stage, even if Mark has interpreted it in accordance with later understanding.

To suggest that the theme of the suffering Son of Man is a Markan one is to isolate part of the evidence. It is of course true that the great majority of the sayings about the death and resurrection of the Son of Man occur in Mark – though almost all of them are taken over by both the other evangelists, who also make editorial additions; it is also true, however, that almost all the so-called 'eschatological' sayings occur in Matthew and/or Luke, and that the content of these is significantly different from the three Markan sayings. Whereas the sayings in Mark suggest vindication, the non-Markan sayings all refer to judgment, and Matthew adapts two of the Markan sayings to fit this theme.[1]

In asking whether Mark is responsible for the tradition about the suffering Son of Man, therefore, we ought also to ask whether he is responsible for this particular emphasis in those 'future' sayings which he has included. The alternative is that the sayings in Matthew and Luke reflect a later development. Has Mark synthesized two different types of sayings about the Son of Man (only one of which goes back to Jesus) into a pattern of suffering–exaltation, or have the other evangelists used tradition which stresses and develops the Son of Man's future role, and so distorted an original pattern which linked this more closely with the theme of present suffering?

It is perhaps significant that whereas in Mk xiv.62 an affirmation is made about the Son of Man – namely that he will be seen in power and glory, and so be acknowledged as vindicated by God – many of the sayings used by Matthew and Luke take the status of the Son of Man as a given factor: he is assumed to be the judge, and what is at issue is when he will come, and whether men and women will be prepared for his coming. In Mk xiv.62 the saying about 'the Son of Man' represents the claim about future vindication made by Jesus at the moment of challenge before the high priest; but in the eschatological sayings found in Matthew and Luke and not in Mark, the phrase is understood to be a well-known title (though one that is used only by Jesus of himself), and it is assumed that his authority as the Son of Man will be accepted by those who hear his words. If a development has taken place it seems probable that it is from the understanding of the Son of Man as one who expects to be vindicated to the belief that he is the one who will exercise authority in judgment.[2] This is precisely the kind of develop-

[1] In Mark Jesus warns of coming judgment, but does not himself act as judge.

[2] Cf. E. Schweizer, 'The Son of Man Again', *NTS* IX (1963), pp. 256–61: 'Only in the course of a "re-apocalyptization" of the eschatology of Jesus, in a Jewish-apocalyptic group of the early church, did the decisive witness in the last judgment become the judge himself' (pp. 259f).

ment which we see taking place between the picture of the one like a Son of Man in Dan. vii and the Son of Man who acts with the authority of God in 1 Enoch.

The beginning of this development can in fact be traced already within the Gospel of Mark itself, as the Son of Man is increasingly understood to be the one who vindicates others, and as the time of vindication shifts from an imminent to a more distant future. A comparison of the three so-called 'eschatological' sayings shows that in Mk xiv.62 the Son of Man himself is to be vindicated – presumably at the resurrection; in Mk viii.38 it is implied that he is to vindicate his followers, and though the original meaning may have been that Jesus expected his disciples to share his suffering and his vindication,[1] Mark's setting of the saying suggests that he has understood it of a subsequent event; just as Jesus suffered and was vindicated, so his followers may expect to suffer and to be vindicated. This time-scale is made explicit in Mark xiii, where the link between the sufferings of Jesus and of his disciples is seen in the way in which theirs 'conform' to his,[2] but where their sufferings are clearly subsequent to the death and resurrection of Jesus, and their vindication belongs to the distant future.

This kind of development is what we would expect if, as seems probable, sayings of Jesus expressing confidence in a future vindication by God were divided after his death and interpreted, on the one hand in terms of the resurrection, and on the other in terms of a future and final scene of vindication, in which the Son of Man came to play a more and more central role.

It is time to return to our original question: if 'the Son of Man' was, as Dr Vermes argues, an acceptable (though unusual) circumlocution for 'I' in Aramaic, and if Jesus would therefore have been understood to be referring to himself, why should he have chosen to use this particular phrase? Has the early Christian community totally misunderstood him in supposing that it was intended as a claim to future vindication and authority? Any satisfactory solution to the problem of the Son of Man must demonstrate not only why Jesus was thought to be referring to himself but also how the term came to be interpreted as denoting a figure who exercised superhuman authority and who would play a central role in the future as judge.

In spite of comparative neglect in recent years, the traditional view that the term refers primarily to Dan. vii still offers a more complete

1 Cf. C. K. Barrett, *Jesus and the Gospel Tradition* (London, 1967), pp. 49–51.

2 Cf. R. H. Lightfoot, *The Gospel Message of St Mark* (Oxford, 1950), pp. 48–59.

answer to the problem than any other explanation. The following factors support this particular solution:

1. It is clear that Dan. vii.13 has influenced many of the Gospel sayings. It is sometimes assumed that any allusion to the Old Testament must necessarily be secondary, but this is an illogical generalization which has transformed a trend in the tradition (to add Old Testament allusions) into a rule (that all such allusions are additions). The reference to Dan. vii certainly belongs to a very early stage of the tradition, and therefore deserves to be considered seriously as original.

2. In Dan. vii the phrase 'one like a Son of Man' is not a title but a claim to a role and status – a claim which is based on a relationship of obedience to God. There are indications, as we have seen, that in the earliest stratum of the Synoptic tradition also, the phrase signified a role rather than a title.

3. In later Jewish literature, one can see how 'the Son of Man', clearly understood as a reference to the passage in Daniel, develops into or towards being understood as a title. The phrase lends itself to the kind of interpretation which we can see developing in the Synoptic tradition.

4. In spite of frequent denials by New Testament scholars that the figure of the 'one like a Son of Man' in Daniel has any knowledge of suffering, the problem which concerns the author of Dan. vii is that of the suffering of 'the saints of the Most High' who are clearly represented by the man-like figure in the vision. We find in this chapter precisely the theme of suffering–vindication which characterizes the Markan understanding of the Son of Man.

5. The 'one like a Son of Man' in Dan. vii represents a community and is to be understood as a corporate figure, even though an individual interpretation was given later to the passage when it was understood to refer to the Messiah. It has recently been argued that the corporate interpretation, as well as the messianic, was known in first-century Judaism.[1] The suggestion has often been made that 'the Son of Man' in the Gospels is to some extent at least a corporate figure,[2] a view

[1] Maurice Casey, 'The Corporate Interpretation of "One like a Son of Man" (Dan. VII.13) at the Time of Jesus', *NT* XVIII (1976), pp. 167–80. His evidence is particularly interesting in view of the fact that he does not himself argue for a corporate interpretation of the phrase in the gospels.

[2] Notably by T. W. Manson, in *The Teaching of Jesus*, 2nd edition (Cambridge, 1935), pp. 211–34 and 'The Son of Man in Daniel, Enoch and the Gospels', *BJRL* XXXII (1950), pp. 171–93. Manson's view has never received much support, partly perhaps because he linked it with the idea that one could trace an historical development from corporate to individual in Jesus' use of the term.

which has received support from Matthew Black.[1] Certainly the Synoptic Son of Man – when he does not stand over against mankind as judge – is closely linked with other men, and seems to be understood as the head of a community.

The weakness of the view which links 'the Son of Man' in the Gospels with Dan. vii is that it seems a very odd way for Jesus to have spoken of himself. This difficulty has led many to the belief that he must in fact have been referring to someone other than himself. Could Jesus have been referring to himself *and* to Dan. vii when he used this phrase, or do we have to choose between these two views?

In a recent article (one of three which he has contributed to the problem of this term) Maurice Casey[2] has argued that the Ethiopic phrases for 'Son of Man' in 1 Enoch are used in exactly the same way as the Aramaic and Hebrew equivalents – i.e. to mean 'man'. The figure referred to, he argues, is not a heavenly one at all, but an exalted man (later identified with Enoch himself); although the phrase 'Son of Man' is used in the sense of 'man', it is chosen because of the influence of Dan. vii.13 upon the author's thought.

We suggest that in a similar way the phrase 'the Son of Man' was chosen by Jesus as a self-designation because of the vital influence of Dan. vii on his thought. The phrase was used in contexts where it was clear that the 'man' referred to was none other than Jesus himself,[3] and the reason why he chose this somewhat unusual way of referring to himself was that the sayings in which it occurs make claims which could not be justified by a simple 'I', since they are based on Jesus' identification with the mission of the people of God, who are symbolized by the 'one like a Son of Man' in Dan. vii. Jesus chose to use this particular Aramaic phrase, not only because it could be understood by his hearers in these particular contexts to refer to himself, but also because it would be understood to point to the Danielic idea of the suffering and vindicated righteous community. As in Daniel, the phrase is better understood as a reference to a role than as a title. At the same time, since it is only the context which can make plain whether *bar nāshā* is

[1] See p. 160, n. 2 above.

[2] M. Casey, 'The Use of the term "Son of Man" in the Similitudes of Enoch', *Journal for the Study of Judaism* VII (1976), pp. 11–29. See also p. 157, n. 3 and p. 166, n. 1 above.

[3] English readers who remember the radio programme 'Itma' will be familiar with an example of the way in which a neutral phrase ('that man') can be given a special nuance. Every listener to the programme was aware that the statement 'It's that man again' in this particular context must refer to Tommy Handley: the phrase 'that man' was therefore transformed by its associations into something approximating to a title.

to be understood as 'I' rather than as 'man', the sayings are not necessarily to be understood as referring exclusively to Jesus. The Son of Man sayings contain a challenge to others to be included and to make a corporate interpretation a reality instead of a possibility.

In 1 Enoch the Ethiopic phrases are preceded by the demonstrative 'that' – an indication, perhaps, that the author is pointing us to the vision of the Danielic Son of Man. In the Synoptic phrase, the pointer to Daniel may have left its mark in the use of the distinctive ὁ – described recently by C. F. D. Moule as one of the 'neglected features in the problem of the Son of Man'.[1] Jesus is not, after all, speaking of himself as any man, but as man understood in terms of Daniel's vision. Jesus can speak of his mission and his future role as 'man' only because he sees himself in the light of 'the Son of Man' whose obedience and authority, suffering and exaltation, are described in visionary terms in Dan. vii.

Appropriate enough within the ministry of Jesus, as an expression of his obedience to God and his trust in him for future vindication, the term ceased to be appropriate in the same way after the resurrection. The Christian community understood it as a title, but did not adopt it for their own use, preferring to use 'Messiah' or 'Son of God' or 'Lord'. Nevertheless, it continued to be important within the tradition of Jesus' sayings, and to be understood as expressing the hope for vindication – now seen as a final vindication taking place at the parousia of the Son of Man.

Is the Son of Man problem really insoluble? It would perhaps be optimistic to hope that any 'solution' will be accepted in the near future as an 'assured result'. But assured results are always dangerous in New Testament scholarship. We shall perhaps move towards a solution, however, if we recognize that there is sometimes merit in very diverse views; like the Son of Man sayings themselves, each may convey part of the truth, distorted when taken on its own, but playing its own part in the total pattern.

[1] C. F. D. Moule, 'Neglected Features in the Problem of "the Son of Man"', *Neues Testament und Kirche*, Festschrift für Rudolf Schnackenburg, edited by J. Gnilka (Freiburg, 1974), pp. 413–28. G. Vermes' claim that the definite and indefinite forms of the phrase were indistinguishable in meaning has been disputed by J. A. Fitzmyer (see p. 157, nn. 1 and 2 above). The use of the definite article is certainly a striking feature in Greek, and as Moule comments, suggests 'something in the traditions of the sayings of Jesus which is more distinctive than simply an Aramaic phrase meaning "a man" or "somebody" or even ... "I"' (C. F. D. Moule, 'Neglected Features in the Problem of "the Son of Man"', p. 21). See also C. F. D. Moule, *The Origin of Christology* Cambridge, 1977), pp. 14–17.

Patristic evidence for Jewish Christian and Aramaic Gospel tradition

A. F. J. KLIJN

An Aramaic Approach to the Gospels and Acts[1] has been and will be an important source of inspiration for many studying the New Testament and its text. With many examples it is proved 'that an Aramaic saying-source or tradition lies behind the Synoptic Gospels'.[2] In this connection it is also said that 'D represents the Aramaic background of the Synoptic tradition more faithfully than do the non-Western manuscripts'.[3] Finally we read that 'the Old Syriac had been influenced at its source by an extra-canonical and apocryphal Gospel tradition of the sayings of Jesus, which may have been non-Hellenistic, transmitted directly from an original Palestinian Aramaic source'.[4]

Not much attention is paid to the evidence from outside regarding this Aramaic tradition. Papias, mentioned in the first edition, is met in the third one in the indices only.[5] Hegesippus is only mentioned in passing.[6] For this reason it seemed appropriate to survey those passages in the early Christian literature which speak about a Gospel tradition in Aramaic or Hebrew in order to determine whether this evidence is of any importance for the subject dealt with in the most famous book written by him in whose honour we are allowed to make this contribution.

Eusebius, *Hist. eccles.* III.39.16, where Papias is quoted speaking about the origin of the Gospel of Mark and Matthew – especially the words *Ματθαῖος μὲν οὖν Ἑβραΐδι διαλέκτῳ τὰ λόγια συνετάξατο, ἡρμήνευσεν δ' αὐτὰ ὡς ἦν δυνατὸς ἕκαστος* – has been investigated innumerable times since it has had to be dealt with in all 'introductions' to the New Testament.[7] The contents of the passage are much more difficult than it

1 M. Black, *An Aramaic Approach to the Gospels and Acts* (Oxford, 1967[3]).
2 *Ibid.*, p. 271. 3 *Ibid.*, p. 277. 4 *Ibid.*, p. 279.
5 See Black, *An Aramaic Approach* . . . (Oxford, 1946), pp. 1, 234, and (Oxford, 1967[3]), p. 355. 6 *Ibid.*, p. 266.
7 See, apart from the 'Introductions', J. Munck, 'Die Tradition über das Matthäusevangelium bei Papias', in *Neotestamentica et Patristica*, Festschrift for O. Cullmann, in Supplements to *Novum Testamentum* VI (Leiden,

would seem at first sight. At the moment everyone agrees that the words *τὰ λόγια* have to be applied to the Gospel as a whole and not to some sayings-source.[1] But not everyone agrees about the meaning of the words *Ἑβραΐδι διαλέκτῳ*. It is generally assumed that our Gospel of Matthew could not have been a translation from an Aramaic original. Therefore, one has to say either that Papias made a mistake or that the words *Ἑβραΐδι διαλέκτῳ* do not mean 'the Hebrew (or Aramaic) language'. This last possibility was suggested by Kürzinger who assumed that the Gospel was written in Greek but with a Hebrew idiom.[2] The end of the passage is usually explained as being a statement about the many efforts to translate the original Hebrew or Aramaic into Greek. It is again not clear what is meant by Papias. Did he know of various editions of the Gospel with differing readings, or did he know about various editions of this Gospel compiled by Jewish Christian sectarians? Also here Kürzinger propounded his own idea, saying that the passage refers to the authors of the canonical Gospels who individualistically interpreted the contents of the Gospel.

The starting point for regarding Papias' statement must be that the Gospel of Matthew was not translated from the Hebrew or Aramaic. If one chooses an explanation which agrees with this fact, the passage loses any significance for the present subject. If one chooses an explanation saying that Papias erred, more than one possibility exists. It is, for example, not necessary to conclude that Papias was really acquainted with a Hebrew or Aramaic original. It is possible that he drew this conclusion because he knew of a tradition according to which Matthew wrote for Jews who believed in Jesus.[3] But all this speculation means that Papias is not a very trustworthy witness for the existence of an Aramaic original Gospel.

Irenaeus writes in his *Adv. haer.* (see also Eusebius, *Hist. eccles.* v.8.2): *ὁ μὲν δὴ Ματθαῖος ἐν τοῖς Ἑβραίοις τῇ ἰδίᾳ αὐτῶν διαλέκτῳ καὶ γραφὴν ἐξήνεγκεν εὐαγγελίου*. It is possible that Irenaeus was either dependent on Papias or that he was acquainted with an Asian tradition.[4]

1962), pp. 249–60; and C. Stewart Petrie, 'The Authorship of "The Gospel according to Matthew": A Reconsideration of the External Evidence', in *NTS* xiv (1967–8), pp. 15–33.

[1] Especially in the light of the words *ὃς* (*scil.* Peter) *πρὸς τὰς χρείας ἐποιεῖτο τὰς διδασκαλίας, ἀλλ' οὐχ ὥσπερ σύνταξιν τῶν κυριακῶν ποιούμενος λογίων*, ...

[2] J. Kürzinger, 'Das Papiaszeugnis und die Erstgestalt des Matthäusevangeliums', in *BZ* n.F. iv (1960), pp. 19–38.

[3] See, for example, Clement of Alexandria in Eusebius, *Hist. eccl.* vi.14.2: *Ἑβραίοις Ἑβραϊκῇ φωνῇ, Λουκᾶν ... αὐτὴν μεθερμηνεύσαντα ἐκδοῦναι τοῖς Ἕλλησιν*.

[4] See J. Kürzinger, 'Irenäus und sein Zeugnis zur Sprache des Matthäusevangeliums', in *NTS* x (1963–4), pp. 108–15, esp. pp. 111–12.

Compared with Papias, Irenaeus added that Matthew published his Gospel among the Hebrews and he omitted that the work was translated. We receive the impression that Irenaeus especially wanted to show for whom the four canonical Gospels were written: Mark for the Romans, Matthew for the Jews, Luke for the Pauline churches and John for Asia Minor. Thus he was not interested in the language in which Matthew was written. He obviously spoke about a Gospel of Matthew familiar to his readers, and that Gospel was written in Greek.[1]

It is remarkable that Irenaeus, *Adv. haer.* I.26.1, writes that the Ebionites only knew of one Gospel, that of Matthew: 'Solo autem eo, quod est secundum Matthaeum, evangelio utuntur' (also in III.11.7).[2] It is not clear where Irenaeus received this information. It is possible that he arrived at this assumption based on the idea that the Gospel of Matthew was written exclusively for Jews. Irenaeus writes that the Ebionites were shown to be wrong by their own Gospel. This obviously refers to Matt. i.23 which speaks of the virgin birth.[3] It is clear that this Gospel in its present form must have been unacceptable to Jewish Christians.

From this it appears that Irenaeus was not interested in an Aramaic origin of Matthew. He only wanted to say that it was meant for Christians of Jewish origin, both orthodox and heretical.

Clement and Origen speak about a Gospel according to the Hebrews. Clement quotes from it in *Strom.* II.ix.45.5 with the introduction: ἧ κἀν τῷ καθ' Ἑβραίους εὐαγγελίῳ . . . γέγραπται. Origen quotes this Gospel three times introduced by the words Ἐὰν δὲ προσιῆταί τις in *In Joh.* II.12,[4] by Εἰ δέ τις παραδέχεται in *Hom. in Jer.* XV.4 and 'si tamen placet alicui suscipere illud' in *In Matth.* XV.14. There is no reason to doubt that this Gospel was written in Greek. The original source, however, must be sought in a Semitic-speaking environment, because the Holy Spirit is supposed to be a female being.[5] Origen apparently did not say that this Gospel was heretical, in contrast to his views about the Gospels of the Egyptians and the Twelve Apostles (*Hom. in Luc.* I.1). We may assume that the Gospel according to the

1 From this Kürzinger (*ibid.*) concluded that both Papias and Irenaeus knew the Gospel of Matthew in Greek only.

2 This passage is not present in the parallel text of Hippolytus, *Refut.* VII.34.1–2.

3 Cf. Eusebius, *Hist. eccles.* VI.17.1, writing that Symmachus, an Ebionite Christian, combated the Gospel of Matthew.

4 The quotation is also met in Origen, *Hom. in Jer.* XV.4; Jerome, *Comm. in Micha* VII.6, *Comm. in Is.* XL.9 and *Comm. in Hiez.* XVI.13.

5 Origen, *In Joh.* II.12; Ἄρτι ἔλαβέ με ἡ μήτηρ μου, τὸ ἅγιον πνεῦμα.

Hebrews was used in Egypt by a group of Christians of Jewish origin who were supposedly still part of the Christian church.

Eusebius too writes about the Gospel according to the Hebrews. He reckons this Gospel *ἐν τοῖς νόθοις* with other writings like the *Acta Pauli*, and he continues that 'according to some people' the Apocalypse of John belongs to the same group. This Gospel was written, according to Eusebius, for the Jews *οἱ τὸν Χριστὸν παραδεξάμενοι* (*Hist. eccles.* III.25.5). Here also we have to draw the conclusion that this Gospel was written in Greek. However, we assume that Eusebius did not know of the Gospel himself in spite of his remark about Papias who had known about the pericope of the adulteress (John vii.53–viii.11), *ἣν τὸ καθ' Ἑβραίους εὐαγγέλιον περιέχει* (*Hist. eccles.* III.39.17). This information was obtained from a tradition which came to Eusebius from some unknown source.[1]

In Eusebius, *Hist. eccles.* IV.22.8, we find the important passage about Hegesippus, of whom it is said that he quoted *ἔκ τε τοῦ καθ' Ἑβραίους εὐαγγελίου*. This is very possible, since Hegesippus belonged to the Greek-speaking, Jewish Christian community of Palestine of the second century. It is obvious that we are dealing again with a Gospel written in the Greek language since the passage continues with the words: *καὶ τοῦ Συριακοῦ καὶ ἰδίως ἐκ τῆς Ἑβραΐδος διαλέκτου τινὰ τίθησιν*. Here Eusebius explicitly speaks about Syriac and Hebrew. The second part of the sentence is not quite clear. He probably speaks of yet another Gospel apart from that according to the Hebrews but this time written in the Syriac language. It is likely that here we are dealing with 'one of the earliest attempts at translation of the Gospel into Syriac'.[2] For the rest the remark deals with traditions, written or oral, still available in Hebrew or Aramaic.

Contrary to Irenaeus' idea that the Gospel according to Matthew was used by the Ebionites is the passage in III.27.4, where Eusebius writes that they used the Gospel according to the Hebrews. This, however, is the result of a misunderstanding on the part of Eusebius. In the passage about the Ebionites he is depending on Origen, Hippolytus and Irenaeus. None of these writers actually connects the Gospel of the Hebrews with the Ebionites, but understandably Eusebius drew this conclusion from Origen's writings in which both the Ebionites and a Gospel used by Jewish Christians are mentioned.[3]

[1] See U. Becker, *Jesus und die Ehebrecherin*, Beiheft zur *ZNTW* XXVIII (Berlin, 1963), pp. 91–117.

[2] See Black, *An Aramaic Approach* . . ., p. 266.

[3] See A. F. J. Klijn and G. J. Reinink, *Patristic Evidence for Jewish Christian Sects* (Supplements to *Novum Testamentum* XXXVI (Leiden, 1973), p. 26.

In his description of the canonical books, Eusebius writes that Origen knew of only four Gospels. He quotes Origen as saying about Matthew γράμμασιν Ἑβραϊκοῖς συντεταγμένον, and that it was given to those who believed among the Jews (IV.25.4).[1] Thus Origen was aware of the tradition we met with in Papias. But also in this passage the emphasis lies upon the distribution of the Gospels among the different nations and regions, which again made it unnecessary for him to pursue the question who was responsible for the translation into Greek.[2]

In *Hist. eccles.* III.24.6, Eusebius writes again about the Gospel of Matthew as having been written for Hebrew Christians in their own language, but he supplements the reference by the remark that Matthew did this because he was about to leave the Jews among whom he was living.[3] Both passages represent the persistent but spurious tradition already met with in Papias.

Eusebius relates a remarkable tradition regarding Pantaenus, who in India discovered among some Christians a Hebrew Gospel of Matthew which was left by Bartholomew (V.10.3). It is, of course, not easy to understand what Indian Christians were doing with a Gospel in Hebrew. It is, however, possible that Pantaenus is speaking about a Gospel in the Syriac language introduced by Syriac Christians and used by the later so-called Thomas Christians, whose liturgy in the Syriac language shows that they were thoroughly influenced by the Syriac language.[4]

A very important remark is found in Eusebius' Theophany where he speaks about a Gospel in Hebrew letters. In this Gospel an altered form of the parable of the talents is recorded in which the threat is not directed at the frugal recipient but at the spendthrift. This clearly also shows that Eusebius did not identify this Gospel with that of Matthew. He writes that this Gospel 'has come to us' (εἰς ἡμᾶς ἧκον) which might

1 The expression 'in Hebrew letters' is identical with 'in the Hebrew language', cf. VI.16.1.

2 It is, therefore, natural that in the various colophons attached to the Gospel of Matthew in the manuscripts of the New Testament we find that the Gospel was written in Jerusalem (K 126) or Palestine (174) and in the Hebrew language (*multi*), and was translated by John (5, 29, 132 and others), James (53) or Bartholomew (293); see C. Tischendorf, *Novum Testamentum Graece* (Lipsiae, 1869[8]), pp. 212–13.

3 See for the traditions about Matthew, Th. Schermann, *Propheten- und Apostellegenden, TU* XXXI (Leipzig, 1907), pp. 269–72, and F. Haase, *Apostel und Evangelisten in den Orientalischen Überlieferungen, Neutestam. Abhandl.* IX B. 1–3. Heft (Münster, 1922), pp. 102, 272.

4 See A. F. J. Klijn, *The Acts of Thomas*, Supplements to *Novum Testamentum* V (Leiden, 1962), pp. 27–9, and A. Dihle, 'Neues zur Thomas-Tradition', in *Jahrb. f. Ant. u. Christentum* VI (1963), pp. 54–70.

show some acquaintance with its existence or contents.[1] In another passage of the Syriac Theophany, he speaks about a Gospel found by him, used among Hebrews and written in Hebrew which said: 'I always choose the best ones for myself of those whom my Father in heaven has given to me.'[2]

Here we meet, for the first time, a Gospel in Hebrew personally known to a Christian author. It was not supposed to be identical with Matthew and was written in Hebrew or Aramaic.

Epiphanius writes about Aramaic and Jewish Christian Gospels several times. With regard to the Ebionites, he says that they accept the Gospel of Matthew (*Pan.* 30.3.7). This tradition was taken from Irenaeus, *Adv. haer.* 1.26.2, but it is not in agreement with other data known to Epiphanius. For from Eusebius he also learned that the Gospel according to the Hebrews had been used by the Ebionites. Erroneously Epiphanius identifies the two, justifying himself by saying that Matthew wrote his Gospel *Ἑβραϊστὶ καὶ Ἑβραϊκοῖς γράμμασιν*, and writes that the Ebionites called the Gospel of Matthew 'according to the Hebrews'.

In the same passage he states that Cerinthus and Merinthus used the same Gospel, and in another passage he adds to these Carpocrates (see 30.14.2). Elsewhere, in his description of Cerinthus, Epiphanius again says that his followers used the Gospel of Matthew (28.5.1). Yet this remark is valueless. Epiphanius only comes to this idea because Irenaeus had said in his passage about the Ebionites that they possessed the same ideas as Cerinthus and Carpocrates and that 'they used the Gospel of Matthew only' (*Adv. haer.* 1.26.1). Epiphanius assumed that Irenaeus was speaking about all three heretics, not seeing that here he was speaking only about the Ebionites again.

But apart from the evidence taken from Christian authors, Epiphanius also knew about a Jewish Christian Gospel, of which he gave some quotations. From these it appears that this Gospel lacked a genealogy and started with the baptism of John the Baptist.[3] Epiphanius compares the contents of this Gospel known to him and the data known to him from other sources. Since he identified his Gospel with that used by the Ebionites and the Cerinthians he had to write that the Cerinthians used the Gospel of Matthew, as we have already mentioned above, but *ἀπὸ μέρους καὶ οὐχὶ ὅλῳ, ἀλλὰ διὰ τὴν γενεαλογίαν τὴν ἔνσαρκον*

[1] Eusebius, *De Theophania*, in Migne, *Patr. Gr.* 24, cols. 685–8.

[2] Eusebius, *Die Theophanie* IV.12, edited by H. Gressmann in GCS, Eusebius III (Leipzig, 1904), p. 183.

[3] See Epiphanius, *Pan.* 30.13.6: *ἡ δὲ ἀρχὴ τοῦ παρ' αὐτοῖς εὐαγγελίου ἔχει ὅτι "ἐγένετο ἐν ταῖς ἡμέραις Ἡρῴδου βασιλέως τῆς Ἰουδαίας ἦλθέν τις Ἰωάννης..."*

(28.5.1). Also, the Gospel of the Ebionites is supposed to be incomplete: *οὐχ ὅλῳ δὲ πληρεστάτῳ* (30.13.2).

In contrast to this he writes elsewhere that Cerinthus and Carpocrates used the Gospel of Matthew especially because of the beginning which records that Jesus was from the generation of Joseph and Mary (30.14.1).

From the above it appears that Epiphanius depends on evidence known to him from previous Christian authors. However, he knew that a Jewish Christian Gospel written in Greek and without genealogy existed. He often tried to combine his knowledge about this Gospel with the evidence handed down to him, without noticing that his sources were speaking about a different Gospel.

Finally Epiphanius writes with regard to the Nazoraeans that they also used the Gospel of Matthew *πληρέστατον Ἑβραϊστί* and *Ἑβραϊκοῖς γράμμασιν* (29.9.4). It is evident that Epiphanius is not personally familiar with this Gospel, since he is uncertain whether it possessed a genealogy or not. He appears to be dependent on a source unknown to us. But it is feasible that the sect of the Nazoraeans used an Aramaic or Hebrew Gospel. A very important question is whether this Gospel can be identified with the Gospel known to Eusebius and mentioned in his Theophany. This would seem to be undeniable.

Jerome writes that he received the Gospel of Matthew from the Nazoraeans and was able to copy it. He tells his readers that this Gospel was written 'in Iudea . . . hebreis litteris verbisque' for those who came to believe among the Jews. He does not know who translated it into Greek. He adds that the Gospel was also present in the library at Caesarea (*De viris ill.* III).

From other passages it is clear that he was indeed acquainted with a Gospel in Hebrew or Aramaic. He often speaks about a Hebrew Gospel or the Hebrew original (cf. *In Matth.* 2, 5; *In Ps. tract.* 135; *Epist.* 20, 5 and *In Eph.* 5, 4). He was of course not quoting from the original Matthew in Hebrew letters since such a writing never existed. Although Jerome sometimes writes that he used the authentic Matthew (*Epist.* 20, 5; *In Matth.* 2, 5 and *In Ps. tract.* 135), he himself is also aware that this is doubtful. This is shown in *In Matth.* 12, 13, where he writes about this Gospel: 'quod vocatur a plerisque Mathei authenticum', and in *Adv. Pel.* III.22, where it is said: 'ut plerique autumnant juxta Mattheum'.

It is, however, likely that Jerome really received this Gospel from the Nazoraeans (*In Is.* 40, 9–11; *In Is. prol.* 65; *In Hiez.* 16, 13 and 18, 5–9; *In Matth.* 23, 35 and 27, 51; *Adv. Pel.* III.2). The identification of this Gospel with another one in the library of Caesarea about which he speaks in *Adv. Pel.* III.2 cannot be definitely verified but it is credible that such a Gospel was present in this library. We can accept that this is the same Gospel as that known to Eusebius and mentioned in his Theophany.

In one of his later writings Jerome is uncertain in which language the Gospel was written. He writes: 'Chaldaico quidem Syroque sermone sed Hebraicis litteris' (*Adv. Pel.* III.2). Such a remark would not be possible if Jerome had been really copying this work, yet in other passages he tells his readers that he translated this work 'not long ago' (*In Matth.* 12, 13; *In Micha* 7, 6 and *De viris ill.* II). This statement is obviously false. It is likely that he translated only an occasional passage from his copy.

Jerome said that this Gospel was also called the Gospel to the Hebrews (*In Matth.* 6, 11 and 37, 16; *In Is.* 40, 9–11; *In Is. prol.* 65; *In Hiez.* 16, 13 and 18, 5–9; *In Micha* 7, 6; *Adv. Pel.* III.2), and that it was quoted by Origen (*De viris ill.* II). Here Jerome made his biggest mistake which resulted in his uncritically borrowing from Origen's quotations of the Gospel of the Hebrews, being of the opinion that it was the same Gospel as the Aramaic one known to him.

Nevertheless we gather from Jerome that he was acquainted with a Gospel in Aramaic used by the Nazoraeans which was also mentioned by Epiphanius.[1] After Jerome, early Christian authors do not show any original knowledge with regard to Aramaic Gospels.

This means that in Eusebius, Epiphanius and Jerome reference is made to an Aramaic Gospel. It is likely that they are speaking about the same work used by the Nazoraeans and present in the library of Caesarea. It is doubtful whether this Gospel was known to Hegesippus, although he might be acquainted with an early effort to render the Gospel into Syriac and traditions in Hebrew or Aramaic in an oral version.

It is, of course, hazardous to venture an opinion concerning the nature of this Aramaic, Syriac and Hebrew Gospel tradition. We may say that inquiries into the material showed that the Nazoraeans and the early Syriac Gospel tradition showed the influence of early West Aramaic usage. A direct influence by these Gospels on the Greek text must be excluded, although the early Syriac versions obviously

[1] The same opinion in A. Schmidtke, *Neue Fragmente zu den judenchristlichen Evangelien*, in *TU* XXXVII (Leipzig, 1911), p. 66; G. Bardy, 'Saint Jérôme et l'Évangile selon les Hébreux', in *Mélanges de Science Relig.* III (1964), pp. 5–36, and P. Vielhauer, *Judenchristliche Evangelien*, in Hennecke–Schneemelcher, *Neutest. Apokryphen* I[3], p. 86.

influenced later Syriac translations. If Aramaic or Hebrew Gospel tradition influenced the Greek text, it came through the direct influence of the Aramaic or Hebrew oral tradition on the Greek text in an environment where both Greek and Aramaic were spoken,[1] thus in early Christian communities with a predominantly Jewish population.[2] This, however, does not imply that where these traditions are found in, for example, the Western Text, this text is better or earlier but only that it developed in an environment where a lively Gospel tradition was present influencing the Gospels written in Greek.

1 See Black, *An Aramaic Approach* . . ., p. 281–6; A. F. J. Klijn, 'John XIV 22 and the Name of Judas Thomas', in *Studies in John* presented to J. N. Sevenster, in Supplements to *Novum Testamentum* XXIV (Leiden, 1970), pp. 88–96, and A. F. J. Klijn, 'Jerome's Quotations from a Nazoraean Interpretation of Isaiah' (in *Judéo-Christianisme*. Recherches Historiques et Théologiques offertes en Hommage à J. Daniélou (Paris, 1972), pp. 241–55.

2 See A. F. J. Klijn, *A Survey of the Researches into the Western Text of the Gospel and Acts*, part two: 1949–69, in Supplements to *Novum Testamentum* XXI (Leiden, 1969), pp. 66–70.

St Jerome's explicit references to variant readings in manuscripts of the New Testament

BRUCE M. METZGER

It is difficult to overestimate the importance of biblical citations made by early church fathers for the textual criticism of the New Testament. Besides patristic testimony which bears on an individual set of variant readings, the wider induction of evidence enables one to isolate and identify 'local texts'. Of still greater importance is the occasional comment made by a father, drawing attention to the existence of variant readings in contemporary copies of the New Testament. Such references enable the modern scholar not only to assess the critical acumen of the patristic writer in choosing among readings, but also to determine more precisely the emergence and currency of one or another alternative reading.

Among the more scholarly patristic writers Origen and Jerome take first place in the Eastern and the Western Churches respectively. In a previous publication a study was made of 'Explicit References in the Works of Origen to Variant Readings in New Testament Manuscripts'.[1] The writings of Jerome deserve similar attention. To be sure, certain aspects of Jerome's work as a textual critic have already been discussed. K. K. Hulley,[2] for example, has collected from Jerome's treatises a wide variety of comments that call attention to various kinds of scribal mistakes in biblical manuscripts. These include copyists' errors arising from (1) faulty word-division, (2) faulty punctuation, (3) confusion of number-signs, (4) confusion of similar letters, (5) confusion of abbreviations, (6) dittography and haplography, (7) metathesis of letters, (8) assimilation, (9) omissions,

1 Published originally in *Biblical and Patristic Studies in Memory of Robert Pierce Casey*, edited by J. Neville Birdsall and Robert W. Thomson (Freiburg im Breisgau, 1963), pp. 78–95, and reprinted, with minor additions, in Metzger's *Historical and Literary Studies, Pagan, Jewish, and Christian* (Leiden and Grand Rapids, Mich., 1968), pp. 88–103.

2 K. K. Hulley, 'Principles of Textual Criticism Known to St Jerome', *Harvard Studies in Classical Philology*, lv (1944), pp. 87–109, esp. pp. 94–101.

(10) transpositions, (11) conscious emendation, and (12) interpolations.

Helpful as Hulley's work is, however, one looks in vain for sustained discussion of instances in which Jerome mentions variant readings in copies of the Scriptures that were current in his day.[1] It is the purpose of the following pages to examine more than two dozen such instances in order to shed light on several important matters, notably: (1) the evaluation of Jerome's sagacity as a textual critic, and (2) the proportion of manuscript evidence for and against a given variant reading extant today as compared with the proportion of manuscript evidence known to Jerome.

In the following discussions citations of the Vulgate are taken from the recently edited text *Biblia sacra iuxta Vulgatam versionem*, edited by Robert Weber and published by the Württembergische Bibelanstalt (Stuttgart, 1969; 2nd edition, 1975). References to works of Jerome not specified by title are to be understood as references to his commentary on the passage being discussed.

1 (Matt. v.22). In his treatise *Against the Pelagians* (II.7) Jerome mentions that in Jesus' statement forbidding anger against one's brother 'most of the ancient copies do not have the qualification *without a cause*' (*in plerisque codicibus antiquis* sine causa *additum non est*). Likewise in his *Commentary on Matthew* Jerome states that 'in certain copies *without a cause* is added, but in the true copies the meaning is plain and anger is totally abrogated' (*in quibusdam codicibus additur* sine causa; *ceterum in veris definita sententia est et ira penitus tollitur*). Among Greek witnesses extant today the great majority add *εἰκῇ* (ℵ^{c} D K L W *Δ Θ Π* fam^{1} fam^{13} Old Latin), while 𝔓$^{67\ vid}$ ℵ* B 2174^{vid} and the Vulgate lack the word.

2 (Matt. vi.25). Jerome states that after Jesus' words 'Be not anxious for your life, what you shall eat', 'some copies' (*codices nonnulli*) add 'or what you shall drink'. Today the shorter text is read by ℵ fam^{1} 892 *al.* and the Vulgate.

3 (Matt. xi.19). Is wisdom justified by her works or by her children? Jerome mentions that in certain copies (*in quibusdam evangeliis*) instead of 'children' one finds 'works'. In his opinion this reading is preferable, for (as he puts it) 'Wisdom seeks not the testimony of the voice but of works' (*Sapientia quippe non quaerit vocis testimonium sed operum*). Today *ἔργων* is read by ℵ B* W, while *τέκνων* is read by the great majority of witnesses, including the Vulgate.

[1] Hulley cites only three examples, *Harvard Studies in Classical Philogy*, p. 92.

4 (Matt. xi.23). Instead of the reading of the Vulgate, 'And you, Capernaum, will you be exalted to heaven?', Jerome supplies the information that 'in another copy we find (*in altero exemplari reperimus*) "And you, Capernaum, which are exalted unto heaven [shall come down to hell]."' The latter reading is preserved today in *Π*^{mg} 700 *al* and the Textus Receptus. The Vulgate follows the reading of א B* D W *Θ al* (μὴ ἕως οὐρανοῦ ὑψωθήσῃ).

5 (Matt. xiii.35). Jerome knows that 'some copies' (*nonnulli codices*) of the Gospel according to Matthew introduce the citation of Ps lxxviii.2 with the words 'which was written through Isaiah the prophet'. This is the reading today of א* *Θ* fam^{1} fam^{13} 33 *al.* In his commentary on Ps lxxviii (lxxvii), he supposes that the Evangelist originally read '... through Asaph the prophet' and that subsequently a copyist 'began to say "Who is this Asaph the prophet?" and thereupon altered the name to the more familiar Isaiah.' The Vulgate reads 'through the prophet' (*per prophetam*).

6 (Matt. xvi.2–3). According to Jerome, the logion concerning the ability to foretell the weather ('When it is evening, you say, "It will be fair weather, ..."') 'is not present in most copies' (*hoc in plerisque codicibus non habetur*). It is, however, included in the Vulgate and in C D (F) G H K L M S U *Δ Π al pler*. The words are omitted in א B V X Y *Γ Ω al.*

7 (Matt. xxi.31). In the Vulgate text of this famous and highly perplexing nest of variant readings concerning the two sons, each of whom was asked to go and work in the father's vineyard, the first says 'No', but afterwards repents; the second says 'Yes', but does nothing. In reply to Jesus' question 'Which of the two did the will of the father?' the manuscripts differ in reading 'the first' or 'the last'. Jerome, who knew of copies in his day that read the nonsensical answer ('the last'), suggested that through perversity the Jews intentionally gave an absurd reply in order to spoil the point of the parable. Although it is generally agreed today that Jerome's supposition attributes far-fetched psychological and overly subtle literary motives to the Jews and/or to the evangelist, one ought still to give attention to his comment, 'It must be understood that in the true copies it does not read "the last" but "the first"' (*sciendum est in veris exemplaribus non haberi* novissimum *sed* primum). Wordsworth and White print *primus*, whereas Weber prints *novissimus.*[1]

1 For a succinct account of the exceedingly complicated state of the Greek evidence, see Metzger, *A Textual Commentary on the Greek New Testament, ad loc.*

8 (Matt. xxiv.36). Jerome treats at length the important variant reading 'neither the Son' knows the hour of the parousia: 'In certain Latin manuscripts there is an addition *neque filius*, although this addition is not present in Greek manuscripts, especially those of Adamantius and Pierius.[1] But because it is read by some manuscripts, it seems that it must be discussed' (*In quibusdam Latinis codicibus additum est* neque filius, *cum in Graecis et maxime Adamantii et Pierii exemplaribus hoc non habeatur additum; sed quia in nonnullis legitur, disserendum videtur*). After adducing other passages in scripture that refer to the wisdom of the Saviour (e.g. Col. ii.3), Jerome concludes that the variant reading should not be adopted, nor is it read by the Vulgate. It is present today in ℵ*,b B D Θ fam13 *al.*

9 (Mk xvi.9). In more than one treatise Jerome gives attention to the ending(s) of the Gospel according to Mark. In his reply to several questions raised by a certain Hedibia, a lady of Gaul who was much interested in the study of scripture, he discusses, among other problems, how one can reconcile the diverse accounts of the resurrection appearances in Matt. xxviii.1 and Mk xvi.1, 2, and 9. He writes (*Epist.* 120, 3): 'There is a twofold solution to this question. Either we reject the testimony of Mark, which is met with in only a few copies of the Gospel – almost all the codices of Greece being without this passage (especially since it seems to narrate what is different from and contradictory to the other evangelists) – or else it must be responded that both [evangelists] state what is true' (*Cuius quaestionis duplex solutio est. Aut enim non recipimus Marci testimonium, quod in raris fertur evangeliis omnibus Graeciae libris paene hoc capitulum in fine non habentibus, praesertim cum diversa atque contraria evangelistis ceteris narrare videatur, aut hoc respondendum quod uterque verum dixerit*).

10 (Mk xvi.14). Until the first decade of the twentieth century no manuscript of Mark was known to be extant that contained in Greek a most remarkable addition after Mk xvi.14. All we had was Jerome's statement that 'in certain copies, and especially in the Greek codices, it is written, according to Mark, at the end of his Gospel: "At length Jesus appeared to the Eleven as they were at table; and he upbraided them for their lack of faith and hardness of heart, in that they did not believe those who had seen him after he had risen. And they began to apologize, saying: 'This world is the substance of iniquity and unbelief,

[1] Adamantius is a surname of honor given to Origen, and Pierius is no doubt the presbyter of Alexandria who lived at Rome after the Diocletian persecution. He was styled 'the Younger Origen' on account of his learning, and was perhaps the teacher of Pamphilus (Eusebius, *Hist. eccles.* VII.32; Jerome, *De viris ill.* 76).

which (or: This world of iniquity and unbelief is under Satan and) does not allow the true virtue of God to be understood because of unclean spirits; therefore now reveal your justice' " ' (*in quibusdam exemplaribus et maxime in Graecis codicibus iuxta Marcum in fine eius evangelii scribitur:* Postea quum accubuissent undecim, apparuit eis Iesus, et exprobravit incredulitatem et duritiam cordis eorum quia his qui viderant eum resurgentem non crediderunt. Et illi satisfaciebant dicentes: Saeculum istud iniquitatis et incredulitatis substantia (v.l. sub Satana) est quae non sinit per immundos spiritus veram dei apprehendi virtutem. Idcirco iam nunc revela iustitiam tuam). Then in 1907 Charles L. Freer of Detroit acquired a copy of the Four Gospels known today as Codex Washingtonianus which contains, at even somewhat greater length, the Greek text of this remarkable saying attributed to the risen Lord.[1]

11 (Luke xiv.27). This verse, which closes with the same five words as does the preceding verse (*οὐ δύναται εἶναί μου μαθητής*), is omitted (because of parablepsis) in M* R *Γ* and many other manuscripts. According to Jerome, however, 'ancient copies' (*antiqua exemplaria*) contained the sentence (*Epist.* 127, 6); it is present in the Vulgate.

12 (Luke xxii.43f). The statement concerning the bloody sweat and the angel from heaven that strengthened Jesus in Gethsemane is lacking in 𝔓[75] ℵ[a] A B T W *al.* The passage must have been missing also in manuscripts known to Jerome, for he states (*Adv. Pel.* II.16) that 'in certain copies, Greek as well as Latin, the following words are found written by Luke, "There appeared to him an angel from heaven to strengthen him; etc." ' (*in quibusdam exemplaribus tam Graecis quam Latinis invenitur scribente Luca:* Apparuit illi angelus; etc.). The passage is present in the Vulgate; among Latin manuscripts, it is lacking (according to Wordsworth and White) only in MS *f*.

13 (John vii.53–viii.11). The *pericope de adultera*, Jerome states (*Adv. Pel.* II.17), 'is found in many of both the Greek as well as the Latin copies of the Gospel according to John' (*in evangelio secundum Iohannem in multis et Graecis et Latinis codicibus invenitur de adultera muliere*). It is included by the Vulgate, though it is lacking in several Old Latin manuscripts. As is well-known, it is absent from 𝔓[66] 𝔓[75] ℵ A[vid] B C[vid] L N T W X Y *Δ* *Θ* *Ψ* 0141 0211 *al.*

14.(Acts xv.29). Whether the Apostolic Decree made reference to abstaining from *πνικτῶν* (ℵ* A* B C 81 614 2412) or from *πνικτοῦ* (𝔓[74] ℵ[c] A[2] E P *Ψ* *al*) or whether the words were omitted altogether (D *al*),

[1] Cf. Caspar René Gregory, *Das Freer-Logion* (Leipzig, 1908).

is disputed. In company with other Western fathers, Jerome (*Com. on Gal.*, 5.2) quotes the text without *καὶ πνικτῶν* and then adds, 'Or, in some copies it is written, "and from things strangled" ' (*sive in nonnullis exemplaribus scriptum est*, et a suffocatis). Unfortunately he does not indicate whether the copies referred to were Latin or Greek or both. The Vulgate includes *suffocato* (so Weber; Wordsworth and White include the word, enclosed within square brackets).

15 (Rom. xii.11). In a letter to Marcella, Jerome defends himself against the charge of having altered the text of scripture, and declares that he has merely brought the Latin version of the New Testament into agreement with the Greek original: 'the Latin manuscripts of the Scriptures are proved to be faulty by the variations which all of them exhibit, and my object has been to restore them to the form of the Greek original, from which my detractors do not deny that they have been translated' (*Epist.* 27, 1). Later in the letter he gives several examples, including a reference to Rom. xii.11f: 'They may say if they will, "rejoicing in hope, serving *the time*", but we will say "rejoicing in hope, serving *the Lord*" ' (*illi legant* spe gaudentes, tempori servientes, *nos legamus* domino servientes). The variant arose because scribes misread *κυρίῳ* (𝔓[46] ℵ A B $D^{b,c}$ P *Ψ al*) as *καιρῷ* (D* F G). The Vulgate reads *domino servientes*.

16 (Rom. xvi.25–7). In his commentary on Ephesians (3.5) Jerome mentions that the doxology, 'Now to him who is able . . .' is found 'in most copies' (*in plerisque codicibus*) of the Epistle to the Romans. By this statement, therefore, Jerome witnesses to the existence of copies that lack the doxology altogether (as is true of F^{gr} G 629). The Vulgate includes the doxology at this place.[1]

17 (1 Cor. ix.5). The text of this passage has been much tampered with by the advocates or the opponents of celibacy. In his discussion in his treatise *Against Jovinianus* (1.26), Jerome first quotes the verse with the plural *γυναῖκας* (as is read also by F G Tertullian and other Western fathers).[2] Then he adds that 'in [the] Greek copies' (*in Graecis codicibus*) one finds, 'Have we no right to lead about women that are sisters, or wives?' (*Numquid non habemus potestatem sorores mulieres vel uxores circumducendi?*). Today the great majority of Greek manuscripts

[1] On the variant see now Harvey Gamble, Jr., *The Textual History of the Letter to the Romans*, a Study in Textual and Literary Criticism (Grand Rapids, Mich., 1977).

[2] This reading, Zuntz thinks, 'is original; the crude expression suits Paul's polemical fervour, and was bound to provoke the various softening substitutes which the other witnesses transmit' (G. Zuntz, *The Text of the Epistles* (London, 1953), p. 138).

(including 𝔓46) read ἀδελφὴν γυναῖκα, which is also witnessed by the Vulgate.

18 (1 Cor. xiii.3). Did Paul write, 'If I give up my body to be burned ...' (καυθήσομαι) or '... that I may glory' (καυχήσωμαι)?[1] Jerome testifies (*Com. on Gal.*, 5.25 *fin.*) that each reading is found in Greek and Latin manuscripts: *Scio in Latinis codicibus, in eo testimonio quod supra posuimus:* Si tradidero corpus meum ut glorier, ardeam *habere pro* glorier. *Sed ob similitudinem verbi, qua apud Graecos* ardeam *et* glorier, *id est* καυθήσομαι *et* καυχήσομαι, *una litterae parte distinguitur, apud nostros error inolevit. Sed et apud ipsos Graecos exemplaria sunt diversa.*

19 (1 Cor. xv.51). Three principal forms of this verse were in circulation during Jerome's day.[2] He states (*Epist.* 119, 2) that the reading 'We shall all sleep, but we shall not all be changed' (א (A) C G 33 1739) and the reading 'We shall not all sleep, but we shall all be changed' (B D^{c} K P Ψ 81 *al*) were each found in Greek copies (*utrumque in Graecis codicibus invenitur*). The third reading, 'We shall all rise, but we shall not all be changed', was current, according to Jerome, in Latin manuscripts, from which he admitted it into the Vulgate. Today it is the reading of D* Old Latin MSS and Marcion.

20 (Gal. ii.5). Jerome testifies that 'according to [the] Greek manuscripts' (*iuxta Graecos codices*) the verse includes the words οἷς οὐδέ, but that a superior sense is obtained if one follows the reading of 'a Latin copy' (*Latini exemplaris*) and omits the two words. Today the omission is witnessed by D* it^{d,e} and several Western patristic writers. The Vulgate, however, includes *quibus neque*, following the overwhelming number of extant Greek witnesses.

21 (Gal. iii.1). Jerome states that 'in certain copies (*in quibusdam codicibus*) it reads, "Who has bewitched you *that you should not obey the truth?*" But because this is not present in the [Greek] copies of Adamantius,[3] we have omitted it.' Today the Textus Receptus, following C D^{c} K L P Ψ most minuscules and MSS of the Vulgate, adds τῇ ἀληθείᾳ μὴ πείθεσθαι from Gal. v.7. Modern editors of the Vulgate properly omit the phrase.

22 (Eph. iii.14). Jerome declares that after *ad Patrem* the words 'of

[1] For a strong case that the reading 'to be burnt' is original, see Zuntz, *ibid.*, pp. 35f; for the case that can be made for the originality of 'that I may glory', see K. W. Clark in *Studia Paulina in honorem Johannis de Zwaan* (Haarlem, 1953), pp. 61f.

[2] A fourth reading, 'We shall not all sleep, but we shall not all be changed', is read by 𝔓46, which looks like an accidental repetition of the negative.

[3] For Adamantius, see p. 182, n. 1, above.

our Lord Jesus Christ' are an addition 'in [the] Latin copies' (*in Latinis codicibus*) and should be rejected as inappropriate in the context. Nevertheless, according to Wordsworth and White, almost all of the oldest manuscripts of the Vulgate include the words, and they are admitted into present-day editions of the Vulgate. The words are absent from 𝔓46 ℵ* A B C P 33 81 1739 *al.*

23 (Eph. v.22). According to Jerome, 'that which is added in Latin copies, "Let them be subject", is not present in Greek copies, since it refers to the preceding words and is understood from "Be subject to one another in the fear of Christ" ' (*hoc quod in Latinis exemplaribus non habetur, siquidem ad superiora refertur et subauditur* subjectae et in timore Christi). Despite what Jerome says concerning the understanding of the Greek, ℵ A P *al* insert *ὑποτασσέσθωσαν*, and the Textus Receptus, following K L and other Byzantine witnesses, inserts *ὑποτάσσεσθε*. Most of the manuscripts of the Vulgate read *mulieres viris subditae sint.*

24 (Col. ii.18). Among the difficult textual problems involved in this verse is the variation between *ἃ μή* (most manuscripts and the Vulgate) and *ἃ* without *μή* (𝔓46 ℵ* A B D* 33). Jerome states (*Epist.* 121, 10) that 'each reading is current in Greek' (*utrumque enim habetur in Graeco*).

25 (1 Tim. i.15 and iii.1). Instead of 'it is a *faithful* saying' (ℵ A D G^gr H K P *Ψ al*) certain Latin witnesses (joined in iii.1 by the first hand of D) read '. . . a human saying' (*humanus sermo*). Jerome, however, defends his version, namely *fidelis sermo*, saying 'we are content to err with the Greeks, that is to say with the apostle himself, who spoke Greek' (*Epist.* 27, 3; cf. 15 above).

26 (1 Tim. v.19). Jerome implies that those who prefer Latin manuscripts 'may see fit to receive an accusation against a presbyter unconditionally; but we will say in the words of [the Greek manuscripts of] Scripture, "Against an elder receive not an accusation *except before two or three witnesses*" ' (*Epist.* 27, 3; cf. 15 above).

27 (Heb. ii.9). The old (and, according to Zuntz,[1] who follows Harnack, the original) reading, 'that he [Jesus], apart from God (*χωρὶς θεοῦ*) should taste death for every man', was current, according to Jerome, 'in certain copies' (*in quibusdam exemplaribus*). The Vulgate reads *gratia Dei*, following the generally accepted Greek reading *χάριτι θεοῦ*.

[1] See Zuntz, *The Text of the Epistles*, pp. 34, 285.

CONCLUSIONS

The data assembled above tend to confirm the generally favorable estimate held by scholars as to Jerome's sagacity as a textual critic.[1] Although he does not always expressly declare his own preference concerning two or more variant readings (6, 9, and 24), when he does do so it is usually for reasons that would be recognized today as valid and persuasive. In some cases intrinsic considerations (*Sachkritik*) tip the scales (1, 3, 20, and 22); in other instances it is presumed transcriptional probabilities (5).[2] In some cases he appeals to the antiquity of manuscripts that support a given reading (1 and 11), or to the presumed excellence of Greek copies of scripture belonging to famous scholars (8 and 21). When Greek and Latin manuscripts differ, he usually prefers the reading supported by the former (15, 19, 25, and 26), but not always (8, 10, and 20). Only rarely is Jerome swayed by considerations that appear to be far-fetched and overly subtle (7).

In several cases the current text of the Vulgate is contrary to the preference stated or implied by Jerome (3, 5, 6, 19, 20, and 22). In some instances such discrepancies may be explained by supposing that Jerome changed his mind; in others it may be that the text of the Vulgate has suffered in transmission.[3]

Jerome uses a wide variety of expressions in referring to the quality and the quantity of manuscript witnesses current in his day. Sometimes he describes them as 'true copies' (1 and 7) and at other times as 'ancient copies' (1 and 11). More often he is content to refer to the proportion of witnesses supporting a reading, as 'almost all copies' (9),

[1] See Hulley's study (p. 179, n. 2 above) and Evaristo Arns, *La technique du livre d'après saint Jérôme* (Paris, 1953), pp. 186ff. In his PhD Harvard dissertation 'Latin Textual Criticism in Antiquity' (1972), James E. G. Zetzel touches upon Jerome only incidentally. For a résumé see *Harvard Studies in Classical Philology*, lxxix (1974), pp. 284f.

[2] More than once Jerome, without specifically mentioning the existence of variant readings in contemporary manuscripts, explains the origin of discrepancies in the biblical record as having arisen from errors introduced by copyists. Thus, in discussing the difference between Mk (xv.25) and John (xix.14) in recording the hour when Jesus was crucified, he lays the blame for the difference upon scribes who confused the signs for numbers in Greek: *Error scriptorum fuit: et in Marco hora sexta scriptum fuit, sed multi pro* ἐπισήμῳ *Graeco putaverunt esse gamma* (*Tract. in Psalm.* 77 (*Anec. Mared.* III.2, p. 60); cf. Sebastián Bartina S.J., 'Ignotum *episèmon* gabex', *Verbum Domini*, xxxvi (1958), pp. 16–37).

[3] Several scholars have argued that such differences imply that someone other than Jerome (was it Pelagius ?) was responsible for producing the Vulgate text of the Pauline Epistles; for a discussion of these theories, see Metzger, *The Early Versions of the New Testament* (Oxford, 1977), pp. 356ff.

'most copies' (1, 6, and 16), 'many copies' (13), 'few copies' (9), and 'another copy' (4). Sometimes he is quite indefinite, referring to certain copies' (1, 3, 8, 10, 12, 21, and 27) or to 'some copies' (2, 5, 8, and 14).

When one considers the proportion of manuscript evidence for and against a given reading that is extant today as compared with the proportion known to Jerome, some rather remarkable reversals are disclosed. Thus, whereas in some instances Jerome declares that most of the ancient copies contain a given reading (1), or do not contain a given passage (6 and 9), the manuscripts that happen to have survived today present just the opposite picture so far as number of witnesses is concerned. Although such disparities of proportion of evidence for and against a reading may of course be due to limitations of Jerome's knowledge, the disquieting possibility remains that the evidence available to us today may, in certain cases, be totally unrepresentative of the distribution of readings in the early church. For this reason, if for no other, modern textual scholars must not fail to give careful attention to explicit comments in the fathers as to variant readings current in contemporary manuscripts. A comprehensive collection of all such references remains an unfulfilled *desideratum* of long standing.[1]

ADDENDUM

The following list is offered by way of making a beginning of collecting evidence from patristic authors who mention variant readings in contemporary copies of the New Testament. Most of the items in the list have been assembled from references in the *apparatus critici* of Tischendorf's *Novum Testamentum Graece*, 8th edition (where the passages in the patristic treatises concerned are identified) and of the United Bible Societies' *Greek New Testament*. Additional items have been culled from a variety of editions, which are in every case briefly identified.

Acacius: 1 Cor. xv.51
Adamantius (*ap.* Jerome): Matt. xxiv.36
Ambrose: Matt. xxiv.36; Luke vii.35, xi.13; Gal. iv.8; Phil. iii.3; Heb. ii.9
Ambrose (pseudo): Rev. xi.2
Ambrosiaster: Rom. v.14, xii.11; 1 Cor. v.3; Gal. ii.5

[1] Suggested at the close of the last century by Eberhard Nestle, *Einführung in das griechische Neue Testament*, 2te Aufl. (Göttingen, 1899), pp. 266f.

Anastasius: Matt. xxvii.18
Andrew of Caesarea: Rev. iii.7, xv.6
Anonymous scholia: Matt. ii.18, xx.28, xxii.12; Mk xi.13; Luke xvi. 19, xxii.43f, xxiv.13; John i.29, vii.53, xxi.25; Rom. viii.24
Arethas of Caesarea: Rom. iii.9 (K. Staab, *Pauluskommentare*, 1933, p. 654); Rev. i.2, iii.7
Athanasius: Matt. v.22; Rom. viii.11; II Thess. ii.9
Augustine: Matt. v.22 and 32, vi.4, x.3, xxvii.9; Luke iii.22; John xvi.13; Rom. v.14, vii.18, xiii.14; I Cor. xv.5 and 51; Phil. iii.3; Col. ii.18
Basil: Luke xxii.36; Eph. i.1
Bede: Acts iii.27, iv.10, v.3, vii.17, viii.37, x.32, xiii.20 and 33, xiv.19, xv.24, xvii.26, xviii.17, xxi.25, xxii.9, xxiv.6–8
Cassiodorus: Gal. ii.5
Chronicon Paschale: John xix.14
Chrysostom: John i.28
Claudius of Turin: Gal. ii.5
Didymus: I Cor. xv.51; II Cor. i.1
Ephraem: Luke i.35
Epiphanius: Matt. i.8, ii.3, ii.11 (Westcott–Hort, volume II *ad loc.*), viii.28; Luke viii.26, xix.41, xxii.42f; John i.28; Eph. i.1
Eusebius: Matt. xiii.35, xxvii.9; Mk i.2, xvi.3, 8ff; John xix.14
Euthalius: Jude 25
Euthymius: Matt. vii.24; Mk xvi.9; John vii.53
Gregory of Nyssa: Mk xvi.2 and 9
Hilary: Luke xxii.42
Irenaeus: Rev. xiii.18
Isidore: Heb. ix.17
Macarius Magnes:[1] Mk xv.34; John xii.31
Macedonius (*ap.* Athanasius): Rom. viii.11
Marcion (*ap.* Epiphanius): Eph. i.1
Maximinus: I Cor. xv.47
Maximus of Turin: I Cor. xv.51
Oecumenius (pseudo): Acts xiv.26; II Pet. i.1
Origen: Matt. ii.18, iv.17, vi.1, viii.28, xvi.20, xviii.1, xix.19, xxi.5

1 In view of the rarity of the only edition of the Greek text of Macarius Magnes' *Apocriticus* (that of C. Blondel, published at Paris in 1876), Macarius' comment concerning the variant at John xii.31 may be cited here: *ὡς ἔχει τινὰ τῶν ἀντιγράφων, 'βληθήσεται κάτω'*. The variant at Mk xv.34 (*ὠνείδισάς με*) is attributed by Macarius to an anti-Christian opponent, thought by modern scholars to have been Porphyry, who comments on the variety among the Gospel accounts in reporting Jesus' Cry of Dereliction.

and 15, xxiv.19, xxvii.16f; Mk ii.14, iii.18; Luke i.46, viii.26–37, ix.48, xiv.19, xxiii.45; John i.3–4 and 28, iii.34; Rom. iii.5, iv.3, v.14, vii.6, xii.11 and 13, xiv.23, xvi.23; Eph. ii.4 (*JTS*, iii (1902), p. 403); Col. ii.15; II Tim. iv.6; Heb. ii.9

Pelagius: Rom. xii.13; I Cor. x.22, xv.51; Col. iii.15; II Thess. ii.3 (Souter, *Pelagius's Expositions*, volume I, 120f)

Peter of Laodicea: Matt. v.44, vi.13, xxvii.16 (edited by G. Heinrici, 1908)

Pierius (*ap.* Jerome): Matt. xxvi.36

Porphyry: see Macarius Magnes and p. 189, n. 1

Primasius: Rev. ii.22

Severus: Mk xvi.9

Socrates: I John iv.3

Theodore of Mopsuestia: Rom. xii.13; Heb. ii.10

Theodoret: Rom. viii.11, xvi.3

Theophylact: II Thess. iii.14; Heb. ii.10, x.1

Victor of Antioch: Mk xvi.9 (J. W. Burgon, *Last Twelve Verses*, p. 288 [American edition, p. 368])

Victor of Vita: I John v.7–8

Victorinus of Rome: Gal. ii.5

The text of Acts x.36

HARALD RIESENFELD

Brackets in the text of the Greek New Testament edited by the United Bible Societies – a modern standard work to which Dr Black has made highly deserving contributions – indicate as a matter of course that problems of textual criticism still remain unsolved. In the majority of cases the choice between the longer reading, which is enclosed in brackets, and the shorter reading is of no great importance. This is precisely why it is difficult to make a decision based on arguments of internal evidence. There are, however, cases where a decision is needed for an adequate understanding of the text, but where we face the dilemma that neither external nor internal evidence provides a convincing basis for a solution of the problem involved in the text.

An instance of this kind of difficulty is given by Acts x.36. *The Greek New Testament* (3rd edition, 1975) reads here *τὸν λόγον [ὃν] ἀπέστειλεν τοῖς υἱοῖς Ἰσραὴλ εὐαγγελιζόμενος εἰρήνην διὰ Ἰησοῦ Χριστοῦ – οὗτός ἐστιν πάντων κύριος – ὑμεῖς οἴδατε, τὸ γενόμενον ῥῆμα καθ' ὅλης τῆς Ἰουδαίας*. As the punctuation indicates, the editors have understood the passage in the following way: 'You know the word which he sent to the children of Israel, preaching the good news of peace through Jesus Christ (he is Lord of all), the word which was proclaimed throughout all Judea' (so RSV and, in a similar way, TEV). This interpretation lies underneath the Greek text of Nestle (25th edition, 1963) as well as that of the British and Foreign Bible Society (2nd edition, 1958). It is favoured in the commentaries by C. S. C. Williams (1957), H. Conzelmann (1963), R. P. C. Hanson (1967) and B. M. Newman and E. A. Nida (*A Translator's Handbook*, 1972).

This understanding implies that the initial *τὸν λόγον* is supposed to be the object of the predicate in the main clause, i.e. *ὑμεῖς οἴδατε*. The object *τὸν λόγον* is in its part determined by a relative clause, *ὃν ἀπέστειλεν* 'which he (i.e. God; cf. verses 34f) sent'. The latter and larger part of the sentence, from *τὸ γενόμενον ῥῆμα* to the end of verse 38, forms then an apposition, which means that the phrase *τὸ γενόμενον ῥῆμα* refers to *τὸν λόγον* at the beginning of verse 36. The weight of external evidence is beyond doubt in favour of the longer reading where *ὅν* is retained.

There remain, however, three difficulties in the sentence if it is understood in the way which is shown by the translation: (1) the absence of a connecting particle together with the initial *τὸν λόγον*; (2) the fact that the final apposition is strangely long and heavily loaded; (3) the incongruity of the two nouns *λόγος* and *ῥῆμα* in a clause where *ῥῆμα* is taken to be an apposition referring to *λόγος*. Is *τὸ γενόμενον ῥῆμα* really a phrase which adequately expounds and elucidates the significance of *λόγος* taken in the sense which has already been given to it by the relative clause? And does *τὸ γενόμενον ῥῆμα* in fact mean 'the word which was proclaimed'?

A slightly differing interpretation of the same sentence has been given by C. C. Torrey.[1] He considers *τὸν λόγον ὃν ἀπέστειλεν . . . διὰ Ἰησοῦ Χριστοῦ* a suspended construction which can be literally translated into grammatical Aramaic: 'As for the word which he sent to the children of Israel, proclaiming good news of peace through Jesus Christ . . . you know what took place (*τὸ γενόμενον ῥῆμα*) . . .' F. F. Bruce (1956) gives his consent to this solution.

Quite another way of understanding is chosen by those scholars who prefer to follow that minority of witnesses (represented not least by B) where *ὅν* is lacking. This text also makes sense if it is rendered, 'He sent his word to the children of Israel, proclaiming good news of peace by Jesus Christ . . . You know what took place throughout all Judea . . .' (so NEB and Jerusalem Bible). Among commentators, K. Lake and H. J. Cadbury (1933) as well as E. Haenchen (1956) are in favour of this interpretation. Once again a number of difficulties remain: (1) the absence of a connecting particle; (2) the exclusion of *ὅν* which from the point of view of textual criticism is *lectio probabilior*; (3) if verse 36 is a main clause, it hardly makes sense in the line of thought developed in verses 34–7.

Rather odd, with regard to grammar as well as content, is the interpretation given by Blass and Debrunner, 'The word which he sent (*τὸν λόγον ὃν ἀπέστειλεν*) to the children of Israel . . . is Lord of all' (*οὗτός ἐστιν πάντων κύριος*), where the accusative *τὸν λόγον* is said to be due to an assimilation to *ὅν*.[2]

Now the obstacles of grammar and textual criticism disappear if we

[1] C. C. Torrey, 'The composition and date of Acts', *HTS*, 1 (1916).

[2] F. Blass and A. Debrunner, *Grammatik des neutestamentlichen Griechisch*, 14th edition, edited by F. Rehkopf (1976).

retain the longer and better reading, i.e. ὅν, and take τὸν λόγον as an apposition resuming the whole statement made in the ὅτι-clause in verses 34–5. It is a well-known fact that appositions can be attached not only to single words but to statements made in clauses. In such a case the nominative or, more frequently, the accusative is used for the apposition.[1] Moreover, if τὸν λόγον is an apposition resuming the preceding ὅτι-clause, the apposition is after all ruled by the main verb, καταλαμβάνομαι, which makes the accusative still more natural. If we choose this interpretation, a comma will have to be put after verse 35 and a full stop after verse 36.

The whole passage, being the first part of Peter's speech in the house of Cornelius at Caesarea, can then be rendered as follows: 'Truly I realize that God does not show partiality, but in every nation anyone who fears him and does what is right is acceptable to him; (this is) the word which he sent to the children of Israel, proclaiming good news of peace through Jesus Christ – he is Lord of all. You know what took place throughout all Judea, beginning from Galilee after the baptism which John preached . . .' (verses 34–7).

If the sentence is taken in this way, the word which God sent to the children of Israel consists of the good news that God does not show partiality, but that whoever fears him and does what is right is acceptable to God, no matter what nation he belongs to. What is made clear in Peter's speech, which in the economy of Acts marks the beginning of the mission to the Gentiles, is that the Gospel which has been addressed to the Jews (by the message and the ministry of Jesus) from its beginning implies the fact that peace (between Jews and Gentiles) has been established by the mission and achievement of Jesus Christ. Therefore he is Lord of all (of Jews and Gentiles equally). It is obvious that the prepositional phrase διὰ Ἰησοῦ Χριστοῦ determines the word 'peace', cf. Eph. ii.14–17, and not the participle 'proclaiming the good news' (see Conzelmann).

This interpretation has the following advantages: (1) no connecting particle is needed, τὸν λόγον being an apposition; (2) the longer reading ὅν can be retained; (3) verses 34–7 make now a continuous line of thought, linking the conviction that the Gospel will have to be proclaimed to the Gentiles with the decisive and justifying event, which makes up the central part of Peter's speech; (4) λόγος in verse 36 receives a reasonable sense, viz. 'message', and is independent of ῥῆμα in verse 37.

The comma after οἴδατε (see *Greek New Testament*) has obviously to

[1] R. Kühner and B. Gerth, *Grammatik der griechischen Sprache*, volume 1 (1898), pp. 284–6; E. Schwyzer, *Griechische Grammatik*, volume 2 (1950), p. 617.

be dropped. Moreover, there is no need of a connecting particle with ὑμεῖς οἴδατε in verse 37. There are other instances in Acts of an emphatic use of personal pronouns at the beginning of a sentence where no particle appears, e.g. iii.25 ὑμεῖς ἐστε οἱ υἱοὶ τῶν προφητῶν, and xx.29 ἐγὼ οἶδα ὅτι εἰσελεύσονται λύκοι βαρεῖς.

In verses 34–7 Peter states that the mission to the Gentiles is inherent in God's will and promise, and that peace between Jews and Gentiles has been established through Jesus Christ. The proof of this fact can be found in the life, the death, and the resurrection of Christ, events which are said to be known to Peter's audience (ὑμεῖς οἴδατε) and which are considered a definite demonstration of God's goodwill and acting power, verses 37–41. In verses 42 and 43 the whole of the argument is summed up and the conclusion is drawn: the apostles have been sent to testify that Christ will be the judge of all but that whoever believes in him will receive forgiveness of sins.

If the interpretation which has been outlined here can be accepted, it might be possible to drop, in a future edition of the *Greek New Testament*, the brackets which now enclose ὅν.

The solution which we have ventured to propose is by no means far-fetched. On the contrary it is strange that no modern translator or commentator seems to have thought of it. Looking through older exegetical works I finally discovered that a nineteenth-century Swedish scholar had translated the passage and commented on it in the way outlined above.[1] From his presentation I could presume that he had not found it out himself. Consequently he must have taken it over. From where? It was satisfying to find the answer: almost certainly it was from J. A. Bengel. In his *Gnomon Novi Testamenti* the famous scholar remarks on Acts x.36: τὸν λόγον ὃν ἀπέστειλε, Hebraismus, ex quo את valet, *hoc est*. As we have seen, it is by no means necessary to suppose here an influence from the Hebrew language. Appositions to a clause are well known in Greek idiom. But Bengel saw that the statement in verse 36 sums up what has been said in verses 34–5.

A concluding remark might not be out of place. As far as I have been able to see, Bengel stands alone amongst his contemporaries with his understanding of Acts x.36. Yet it is extraordinary that his achievement in respect of this passage has not been taken over and carried on in the current of New Testament scholarship. A possible explanation is the fact that Bengel's note is extremely condensed in its Latin form and perhaps not easy to understand. Therefore his insight might have escaped the attention of posterity.

[1] H. M. Melin, *Det Nya Testamentet* (1865).

Traditional ethical patterns in the Pauline and post-Pauline letters and their development (lists of vices and house-tables)[1]

E. SCHWEIZER

I. LISTS OF VICES ('LASTERKATALOGE')[2]

1. 1 Thess. iv.3–6

In a missionary situation converts separate themselves from their fellow-citizens. Marks which distinguish them from those who have not accepted the new faith become, therefore, important. Hellenistic Judaism emphasized in this way the absence in its midst of idolatry and fornication, which was often combined with heathen festivals (Wisd. xiv.12; Ep. Jer. xliii). Sometimes greediness, often mentioned in Hellenistic lists, has been added. Thus, we find the three of them, for instance, in Test. Dan. v.5–7 and CD iv.17f. Their absence distinguishes also the young Christian congregations from their environment.

It is not surprising that they also form the first group of vices which we find in the Pauline letters,[3] although 'idolatry' is only hinted at when the apostle speaks of the 'heathen who do not know God'. The warning against these vices belongs to Paul's first missionary teaching and is traditionally connected with a forewarning about the Lord's coming judgment (verses 2, 6; cf. Wisd. xiv.30; IQS iv.11–14; slav. En. x.6). There are some new overtones, though. First, the power behind this new life is not simply the enthusiasm of a convert, but God's own Spirit (verse 8). Second, its goal is not a perfect group of converts, but love towards the brethren and challenge to those outside, which might induce

1 Being no specialist in the fields in which Matthew Black excels, I am not able to contribute anything valuable in these areas; but just because this is so, my essay may express my deep gratitude to him for so much in his work from which I have learned.

2 For all details and references cf. my essay 'Gottesgerechtigkeit und Lasterkataloge bei Paulus (inkl. Kol und Eph)', in *Rechtfertigung*, Festschrift für E. Käsemann (Tübingen, 1976), pp. 461–77.

3 *Πλεονεξία* (greed) is so typical for these lists that a reference to adultery in verse 6 (RSV) is very improbable.

them also to find their way to Jesus (verses 9–12). This is why the apostle does not speak of something extraordinary of which the church might boast. He points to traditionally accepted vices which everybody is expected to avoid and shows simply that the power to abstain from them has been given to his readers. Even more important is the whole context, which expresses the hope that they will grow in their new life. In short, although there are marks which distinguish the church from the non-church, the newness of their lives is nothing to boast about; it exists only as long as they grow in it.

2. 1 Cor. v.9–13

In the chronologically second passage we find the same triad of 'idolaters, fornicators and the greedy', supplemented and interpreted by 'robbers'. Most interesting is the fact that it does not speak of the world, in which these vices might be expected. It says, on the contrary, that to judge the world is none of the church's business, but belongs to God alone. To make himself quite clear, Paul repeats the list and states that he speaks of idolaters, fornicators, the greedy and robbers within the church, but adding now two more types of transgressors of God's law, namely the 'revilers and drunkards', types that might be found in the church more often than idolaters and robbers. This means that a first decision which has been taken once for all, like giving up idols, must be repeated time and time again, because the fundamental heathen vices, from which the converts have definitely separated themselves, continue to creep back in a more subtle form, for instance as calumny of the brethren or of those outside, or as uncontrolled drunkenness. The function of the traditional list of vices has totally changed with Paul; no longer does it distinguish the perfect church from the imperfect world; on the contrary, it serves to remind the church of the fact that vices, which it thinks to have left behind for ever, easily creep back.

3. 1 Cor. vi.9–11

The same list is repeated in the following chapter, enlarged by 'adulterers and homosexuals' – interpreting the traditional 'fornicators' – and by 'thieves' – interpreting the traditional 'greedy'. Traditional is also the warning that 'they will not inherit the kingdom of God' (cf. Gal. v.21; Eph. v.5, also Rev. xxi.7; slav. En. x.6 and Matt. xxv.34). The list has grown again; offences which may turn up in the church have been inserted. What is the function of this list? Paul reminds the Corinthians of their definite break away from all that: 'Such were some of you, but you were washed, sanctified, justified.' And yet, he does so in a context which treats the problem of church members going to court against one another and points to the Corinthian slogan 'All things are allowed', which they understand as liberty for going to prostitutes. Again, Paul deals with the same questions: How does the sanctification and justification conferred upon them in baptism live on in everyday life? How will God's definite election to a new life go on and prevail?

4. II Cor. xii.20f

Paul's second letter, written not much later, contains a totally different list. It mentions typical acts of unbrotherly behaviour within a community: 'quarrelling, jealousy, anger, selfishness, slander, gossip, conceit, disorder'. Again, it is in some way a traditional group; the first three items are repeated in Gal. v.20 and similarly in Rom. xiii.13 and Col. iii.8; and Ecclus. xl.5, xxviii.10, xxx.24; Prov. xxvii.4, vi.34 and IQS iv.9–11 are not very different. In II Cor. xii nothing is said about gross sins like idolatry or fornication. This is because the context is totally different from that of the former passages. Here, Paul speaks of what he is afraid to find in the church when he comes. The typical sins of the church belong, as it seems, not so much to the area of clear-cut immoral acts, but to that of unbrotherliness. And yet, surprisingly enough, the main reproaches of the old, traditional triad turn up again in the very next verse: their living in such unbrotherly demeanour shows that they have not yet really given up their 'impurity, fornication and licentiousness'.

5. Gal. v.19–22

Gal. v brings a much longer list. Verse 15 tells us that quarrels have arisen in the congregation. Thus it is not surprising that 'quarrelling, jealousy and anger', which head the list in II Cor. xii, appear again, together with other offences against the brotherhood, including 'drunkenness and carousing', which will turn up again in Rom. xiii.13 (and similarly in I Pet. iv.3). Before Paul comes to these terms, however, he starts with the two principal vices and specifies first 'fornication, impurity, licentiousness', then 'idolatry and sorcery'. He even refers his readers to his initial teaching and to his warning that such people 'will not inherit the kingdom of God'. That means again: in the discord of the church, the principal heathen vices come to life again. And yet this is not simply a moral statement. Strangely enough, it is exactly in this context that Paul reminds them of the fact that they are no longer under the law (verse 18). What Paul wants to explain to them goes much deeper. What they need is not new moral admonition, but the proclamation of their liberty under the lordship of God's grace and Spirit; for the fact that they 'bite and devour one another' shows that they no longer live under the rule of God's justification. What the apostle opposes to their discord with all its vices is therefore not a list of virtues, although scholars usually call it this, but 'the fruit of the Spirit'. It is fruit, not work, something which is not 'performed', but is growing. 'Fruit' is a singular over against the plurality of 'the works of the flesh', i.e. one whole and all-including way of life, in which morally good deeds are not to be boasted of, and in which morally wrong deeds are healed and integrated. 'Fruit' finally designates a behaviour which is not 'plain' as the works of the flesh are; i.e. the newness of the life of the Spirit becomes certainly visible in concrete acts, but never in such a way that one could point to unambiguous marks of a new and perfect morality. Just because it is the life of the Spirit, man possesses no yardstick of his own to measure and to judge it. The only criterion is the one which Paul mentions in the same context: 'The whole law is fulfilled in one word: You shall love your neighbour as yourself' (verse 14). Hence, he calls them back, not to extraordinary performances, but to 'faith working through love' (verse 6). All that he can say is therefore: 'Live as those that you are', or in his own words: 'Since we are living in the Spirit, in the Spirit let us walk!' (verse 25).

6. *Rom. xiii.13*

Much the same is to be said about the end of Rom. xiii. The emphasis on offences against the common life of the church is again typical. 1 Peter iv.3 will repeat the first four terms in chiastic order, followed also by two more vices, which, however, are different from those mentioned in Rom. xiii.[1] As in Gal. v, the list is preceded by the statement that love fulfils the law, and followed by a warning against the desires of the flesh. As in Gal. v, it becomes quite clear that Paul does not simply deal with moral requirements. What should happen is much more; they should 'put on the Lord Jesus Christ' (verse 14) and, in this way, pass from the reign of darkness into that of light; i.e. they are not merely to put on some virtues, but Jesus Christ himself; they are not merely to enter a more perfect state of moral conduct, but a new 'world'. This cosmic language roots in Hellenistic-Jewish ideas. Philo, older contemporary of Paul, speaks of God's Logos who 'puts on' the universe with its five elements, as the individual soul puts on the body and the wise man puts on the virtues (*Fuga* 110). The act of creation, in which God's life-

[1] A. Vögtle, 'Die Tugend- und Lasterkataloge im NT', *NTA* 16 4/5 (1936), p. 44.

giving Logos enters the world of created things, is paralleled with the birth of individual man and with his rebirth to real wisdom.[1] This shows how much the cosmic language of entering a new world is in the background of Paul's summons definitely to leave the old world of vices and to 'put on' Jesus Christ.

7. Rom. i.29–31

Even more suggestive is the context of this passage. The traditional warning against the coming wrath of God is actually the heading of the whole second half of this chapter. However, this eschatological wrath of God has already come with and in the proclamation of the Gospel, because this reveals man as he is. The traditional pattern of catalogues of vices is still detectable. Paul starts with the basic vice of idolatry, out of which fornication and similar vices arise (verses 22–4 and again 25–7), before he comes to his enumeration of all the various vices (verses 28–31). And yet this is absolutely different from all usual paraenesis. First, idolatry is not simply one, if the first, vice among others; for Paul, leaving God and filling his place with created things is *the* sin. All the so-called vices are not sins in the proper sense of the word. They are but consequences to which God gave up those who had already given him up. Thus the list of vices loses its moral pathos. They are but signs of a fundamental decision of man which goes much deeper. And second, the function of this more or less traditional list has changed totally. It distinguishes no longer a morally perfect people of God from the Gentiles, nor does it call this people to an even more intense moral effort. On the contrary, it shows that this is the situation of man wherever he lives, as long as God's righteousness does not break into his life. Therefore, the morally less abominable sins of malicious gossips etc. are signs of man's perdition without God, as well as the everywhere detested vices of murder etc.

8. Col. iii.5–8

Col. iii is, perhaps, the most interesting example of the development of the traditional formulae. First, the two sets of vices are, again, to be distinguished in our text. There is a first one, containing the traditional triad of 'fornication, greed and idolatry', combined with the typical warning against God's coming wrath. The first vice is interpreted, as we found before, by three more terms, 'impurity, passion and evil desire'. To the second one, 'greed', an explicatory note is added which introduces

[1] Cf. the excursus to Col. iii.5 in my commentary *Der Brief an die Kolosser* (Zürich/Neukirchen, 1976); to be published in English by S.P.C.K.

the third traditional vice, namely 'greed which is idolatry'. This shows both the dependence on a traditional pattern of three basic vices[1] and the new theological understanding of all the various sins as variants of the one sin, of the transgression of the first commandment. When man has lost God, he is at the mercy of all things, because his own covetousness takes the place of God. Of these basic sins of 'fornication, greed and idolatry', the author of our letter says that the Colossians have once walked in them, and he continues, true to the usual pattern: 'But now . . .'. Here, however, it is not the description of their new life that follows, but on the contrary a new imperative, introducing the second set of sins which are typical for life in the community. Thus again, the function of the list is quite different from the usual pattern. Here also, it does not distinguish the morally high standard of the elect from the abominable immorality of the world. On the contrary, it declares the 'finer' sins of gossip and unkindness as virtually identical with the basic vices of fornication, greed and idolatry; for, the text runs: 'But now, put them (the fundamental vices) all away: anger, wrath, malice, slander and foul talk.' Thus, in the foul talk of the members of the church against one another the heathen sins that they have left behind in baptism are creeping in again.

Second, even more important is another observation. Col. iii does not contain a merely radicalized moral admonition either. Unfortunately the translation of the participles in verses 9 and 10 is not clear. Do they refer to the fact that the Colossians have already and definitely put off the old man and put on the new, or do they call them to do so now? Be that as it may, what the author wants them to take is certainly a definite and all-including step into the new world in which there is neither Greek nor Jew, neither circumcised nor uncircumcised, neither barbarian nor Scythian, neither slave nor free man, but Christ, all in all (verse 11). Again we are back to the cosmic concept of migration into a new world, and all the specified sins are but signs of a disastrous return from that new land to the old country. This cannot be healed simply by a new moral exertion; rather, the Colossians are to come back to Christ himself, to faith which expresses itself in love, i.e. in their common life as the body of Christ.

9. *Eph. iv.17–19; v.3–5*

The passage of Col. iii is mirrored in Ephesians. The same motives are to be found there, although not so clearly united in one place. The context reminds the readers again of their baptism, to which they should

[1] Besides, this is the only occurrence of the root πλεον- in our letter.

return in their whole conduct: 'Awake, O sleeper, and arise from the dead . . .' (verse 14). Before we draw our conclusions, we shall discuss another traditional pattern, which turns up for the first time in the letter to the Colossians.

II. THE HOUSE-TABLES[1]

1. The origin

Since the times of Dibelius and Weidinger, the Stoic parallels have been known. The same three groups which we find in Col. iii.18–iv.1 – wives and husbands, children and parents, slaves and masters – are mentioned by Aristotle, Seneca, Plutarch, although usually combined with the summons to serve the gods, the emperor and one's country, and with social obligations towards friends and relatives. Even more important is the fact that in all these references – with one exception in Seneca and some passages in Epictetus, a former slave, who considered himself as virtually baptized (*Diss.* II.9, 20f) – it is always the male, adult and free individual that is told how to act over against his wife, his children, his slaves. He is addressed in the typical style of Hellenistic diatribe, which argues with the reader in order to convince him that its advice is really for his good, because it harmonizes with the all-embracing divine order of the cosmos.

The pattern changed, at least partly, when house-tables were taken up in Hellenistic Judaism, as Lohmeyer and Schroeder have shown, possibly because they have been grouped from the beginning around the commandment to honour one's parents, addressed to children as a call to subordination. Whereas the Old Testament and the earliest period of Judaism know of no house-tables, since the law suffices to rule all family life, we find, for instance with Philo, this Hellenistic pattern in the Jewish diaspora, but now including the call to subordination and therefore addressed to both parties, parents and children, husbands and wives, masters and slaves. We still find, as in the Hellenistic models, the relations with God and one's country, to friends and relatives usually combined with these three groups.

However, the background of these Hellenistic-Jewish house-tables is a different one. It is the Old Testament, which sides time and time again with the weak, the minor, the unfree. Throughout the Old Testament,

1 For all details and references cf. my essay 'Die Weltlichkeit des Neuen Testamentes: die Haustafeln', in *Beiträge zur alttestamentlichen Theologie*, Festschrift für W. Zimmerli (Göttingen, 1977), pp. 397–413, and also the excursus to Col. iii.18–iv.1 in my commentary (cf. p. 199 n. above).

Israel is reminded of her own slavehood in Egypt lest she forgets the hard fate of her slaves. It is always the married life of the neighbour which is protected, not the perfection of one's own marriage, and the authority of parents over their children is always limited by the first commandment. No doubt authors like Plutarch also know about the needs of wives and children, and Epictetus has suffered as a slave himself. And yet the aim of the Greek house-tables is the self-perfection of the male, adult and free man, who, in order to reach this stage, should remember the right attitude towards inferiors and their needs. For a group that has been shaped by the Old Testament, the central interest is no longer that perfect inner freedom of the individual who would free himself as much as possible from all ties, but rather the protection of those who are weak, helpless and unfree. This includes, as we have seen, the fact that the partner is always taken seriously and that all human beings, and consequently wives and children and slaves, as well as men, are considered ethically responsible subjects.

No doubt Hellenistic patterns have reached the New Testament, mediated by Hellenistic Judaism. Why have they been taken over ? The teaching and the whole life and death of Jesus, to which Rengstorf and Goppelt pointed, have certainly been a decisive factor. Jesus, who taught his disciples that 'whoever wanted to be great should be servant, or to be first should be slave to all, because the Son of Man had not come to be served, but to serve and to give his life as a ransom for many' (Mk x.43–5), has shaped the new understanding of what living together means. Especially, his view of married life may have led to it being given a favoured place in the house-tables. This is not *the* source of this pattern, though, because as far as we know Jesus hardly said anything about parentage and about the relation of slaves to masters. Even less probable is an origin of the house-tables in a primitive Christian catechism, as Seeberg and Selwyn suggested; for they appear only in writings of the Pauline school. The over-enthusiastic reception of the Pauline doctrine of freedom, as we find it in Corinth, may have been an essential factor leading to the house-tables, but again, it cannot be the only one, because emancipation of children was certainly not at stake there; true as it is, the disdain of earthly life and of its obligations in the Corinthian and other Pauline congregations urged Paul's co-workers and successors to emphasize the ethics of the house-tables.

2. *The first house-table: Col. iii.18–iv.1*

When in Col. iii a house-table turns up for the first time in the New Testament, some differences from earlier models are visible at once.

Firstly, wives, children and slaves are addressed equally with their husbands, fathers and masters. This is not totally new, as we have seen, but I know of no example which does so in such a thoroughgoing way. This means that wives, children and slaves are ethically responsible partners and able to do 'what is fitting', as well as the male, adult and free man. This is actually a revolutionary step beyond Hellenistic house-table ethics.

Secondly, the readers are admonished 'in the Lord'. A mere verbal reference to Christ changes nothing, of course. It is, however, connected with a clear change in style. The arguing of Hellenistic diatribe which tries to prove that living in such and such a way would be in conformity with the order of nature and therefore lie in the interest of the reader, disappears in favour of a reference to the goodwill of God who protects the weak, the unimportant, the unfree. The New Testament does not preach a universal cosmic order to which man has to adjust, but love and service towards God as the basis of all life. Therefore the cultic and patriotic obligations, which in the Greek parallels usually take the first place, are dropped in the New Testament.

Thirdly, the Colossian house-table is but the explication of what it means 'to do whatever one does, in word and deed, in the name of the Lord Jesus, giving thanks to God the Father through him' (verse 17), and this in its turn is a summary of the description of the divine service of the Christian church, in which all members may be teachers, spiritual counsellors and music directors (verse 16). Thus, the house-table explains that this divine service goes on in everyday life. 1 Peter even introduces its house-table by the declaration of the general priesthood of all believers, which consists not so much in priestly acts within the church, as in missionary service to the world outside. This leads to the next point.

Fourthly, New Testament house-tables have, probably, been formed first against the danger of an actual delusion about the baptized as living already in heaven, so that this world and its needs would be of no importance at all for Christians. In the Colossian church, to which this first house-table is addressed, asceticism was highly praised as a means to keep the soul as pure as possible from all contact with the world and its elements, and to enable it to ascend, after having left the earthly and material body,[1] through all four elements to heaven. Against all this, the 'good worldliness', as W. Zimmerli puts it, of the Old Testament, its openness towards this world and its problems, is echoed in the New Testament house-tables. They remind the reader of the positive way in which the Old Testament looks at creation and, therefore, also at

[1] Cf. the excursus to Col. ii.8 in my commentary (cf. p. 199 n. above).

marriage, at human propagation and at human work. There is no idea of an ascetic restraint from this world and all that it offers, from the experience of love and desire and fertility. The Wisdom literature expresses this view very clearly and sees man in the context of God's creation. Gen. i and ii, the creation of man as male and female and the encounter of the two, remain crucial texts for understanding man and world. In a similar way, the first house-table in the New Testament declares that marriage, fertility and work are part of God's good creation, and this is one of the points where the switch has been thrown to the right track for centuries to come. This is the more surprising, because the author of our letter summons his readers 'to set their minds on things which are above' (verse 2). Yet his idea of a life ruled from above where Christ is reigning is exactly that of a life in marriage, parenthood and everyday work.

Fifthly, this life is not described in ideals, but in very concrete statements. To be sure, this makes them vulnerable, and many of them are obsolete today. But ideal theories block the way to real and practical engagement. The Stoic maxim that the innermost self of a slave remains always free, and puts him essentially on the same level as any free man, has been repeated time and again, also in the church, in order to avoid any social change.[1] When the letter to the Colossians tried to formulate in practical terms what 'love which binds together in perfect harmony' (verse 14) really meant, it did so in terms of generally accepted principles of that time. These have certainly been selected, as we have seen, cultic and patriotic obligations or interest in high society having been dropped; they have also been reshaped, the male, adult and free individual no longer being the only addressee of an argument from the cosmic order. Nonetheless this means that there were never totally new religious principles, taught directly from heaven and therefore valid for all times and all situations. The church tried to say as clearly and as plainly as possible what should be done in a given time and a given situation.

3. The further development

House-tables are also to be found in later epistles, including the apostolic fathers, but disappear again after that time. Strangely enough they play no significant role in the church, up to the nineteenth and twentieth centuries, when they are used in defence of 'law and order'.[2] Even

[1] Chrysostom, *Homily* x.2, *PG* 62, 367; Theodoret, *PG* 82, 621B; Oecumenius, *PG* 119, 48D; E. F. Scott in MNTC (1930), p. 81 (cf. my commentary part C, chapter IV, paragraph 4).

[2] It makes no big difference whether this 'law and order' is of conservative or revolutionary origin; cf. my commentary, *ibid.*

stranger is the fact that, just as the house-tables have been Christianized, so they have also been paganized.

Firstly, it was a most important biblical insight that wives, children and slaves were fully responsible persons, not less than their husbands, fathers and masters. In 1 Pet. ii.18–25; Tit. ii.4f and Pol. Phil. iv.2, however, the subordination of slaves or wives is taught without a word to their masters or husbands. That 1 Pet. ii.14–17 discusses also the relation to the civil authorities is certainly not wrong; and yet, it appears in dangerous combination with the reverence due to God. It is true that this is understood as a specification of the Christian obligation 'to be subject to every human creature for the Lord's sake' (verse 13; cf. also Tit. iii.1f), that 'honouring the emperor' (as 'all men') is not the same as 'fearing God' and that Old Testament terminology excludes an identification of emperor and God. It is also remarkable that Tit. iii.1 still separates the summons to be submissive to rulers and authorities from the house-table. Nonetheless this leads to the second point.

Secondly, Christianization becomes definitely visible when submission to church authorities is taught. In 1 Pet. v.1–5 this is still done in an extra paragraph not directly connected with the house-table, but already in Tit. ii.2–8 both areas are more or less combined, and in 1 Clem. i.3; xxi.6–8; Ign. Pol. vi and Pol. Phil. iv–vi presbyters, bishops and deacons appear actually in a house-table. The hierarchic order in church and home shapes the life of the Christian more and more.

Thirdly, much more dangerous is the return of the traditional Hellenistic idea of an all-embracing cosmic order. Even the wonderful and deep interpretation of married life in the light of Christ's love towards the church in Eph. v.22–33 could also lead to the concept of a universal hierarchy in which women are subject to men as these to Christ (cf. already 1 Cor. xi.3). When Eph. vi.2f adds 'the first commandment with a promise' of the decalogue in order to underline the necessity of honouring one's parents, and speaks, in a formula which soon became a too easily repeated phrase full of biblical authority, of 'discipline and instruction of the Lord', it is another step towards a well cemented authoritarian order, valid for all time. Admittedly it need not be understood in this way, but it can be. Eph. v still knows that the lordship of Christ is expressed in his service up to the cross, and 1 Pet. ii.18–iii.1 uses it as an example for the slaves and stresses the active role of wives who win over their husbands for their faith, without a word being said, but as soon as this is forgotten, the old background of a universal cosmic order, fixed for all time, comes to life again. This is definitely so, when 1 Clem. xx lays the foundation of the house-table by pointing to the order of the universe, in which every star runs his prescribed course. The repaganization is perfect.

Fourthly, combined with this development and even more disastrous is the re-interpretation of the maxim that all service is finally rendered to the Lord himself, because, little by little, the human lords replace the heavenly one. When Col. iii.23 calls the slaves 'to work heartily, as serving the Lord and not men', it gives them in some way also liberty, freeing them from incessant staring at their masters and their questionable acts. When Eph. vi.5 repeats this in the form 'Be obedient to ... your earthly masters ... as to Christ', it is much more ambiguous. Does it still mean that their obedience to the masters should be like that to Christ, or does it say that obedience to the masters is actually obedience to Christ? At the same time, 'fear and trembling' applies to these earthly masters, and not as in Col. iii.22 to the heavenly one. 1 Pet. ii.21–5 sees, as we have said, Christ as the example of the slaves, without saying anything to their masters. Has service to the next higher class of society become identical with service to God? Tit. ii.9 does not speak, as Col. iii.20 does, of what is 'pleasing in the Lord', but of what pleases the earthly masters. These are, in Did. iv.11, already the 'type', i.e. the model and exact replica of *the* Lord, and Barn. xix.7 expands this 'typology' to all kinds of superiors. Both add biblical phrases about fearing the Lord and hoping in him. In Pol. Phil. v.3 presbyters and deacons take the place of God, and in Ign. Pol. vi.2 the military order appears as the cosmic one does in 1 Clem. xx.

Fifthly, all this is connected with a formal repaganization. The style becomes more and more assimilated to that of the Stoic parallels. In 1 Clem. i.3; xxi.6–8 admonitions to wives and children are actually inserted into the address to men; Did. iv.9f and Tit. ii, like Hellenistic models, deal more or less exclusively with the obligations of man towards his inferiors, and Ign. Pol. iv–vi teaches Polycarp how to act towards widows, slaves, women and men, who are all subject to the bishop.

Thus, on the one hand, only slaves or children are admonished without a word to their respective masters and parents; on the other, only male, adult and free individuals are addressed. Both facts show the same development. Christianization and paganization go hand in hand. The 'good worldliness', in which some principles of common life have without much ado been taken up as generally accepted rules, profane in themselves but sanctified by faith, has been lost. The more these rules were changed to eternal divine orders, the more the pagan belief in a divine cosmic hierarchy crept back and the less the biblical openness to the weak, the minor, the unfree could prevail. Surprisingly enough, this development stopped more or less after the second century and came to life again only in the nineteenth and twentieth centuries, when the so-called ethical progress of mankind, including democracy with 'law and order', was identified with the coming Kingdom of God. Then, the house-tables were interpreted anew as defence against all revolution, as basis of the superiority of man and of an order with discipline and authority considered to be 'the first law of heaven'.[1]

III. CONCLUSIONS

1. The New Testament shares with the Old a 'good worldliness', and this in two respects: (a) Lists of vices and house-tables are traditional patterns of the Jewish and heathen world in the first century A.D. The New Testament took them up, selecting and reshaping, but basically accepting them. (b) On the whole, the lists of vices contain no typically religious or cultic offences; they rather emphasize sins against the common life in the brotherhood. House-tables even originated, probably, in defence against a movement which tried to abandon this world and to flee into a heavenly, religious world of its own. They call the church back to its divine service in marriage, parentage and everyday work.

2. This means that these patterns are not fixed for ever. Even within the New Testament they change considerably. Details are picked up sometimes at random, sometimes according to a specific situation. The church has, therefore, to ask time and again which of the ethical values of the modern world should be taken up, which revised, which dropped. What are the criteria for doing so?

3. The goal of these ethical instructions is not the perfection of a pure soul or even of a pure church. In this respect, the function of the lists of vices has been changed; they no longer distinguish an outstanding group of high moral standards from the abominable immorality of the world, but serve to show the church how much this world is still living in its midst. House-tables describe what Jewish or heathen authors would equally recommend and what could actually also be found in their culture.

4. The real interest of the New Testament is the common life in church and home, i.e. the brother who must not be hurt. There is a kind of hierarchy of vices and virtues, but a very strange one. On the

[1] *Handbuch der Bibelerklärung* (Calw, 1900), III, p. 414; J. Huby, *Saint Paul. Les épîtres de la captivité* (VSal 8) (Paris, 1947), p. 100; W. H. G. Thomas, *Studies in Colossians and Philemon* (Grand Rapids, Mich., 1973), pp. 122f.

one hand, there are signs which distinguish the church from the non-church. The traditional triad of vices – idolatry, fornication, greediness – is intolerable in the church; by the same token, the divine service of preaching the word of Christ, praying and singing to him is the church's indispensable mark. In a missionary situation these items are therefore of first importance. Likewise, in specific circumstances like those under the rule of Hitler, specific points, as for instance the attitude towards Jews, become most important and actually separate church and non-church. On the other hand, the Pauline lists of sins are more interested in the 'finer' sins of gossip, unkindness etc., because they make living together impossible, and the house-tables deal exclusively with the everyday situation at home. In some way, the New Testament lists of vices and house-tables speak of trivialities. Trivial matters, however, under normal circumstances, form our life much more than outstanding acts like murder, and therefore become most important for life in the church and home. It is just these trivial matters that may hurt or help our brethren more than anything else, and since Old and New Testament are interested in their well-being and not in the morally perfect state of our own souls, these trivialities become so utterly central in their ethical instruction.

5. This means that the question whether this or that should be considered sinful or not in the Christian church is not of first importance. It is much more a question of living within the new world of Christ or outside it. Gossip may be quite harmless, but gossip may also render our common life insupportable and then it is a sign of real falling away from Christ's world. This is serious indeed. Therefore, neither lists of vices nor house-tables are used for an appeal to increased moral exertion; they rather call the church back to the new world which has already been established in Jesus Christ, and to faith as it expresses itself in hearing the word of Christ, praying and singing, and becomes in this way, to formulate it in the words of Gal. v.6, 'faith working through love'. Faith knows that there are times in which some acts can be clearly defined as intolerable or indispensable in the church: worshipping or abandoning idols, persecuting or helping the Jews, for instance. But this will never lead to the conclusion that other acts could not become even more intolerable or necessary, although their pernicious or blessed consequences are not so easily visible.

6. Jesus' disciples take their ethical obligations seriously, but never possess a rigid and definitely fixed ethical code. On the whole, they share with their world and time the same ethical values and warnings against unethical conduct. But they are able to detect why such and such a

person had to act differently, and they are ready for an understanding discussion. They are also open to detect that a blameless way of life according to the accepted ethical standards may be a disastrous violation of God's will, and are ready to attack this, if necessary. They go sometimes a long way with a 'worldly' group, but remain always sensitive to what God really wills, and therefore ready to protest at any point. They know that they are not expected to keep their souls as pure as possible – it was a Roman officer in command of an execution squad in an extremely unjust case that first confessed Jesus as the Son of God – but to live in faith and thus in love towards their fellow men, in normal situations first of all to those whom they encounter in the everyday life of church and family and business.

A Greek characteristic of prophecy in the Fourth Gospel

W. C. VAN UNNIK

The conversation of Jesus with the Samaritan woman in John iv.4ff is remarkable in many respects: because of its structure, its change of topics and the statements made. In this paper I wish to concentrate on one particular point, namely the manner in which the interview is brought to a close and on what is said there about the Messiah.

This final part of the conversation, verses 25–6, comes after the discussion on the (place of the) true adoration of God (verses 19–24) and has no direct connection with this preceding section. The last word of Jesus is, as so often in the discourses of the Fourth Gospel, a declaration from his side about his own person. But in this case the revelation it gives can only be understood on the basis of what the woman has said; it is complementary to her statement. She mentions an article of her 'creed' (οἶδα)[1] and Jesus solemnly declares (ἐγώ εἰμι!)[2] that he, her interlocutor, is that expected Messiah.

This complementary aspect must be underlined. Walter Bauer's remark, that the word of the woman is recorded in order to make Jesus' pronouncement possible, is only partly correct,[3] because it reduces the value of her declaration. Here we find a case of 'glove and hand': she expresses a general truth about what is to be expected of the Messiah, and it is the person of this Jesus who meets the requirement.

1 There is a well-attested variant reading οἴδαμεν, see the critical apparatus in K. Aland–M. Black–C. Martini–B. M. Metzger–A. Wikgren, *The Greek New Testament* (United Bible Societies, 1975[3]), p. 334. The choice between these two readings is difficult, cf. B. M. Metzger, *A textual commentary on the Greek New Testament* (London–New York, 1971), p. 207. The plural brings out the 'credal character' more clearly, cf. iii.2; iv.22; on the other hand the singular is more logical. Since this point has no direct bearing on the contents of this paper, I follow the reading as printed in the UBS and Nestle–Aland text (for οἶδα as an expression of firm faith, cf. also John xi.22, 24).

2 See on this formula the excursus of R. Schnackenburg, *Das Johannesevangelium II. Teil* (Freiburg–Basel–Wien, 1971), pp. 58ff and the literature mentioned there.

3 W. Bauer, *Das Johannesevangelium* (Tübingen, 1933[3]), p. 71.

So these verses are an excellent illustration of what the author defined as the purpose of his Gospel: 'that you may believe that Jesus is the Christ (xx.31).[1] And the importance of this illustration is underscored by the twofold way in which the great title is expressed: *Μεσσίας ἔρχεται, ὁ λεγόμενος Χριστός*, Semitic and Greek (cf. i.41).[2]

But the most remarkable feature in this passage is not so much the word of Jesus which finds its parallels elsewhere in this Gospel with its frequent use of the ' "I am" formula', but the characteristic of the Messiah: *ὅταν ἔλθῃ ἐκεῖνος, ἀναγγελεῖ ἡμῖν ἅπαντα*, which is put in the mouth of the Samaritan woman. This description of the activity of the Messiah is not a casual remark, but decisive for the subsequent story in the Gospel. The interview between Jesus and the woman may have come to a close, but the revelation of Jesus is not the last word the evangelist wants to convey to his readers as his message. The conversation has an after-effect which has also a direct relation with the purpose of the Gospel.

In verses 28–9 we are told that the woman returned to the city and gave her report. She did not summarize the whole conversation, but just the last item, which is the only thing that matters: *ἴδετε ἄνθρωπον ὃς εἶπέν μοι πάντα ὅσα ἐποίησα. μήτι οὗτός ἐστιν ὁ Χριστός;* (verse 29). The formulation here is interesting: she speaks about a human being who must be avowedly[3] the Messiah, because he has told her all (*πάντα*) she had done. So the distinctive mark of the Messiah is the fact that he can tell everything (*πάντα*) and this general rule is applied to her particular case. She has made the proof herself. This reflects that part of the conversation which has been related in verses 16–19. This passage shows that the words 'all that I ever did' get a special meaning. The word 'all' does not comprise her every word or action since her birth, but one particular, most important part of it, viz. her sexual life. This stranger Jesus (cf. verse 9), who could not possibly know this by normal ways, tells her that nevertheless he does know. Then she discovers (that is the meaning of *θεωρῶ* here) that that stranger must be a prophet. He knows things hidden from ordinary eyesight, things past. But on this ground, where she could control him, she has also accepted his claim that he

[1] W. C. van Unnik, 'The purpose of St John's Gospel', in *Sparsa Collecta* i (Leiden, 1973), pp. 35ff.

[2] The expression *ὁ λεγόμενος* is somewhat strange, see R. Bultmann, *Das Johannesevangelium* (Göttingen, 1950[11]), p. 141 (note 5)–142.

[3] On *μήτι* introducing a question see F. Blass–A. Debrunner–R. W. Funk, *A Greek Grammar of the New Testament and other early Christian Literature* (Cambridge, 1961), pp. 220f; its use here differs from the general rule, that it introduces questions where a negative answer is expected; but there are other instances for this modified meaning as indicated *loc. cit.*

answers the requirement laid down in the rule that the Messiah 'will make known all things' without restriction.

The importance of this declaration by the woman is enhanced by the end of the story. It is brought home to the readers of the Gospel in a very effective way, namely by holding them in suspense. The answer made to the question put in verse 29b is not an affirmation in words, but the somewhat dry remark: 'They went out of the city and went to him' (verse 30). The reader is left in the lurch, because no further reasons for the behaviour of the Samaritans are given: do they go out of sheer curiosity or because of something else? No answer is given before verses 29ff, for the evangelist first diverts his readers in another direction, to the conversation of Jesus with his disciples on a different topic (verses 31–8). After this fairly long interlude the attention shifts back to the Samaritans: the indication ἐκ τῆς πόλεως (verse 30) is resumed in verse 39 and so the thread is taken up. In two stages which show a parallelism on different levels (verse 39: πολλοί – διὰ τὸν λόγον τῆς γυναικός/ verse 41: πολλῷ πλείους – διὰ τὸν λόγον αὐτοῦ) the story is brought to a climax. The leading thought is the verb ἐπίστευσαν (verses 39, 41; cf. verse 42 πιστεύομεν) which is the ever-returning theme of the Gospel, as is immediately seen from a concordance, *s.v.*, and is expressed by the author himself in formulating his purpose (xx.31 ἵνα πιστεύσητε). The initial step to this faith is given by the word of the woman which is repeated here (verse 39: εἶπέν μοι πάντα ἃ ἐποίησα) and introduced by another weighty word from the author's vocabulary (verse 39: μαρτυρούσης).[1] Also in this case repetition means underscoring, and her word in verse 29 is not just an interesting saying, but ranked among the 'witnesses' about Jesus the Christ. But this is only the first step, because it is *about* Jesus (verse 42: διὰ τὴν σὴν λαλιάν); the final step is reached in the personal encounter and leads to a confession of faith (verse 42: αὐτοὶ γὰρ ἀκηκόαμεν, καὶ οἴδαμεν ὅτι οὗτός ἐστιν [cf. 29] ἀληθῶς ὁ σωτὴρ τοῦ κόσμου).

Both for its setting in the characterization of the Messiah–Christ and for its central role in the events of this part of St John's Gospel the combination 'to announce' or 'to tell all things'[2] is extremely important and calls for some careful consideration.

The criterion as it is formulated in verse 25 is also very remarkable from another point of view: the Messiah ἀναγγελεῖ ἡμῖν ἅπαντα.

[1] The importance of this verb for the theology of the Fourth Gospel appears from its frequent use, as is shown by the concordances, *s.v.*

[2] There is no difference between ἅπαντα and πάντα.

The verb *ἀναγγέλλω*[1] has the meaning 'to make known', 'to announce', sometimes 'to proclaim'. It is often used in the Septuagint,[2] mostly translating the verb הגיד; in many cases something that was hidden from the recipient is implied.[3] It is not a word that was restricted to the religious sphere, but could be used for all sorts of information. Therefore it is not strange that in the report of the woman the very simple word *εἶπεν* serves as an equivalent, whereas in Jesus' answer, verse 26, it is replaced by *λαλῶν*.[4] For the use in St John's Gospel see v.15: the healed man did not know who had healed him, but after he has met Jesus a second time *ἀνήγγειλεν τοῖς Ἰουδαίοις ὅτι Ἰησοῦς ἐστιν κτλ.*

Chapter xvi.13–15 about the Holy Spirit *ὅσα ἀκούσει λαλήσει, καὶ τὰ ἐρχόμενα ἀναγγελεῖ ὑμῖν* (cf. Isa. xliv.7: *τὰ ἐπερχόμενα πρὸ τοῦ ἐλθεῖν ἀναγγειλάτωσαν ὑμῖν*)...*ἐκ τοῦ ἐμοῦ λήμψεται καὶ ἀναγγελεῖ ὑμῖν. πάντα ὅσα ἔχει ὁ πατὴρ ἐμά ἐστιν. διὰ τοῦτο εἶπον ὅτι ἐκ τοῦ ἐμοῦ λαμβάνει καὶ ἀναγγελεῖ ὑμῖν.* Here again it is parallel to *λαλεῖν* and the meaning is: to make known. Its particular stamp is given by the context and the relation between the Father, Jesus and the Spirit.

So the special office of the Messiah–Christ, according to iv.25, is 'to make known all things'. This word *ἅπαντα* is not explained by any further apposition and is used in an absolute form. The woman did apply it, as we saw, to her past life. From Jesus' answer in verse 26: *ὁ λαλῶν σοι*, we may conclude that it should also be applied to the future: the water of life (verse 14) and the real adoration (verse 23). But these are specifications of that absolute statement 'all things'. The office of the Messiah–Christ is formulated here in a very general way: 'to make known to us all things'.

This description of his task is striking and remarkable, for so far no parallels have been found in Jewish Messianology. The texts adduced by Billerbeck[5] do not speak of such an office: the King–Messiah will not teach the Israelites, but give thirty commandments to the Gentiles and reassemble the Diaspora. But this is quite different from 'making

[1] See the article on this verb by J. Schniewind, in *TWNT* I, pp. 61ff.

[2] In the concordance of E. Hatch–H. A. Redpath four columns!

[3] Cf. eleven cases in Daniel ii (the dream of Nebuchadnezzar) and three cases in Daniel v (the mysterious handwriting).

[4] See for some parallels in usage: II Sam. xxiv.13 the prophet Gad goes to David *καὶ ἀνήγγειλεν αὐτῷ καὶ εἶπεν αὐτῷ . . .*; Jer. xvi.10 *καὶ ἔσται ὅταν ἀναγγείλῃς τῷ λαῷ τούτῳ ἅπαντα τὰ ῥήματα ταῦτα καὶ εἴπωσιν πρός σε Διὰ τί ἐλάλησεν κύριος ἐφ' ἡμᾶς πάντα τὰ κακὰ ταῦτα;*

[5] See the material in H. L. Strack–P. Billerbeck, *Kommentar zum Neuen Testament aus Talmud und Midrasch* (München, 1924), volume II, p. 438; the number of texts given there is very small indeed.

known all things'. In these texts the faintest resemblance to the task assigned to the Messiah in John iv.24 is missing.

But since a Samaritan woman is speaking here, it is in the direction of Samaritan eschatology that commentators turn for light. And not in vain, so it seems, for the Samaritans expected the appearance of the *Ta'eb* = Restorer who is, according to the terminology of the commentaries, the Messiah of the Samaritans. So, for example, the once well-known Orientalist and New Testament scholar Adalbert Merx wrote a book under the title *Der Messias oder Ta'eb der Samaritaner*.[1] The same terminology is found in many other publications. There are good reasons, however, to question this kind of terminology in which 'Messiah' is an equivalent for the Samaritan term *Ta'eb*.

We must be on our guard, lest we fall into the trap of terminological confusion. In the Samaritan sources the noun 'Messiah' is never used as the name of the eschatological redeemer-figure.[2] If then notwithstanding this fact the *Ta'eb* is called 'Messiah', this latter term is applied in a broader sense, as a *religionsgeschichtliche* category ('Messiah' = eschatological redeemer; 'messianic' = eschatological). But such a transference from its original home in Judaism to a Samaritan context is dangerous, because it suggests that the Samaritans had more or less the same conception of that figure as the Jews. And this is not the case. An authority on Samaritan theology, John Macdonald, is quite correct in saying: ' "Messiah" is hardly the right term in the Samaritan case: for their concept of the "one who is to come" is not quite like that of Judaism and Christianity. Their "coming one" is only a restorer and not an anointed figure of some royal house.'[3] And we may add: he could not be, since the Jewish and Christian concept of the Messiah is based on writings which the Samaritans did not accept (the prophetic books of the Old Testament). Hence it is better to avoid a confusion by keeping both names 'Messiah' and *Ta'eb* apart.

What did the Samaritans expect when they believed in the coming of this *Ta'eb*? The fulfilment of the prophecy in Deut. xviii.18: 'I will raise up for them a prophet like you from among their brethren; and

1 A. Merx, *Der Messias oder Ta'eb der Samaritaner* (Giessen, 1909).

2 The only text which speaks of a Christ–Messiah of the Samaritans is Justin Martyr, *Apologia* liii.6: *'Ιουδαῖοι δὲ καὶ Σαμαρεῖς, ἔχοντες τὸν παρὰ τοῦ θεοῦ λόγον διὰ τῶν προφητῶν παραδοθέντα καὶ ἀεὶ προσδοκήσαντες τὸν Χριστόν*. In spite of the fact that Justin came from Nablus (but of a pagan family! – lv.3), his information is wrong; he states that the Samaritans accepted the prophets, meaning of course those of the Old Testament, which is not the case. The testimony of John iv.25 cannot be employed in the context of our paper, because that would lead us to circular reasoning.

3 J. MacDonald, *The Theology of the Samaritans* (London, 1965), p. 361.

I will put my words in his mouth, and he shall speak to them all that I command him.'[1] This word had such an importance for the Samaritans that it formed part of their version of the Ten Commandments.[2] Though the Samaritan sources are late (from the end of the third or beginning of the fourth century), it may well be and is quite feasible that this belief did exist already at a much earlier date. Josephus (*Ant. Jud.* xviii.85) gives the report of an event among the Samaritans in the days of Pontius Pilate, which may well be explained as the appearance of a *Ta'eb*.[3]

Of this *Ta'eb* it is said by Markah, *Memar* iv.12, that he would reveal the truth, which, so Macdonald says, 'may remind one of the statement in John iv.25'.[4] But though by a certain reasoning 'all' and 'the truth' may be equated, the formulation is not the same. John knows the term 'to speak the truth' (viii.40, 45; ix.46; xvi.7), but that is not used here. This difference is the more striking, because we have to do here with a kind of credal formula. What is the origin of ἅπαντα in this connection? It is a curious fact that this point is hardly ever discussed in the commentaries, although it plays an important part in the text (see above, p. 212). Leon Morris referred to that selfsame text Deut. xviii.18 on which the Samaritan belief was built.[5] There indeed the word 'all' is found in the original texts and the translations based upon it: (MT + Sam. + Targum) = 'he shall speak to them all that I command him' (also Vg.: *omnia quae illi praecepero*). But the LXX has a different reading and omits the word 'all': καὶ λαλήσει αὐτοῖς καθότι ἂν ἐντείλωμαι αὐτῷ.[6]

1 Billerbeck, *SB*, volume II, p. 626: 'Dt.18, 15 u. 18 wird in der rabbinischen Literatur äußerst selten erwähnt'; on pp. 626f he gives the references. Cf. also H. M. Teeple, *The Mosaic eschatological prophet* (Philadelphia, 1957).

2 See the text in M. Gaster, *The Samaritans* (London, 1925), pp. 185ff. Cf. H. Odeberg, *The Fourth Gospel* (Uppsala–Stockholm, 1929), pp. 182ff; J. Macdonald, *Theology*, pp. 364ff.

3 A text of Josephus is often quoted in this connection: there was disturbance among the Samaritans: 'a man who made light of mendacity and in all his designs catered to the mob, rallied them, bidding them to go in a body with him to Mount Gerizim, which in their belief is the most sacred of mountains. He assured them that on their arrival he would show them the sacred vessels which were buried there, where Moses had deposited them.'

4 Marqah, *Memar* iv.12, in *Memar Marqah, the teaching of Marqah*, edited and translated by John Macdonald, volume II (Berlin, 1963), p. 186: 'The Taheb will come ... to manifest the truth', which, so Macdonald, *Theology*, p. 365, says, 'may remind one of the statement in John iv.25'. R. Schnackenburg, *Das Johannesevangelium*, I. Teil (Freiburg i.B., 1965), p. 476 *in loc.* refers to this text.

5 L. Morris, *The Gospel according to John* (London, 1972), p. 273, n. 64.

6 Cf. II Sam. xxiv.19 (of the prophet Gad) καθ' ὃν τρόπον ἐνετείλατο αὐτῷ κύριος = in Hebrew כאשר צוה יהוה.

Now this difference may be due to a copy of the Hebrew text which had כאשר instead of כל־אשר, leaving out the *lamed*. It is conceivable that John or his *Vorlage* followed here the original. However, John has ἅπαντα (πάντα in verses 29, 39) alone, in an absolute sense, without the addition and restriction 'that I command him'. Was this nevertheless implied? In view of the application the woman gives in verse 29 this is hardly conceivable. Was that knowledge of her past life that Jesus apparently possessed and by which he is accepted as the Christ, part of that command of the Lord?

So we must look elsewhere to find an explanation for this absolute ἅπαντα–πάντα which plays such an important role in this story. This usage of πάντα in this passage does not stand alone in the Fourth Gospel. The following texts may be mentioned in this connection.

Chapter xiv.26 about the Holy Spirit: ἐκεῖνος ὑμᾶς διδάξει πάντα καὶ ὑπομνήσει ὑμᾶς πάντα ἃ εἶπον ὑμῖν. Chapter xvi.30: The disciples gladly acknowledge the fulfilment of Jesus' promise that he will speak plainly and not in figures, and they add: νῦν οἴδαμεν ὅτι οἶδας πάντα καὶ οὐ χρείαν ἔχεις ἵνα τίς σε ἐρωτᾷ, 'By this we believe that you came from God.' This is a reflection on verses 17–19: 'Is this what you are asking yourselves, what I meant by saying . . . ?' The answer has been given; the disciples acknowledge his omniscience and believe his divine origin.[1]

Chapter xviii.4: In Gethsemane when Judas with a band of soldiers comes to arrest Jesus: then Jesus εἰδὼς πάντα τὰ ἐρχόμενα ἐπ' αὐτόν came forward.

Chapter xxi.17: the third time that Peter must answer the question whether he loves Jesus: Lord πάντα σὺ οἶδας, you know that I love you. In the three last texts it is remarkable that this πάντα is always combined with the verb 'to know'; it is used in relation with something that is unknown, because it is hidden in the heart of men or in the future. Therefore it is a superhuman, a prophetic insight. The same idea lies behind the word in iv.25, for he can make known all things only on condition that he knows them.

In the same line lies the promise that the disciples will be taught all things by the Holy Spirit. In this connection we may also refer to 1 John ii.20: καὶ ὑμεῖς τὸ χρῖσμα ἔχετε ἀπὸ τοῦ ἁγίου, καὶ οἴδατε πάντα. Or should we read the last word as πάντες? That is very hard to decide on

[1] This reminds one of John ii.25: οὐ χρείαν εἶχεν ἵνα τις μαρτυρήσῃ περὶ τοῦ ἀνθρώπου. αὐτὸς γὰρ ἐγίνωσκεν τί ἦν ἐν τῷ ἀνθρώπῳ. Although there is a parallelism in thought, the 'formulation' is different and precisely this word πάντα is missing (it is not the same as πάντας in verse 24 = all men). 'To know what is in man' is more restricted than 'to know all things'.

purely text-critical grounds.[1] It would take us too far afield, if we were to discuss that point more fully here. At any rate, whatever may be the correct reading, we may safely say that either in the first or in the second century, when this variant was made, this connection of the verb 'to know' with 'πάντα' was well-known[2] (cf. verse 27: τὸ αὐτοῦ χρῖσμα διδάσκει ὑμᾶς περὶ πάντων, which is parallel to John xiv.26).[3]

Interesting also is the remark in the 'captatio benevolentiae' of Jude 5: the author will not teach, but only remind his readers of certain facts; there is no need for such a teaching, because 'they know all things' (εἰδότας ὑμᾶς πάντα). Is this just a somewhat exaggerated sign of respect or is it an indication of what the author assumes about the status of his Christian readers? Hans Windisch collected some parallel material which makes it clear that there is something more behind this expression than the simple information that the readers actually did not need instruction.[4]

In commenting upon Jude 5 my former teacher did not associate the expression as used in that epistle with the texts in the Fourth Gospel, and besides that the material can be considerably expanded. Though I do not claim that the collection offered in this paper is complete, it is sufficient to enable us to grasp what the original Greek readers understood, when it was said of somebody: 'he knows all things' (οἶδεν

[1] See the text-critical note in UBS edition (cf. p. 211, n. 1 above), p. 816 with the commentary by B. M. Metzger, *A textual commentary*, p. 710; see also the special note of R. Schnackenburg, *Die Johannesbriefe* (Freiburg i.Br., 1953), pp. 135f.

[2] J. L. Houlden, *A commentary on the Johannine Epistles* (London, 1973), p. 79, n. 1 thinks that 'some manuscripts and ancient versions go further in a "Gnostic" direction' in altering πάντες to πάντα, but he does not give any evidence for this suggestion. The term πάντα εἰδώς does not belong to the typically 'gnostic' vocabulary and has, as will be seen in the course of this paper, different connotations. If πάντες was the original reading, it has been changed to πάντα, because that was a well-known combination and it helps to remove a difficulty, viz. that with the reading πάντες the verb οἴδατε has no object. These reasons give a good explanation for that change, whereas it is hard to account for adopting πάντες instead of πάντα.

[3] Cf. the gnostic book 'Das Wesen der Archonten', pp. 96f, translated by M. Krause, in *Die Gnosis*, Bd. II, ed. W. Foerster (Zürich–Stuttgart, 1971), p. 61: '[Der Geist der] Wahrheit, den der Vater ihnen gesandt hat, jener wird sie über alles belehren. Und er wird sie mit dem Salbe des ewigen Lebens salben, die ihm von dem Geschlechte gegeben wurde, das keine Königsherrschaft hat'. We cannot enter into a full discussion of this text for the present moment, but it seems clear that it is dependent upon John xiv.26 and 1 John ii.20.

[4] H. Windisch–H. Preisker, *Die Katholischen Briefe* (Tübingen, 1951[3]), p. 40; he mentions *Enoch* i.2; Homer, *Odyss.* xii.191; Dio Chrys., *Or.* xxxiii.4; Hippolytus, *Ref.* I.i.4, 1; Philostratus, *Vit. Apoll.* iii.18; Celsus, *ap.* Origen, *c.C.* i.12 in this sequence, but without further comments or order.

πάντα). The expression 'the original Greek readers' was deliberately chosen, because so far no such term for omniscience has come to my notice in the sphere of the Old Testament and later Palestinian Jewish literature.

We may start with two interesting texts from the famous contemporary of St John, Dio Chrysostom who here, as so often in his orations, gives a lively picture of life in Asia Minor in his time.[1] In the first Oration to the people of Tarsus 4 (*Or.* xxxiii.4) he remarks: *Δοκεῖτέ μοι πολλάκις ἀκηκοέναι θείων ἀνθρώπων, οἳ πάντα εἰδέναι φασὶ καὶ περὶ πάντων ἐρεῖν*, 'how they have been appointed and what their nature is, their repertoire including not only human things and demi-gods, but gods, yes, and even the earth, the sky, the sea, the sun, the moon and the other stars – in fact the entire universe – and also the processes of corruption and generation and ten thousand other things'; he goes on to criticize their oratory as bombast. In *Or.* xxxv.2 Dio says: 'For at present quite possibly people suspect that I am one of your wiseacres, one of your know-it-alls' (*τῶν σοφῶν ἀνθρώπων καὶ πάντα εἰδότων*).

These texts are extremely illuminating for the situation. They show that there were people going around as 'divine men'[2] who boasted that they 'know all', clever chaps[3] (later we shall meet one of them; see p. 220). The former text gives us an insight into what these people discussed, the topics of which they claimed to have special knowledge, the secrets of divine and cosmic life, what was comprised in this single and simple word *πάντα*. Therefore when we hear in the New Testament the term *εἰδὼς πάντα*, it was not an unfamiliar phrase. Certain people used it as self-advertisement and those people Dio holds up to ridicule.

[1] G. Mussies, *Dio Chrysostom and the New Testament* (Leiden, 1972), p. 167, mentioned these texts under 1 Cor. xiii.2: *καὶ ἐὰν ἔχω προφητείαν καὶ εἰδῶ τὰ μυστήρια πάντα καὶ πᾶσαν τὴν γνῶσιν*, but did not refer to the Johannine passages – where they would have been more appropriate – because of the absolute use of *πάντα*. But *ad sensum* St Paul's word offers an excellent parallel and helps as we shall see to explain that word 'all things'. J. J. Wettstein, *Novum Testamentum*, volume 1 (Amstelaedami, 1751), p. 935, *ad* Joh. xiv.26, refers to Nonnus, *Dionysiaca* xv (without number of the verse; the reference is wrong and should be xl.429). This is the only classical parallel he gives in his notes on St John's Gospel, and it may be said that it is not very illuminating. *Ad* John iv.25 he quotes the medieval Jewish philosopher Maimonides!

[2] The famous book of L. Bieler, *ΘΕΙΟΣ ΑΝΗΡ, Das Bild des 'göttlichen Menschen' in Spätantike und Frühchristentum* (Wien, 1935–6) does not mention this testimony of Dio Chrysostom nor does it offer any help for the present theme in general.

[3] The word *σοφός* is used here in its unfavourable sense as often in Greek, see H. G. Liddell–R. Scott–H. S. Jones, *A Greek–English Lexicon* (Oxford, 1940[9]), p. 1622, *s.v.* ('shrewd').

Indeed, this kind of boasting was in general not highly appreciated. Heraclitus for example was censured for it; see the doxography in Hippolytus, *Refutatio* I.4, I: *αὐτὸν μὲν γὰρ ἔφασκεν τὰ πάντα εἰδέναι, τοὺς δὲ ἄλλους ἀνθρώπους οὐδέν*, and later the criticism by Proclus, *In Platonis Timaeum*, folio 106 E: Heraclitus *ἑαυτὸν πάντα εἰδέναι λέγων πάντας τοὺς ἄλλους ἀνεπιστήμονας ποιεῖ.* This is a summarizing judgment passed on the Ephesian philosopher by later historians of philosophy, for among the remaining fragments it is not so clearly stated.[1] Aristocles[2] saw a sign of decline in the development of philosophy after Socrates in the fact that there were so many conflicting ideas, e.g. *οἱ μὲν εἰδέναι πάντα ἐκόμπαζον, οἱ δὲ ἁπλῶς μηθέν* (fr. 1 *ap.* Eusebius, *Praep. Evang.* xi.3, 4). When Celsus said that he did not need to ask questions of the Christians in order to learn something, his reason being, *πάντα γὰρ οἶδα*, he is severely criticized by Origen; he would not have said so, the church father declares, had he known anything of the Christians (*c. Celsum* i.12).

Nevertheless, in Philostratus, *Vita Apollonii Tyan.*, it is accepted as a true claim. This is self-evident, because Apollonius, who is in many ways *the* type of a '*Theios Anēr*', is pictured here as a true messenger of God. He says (vii.18): *ἐγὼ δὲ γιγνώσκω μὲν πλεῖστα ἀνθρώπων, ἅτε εἰδὼς πάντα.*[3] The whole biography is full of examples of Apollonius' superhuman knowledge. It is also claimed by the Indian sages: *πάντα γινώσκομεν, ἐπειδὴ πρώτους ἑαυτοὺς γινώσκομεν* (iii.18). That is not criticized, but is evidence of their great wisdom. In the *Greek Baruch* i.4 an angel is sent by God to Baruch: *ὅπως ἀναγγείλω*[4] *καὶ ὑποδείξω*[5] *σοι πάντα τοῦ θεοῦ.*

In another way we meet the same formula in the opening passage of the third part of II Enoch, a book of uncertain dating, but probably

[1] E. Diehl in his edition, *Procli Diadochi In Platonis Timaeum commentaria*, volume I (Lipsiae, 1903), p. 351, referred to fragment I in the collection of H. Diels, *Die Fragmente der Vorsokratiker*, edited by W. Kranz, volume I (Berlin, 1951[6]), p. 150, taken from Sextus Empiricus, *Adv. Mathem.* vii.132, but there is no literal conformity and the words *τὰ πάντα εἰδέναι* are missing there. On this fragment see W. K. C. Guthrie, *A History of Greek Philosophy*, volume I (Cambridge, 1962[2]), pp. 424f, who does not mention the testimonies of Hippolytus and Proclus. Whatever may be their worth for our knowledge of the real Heraclitus, they are important for their conception of the term we are investigating.

[2] Peripatetic philosopher in the second century A.D.; see W. D. Ross, in N. G. L. Hammond–H. H. Scullard, *The Oxford Classical Dictionary* (Oxford, 1970[2]), p. 111, *s.v.* (2).

[3] G. Petzke, *Die Traditionen über Apollonius von Tyana und das Neue Testament* (Leiden, 1970), pp. 175f.

[4] Cf. John iv.25; see p. 213f above.

[5] Cf. John v.20 *ὁ γὰρ πατὴρ . . . πάντα δείκνυσιν αὐτῷ ἃ αὐτὸς ποιεῖ.*

going back to an origin in Alexandrian Judaism.[1] A reference to this introduction is found in Clemens Alexandrinus, *Ecl. proph.* 2 and Origen, *De Principiis* iv.35, so that it was in existence in the second century A.D. at least.[2] In his admonition to his children Enoch says (xi.1): 'I know all things, for this is from the Lord's lips' (according to A; the reading of B is: 'I know all things from the Lord's mouth'), followed in version A by verse 2: 'I know all things, and have written all things into books, the heavens and their end, and their plenitude', after which follows a long description of what he saw of the physical world (version B is somewhat shorter, but is in the main parallel). In passing we observe that this recalls the topics mentioned by the 'divine men' in Dio's account (see above, p. 219). It is also worthwhile to quote from the preceding passage in which Enoch introduces himself to his children as the man who has seen the Lord (xxxix.2–8; cf. xxii where the anointing of Enoch is told and his installation as writer). He describes his task as to 'announce to you not from my lips, but from the Lord's lips, all that is and was and all that is now, and all that will be till judgment-day' (version A; in B the text is somewhat shorter: 'all things that are and that will be till judgment-day'). Here the formulation of this theme is set forth in the threefold formula which is often found in Hellenistic texts to describe the work of a prophet[3] (some examples will appear in the following pages). The question whether A or B offers the original text can be left open, for even if B has a right of priority,[4] the version of A proves that in certain circles where this version was current a certain well-defined conception of the phrase 'to know all things' as an expression for the charge of a prophet was existing. There can be no doubt that the figure of Enoch is seen in that light, as God's messenger. In the light of Hellenistic parallels the terminology is very telling and betrays its provenance. In this text it is striking that the claim of the prophet 'I know all things', is supplied by the express saying 'from the Lord's mouth' (or 'lips'); the same

1 O. Eissfeldt, *The Old Testament, an Introduction*, translated by P. R. Ackroyd (Oxford, 1965), p. 623; Th. C. Vriezen–A. S. van der Woude, *Literatuur van Oud-Israel* (Wassenaar, 1973⁴), pp. 350f; see also N. Forbes–R. H. Charles, in R. H. Charles, editor, *The Apocrypha and Pseudepigrapha of the Old Testament*, volume II (Oxford, 1913), pp. 426, 439.

2 See the quotations in Forbes–Charles, *The Apocrypha and Pseudepigrapha*, p. 455, note.

3 I may refer here to my article: 'A Formula describing Prophecy' in *New Testament Studies* ix (1962–3), pp. 86–94 (since the publication of that article I have collected many more relevant texts which I hope to publish elsewhere and which confirm the conclusions reached before).

4 A. Vaillant, *Le livre des Secrets d'Hénoch* (Paris, 1952), p. iv (French translation on pp. 39–41).

addition in xxxix.2. Has this double supplement a polemical undertone, directed against 'divine men' in the pagan world? At any rate it wards off a possible misunderstanding, as if the prophet knew these things by his own intelligence; it underlines his dependence and the source of his inspiration, the character of his mission: he has received it from the Lord himself.[1]

In the same line – not of self-advertisement, but of a personal witness to his calling – lies the statement of an Essene prophet, as recorded in an interesting passage of Josephus, *Ant. Jud.* xv.373ff: when Herod was in his youth, that prophet had predicted his future kingship and had recommended justice, piety etc. as virtues for his behaviour as king, but he had added: ἀλλ' οὐ γὰρ οἶδά σε τοιοῦτον ἔσεσθαι, τὸ πᾶν ἐπιστάμενος. The prophet's foreknowledge of the fact that Herod later as a king will not show forth these virtues, is not accidental, but a demonstration of his nature as a prophet: 'who understands the totality'.[2] This reason is

[1] As was indicated above (p. 218, n. 4), Windisch also referred to I Enoch i.2. The interpretation of this text, particularly with regard to the point at issue, is difficult, because there is a divergence in reading among the textual witnesses: (a) Aramaic fragment, as published and translated by J. T. Milik with the collaboration of Matthew Black, *The Books of Enoch, Aramaic Fragments of Qumran Cave 4* (Oxford, 1976), p. 142: 'and from the words of (the Watchers) and the holy ones (I heard) it all; (and because I heard from them, I knew and I understood everything . . .)', cf. also Plate I. It is clear that only a few words are left, but for our purpose it is important that the word 'all' is preserved. (b) Greek text, as published by M. Black, *Apocalypsis Henochii Graece* (Leiden, 1970), p. 19: ἁγιολόγων ἁγίων ἤκουσα ἐγώ, καὶ ὡς ἤκουσα παρ' αὐτῶν πάντα καὶ ἔγνων ἐγὼ θεωρῶν.

(c) Ethiopic text as translated by R. H. Charles, *The Apocrypha and Pseudepigrapha*, volume II, p. 188: 'which the angels showed me and from them I heard everything and from then I understood as I saw . . .' In Charles' edition of the Greek fragment (R. H. Charles, *The Book of Enoch* (Oxford, 1893), p. 326), the reading is: ἤκουσα (ἀγγέλων ἐγὼ καὶ ὡς ἤκουσα) παρ' αὐτῶν πάντα, the bracketing meaning 'corrupt additions' (p. 325). According to Milik, *The Books of Enoch*, p. 144 'the pronoun πάντα = כל has been omitted by the Greek translator (or a Greek copyist) before or after ἤκουσα ἐγώ, because it is taken up again immediately afterwards'; he suggests as the original reading in Greek: ὡς ἤκουσα παρ' αὐτῶν, πάντα ἔγνων. If we had only the Greek and Ethiopic texts to go by, one might suspect here that a line was dropped in an ancestor of E by way of homoioteleuton, but in view of A that seems impossible. However, with regard to the point at issue we must conclude that the use of 'all' here, although it is found in the introduction to an apocalypse, is different from that which we met in the texts discussed so far. If we have to follow A, then 'all' is determined by a possessive which points to the 'vision' in the preceding clause; if we interpret according to G, 'all' is determined by the relative ὡς. It has not the absolute meaning here as in the passage πάντα εἰδώς.

[2] The translation of R. Marcus in the Loeb edition of Josephus, volume VIII (1963), p. 183: 'I know that you will not be such a person, since I understand the whole situation', is not correct, for it does not do justice to the formula: τὸ πᾶν ἐπιστάμενος.

sufficient to guarantee the truth of his verdict in this case. The word εἰδώς is replaced here by its equivalent ἐπιστάμενος, probably for stylistic reasons (it is preceded by οἶδα). This prophet does not add this clause to enhance his own glory, but gives a simple statement of fact to answer Herod that his words are true. In Josephus' report it is given without further comments; that is an indication that it was a phrase, to describe the nature of a prophet, that was understood by his readers.

The expression as used by Josephus is also found in the *Pseudo-Clementine Homilies*, together with its equivalent πάντα εἰδώς, as standing descriptions for the 'true prophet'. A full analysis of the role and work of this key figure in that still enigmatic literature falls outside the scope of this paper,[1] but the message conveyed by these epithets is made clear by the contexts in which they occur. To begin with it is remarkable that the formula has a somewhat expanded form: πάντα πάντοτε ἐπιστάμενος or εἰδώς. Why? There was, as will be seen, a good reason for that addition, viz. to distinguish this prophet from others who also claimed to 'know everything'. This need of distinction shows the diffusion of the formula and the rivalry that existed. The first text is found in *Hom.* II.6, 1: Peter had explained that the real blessings in life can only be possessed by knowing things as they are and the road to this knowledge is to become acquainted with the prophet of the truth (chapter 5). Then he gives this definition: προφήτης δὲ ἀληθείας ἐστὶν ὁ πάντοτε πάντα εἰδώς, which is followed by an explanation of πάντα: τὰ μὲν γεγονότα ὡς ἐγένετο, τὰ δὲ γινόμενα ὡς γίνεται, τὰ δὲ ἐσόμενα ὡς ἔσται, and some ethical qualities. It is curious to find here the well-known threefold formula, so often describing the mystery of existence into which the prophets had an insight.[2] The true prophet shows forth the truth as the sun its light. Then Peter argues that 'all therefore who ever sought the truth, trusting to themselves to be able to find it, fell into a snare. This is what both the philosophers of the Greeks, and the more intelligent of the barbarians, have suffered' (chapter 7). A second very important passage is found in *Hom.* III.11, 2–15, 1. It starts by repeating that truth can only be found from a prophet of truth; προφήτης δὲ ἀληθής ἐστιν ὁ πάντα πάντοτε εἰδώς. It is not simply a matter

[1] L. Cerfaux, 'Le vrai prophète des Clémentines', in *Recueil Lucien Cerfaux*, volume I (Gembloux, 1954), pp. 301ff did not deal with the problem that interests us here.

[2] See my article 'A formula describing prophecy' (see p. 221, n. 3 above), p. 89. I should add here also *Hom.* II.10, 1: εἰ προφήτης ἐστὶν καὶ δύναται εἰδέναι ὡς ἐγένετο ὁ κόσμος καὶ τὰ ἐν αὐτῷ γινόμενα καὶ τὰ εἰς τέλος ἐσόμενα, ἐαν ἡμῖν ᾖ τι προειρηκὼς ὃ εἰς τέλος ἐγνώκαμεν γεγενημένον, καλῶς αὐτῷ ἐκ τῶν ἤδη γεγενημένων καὶ τὰ ἐσόμενα ἔσεσθαι πιστεύομεν οὐ μόνον ὡς γινώσκοντι, ἀλλὰ καὶ προγινώσκοντι.

of prediction that qualifies him, but 'whether his foreknowledge can stand apart from other cause. For physicians predict certain things, having the pulse of the patient as matter submitted to them; and some predict by means of having fowls, and some by having sacrifices, and others by having many various matters submitted to them; yet these are not prophets' (chapter 11). In chapter 12 it is set forth that 'the foreknowledge of the one true Prophet does not only know things present (*τὰ παρόντα ἐπίσταται*), but stretches out prophecy without limit as far as the world to come'; his words are not dark or ambiguous; they need no explanation by another prophet,[1] but are clear and simple as 'our Master being also a prophet *ἐνφύτῳ καὶ ἀεννάῳ πνεύματι πάντα πάντοτε ἠπίστατο* (12, 3). Therefore he made statements respecting future events; as a faultless prophet he watched all things closely with the eye of his soul, and knows them, even if he does not utter them (*πάντα κατοπτεύων ἐπίσταται λανθάνων*)'. This raises the question, whether his prophetic inspiration is permanent or not; and here it becomes clear why the word *πάντοτε* was added.[2] It would be a grave mistake to hold the view that the true prophet did not *always*, but only sometimes, possess the Holy Spirit. Here lies an important criterion of distinction with false prophets (chapter 13).

In the next paragraph the wording and the train of thought are somewhat difficult, though the underlying problem is quite clear. What is the right criterion to find out if and when the prophet has the Holy Spirit? Is he void of the Spirit when his saying is proved to be wrong? Must he be trusted as possessing the Spirit, when among many predictions some come to pass? The answers are very difficult, because the words of these prophets are a mass of obscure, ambiguous utterances in which past and future are mixed up, which are without sequence or proper form (chapter 14). But with the true prophet it is quite different: our teacher *οὐδέν τι τοιοῦτο ἐγοητεύσατο, ἀλλ' (ὡς φθάσας εἶπον) προφήτης ὢν ἐνφύτῳ καὶ ἀεννάῳ πνεύματι πάντα πάντοτε ἐπιστάμενος τεθαρρηκὼς ἐξετίθετο*. Though it is impossible to go into detail here and discuss these two passages in relation to prophetic phenomena contemporary

[1] It is interesting to compare these words with the injunctions of St Paul, 1 Cor. xiv.13: *ὁ λαλῶν γλώσσῃ προσευχέσθω ἵνα διερμηνεύῃ*; 27: *εἴτε γλώσσῃ τις λαλεῖ, κατὰ δύο ἢ τὸ πλεῖστον τρεῖς...καὶ εἷς διερμηνευέτω*; 28: *ἐὰν δὲ μὴ ᾖ διερμηνευτής, σιγάτω ἐν ἐκκλησίᾳ, ἑαυτῷ δὲ λαλείτω καὶ τῷ θεῷ*.

[2] This important text, *Hom.* III.13, 2f, reads as follows: 'If we should hold, as many do, that even the true Prophet, not always but sometimes, when He has the Spirit, and through it, foreknows, but when He has not is ignorant, if we should suppose thus, we should deceive ourselves and mislead others.' *τὸ γὰρ τοιοῦτον μανικῶς ἐνθουσιώντων ἐστὶν ὑπὸ πνεύματος ἀταξίας, τῶν παρὰ βωμοῖς μεθυόντων καὶ κνίσης ἐνφορουμένων*. For this *ἀταξία* cf. 1 Cor. xiv.33.

with the author, it will be clear what is meant by the phrase: *πάντα πάντοτε εἰδώς*. The true prophet, the teacher of the Christian, has like every prophet a real knowledge of past, present and future, though he has nothing in hand to go by, and he has the Spirit, not at certain periods, but permanently. The most simple phrase *πάντα εἰδώς* was insufficient to give a safe guideline in finding the true prophet. Now the decisive quality is that for him the Spirit is inborn and ever-flowing, without interruption and therefore trustworthy. But it is clear that this addition of *πάντοτε* was a later addition to meet difficulties arising from the simple phrase when applied to practical reality. An interesting application of Jesus' omniscience is found in *Hom.* VIII 21, 4 in the story of Jesus' temptation (cf. Matt. iv.3, 9): the 'temporary king' offers Jesus all the kingdoms of the earth on condition that he falls in adoration of the devil; but Jesus *πάντα εἰδώς* refused to adore him and rejected what he had offered. Here the short cut to temporary success is contrasted with that 'all'. Jesus sees through the offer made to him, because he knows that eternal totality. Concerning Jesus' apostles who continue his teaching and make clear the proofs of what he had revealed very briefly, the word in *Hom.* XVII 7, 1 is important: Jesus *εἰδὼς οὖν ἡμᾶς εἰδότας πάντα τὰ ὑπ' αὐτοῦ ῥηθέντα καὶ τὰς ἀποδείξεις παρασχεῖν δυναμένους* sent them to the Gentiles. Here we find the formula (also met in the New Testament, see p. 217f), but specified by the addition 'that was spoken by him'. They do not 'know all things' by themselves, but know all his words, can transmit them and demonstrate their truth.

This use of the word *πάντα* in relation to prophetic insight was widespread in the Greek–Hellenistic world. Here follow a few examples:

Sophocles, *Oedipus Rex* 300, where Oedipus addresses the seer Teiresias in these words: *ὦ πάντα νωμῶν, Τειρεσία, διδακτά τε / ἄρρητά τ' οὐράνιά τε καὶ χθονοστιβῆ*. Teiresias is blind, but nevertheless he sees more than other men, he has an all-embracing insight into what is taught (by men) and what may not be divulged,[1] of things in heaven and on earth.

Euripides, *Helena* 922f. Helena reproaches the prophetess Theonoe: *αἰσχρὸν τὰ μέν σε θεῖα πάντ' ἐξειδέναι / τά τ' ὄντα καὶ μέλλοντα, τὰ δὲ δίκαια μή*. Here it is remarkable to see that *πάντα* is combined with things divine and made more explicit by the addition of two parts of the 'threefold formula' which was known long before the times of Euripides, e.g. Homer, *Iliad* I.70.[2] Vergil, *Georgica* IV.392f about the semi-divine prophet Proteus: *novit namque omnia vates / quae sint, quae*

[1] See Liddell–Scott–Jones, *A Greek–English Lexicon*, p. 246: 'things profane and sacred'.

[2] See my article, 'A formula describing prophecy' (see p. 221, n. 3 above), p. 92.

fuerint, quae mox ventura trahantur. Here again the word *omnia* is explained by the 'threefold formula'.

Quintus Smyrnaeus,[1] *Posthomerica* IX.331f, on the prophet Calchas, οὐ γὰρ ἄϊδρις / μαντοσύνης ἐτέτυκτο θεὸς δ' ὡς ᾔδεε πάντα (cf. below p. 227).

Hesychius, the Greek lexicographer, *s.v.* Χαλδαῖοι· γένος μάγων πάντα γινωσκόντων. Whatever may be the historical value of this note, the use of the phrase is significant.

Berlin Magical Papyrus 1.15 (edited by Preisendanz, *Papyri Graecae Magicae*, volume I (Leipzig–Berlin, 1928), p. 2; papyrus from the fourth–fifth century, the text itself may be older): about a *paredros daimon* ὃς τὰ πάντα μηνύσει σοι ῥητῶς: he is the source of inspiration of the soothsayer.

London Magical Papyrus 1.286ff (Preisendanz, *Papyri Graecae Magicae*, volume I, p. 190; papyrus from the fourth century, the text itself may be older): the soothsayer declares that he will not let the god give an oracle before he knows exactly what is in the minds of all people from Egypt, Syria, Greece and Ethiopia who come to consult him,[2] ὅπως αὐτοῖς ἐξαγγείλω τὰ προγεγονότα αὐτοῖς καὶ ἐνεστῶτα καὶ τὰ μέλλοντα αὐτοῖς ἔσεσθαι[3] and all their circumstances, and in order that I can read a sealed epistle[4] καὶ ἀπαγγείλω αὐτοῖς πάντα ἐξ ἀληθείας.[5] This promise is highly interesting, because it gives a lively impression of the work such a diviner did. The language is typical of a prophet (threefold formula – πάντα not applied, however, to the history of the world, but to the lives of individuals, αὐτοῖς). Another remarkable feature in this text is the wide circle from which the clientèle is drawn.

Many years ago Richard Reitzenstein drew a parallel between this

[1] Epic poet who lived in the fourth century A.D.; see W. F. J. Knight, in *Oxford Class. Dict.*, p. 908, *s.v.*

[2] The verb ἐπερωτάω is often used in the special sense of 'consulting an oracle, diviner', see H. Greeven, in *TWNT* volume II, p. 685, *s.v.* Mark the contrast in Hermas, *Mand.* xi.5: πᾶν γὰρ πνεῦμα ἀπὸ θεοῦ δοθὲν οὐκ ἐπερωτᾶται, ἀλλ' ἔχον τὴν δύναμιν τῆς θεότητος ἀφ' ἑαυτοῦ λαλεῖ πάντα (this πάντα has a different meaning from that discussed in this paper; it is 'all the words the prophet utters'); 8: where it is said of the true prophet: οὐδενὶ οὐδὲν ἀποκρίνεται ἐπερωτώμενος. See on this Mandate the monograph of J. Reiling, *Hermas and Christian Prophecy* (Leiden, 1973).

[3] Note the threefold formula plus αὐτοῖς; see my remarks, 'A formula describing prophecy', pp. 90f.

[4] In this form the questions were given into the hands of the soothsayer on the understanding that the god would read them and give the answer through the diviner as an instrument that did not know the contents of the letters; see below, p. 227.

[5] N.B. here the verbs ἐξαγγέλλω–ἀπαγγέλλω as synonyms for 'to make known'; for the relation of the latter verb with ἀναγγέλλω (see above p. 214), cf. Schniewind, TWNT vol. I, p. 61.

papyrus-text and Lucian, *Alexander Pseudoprophetes* 20:[1] both prophets receive questions written in sealed letters, to which the oracle had to give answer. Both prophets made a wide appeal in the world of their days. Now in the text of Lucian we are told how Alexander managed to open those letters by clever tricks, to read their questions, to put the seal in order again and formulate the right answer. The people are stupefied: how could this well-guarded secret question be known? Their conclusion is: he must be a god (*πόθεν γὰρ οὗτος ἠπίστατο ἃ ἐγὼ πάνυ ἀσφαλῶς σημνάμενος αὐτῷ ἔδωκα ὑπὸ σφραγῖσιν δυσμιμήτοις εἰ μὴ θεός τις ὡς ἀληθῶς ὁ πάντα γινώσκων ἦν;*). The way in which this conclusion is formulated is highly relevant for our purpose: he who 'knows everything' must be some god (cf. above p. 219), here incarnate in the person of Alexander, whose aim it was to be recognized as such.[2] Here a divine quality is ascribed to this 'knowing everything': he who possesses this gift is not only a servant of God, his prophet, but a god himself.

This connection is not strange to Greek religious feeling, but was known down through the ages. It is already found in Hom., *Iliad* II.484ff of the Muses, who gave inspiration: *ἔσπετε νῦν μοι, Μοῦσαι. . . / ὕμμες γὰρ θεαί ἐστε, πάρεστέ τε ἴστε τε πάντα,* men can only listen and know nothing. *Odyss.* IV.379 a general statement: *θεοὶ δέ τε πάντα ἴσασιν.*[3] *Odyss.* XII.189: the Sirens boast that they know all that happened in the war between Greeks and Trojans. Also in Pindar, *Paean* IX.54f the Muses are addressed: *ἴσθ' ὅτι, Μοῦσαι, πάντα.* The thought that the gods know everything is widespread. Very telling is the sentence of Xenophon, *Cyrop.* I.6, 46: *θεοὶ δὲ* (in opposition to human wisdom) *ἀεὶ ὄντες πάντα ἴσασι τά τε γεγενημένα καὶ ὅτι ἐξ ἑκάστου αὐτῶν ἀποβήσεται, καὶ τῶν συμβουλευομένων ἀνθρώπων οἷς ἂν ἵλεῳ ὦσι, προσημαίνουσιν ἅ τε χρὴ ποιεῖν καὶ ἃ οὐ χρή* (but not to all men, because there is no force compelling them to care for those they do not like). This text shows all elements together: 'knowing all things' – the 'threefold formula' (that is found in many variations) and the divine guidance by divination. It falls beyond our present scope to discuss the difference made here between groups of men.

1 R. Reitzenstein, *Die hellenistischen Mysterienreligionen* (Leipzig–Berlin, 1927[3]), p. 239, n. 1.

2 This is different from what is said about Pancrates in Lucian, *Philopseudes* 34: *θαυμάσιος τὴν σοφίαν καὶ τὴν παιδείαν πᾶσαν εἰδὼς τὴν Αἰγυπτίων*, cf. Acts VII.22 and the note of H. Conzelmann, *Die Apostelgeschichte* (Tübingen, 1972[2]), p. 53.

3 Nevertheless, there are many 'instances of the apparent ignorance of the Homeric gods', see A. S. Pease, *M. Tulli Ciceronis De Divinatione* (reprint, Darmstadt, 1963), p. 244 with the references to discussions of that topic.

From the Apocrypha of the Old Testament three texts which contain this phrase can be quoted (it is not found, as far as I can see, in the Septuagint translation of *Tenach*). Therefore the phrase occurs only in texts that reached us from or through Hellenistic Judaism:

Baruch iii.22: who is the man who finds Wisdom?

ἀλλ' ὁ εἰδὼς τὰ πάντα γινώσκει αὐτήν·
ἐξεῦρεν αὐτὴν τῇ συνέσει αὐτοῦ.

Susanna 42 Theodotion (not in LXX): Susanna cried out with a loud voice and said: Ὁ θεός, ὁ αἰώνιος, ὁ τῶν κρυπτῶν γνώστης, ὁ εἰδὼς τὰ πάντα πρὶν γενέσεως αὐτῶν thou knowest that they have false witness against me.

Wisdom of Solomon ix.11: in a prayer to God to send his wisdom:

οἶδε γὰρ ἐκείνη πάντα καὶ συνίει
καὶ ὁδηγήσει με ἐν ταῖς πράξεσί μου σωφρόνως
καὶ φυλάξει με ἐν τῇ δόξῃ αὐτῆς.

In two of these texts the phrase is used as a name for God, in one for his Wisdom that can be sent to guide men.

For Philo we may quote from his treatise *Quod deterius potiori insidiari soleat* 17, 57: he discusses why God put a question to Cain (Gen. iv.9) whereas: πάντα δὲ θεῷ γνώριμα, οὐ τὰ παρόντα μόνον καὶ παρεληλυθότα ἀλλὰ καὶ μέλλοντα (again the tripartite formula!). For texts from Hellenistic Judaism where the phrase is applied to men cf. p. 220f. It was known there like other epithets of God such as ἐπόπτης, παντοκράτωρ.

The material offered in this paper to elucidate the phrase πάντα εἰδώς as applied to a certain person may lead us to certain conclusions, even though it is far from complete. From the testimonies assembled from very different ages and circles we see that this expression was frequently used for people who had a very special relation to the gods 'who know all things'; they are prophets. They possess a knowledge of 'all things', hidden[1] and visible for all men. This word 'all things' stresses of course the first element; it is the particular gift of these prophets that they know 'all mysteries' which are often defined by a well-known formula as 'past, present, future'.[2]

[1] Cf. Paul, I Cor. xiii.2, see p. 219, n. 1 above and the supposition in Luke vii.39, though there πάντα is not used. In a very limited sense it is used, e.g. in Tacitus, *Annales* xi.32: *gnara Claudio cuncta* of a certain plot against him, and is the trick of secret services to trap people into confessing by saying: 'we know all things'. That has nothing to do with the subject of this paper, though there is a similarity of words, because it means: all details of a certain matter, but not insight into the mystery of life.

[2] In the light of this phrase πάντα εἰδώς the opposite in I Timothy vi.4 μηδὲν ἐπιστάμενος offers a striking contrast.

From the contexts in which the Fourth Gospel uses this phrase it appears that the author knew the contents of the expression and that he wrote for readers who must have been familiar with that phrase. A special feature in this Gospel, viz. that Jesus himself never uses this phrase, but that it is always applied to him by others is not fortuitous, but significant: Jesus does not belong to that class of people who advertise themselves as such (cf. p. 219f), but others discover his exceptional quality.

It is interesting to see that in John iv.19 the Samaritan woman first addresses Jesus as a prophet and then at a second stage brings in that word about the Messiah: He who can 'make known all things' (and therefore must 'know all things'). From this passage of John iv it follows that his prophecy was of a special character. What was the difference? So far I have not found a direct answer in the texts. The best solution of this problem may be found in the distinction made in the Pseudo-Clementines between the true prophet and others: the former had this gift permanently (see p. 223f), while the others may have it at special occasions, but not continuously. This last question, which would lead us to a study of Messianism in general, may be left for further research.[1]

When the term is applied to Christians (see above, p. 217f) it seems to have been a current expression; one could appeal to this quality of the Christians and the knowledge they possessed. To them the promise of the Holy Spirit (cf. John xiv.26) had been fulfilled; as baptized Christians they shared in what Jesus Christ had possessed.

This paper in honour of the Principal Emeritus of St Mary's College is written with the same warm feelings which prompted the closing lines of my former contribution to his first *Festschrift*. It has been a great experience to enjoy the fruits of his scholarship and the warmth of his friendship. *Gratias tibi ago, Matthaeus, verbi divini minister!*

[1] See in this context the monograph of F. Schneider, *Jesus der Prophet*, (Freiburg/Schweiz–Göttingen, 1973).

On investigating the use of the Old Testament in the New Testament

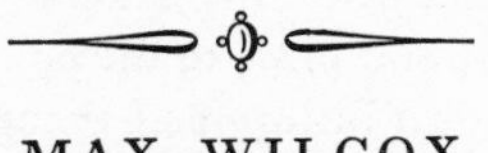

MAX WILCOX

It is a great privilege and pleasure to share in this *Festschrift* in honour of Matthew Black, the more so for one who has known him for some twenty-five years as teacher, colleague, and above all, friend. And in this context what more fitting way than with an essay on a subject to which Matthew Black has so greatly contributed?

Old Testament quotations and allusions, reminiscences and motifs, appear in some profusion throughout much of the NT. Nevertheless they present us with no one OT textual tradition, they stem from a rather restricted set of OT passages, and they are used in many places in ways which may seem unconvincing if not eccentric to the modern mind. It is no surprise that those who have studied them should display a wide diversity of interest and approach. We cite three of them by way of example: H. B. Swete, Rendel Harris, and C. H. Dodd. Swete's primary (though not exclusive) interest lay in the bearing of the OT material in the NT on the problem of establishing the Bible text used by NT writers (and/or their sources).[1] Rendel Harris saw the OT quotations (and allusions) in the light of later patristic collections of proof texts and thus came to identify them as evidence for a lost 'testimony book' (or books), compiled for use in controversy with the Jews; he did not, however, overlook the possibility of its having had earlier roots.[2] Dodd rejected the idea that they were a primitive anthology of isolated proof texts;[3] rather, they were the outcropping signs of the use of a selection of 'certain larger sections' of the OT, these latter to be understood as 'wholes'.[4] The selection arose from the church's interpreting the OT in terms of the *kerygma*: 'the determinate counsel of God' was now

1 H. B. Swete, *An Introduction to the Old Testament in Greek* (Cambridge, 1900), pp. 380–405, 452–61.

2 R. Harris, *Testimonies*, part I (Cambridge, 1916); part II (Cambridge, 1920).

3 C. H. Dodd, *According to the Scriptures* (London, 1952), p. 126.

4 *Ibid.*

fulfilled in the facts of the Gospel. This OT material, common to all the NT writers, formed 'the substructure of all Christian theology'.[1]

Dodd's book appeared in 1952, just as the finds at Qumran were beginning to make their presence felt. In particular, the treatment of scripture in 1QpHab showed how another apocalyptically minded Jewish sect, close in time and place to the emergent church, saw in the words of Habakkuk its own history and thought prefigured, or rather, disclosed. The concept of the *midrash pesher* quickly came into use, especially through the work of Krister Stendahl, E. Earle Ellis and others.[2] At much the same time, however, other scholars had been working on the Targumim and the Midrashic literature: we think of Renée Bloch, Paul Kahle, Roger Le Déaut, and Geza Vermes, among others.[3] Study of the Palestinian Pentateuch Targum fragments from the Cairo Geniza had convinced Kahle that the tradition (or traditions) enshrined in them represented ancient Jewish material, contrary to the hitherto prevailing view that the Palestinian Targumim were post-talmudic, even mediaeval, productions.[4] Renée Bloch saw that midrash was not a late development but was a process – a way of thought – inherent in the emergence of all post-exilic Jewish literature, biblical or otherwise, and wholly inseparable from the very formation of Holy Scripture. Its most essential characteristic was that of 'actualisation' – the updating of the words of scripture to enable them to speak to people of its own time.[5] The NT and the Qumran literature attested the same process at work: indeed, nothing was more characteristic of this than

[1] *Ibid.*, p. 127.

[2] Krister Stendahl, *The School of St. Matthew* (Uppsala, 1954; 2nd edition, Lund, 1967); E. Earle Ellis, *Paul's Use of the Old Testament* (Edinburgh, 1957); Barnabas Lindars, *New Testament Apologetic* (London, 1961); and others.

[3] Paul E. Kahle, *The Cairo Geniza* (London, 1947), esp. pp. 117–32; Renée Bloch, 'Écriture et tradition dans le Judaïsme: Aperçus sur l'origine du midrash', *Cahiers Sioniens* viii (1954), pp. 9–34; 'Note méthodologique pour l'étude de la littérature rabbinique', *RSR* xliii (1955), pp. 194–227; 'Ezéchiel xvi: exemple parfait du procédé midrashique dans la Bible', *Cahiers Sioniens* ix (1955), pp. 193–223; 'Quelques aspects de la figure de Moïse dans la tradition rabbinique', *Cahiers Sioniens* ix (1955), pp. 93–167; 'Note sur l'utilisation des fragments de la Geniza du Caire pour l'étude du Targum palestinien', *REJ* n.s. xiv (= cxiv) (1955), pp. 5–35; ' "Juda engendra Pharès et Zara, de Thamar" (Matth. 1, 3)', in *Mélanges bibliques rédigés en l'honneur de André Robert*, (Travaux de l'Institut catholique de Paris, 4,) (Paris 1957), pp. 381–9; Geza Vermes, *Scripture and Tradition in Judaism*, Studia Post-Biblica, 4 (Leiden, 1961; 2nd edition, Leiden, 1973); Roger Le Déaut, *La nuit pascale: essai sur la signification de la Pâque juive à partir du Targum d'Exode XII 42*, Analecta Biblica, 22 (Rome, 1963); Martin McNamara, *The New Testament and the Palestinian Targum to the Pentateuch*, Analecta Biblica, 27 (Rome, 1966).

[4] P. E. Kahle, *The Cairo Geniza*, pp. 117–32.

[5] R. Bloch, 'Écriture et tradition . . .', *Cahiers Sioniens* viii (1954), p. 33.

the utilization of the OT in the NT – it was always a question of 'actualisation midrashique' (that is, midrashic updating).[1] Not surprisingly, study of the Targumic literature revealed that it preserved certain exegetical traditions also detectable in parts of the NT.[2] The discovery of Codex Neofiti I in 1956 by A. Díez Macho gave an enormous boost to this line of approach, for hitherto the Palestinian Pentateuch Targumim had been known only in fragmentary form.[3] Here at last was a complete MS of this targum-type. To all of these fields Matthew Black contributed: the language of the Targumim and their style, Qumran, and the links of both with the NT alike in language and thought.

This paper is not an attempt at a review of the history of the problem of the use of the OT in the NT. Rather, it seeks to examine the presuppositions underlying various contributions to the debate, in the hope of finding some coherent overall approach to the question.

First of all there is the question of the basis (if any) of selection of the OT quotations and allusions. Rendel Harris' theory looked for a clue to this in the collections of OT references found in various early patristic writings, and to this extent his approach had a certain objectivity. There did appear to be evidence for the existence and use of more or less fixed collections or perhaps 'selections' of OT quotations and allusions (including a few seemingly mixed ones) running through the literature from the NT onwards. But just *who* did the selecting? The NT writers or any one or group of them? Or did they find the 'selection' ready-made? The presence of some of the same 'testimonies' in different parts of the NT suggested that the selection was in some way earlier than the books of the NT.[4] Harris thought the aim of the selection was apologetic, and he was inclined to attribute it to Matthew the apostle.[5] Be that as it may, he did raise a further vital and related question here: what was it that gave the initial impetus to this job of selecting *testimonia*? In answer he turned to the Stone *testimonia*, among the oldest of them, and argued that in their case they were to be traced in the Gospels to Jesus' own words: thus,

> we may say that all the Stone and Rock testimonies, and they are many and early, go back to a Saying of Jesus which incorporated

[1] *Ibid.*

[2] Cf. R. Bloch, ' "Juda engendra Pharès et Zara, de Thamar" (Matth. 1, 3)', (*cit. supra*, p. 232, n. 3), and especially the works of Vermes, Le Déaut and McNamara, listed on p. 232, n. 3.

[3] Codex Neofiti I is hereinafter referred to as Tg.N.

[4] R. Harris, *Testimonies*, I, p. 25; cf. also *ibid.* II, p. 83.

[5] *Ibid.*, I, pp. 108–28; II, pp. 10, 90, 108.

> a Saying of a Prophet or Psalmist. It is Jesus, if we may say so, who sets the Stone rolling. . . .[1]

This brings us to a very important point: even if we were to agree with Harris here, how was Jesus able to use such OT passages at all in such a way, unless certain exegetical methods and traditions were shared by him with his audience? His arguments would otherwise have hung completely in the air. Now in the case of the Stone *testimonia* it happens that we know that some of them at least had already been linked together and given an eschatological twist, as the Qumran literature shows.[2] That is, in this one instance at any rate Jesus (or possibly the primitive church) apparently took up and re-interpreted a known Jewish exegetical tradition. That it was not merely a Qumran motif appears from the fact that Tg. Ps. cxviii.22–3 quite clearly refers the 'stone' to the scion of David and implies the same pun, *'eben* (stone)/*ben* (*'eben*) (son) as underlies Mk xii.6, 10a, par.[3] The fact that the link between Mk xii.6 (son) and 10a (stone) is possible only in Hebrew strengthens the case for the origin of the Stone *testimonia* within an early Jewish exegetical tradition. As if to complete a defence of Harris' general position we may refer to the evidence of 4QTestimonia, showing that the principle of writing down collections of key texts was not without precedent in or just before the NT period.

But are we to limit ourselves to the view that the texts concerned were wholly isolated from their contexts, as Harris seemed to think? Or are we perhaps to go along with Dodd and look rather to a method of exegesis involving the utilization of large sections of the OT, used and viewed as 'wholes', the outcropping quotations and allusions merely acting as pointers to those wholes? Now Dodd was surely right to stress (1) the importance of taking allusions and other quotations without formal introductory words seriously, (2) the need to see that when this was done the resultant material began to show a pattern of belonging to certain wider sections of the OT, and (3) that the so-called *testimonia* were thus not so isolated as they might otherwise have

[1] *Ibid.*, II, p. 96. The passages intended are Isa. xxviii.16 and viii.14 (cf. Harris' discussion, *Testimonies*, I, pp. 26–32). In *Testimonies*, II, on p. 96, he adds references to Ps. cxviii.22, 23 and Dan. ii.44. The whole discussion is most instructive.

[2] 1QS viii.7 (cf. Isa. xxviii.16); possibly 1QH vi.26. Cf. Matthew Black, 'The Christological Use of the Old Testament in the New Testament', *NTS* xviii (1971–2), pp. 1–14, esp. pp. 11–14; E. Earle Ellis, 'Midraschartige Züge in den Reden der Apostelgeschichte', *ZNTW* lxii (1971), pp. 94–104, esp. pp. 100–4; and Max Wilcox, 'Peter and the Rock: a fresh look at Matthew xvi. 17–19', *NTS* xxii (1975–6), pp. 73–88, esp. pp. 84–8.

[3] Cf. Wilcox, 'Peter and the Rock', *NTS* xxii, esp. pp. 85–8.

appeared. We shall have cause to look at some of these points later. Dodd's approach, however, was far too heavily dominated by his *kerygma* theory. We cite his words:

> There remain only two of our fifteen primary *testimonia* which we have not yet examined in their scriptural context: the promise to Abraham, Gen. xii.3, xxii.18 (see pp. 43–4) and the prediction of the 'prophet like Moses' in Deut. xviii.15, 19 (see pp. 53–7). The result of such investigation is negative. In each case the passage cited is isolated, and the context in which it occurs is not otherwise employed to elucidate the ideas of the *kerygma*.[1]

This is not all: the next sentences are even more striking:

> The prediction of the 'prophet like Moses' had little significance for the development of New Testament theology. The story of Abraham in a general way is in the background of many passages of the New Testament, but apart from the promise of the blessing of the Gentiles it does not appear that particular passages from it were employed to elucidate the *kerygma*.[2]

That is, he assumed that the guiding principle of selection was that of relevance to 'the *kerygma*'. The view, 'if it is not in the (!) *kerygma* it does not matter for NT thought' is a value judgment, rather than an empirical statement. It is also odd that he overlooked the presence of the allusion to Gen. xxii.16 in Rom. viii.32a. Our essential point here is one of method. Dodd set out from the view that the church began with the *kerygma* and then went to the OT to marshal evidence to show that the events of that *kerygma* had happened '"by the determinate counsel and foreknowledge of God" (Acts ii.23)'; that is, he proceeded from the assumptions (1) that it was the Church which began the enterprise, and (2) that that enterprise was aimed from the start at finding support for the confessional statement which he identified as the *kerygma*.

Such considerations if valid at all may have affected the relative concentration of emphasis on certain particular texts, but we should be highly doubtful if they were the actual starting points of the procedure. For even if the church's aim in using OT material was in fact apologetic, as Harris, Dodd and others have claimed, that would only reinforce the case that its starting point would have had to be what was already common ground between Jew and Christian. But this does not mean merely the OT, but rather the OT understood in the light of the then accepted exegetical traditions – what A. Díez

[1] C. H. Dodd, *According to the Scriptures*, p. 107. [2] *Ibid.*

Macho has called 'the deraš pešat of ancient Jewish exegesis'.[1] That is, far from scouring the OT in search of texts to bolster up the statements of the *kerygma*, the early church would have needed to start with the exegetical traditions of contemporary Jewish thought concerning the Messiah and the end events, and then argue that these had found their proper interpretation (and hence 'realization') in the person and role of Jesus of Nazareth. In this way the scripture would have been seen to speak (anew) to the situation now called forth in and by the 'Christ event'. On this analysis the elements of the so-called *kerygma* would appear as an end product rather than a starting point. That such a procedure was not without contemporary models we may see from the Qumran literature.

If we argue thus, however, we shall be led to assume that at least in basic form much of the OT material used in the NT was as it were 'preselected': not all of it, to be sure, for we must allow for the introduction of new elements as the debate proceeded. But the starting points of that debate will have been laid down in advance in passages of scripture already viewed within current streams of Jewish exegetical tradition as in some sense 'messianic'.[2] Yet if so, we are warned against proceeding from *kerygma* to scripture.

Further support for this approach appears from the fact that not all use of the OT in the NT is in fact in any serious sense 'christological'. We refer, for example, to the passages dealing with divorce and remarriage, circumcision, duties to parents etc. in the Gospels. Here in a number of cases the context is closely related to current Jewish halachic exegesis.[3] But if so in these cases, why should it have been otherwise in the 'christological' ones?

On the other hand Dodd was surely right to take note of allusions

[1] A. Díez Macho, 'Deráš y Exégesis del Nuevo Testamento', *Sefarad* xxxv (1975), pp. 37–89, esp. p. 39.

[2] Cf. R. Bloch, ' "Juda engendra Pharès et Zara, de Thamar" (Matth. 1, 3)', *Mélanges bibliques* . . . , p. 388: the Jewish exegetical tradition behind Matt. i.3 saw Tamar not only as an ancestress of the Messiah, but as fervently desirous of this favour, 'this share in the messianic blessing' (so Bloch). The apparent sin of Judah and Tamar is seen as due not to 'the will of the flesh' or 'the will of man' (if we may so put it), but to the will of God: it is thus not sin at all. Frag. Tg. (Cod. Nor.) has: 'Tamar my daughter-in-law is innocent: the pregnancy is from me (i.e. Judah)', but Bodl. MS Hebr. c. 75 (P) reads: 'A Bath-Qol came down and said: "You are both innocent: this thing (i.e. the pregnancy) is from Me".' Many more cases might be cited.

[3] On divorce and remarriage, see Mk x.1–12 par. and esp. Matt. v.32; xix.9 (cf m. Gitt. ix.10); on circumcision, John vii.22–3 (cf. Mekh. to Exod. xxxi.12, 13, edited by Horovitz, p. 340, lines 11–13; t. Shab. xvi.16, edited by Zuckermandel, p. 134; b. Shab. 132a, b. Yoma 85b, etc.).

and quotations without introductory formulae as well as of explicit ones, and his instinct was correct to look at wider sections of the OT 'understood as wholes' rather than 'isolated texts'. A formal quotation by its very nature directs the reader or hearer to a specific passage (or passages) of scripture, and that passage may indeed be but one of a collection of isolated texts, on the lines suggested by Harris. An allusion or a quotation without an introductory formula tends rather to assume that the readers or hearers have a certain familiarity with the wider context and probably with its current exegetical interpretation(s) also: it acts as a cue to that context, but it can do so only if it is recognized for what it is. It is thus all the more surprising that Dodd overlooked the allusion to Gen. xxii.12, 16 in Rom. viii.32a, 'He who did not spare his own son...': this statement acts as a cue to the whole Akedah section, Gen. xxii.1–19.[1]

Explicit quotations are, of course, simplest to isolate and investigate. However, they are also much more liable to assimilation in the course of transmission either to some form of the LXX or to other parallels within the NT itself, and so on.[2] Allusions are harder to identify with certainty and may thus be somewhat more resistant to such 'correction'; on the other hand, determining where they actually start and finish is correspondingly much more a matter of subjective decision. This is further complicated by two factors. First, quite apart from anything which has been said before in this paper, the NT does seem on occasion to display a 'naive' or 'uninstructed' use of OT language – apparent reminiscences or allusions may be little more than the sort of language early Christian pious people used, without any deeper intention. Secondly, interpretative elements, biblical or otherwise, may have entered right into the very fabric of an allusion or apparently deviant quotation. We may cite the following example from Qumran, 1QS ii.2–4 (cf. Num. vi.22f):

> ... and they say, '*May he bless thee* with all good, *and keep thee* from all evil and *may he make* thine heart *shine* with understanding of life and *may he give thee grace* through eternal knowledge and *may he lift up the face* of his loving-kindness *towards thee* for eternal *peace*.'[3]

The other side of the same coin is the question how far individual elements from a larger (and well known) context may on occasion have been taken and used as a means of interpreting their new (NT) context,

[1] The form in Rom. viii.32a differs slightly from the LXX of Gen. xxii.12, 16, in reading the emphatic 'his own son' (τοῦ ἰδίου υἱοῦ).

[2] Cf. Wilcox, *The Semitisms of Acts* (Oxford, 1965), pp. 18–19.

[3] Elements from Num. vi.22–4 are italicised.

much as we might today use other 'allusions' – in quotation marks or italics – to make a point: for example, to speak of solving the problem of the use of the OT in the NT 'at a stroke'. In the NT there are many allusions of this type, e.g. Mk xiv.24:

> And he said to them, 'This is my *covenant-blood* which is shed for *many*' . . .

We resolve the awkward phrase τὸ αἷμά μου τῆς διαθήκης (cf. Exod. xxiv.8; Zech. ix.11), and also possibly link the term 'many' (πολλῶν) with Isa. liii.11, 12. Examples of this kind of procedure may be cited from the Qumran Scrolls and the Targumim: it is no NT peculiarity. We shall return to this later.[1]

Factors like these complicate the matter of determining the textual affinities and indeed the precise verbal limits of allusions, but we ignore them at our peril.

We turn now to the question of textual tradition represented by any given element of OT material used in the NT. It is true that a good number of OT quotations and allusions in the NT broadly (and sometimes precisely) present a text form akin to that of the LXX, the more especially to the so-called A form of it.[2] Others seem to presuppose a textual tradition like that of the MT or perhaps one of the known alternative Greek versions. Others again display links with certain of the Targumim while a further sizeable block of material presents a rather more complex pattern of agreements and disagreements. Before we assign such complexities to 'loose citation', 'memory', or other such hypotheses of last resort, we must give full weight to certain well known and basic facts:

(1) The NT, because it is written in Greek, can give its OT references only in transliteration or translation. If the latter, that translation may coincide with, or appear to be modelled upon, a known Greek OT version, or it may not, but be an independent version due either to the writer in question or to his source(s).[3]

(2) The Hebrew text of the OT is known to have circulated in more than one form, one of which seems to have been close in parts to that which formed the basis of our LXX.

(3) Other non-LXX Greek versions of the OT are known to have existed.

[1] See below, p. 240.

[2] See, for example, T. Holtz, *Untersuchungen über die alttestamentlichen Zitate bei Lukas*, TU 104 (Berlin, 1968), pp. 166–9.

[3] Cf. Wilcox, 'The Judas-Tradition in Acts i.16–26', *NTS* xix (1972–3), pp. 438–52, esp. pp. 449–52.

There was thus a wide range of possible choice (if that is the right word here) available, from which OT material might have been taken, and we know from Justin and the Mishnah that this did in fact occur.[1] On the other hand, in certain cases at least the apparently slight variations in wording involved became the basis of scholarly and apologetic disputation.[2] It was not a matter of indifference but, so it seems, of deliberate choice, and the detail of the text appears to have been made to bear considerable weight. The variety of text reflects the state of things in the pre-canonical period. In a way, text and interpretation go hand in hand.

This comes out clearly when we investigate the Targumim, especially the so-called Palestinian Pentateuch Targumim. Here the one element of underlying Hebrew original may be represented by a variety of different Aramaic words and phrases (in the various MSS and text forms). The coincidence of a NT reading with one or other such Targumic authority represents not so much use of that particular Targum or its putative ancestor as the preservation by both the NT and the Targumic authority concerned of an element of early Jewish exegetical tradition. This is strikingly displayed in the case of the so-called Targum Pseudo-Jonathan (BM Add. MS 27031), a targum clearly subject to much late revision, yet having a number of very interesting points of agreement with OT textual traditions and interpretations preserved in the NT.[3]

Closely linked with the previous point is another, namely that the NT in a number of places reflects or assumes knowledge of Jewish exegetical traditions preserved for us in the Targumim. We do not mean attempts to *translate* the Hebrew text of the OT, but rather to give one or other of its early interpretations, or to reflect elements – not uncommonly stereotyped in form – preserved in the Midrashim which have developed out of the OT text in question. These interpretations may be constructed of biblical or non-biblical material. For the latter, the

1 Thus Justin, *Dialogue*, xliii, on the meaning and text of Isa. vii.14, and m. Gitt. ix.10, giving two different interpretations of Deut. xxiv.1. (See next note.)

2 Thus m. Gitt. ix.10, although using the MT of Deut. xxiv.1 in the actual quotations it gives, preserves two readings, *'ervat dabar* (some indecency, some indecent matter) and *d^ebar 'ervah* (a matter, question, of indecency), which then justify the views of the Schools of Hillel and Shammai respectively. Note how Matthew agrees here with the Shammaitic reading.

3 See, for example, M. McNamara, *The New Testament and the Palestinian Targum to the Pentateuch*, pp. 258–9, and *Targum and Testament: Aramaic Paraphrases of the Hebrew Bible: A Light on the New Testament* (Shannon, 1972), p. 179. Also, M. Wilcox, *Semitisms*, pp. 27, 28.

classical instance is Tg. Pseudo-J. Deut. vi.4ff, where the traditional interpretation actually replaces the biblical text in its entirety.[1] The 'biblical' type occurs, for example, in Tg. 1 Sam. xiii.14, where the words *kilbabo* (according to his heart) are rendered 'doing his wishes' (*'abed r^e^vatheh*) (cf. Isa. xliv.28). It is interesting that *both* forms occur alongside one another in Acts xiii.22.[2] Thus, what at first sight looks like a 'mixed quotation' turns out to be an interpreted one: the 'mixing' is not accident but design, following a Jewish exegetical tradition. Such traditions also appear in 1 John iii.12, where we hear that Cain killed his brother Abel 'because his own works were evil, but his brother's works were good' – strikingly close to Pal. Tg. Gen. iv.8, against the vaguer MT and also against the LXX, which refers rather to his 'offerings'.[3] Similarly Acts i.16a, 17–19, takes up a stereotyped motif – a pair of lines – preserved in the traditional midrash of the Palestinian Targumim to Gen. xliv.18, and then proceeds to give it a further haggadic development.[4] Phenomena such as these abound in the haggadic portions of the Targumim.[5]

Now, following on to the last point, we should note that in the haggadic material in the Palestinian Pentateuch Targumim, certain biblical allusions and non-formal quotations are found as stereotypes common to more than one such block of material. The same is also true of certain lines and phrases not biblical in nature. These 'stereotypes' – biblical and non-biblical alike – are in turn used as 'key lines' to cue in the thought of those other passages. The sheer fixity of these elements suggests that they are on the way to achieving a degree of 'canonicity'. Examples may be cited from Pal. Tg. Gen. xxxviii.25, 26; xliv.18; Num. xxii–xxiv; etc.[6]

We may therefore ask whether an OT allusion in a NT passage may

[1] This tradition, found also in m. Ber. ix.5, may underlie the story of the Rich Young Ruler, Mk x.17–22, 23–31, par.

[2] Cf. M. Wilcox, *Semitisms*, pp. 21–2; 'A Foreword to the Study of the Speeches in Acts' in *Christianity, Judaism and other Greco-Roman Cults: Studies for Morton Smith at Sixty*, edited by J. Neusner, part 1, New Testament (Leiden, 1975), pp. 206–25; esp. pp. 220–1.

[3] 'If your works are good in this world, will it not be loosed and forgiven you in the world to come, but if your works are not good in this world, on the day of the Great Judgment your sin will be retained' (So Tg. MS Paris 110).

[4] Cf. M. Wilcox, 'The Judas-Tradition . . .', *NTS* xix (1972–3), pp. 438–52.

[5] See the valuable discussion of these matters by M. McNamara, *The New Testament and the Palestinian Targum to the Pentateuch*, chapters vi–viii, pp. 155–252.

[6] In Tg.N. Num. xxiii.9–10, the set expressions 'the sand of the sea(shore)' and 'the stars of the heavens' (cf. Gen. xxii.17) are used to define 'Israel'. Something of the same phenomenon appears in Rev. vi.15, etc.

not similarly be intended (1) as a pointer to (the) traditional interpretation(s) of the section of the OT from which it comes, and/or (2) as a peg upon which to hang subsequent development. Now this is borne out by the facts. But what of stereotyped non-biblical material appearing in the Targumic haggadot? For example, the reference in Pal. Tgg. Gen. xxxviii.26 (and 25) to the Rabbinic dictum, 'The measure by which a man measures, (by it) it is measured (i.e. they measure) to him'?[1] Are they not elements of Jewish halachic and haggadic tradition in the process of hardening into authoritative statements almost akin to the biblical material itself?

This last point raises the question whether we find in the NT any equivalent material, used with authority and in a way as a means of interpreting OT passages. We suggest that it is in the words of Jesus and to some extent in portions of the basic NT confessional statement (the so-called *kerygma*) that the nearest parallel is to be found. That is, when the NT uses the OT in connection with the words of Jesus and/or the basic confessional statement, its justification for so doing lies in its interpreting scripture by current exegetical tradition and by the growingly canonical elements of primitive Christian 'scripture'. Thus, the primitive church's acceptance of the authority of Jesus, his words and deeds, enabled it to *pesher* the OT in terms of him.[2]

There is one further parallel between the NT and Targumic uses of the OT. We saw earlier how Dodd stressed that the OT passages used *kerygmatically* were concentrated into certain fairly restricted portions of the OT. Now it is an interesting feature of the haggadic material of the Palestinian Pentateuch Targumim that it too is found concentrated into various verses, relatively few in number, and not scattered evenly over the whole of the Pentateuch. (For example, there are quite extensive haggadic expansions at Gen. iii.15, 22, 24; iv.7, 8, 23–4 (25); xv.1, 17; xvii.1; xxii.10, 14; xxvii.40, 41; xxviii.10, 12; xxx.22; xxxiv.31; xxxv.9; xxxviii.25, 26; xl.12, 18, 23 xlii.36; xliv.18 (and Tg.N.19); xlviii.22; xlix.1, 2 (3), 4, (7), (10), 18, 21, 22; l.1. Exod. xii.42; xiii.17; xiv.29; xvi.15; xix.6; etc.). Further, these haggadic portions are not infrequently linked more closely in thought and language than may appear at first sight. In the larger and more basic blocks of material that link is often a common interest in the Messiah, the two worlds, the

[1] Cf. M. McNamara, *The New Testament and the Palestinian Targum to the Pentateuch*, pp. 138–42.

[2] A. Díez Macho, 'Deráš y exégesis del Nuevo Testamento', *Sefarad* xxxv (1975), p. 42, sees two aspects to the process of interpretation: (a) from the OT passages to the Christ-event, (b) from the Christ-event to a re-evaluation of the OT.

great judgment, the reward of the righteous and the punishment of the wicked.[1] Thus in one stream of Targumic tradition to Gen. xliv.18, Judah approaches Joseph, 'emboldened and mighty as *a lion...*' (presumably an allusion to Gen. xlix.9). In Tg. Gen. xlix.10 the Messiah is to arise from Judah, while in Pal. Tg. Gen. xxxviii.25, 26 as we noted earlier the aim of the exercise is to argue that the union of Judah and Tamar was no mere act of human weakness but was part of the divine plan for the raising up of Messiah from the offspring of Judah.

Thus, consideration of the scope and origin of an OT allusion or quotation in the NT demands close attention to known Jewish exegetical traditions relating to the passage or passages concerned. The very text itself in the form in which it appears in the NT may reflect aspects of that interpretation and may have been modified by them. Roger Le Déaut has observed that an important feature of Targum is that it includes the traditional interpretation in the translation itself, in that 'the Bible was received and transmitted with an exegesis from which it was inseparable'.[2] It would be a serious error to overlook the possible operation of similar factors in the case of OT material used in the NT.

So far we have been looking mainly at OT material used 'Christologically' in the NT, although we have also referred to passages where it forms part of a halachic discussion, and in addition to cases of a 'naive' or 'uninstructed' use. We should now add to this places where Jewish exegetical traditions are referred to as part of the ordinary stock of ideas assumed on the part of the hearers or readers of a NT book, and apparently used as illustrations. We mention as an example II Tim. iii.8–9 (referring to Jannes and Jambres as opponents of Moses).[3] We may thus state that the use of the OT within the NT is to be seen as developing, at least in its earlier stages, out of the contemporary Jewish Bible exegesis as a whole. Here we ask two questions: (1) how far NT exegesis of the OT forms part of that traditional Jewish pattern, and (2) where it deviates from that scheme to produce its own distinctive interpretations, what factors enabled it to justify that parti-

[1] Cf. McNamara, *The New Testament and the Palestinian Targum to the Pentateuch*, pp. 238–52.

[2] R. Le Déaut, 'Un Phénomène spontane de l'herméneutique juive ancienne: le targumisme', *Biblica* lii (1971), pp. 522–3.

[3] Tg. Pseudo-J. Exod. vii.11 (cf. also Exod. i.15 and Num. xxii.22). For discussion of the tradition, see R. Bloch, 'Note méthodologique pour l'étude de la littérature rabbinique', *RSR* xliii (1955), pp. 194–227, esp. pp. 212–25, and M. McNamara, *The New Testament and the Palestinian Targum to the Pentateuch*, chapter iii, pp. 70–96.

cular exegetical development. Here we proceed on certain assumptions. First, we hold that NT writers, when giving their OT exegesis a specifically Christian twist, were concerned to carry conviction, and were not merely making bald statements: what they said formed part of a continuing debate between Christian and Jew, Christian and Christian, and later, 'orthodox' and 'heretic'. We also accept that in the NT period there was still a sense in which the OT had not been fixed, either in textual tradition or in canon. Further, we maintain that there are strong grounds for believing that from a very early date, if not from the outset, certain at least of the sayings of Jesus had an authority approaching that of scripture itself within the church,[1] which could then justify using scripture (and its traditional exegesis) along with Jesus sayings to expound one another. One central problem, however, remains: unless the Jesus material in question included some specific 'messianic' claim, what fact or assertion enabled the primitive church to appropriate to Jesus the exegetical traditions which Judaism linked with the Messiah? We suggest that that fact was none other than the assertion of the resurrection (in whatever form the statement was originally made) and the resultant implication that in Jesus the 'new age' (the world to come) had dawned, the great judgment had begun: in short, that Messiah had come. That is, early Christian Bible-exegesis is part of the contemporary Jewish Bible exegesis, distinguished from the latter first and foremost by acceptance of the resurrection and the resultant implied 'messianic' role of Jesus.

To conclude then, we see two main tasks before us: (1) to identify and isolate the OT material in the NT, together with Jewish exegetical material present with and/or within it, and (2) to examine how far the NT represents a consistent haggadic development of that material in the light of the confessional statement of the resurrection. The first of these involves patience and study of the sources; the second may open new questions about the nature of the Jesus material in the Gospels and also about the origins of NT christology itself.

[1] Cf. M. Wilcox, 'The Composition of John 13: 21–30', in *Neotestamentica et Semitica: Studies in Honour of Matthew Black*, edited by E. E. Ellis and M. Wilcox (Edinburgh, 1969), pp. 143–56, esp. pp. 152–6, and 'The Denial-Sequence in Mk xiv. 27–31, 66–72', *NTS* xvii (1970–1), pp. 426–36, esp. pp. 432, 434–6.

Philippians in Fayyumic

R. McL. WILSON

For the practical purposes of New Testament textual criticism, a reference to the Coptic versions means in the main the Sahidic and the Bohairic.[1] Only these two versions can really be called accessible, although Horner's editions have their defects. That of the Sahidic in particular is something of a patchwork, pieced together from many fragments, and there are some quite considerable gaps. We now have complete manuscripts in Sahidic of all the books of the New Testament except the Apocalypse, and in some cases several manuscripts.[2] Reference may be made to Thompson's edition of Acts and the Pauline Epistles, and Quecke's of Mark[3] (an edition of the manuscript of Luke is in preparation). Even so, this is no more than the preliminary groundwork for a proper critical edition. We still have no convenient and complete modern edition of any Coptic version, and there are manuscripts still unpublished. As Gerd Mink has put it, 'Der Forschungsstand ist im Bereich des Verhältnisses der griechischen und koptischen Überlieferung gegenüber dem Materialstand erheblich zurückgeblieben.'[4]

With the other dialects the situation is even worse. An edition of the Subachmimic version of John was published by Thompson, and an extensive fragment from a Michigan papyrus by Elinor M. Husselman.[5]

[1] On the Coptic versions generally, see Gerd Mink, 'Die koptischen Versionen des Neuen Testaments', in *Die alten Übersetzungen des Neuen Testaments, die Kirchenväterzitate und Lektionare*, edited by K. Aland (Berlin, 1972), pp. 160ff; K. Aland, 'Das koptische Neue Testament', in *Bericht der Stiftung zur Förderung der neutestamentlichen Textforschung* (Münster, 1977), pp. 49ff.

[2] Aland, 'Koptisches NT', p. 51.

[3] H. Thompson, *The Coptic Version of the Acts of the Apostles and the Pauline Epistles in the Sahidic Dialect* (Cambridge, 1932); Hans Quecke, *Das Markusevangelium Saïdisch* (Barcelona, 1972). Another manuscript of Acts has been published by F. Hintze and H. M. Schenke, *Die Berliner Handschrift der sahidischen Apostelgeschichte* (P. 15926) (TU 109) (Berlin, 1970).

[4] Mink, 'Koptische Versionen', p. 176.

[5] H. Thompson, *The Gospel of John according to the Earliest Coptic Manuscript*, (London, 1924); E. M. Husselman, *The Gospel of John in Fayumic Coptic*,

For the rest one must first identify the available fragments in the lists published by Vaschalde, or in Till's supplement,[1] and then locate them in their published form, often in widely scattered and not easily accessible journals. The Münster Institute for New Testament textual criticism has however already set in train a systematic search for unpublished New Testament manuscripts in Coptic,[2] and a considerable quantity of material is available on microfilm. Here again we are only at the preliminary stage, and much remains to be done. There is for example the question of the age and history of the various Coptic versions,[3] and that of their relationship one to another.[4] The latter is complicated by the problem of identifying the dialect to which a particular manuscript belongs: is the Michigan John, for example, Fayyumic or Middle Egyptian?[5] Older studies frequently conveyed the impression that Sahidic was the dominant dialect in the early centuries, and was gradually superseded by Bohairic, with the further impression that the Bohairic was therefore later in development. The former impression would appear to be correct, but the discovery of older Bohairic manuscripts, and of affinities between the Bohairic and other versions of an early date, has brought the latter very much into question. Mink for example can speak of a proto-Bohairic version in his analysis of a passage in John.[6]

Many years ago, the late Paul E. Kahle jun. made a collection of all the published New Testament fragments in Fayyumic. Through the agency of Principal Black, this collection, after Kahle's death, was entrusted to the present writer to prepare for publication. The problems encountered, and pressure of other work, have delayed the completion of the project, but work is in progress and it is hoped that the task will soon be finished. In the meantime perhaps this brief study, *quantulacunque*, may serve as ἀπαρχή and ἀρραβών, and provide an appropriate tribute.

Philippians has been chosen for the study because two fragments are

P. Mich. Inv. 3521 (Ann Arbor, 1962). Mink notes: 'Allerdings ist seine Sprache nur unter Vorbehalten dem fajjumischen Bereich zuzuweisen' (167).

1 'Ce qui a été publié des versions coptes de la Bible', *Revue Biblique*, 1919–22 (Sahidic); *Le Muséon* 43 (1930) (Old Testament); 45 (1932) (Bohairic); 46 (1933) (Fayyumic and Achmimic); W. C. Till, 'Coptic Biblical Texts published after Vaschalde's Lists', *BJRL* 42 (1959), pp. 220ff.

2 Aland, 'Koptisches NT', p. 52.

3 Mink, 'Koptische Versionen', pp. 181ff.

4 *Ibid.*, pp. 177ff.

5 See p. 245, n. 5 above.

6 Mink, 'Koptische Versionen', pp. 274ff, esp. p. 288. See also R. Kasser, *L'Évangile selon saint Jean et les versions coptes*, with Mink's comments, pp. 166ff, 183ff.

available for much of the opening chapter. The whole of the chapter, with part of the first two verses of the second chapter, was published by Zoega in his catalogue of the manuscripts of the Museo Borgiano.[1] In addition fragments from a Michigan papyrus were published by Worrell.[2] The text in both cases comes from a manuscript which contained other Pauline epistles, since in Zoega the first column contains part of Eph. vi, followed by the title *πρὸς Ἐφεσίους* in an ornamented border, the title *πρὸς Φιλιππησίους* (*sic*), and then Phil. i.1–3. Similarly the Michigan fragment contains in its first column Eph. vi.19–24. Since column 2 begins in the middle of the second verse of Philippians, the beginning of the letter here also must have stood in column 1.

It is not possible to print a full collation, both for reasons of space and because it would involve the use of exotic script; nor would it be of much use to those who have no Coptic! A couple of verses may however be given in transcription[3] (Z = Zoega; S = Sahidic; M = Michigan; B = Bohairic), to give some idea of relationships. (See table on p. 248.)

Even from this brief extract it is immediately clear that Zoega's text matches fairly closely with the Sahidic, whereas the Michigan fragment goes with the Bohairic. Merely dialectic and orthographical variations must of course be discounted, but attention may be drawn in particular to the omission in the two latter texts of any equivalent for *ὅτι* in verse 18, and to the three inversions in the latter part of this verse.

A rough and ready indication of affinities is provided by the use of loan words, i.e. cases in which one or other text retains the Greek word where others use the Coptic equivalent. Out of a total of 87 counted, 53 are retained by all four. S retains the loan word with Z against B 18 times, with two further cases where it stands alone. Z goes against S once where B agrees with S, omitting a *δέ* in verse 15; in verse 19 Z again omits *δέ* where S retains, but here B reads *γάρ*. B retains a loan word against S and Z 14 times. In most of these cases the text of M is not extant, but in 4 cases it agrees with B in using a Coptic word where S and Z retain the Greek. It is therefore all the more curious that M in one case should agree with SZ against B, in retaining the loan word *θλῖψις* in verse 17. It would of course be dangerous to draw far-reaching conclusions from a brief sample, but the evidence is enough to call in question any idea of a single uniform Fayyumic version. Nor

[1] G. Zoega, *Catalogus codicum Copticorum manu scriptorum* (Rome, 1810; reprint with introduction and bibliographical notes by J. M. Sauget, Hildesheim/New York, 1973).

[2] W. H. Worrell, *BSAC* vi, p. 134.

[3] The transcription uses the 'approximate phonetic values' given in C. C. Walters, *An Elementary Coptic Grammar* (Oxford, 1972), p. 1.

Z	[18]shale	oun	gar	shōpi	plēn	je	hn	smat	nim	eite	hn	oulaigi	eite	hn
S	share	ou	gar	shōpe	plēn	je	hn	smot	nim	eite	hn	ouloige	eite	hn
M		ahaf	gē		plēn		hn	smat	nibi	ite	hn	oulaigi	ite	hn
B		ahof	je		plēn		hen	smot	niben	ite	hen	oulōiji	ite	hen

Z	oumēi	setasheaeish	mpechs.	auō	tileshi hm pei.	auō	an tinaleshi.
S	oume	setasheoeish	mpechs.	auō	tirashe hm pai.	auō	on tinarashe.
M	oumetmei	pchrs	sehiaish mmaf.	auō	hm pei tileshi	auō	eieleshi an.
B	oumethmēi	pchs	sehiōish mmof.		hen phai tirashi	alla woh	eierashi on.

Z	[19]tisooun		je	pei	nashōpi	nēi	nououjei	ebol	hitm	petnasops mn
S	tisooun	de	je	pai	nashōpe	nai	euoujai	ebol	hitm	petensops mn
M	ti[mi		je	pei	neshōpi	nei	e]o[uoujei	eb]al	hitm	petent[ōbh mn]
B	tiemi	gar	je	pai	nashōpe	nai	euoujai	ebol	hiten	petentōbh nem

Z	techorekia	mpepna	nis	pechs.
S	tchoregia	mpepna	nis	pechs.
M	psehni	nte p[pna	nis	pchrs].
B	psahni	nte ppna	nte	is pchs.

is it the case that Z is simply a transposition of S into the Fayyumic dialect, since there are differences which require to be analysed in detail. The problems are more complex than might appear at first sight.

Regarding the general character of the version, there are some free renderings and a few translation errors, but on the whole the Coptic is remarkably faithful to the Greek original. In using the version for purposes of textual criticism, of course, due account must be taken of the idiosyncrasies of Coptic idiom.[1] Thus in i.7 'because you are in my heart' is a free rendering of *διὰ τὸ ἔχειν με ἐν τῇ καρδίᾳ ὑμᾶς*; the possessive 'my' is the normal usage in Coptic, and does not imply a possessive in the underlying Greek text (as it happens, the natural English translation would be 'because I have you in my heart'). Final evaluation will require investigation of the methods of the translator as well as the habits of the scribe or scribes, before it is possible to work back with confidence to the Greek original, but a provisional list may give some indication of the variants so far detected:

1. to all the saints who are in Philippi (om in Christ Jesus, against SB).
2. God the Father (our Father SB Mich., but one B MS has 'the').
3. over you all (at every remembrance of you SB Mich.).
   in my prayers at all times for you (all my prayers at all times for you all SB Mich.).
6. Jesus Christ (with SB and Greek MSS against 𝔓[46] BD et al.)
7. you are partakers with me in grace (om all, against SB).
8. the bowels of Christ (om Jesus). There is variation within the Coptic tradition here: both S and B include the name, but Thompson's MS omits and some Bohairic MSS invert the order.
11. The praise of God (SBZ agree with the majority Greek reading; see the UBS apparatus).
14. Z omits 'in my bonds' against SB.
    to speak the word of God: SBZ provide support (1) for the inclusion of the genitive and (2) for 'of God' rather than 'of the Lord'. It is doubtful if they are relevant for the question of word order.
15. Z omits 'out of goodwill' against SB.
18. SZ appears to support *πλὴν ὅτι*, whereas BM have simply *πλήν*. BM have several inversions of order against SZ.
23. om. *γάρ*.
25. your faith SZ against B.
27. Z omits the first *εἴτε* with B against S.

[1] Cf. the examples discussed by Mink, 'Koptische Versionen', pp. 188ff.

Some of these may be due to scribal error, or to a mistake by the translator, but when there is agreement between two or more of the Coptic witnesses such an explanation becomes less likely – unless they all betray the hand of an original translator or early copyist. The differences however are such as to make derivation from a common source or a common tradition highly unlikely. For textual criticism, of course, the important variants are those where the Coptic evidence stands clearly and incontrovertibly in line with one branch rather than another of the Greek tradition.

INDEXES

(COMPILED BY JOHN D. GRASSMICK)

AUTHORS

PASSAGES CITED

A. THE OLD TESTAMENT

B. THE NEW TESTAMENT

Tabula Gratulatoria

Barbara Aland
K. Aland
George W. Anderson
Sasagu Arai
R. S. Barbour
C. K. Barrett
Ernest Best
Hans Dieter Betz
M. C. Blackwood
Peder Borgen
F. Bovon
William D. Bray
Raymond E. Brown
F. F. Bruce
Jean Carmignac
David R. Catchpole
M. A. Chevallier
Raymond F. Collins
E. Cothenet
John M. Court
C. E. B. Cranfield
Nils Alstrup Dahl
M. de Jonge
J. Duncan M. Derrett
Erich Dinkler
John W. Drane
James D. G. Dunn
J. Duplacy
Jacques Dupont
E. Earle Ellis
Eldon Jay Epp
Owen E. Evans
Gordon D. Fee
Joseph A. Fitzmyer S.J.
R. T. France
G. W. S. Friedrichsen
W. Ward Gasque
A. S. Geyser
Charles H. Giblin S.J.
M. E. Glasswell
Erich Graesser
Pierre Grelot
F. Gryglewicz
Dikran Y. Hadidian
Ferdinand Hahn
R. J. Hammer
L. Hartman
Victor Hasler
A. J. B. Higgins
David Hill
T. Hirunuma
Harold W. Hoehner
Traugott Holtz
Morna D. Hooker
Claus-Hunno Hunzinger
Richard L. Jeske
Aubrey R. Johnson
René Kieffer
A. F. J. Klijn
Robert A. Kraft
Edgar M. Krentz
Georg Kretschmar
Gerard J. Kuiper
F. Lang
Edwin Larsson
B. C. Lategan
M. Lattke
A. R. C. Leaney
Ragnar Leivestad
Louis Leloir
Xavier Léon-Dufour
Barnabas Lindars S.S.F.

Richard N. Longenecker
Robert W. Lyon
I. Howard Marshall
James P. Martin
J. Louis Martyn
B. A. Mastin
Kikuo Matsunaga
John Mbiti
J. McHugh
Bruce M. Metzger
R. Morgan
Leon Morris
C. F. D. Moule
Robert P. R. Murray
F. Neirynck
Eugene A. Nida
Bent Noack
Birger Olsson
V. Parkin
C. Perrot
R. Pesch
T. E. Pollard
J. K. S. Reid
Jannes Reiling
Harald Riesenfeld
Karl Heinrich Rengstorf
Martin Rese
J. R. Richards
B. Rigaux
Y. Herman Sacon
A. Sand
R. Schnackenburg
Bernardin Schneider
John H. Schütz
B. Schwank
Stephen S. Smalley
D. Moody Smith
G. N. Stanton
Peter Stuhlmacher
Ray Summers
J. P. M. Sweet
Richard E. Taylor
Theophilus M. Taylor
Margaret E. Thrall
Bastiaan Van Elderen
W. C. Van Unnik
A. Voegtle
Gunter Wagner
David H. Wallace
A. J. M. Wedderburn
Max Wilcox
Amos N. Wilder
R. McL. Wilson
J. A. Ziesler